# AT THE CROSSROADS

# AT THE CROSSROADS

## MEXICO AND U.S.

## IMMIGRATION POLICY

EDITED BY

FRANK D. BEAN

RODOLFO DE LA GARZA

BRYAN R. ROBERTS

SIDNEY WEINTRAUB

Rowman & Littlefield Publishers, Inc.
Lanham • Boulder • New York • London

ROWMAN & LITTLEFIELD PUBLISHERS, INC.

Published in the United States of America
by Rowman & Littlefield Publishers, Inc.
4720 Boston Way, Lanham, Maryland 20706

3 Henrietta Street
London WC2E 8LU, England

British Cataloging in Publication Information Available

**Library of Congress Cataloging-in-Publication Data**

At the crossroads : Mexico and U.S. immigration policy / edited by
  Frank D. Bean ... [et al.].
      p.     cm.
  Includes bibliographical references and index.
  ISBN 0-8476-8391-5 (cloth : alk. paper). — ISBN 0-8476-8392-3
(paper : alk. paper)
    1. United States—Emigration and immigration—Government policy.
. 2. United States—Emigration and immigration—Economic aspects. 3. Mexico—
Emigration and immigration. 4. Mexicans—United States.  I. Bean, Frank D.
JV6483.A75     1997
325'.273'0972—dc21                                    96-50203

ISBN 0–8476–8391–5 (cloth : alk. paper)
ISBN 0–8476–8392–3 (pbk. : alk. paper)

Printed in the United States of America

⊖™ The paper used in this publication meets the minimum requirements of American
National Standard for Information Sciences—Permanence of Paper for Printed Library
Materials, ANSI Z39.48–1984.

# Contents

# Acknowledgements

T he chapters in this book consider the circumstances and key issues that influence the viability and desirability of policy choices available to the United States and Mexico as the two countries wrestle with the issues stemming from the continuing flow of Mexican legal and undocumented migrants to the United States. The authors of the chapters in this volume individually and collectively analyze the migration flows and weigh the advantages and disadvantages of the various policy options that have been proposed to influence the flows. As is always the case in projects of this kind, many persons and institutions have made it possible for this endeavor to come to fruition. The editors gratefully acknowledge the support of the Ford Foundation, the Hewlett Foundation, the Pew Charitable Trust, and the University of Texas at Austin, each of which provided funding that contributed to the preparation of the volume. The editors also extend special thanks to Charles W. Haynes, Peter Hendricks, Sydel Howell, James O'Brien, and (especially) Penne Restad, who assisted in the preparation of the final chapter. Other persons who deserve a strong vote of appreciation for their assistance include Carolyn Blackwell, Cynthia Bock-Goodner, Cecilia Dean, Gloria Hill, Molly Martin, Maureen Meko, Terry Sherrell, and Karen Wilkinson. Jennifer Knerr of Rowman and Littlefield has been particularly helpful. To anyone whose assistance we have overlooked, we apologize. Any errors or shortcomings, of course, are the responsibility of the editors.

*Frank D. Bean*
*Rodolfo O. de la Garza*
*Bryan R. Roberts*
*Sidney Weintraub*

# Introduction

*Frank D. Bean, Rodolfo O. de la Garza,*
*Bryan R. Roberts and Sidney Weintraub*

T he direction that U.S.-Mexican relations will take in the future is uncertain.
The outcome—whether relations become more cooperative and emphasize
increased integration between the two countries or become more negative
and promote a growing separation—has the potential to affect aspects of social
and economic life in the United States. The rising importance of Mexico to the
United States is reflected in the recent U.S. publication of a raft of books on
Mexico (e.g., Oppenheimer, 1995; Castañeda, 1995; Fuentes, 1996). It is also
illustrated by the high priority the Clinton administration gave in 1993 to the
passage of the North American Free Trade Agreement (NAFTA) (an initiative
begun in a previous Republican administration) and by the loan guarantee package
put together by the U.S. government to assist the Mexican government through
the economic difficulties created by the peso devaluation of December 1994. As
Oppenheimer (1995) notes: "No single country in the post-Cold War era affects
the U.S. national interest in more ways than Mexico" (p. xi).

One of the most important of these ways, perhaps the most important, is
Mexican migration to the United States. This migration is occurring at the same

time that the issue of immigration in general has risen markedly on the U.S. public policy agenda. A number of books have also appeared recently on the general subject of immigration (e.g., Brimelow, 1995; Teitelbaum and Weiner, 1995; Beck, 1996). Further evidence of the rising importance of immigration issues in the United States over the past ten years is reflected in the passage of the 1986 Immigration Control and Reform Act (IRCA) to try to curb illegal immigration to the United States (Bean, Vernez, and Keely, 1990), and in the passage of the 1990 Immigration Act (IMACT) to increase economic-related while limiting overall immigration. And the 1990 act, in anticipation of continuing concerns about immigration, also established the U.S. Commission on Immigration Reform to study immigration and its consequences and to formulate recommendations to Congress for possible future reforms (Bean and Fix, 1992). California's passage of Proposition 187, which seeks to limit the access of undocumented migrants to social services, together with the passage by both houses of Congress in 1995 of bills designed to control undocumented migration also demonstrate that the salience of immigration as a major U.S. public policy issue remains high.

Given the significance of Mexico for the United States and the prominence of immigration as a public policy concern, the intersection of these two issues is of special interest. That is to say, the role played by *Mexican migration* to the United States, including both legal and illegal migration, is of particularly crucial significance to the United States. Interestingly, however, when general immigration issues are considered, the question of Mexican migration is often given only partial consideration because legal Mexican immigration is either ignored or under-emphasized. This is illustrated in the foci of the two major immigration-related studies mounted by the U.S. Commission on Immigration Reform. One of these is being conducted by the National Research Council and examines the demographic and economic effects on the United States of *immigration in general*. The other is being carried out by the Mexico/U.S. Migration Study Commission and focuses predominantly (though not exclusively) on *undocumented* Mexican migration. In a similar vein, the U.S. Congress has focused its *explicit* attention on illegal migration, concentrating its legislative efforts in 1995 on border control and on efforts to slow illegal immigration. The de facto effect of this focus is to emphasize only one part of Mexican migration—the undocumented part. Very little of the congressional reform package targets *legal immigration* in general, and legal Mexican immigration in particular. Little policy attention has been devoted explicitly to the consideration and reform of both legal and undocumented Mexican migration considered in tandem.

This book seeks to redress this imbalance by focusing specifically on Mexican migration to the United States and its significance for U.S. policy and U.S.-Mexico relations. Mexican migration currently holds center stage in the public controversies over U.S. immigration policy, if not always in policy discussions about possible reforms. Indeed, in many instances, the immigration question has become almost synonymous in the public eye with Mexican migration, as evidenced by public support for measures to tighten border controls and to restrict migrants' use of educational, health, or welfare services, as in the provisions of California's Proposition 187. And recent statistics seem to indicate there is in fact some basis for the public's perceived importance of Mexican migration. For example, in 1995, the Mexican foreign-born made up 28 percent of the total foreign-born population in the United States, the largest single national component. And the very rapid growth of Mexico's population from about 67 million persons in 1980 to about 95 million today adds to public concerns by dramatizing the potential for even higher future levels of migration.

The high profile of Mexican migration in U.S. policy is of relatively recent origin. Mexican migration to the United States has, of course, a long history. Since the turn of the century, Mexican migrants have come to the United States to work on railroad construction, in mines, and on the farms of the developing agriculture of the Southwest (Cardoso, 1980). They worked in the steel and meat-packing industries of the Midwest, though most Mexican migrants were concentrated in the American Southwest, including Texas. Yet, until recently, Mexican migration was comparatively small and, in practice if not always in law, relatively unrestricted, with exceptions such as the repatriation of large numbers of Mexican migrants in the 1930s and again in 1954. Compared to the massive immigrations from Europe in the last half of the nineteenth century and the first decades of the twentieth century, Mexican immigration contributed, until recently, only a small part of U.S. population growth. Its pre-Second World War peak occurred in the 1920s, when the economic disruptions caused by the Mexican Revolution (1910-20) and the civil wars that followed led many Mexicans to migrate to the United States in search of jobs. In the 1920s, 459,000 Mexicans were registered as immigrating to the United States, equivalent to 3.2 percent of the total population of Mexico in 1921. These numbers of Mexican immigrants were not to be surpassed until the 1970s, but they were not exceptional. Several European countries, including Italy, Germany, and the United Kingdom, contributed similar numbers of immigrants, and twice that number of immigrants came from Canada in the 1920s. Even Ireland, long past the peak of its contribution to U.S. population growth, sent a higher proportion of its population as immigrants to the United States than did Mexico in these years. Some 5.2 percent of the Irish population immigrated to the United States in the 1920s, despite the attainment of Irish Independence, which removed one of the major ostensible causes of Irish emigration.

Not only was Mexican migration not particularly large, but much of it was temporary in nature. Mexican immigrants have had one of the lowest naturalization rates of any immigrant group (Jasso and Rosenzweig, 1990: Table 2.1). Census figures also suggest substantial emigration out of the United States by Mexican immigrants. While 728,000 Mexicans are recorded as immigrating to the United States between 1901 and 1930, the numbers of the Mexican-born population in 1930 amounted to 641,000, and these would have included many who had not documented their immigration. By 1950, the Mexican-born in the census had dropped to 452,000, reflecting not only mortality and the low level of immigration after 1930, but the forced repatriation of Mexicans in the 1930s. Estimates of Mexican migration to the United States have usually put the amount of return migration to Mexico as about three quarters of the total flow.

Mexican migrants to the United States until the 1960s were predominantly employed in types of work that were temporary and seasonal in nature. The rapid expansion of Californian agriculture depended on a seasonal labor force. Fruit and vegetable production could not employ people year round and, consequently, it was attractive to only the entrants into the labor force, immigrant or not, who had no other sources of work. For most workers in California, seasonal work in agriculture was a step toward finding more permanent work in either the rural areas or the cities. Thus, turnover was high. The difficulties of recruiting a labor force from California's resident population made Mexican migrant labor an attractive option for farmers. It was also attractive for the migrants themselves, who could earn much higher wages than in Mexico and could save enough to maintain their family in the village and, at times, enable them to invest in land or animals. So long as the Mexicans wished to return, the arrangement suited both sides. Until the 1970s, most Mexican migrants did wish to return; but in the last two decades, Mexican immigration became not only greater in volume, but included a greater component of permanent immigration. The chapters in this volume focus on these last two decades and on the reasons for and implications of the shift in the character of Mexican migration.

It is at this juncture that Mexican migration becomes an important, if not always explicit, issue for U.S. immigration policy. Other shifts in the flows of immigrants in the 1970s and 1980s played a part in changing immigration policy in the 1980s, particularly the increases in immigration from Asia. However, the major piece of legislation in the 1980s, the Immigration Reform and Control Act of 1986 (IRCA), and the policy debates around it, were substantially affected by the peculiar challenge posed by Mexican immigration. Whereas previous immigration policies toward Mexico had tended to operate on the adage "If it ain't broke, don't fix it," IRCA involved a determined effort to find a solution to what were perceived to be immigration problems raised by Mexican migration.

Confronted with the reality of millions of undocumented Mexicans residing in the United States and the prospect of many more following them, IRCA, through legalization and employer sanctions, recognized the de facto situation of Mexican migrant settlement while seeking to limit employer demand for further immigration. As various of the contributors to this volume point out, NAFTA was, in policy terms, a further arm of this strategy. By promoting economic development in Mexico, it was hoped that NAFTA would, in the medium and long term, diminish the pressures on Mexicans to migrate to the United States. The validity of this assumption can be tested only in a longer time frame than the three years NAFTA has been in effect.

## The Historical Background to Mexican Emigration

Until the Revolution of 1910, Mexico's agrarian system effectively tied rural inhabitants to the land. Land holding was heavily concentrated among the few and the vast majority of the rural population either possessed no land or had land holdings insufficient to maintain a family. This "landless" population subsisted through various forms of sharecropping arrangements and seasonal labor on plantations, complemented by small-scale craft, service, and commercial activities. This subsistence depended on making use of the labor of almost all members of the household, from very young to very old. Such a pattern of rural survival discouraged the permanent migration of whole families—the young and able-bodied would migrate seasonally but leave children, wives, and the elderly to make a meager subsistence in the village economy. This pattern of survival was already being disrupted before the Mexican Revolution as railroads and Porfirio Díaz's economic modernization expanded commercial agriculture and opened rural areas through more intensive trading networks. These disruptions and the greater population mobility they produced were to be factors in causing the Mexican Revolution. The fighting of the revolutionary years and the accompanying economic and social instability made previous strategies for rural survival even more difficult to sustain: local and regional economies offered few job opportunities, harvests were disrupted and destroyed, and commerce became more difficult. Instability in many parts of Mexico continued until the end of the 1920s, particularly in the Center-West of Mexico, where the Catholic, counter-revolutionary *Cristiada* pitted villages against each other and against central government. Long-distance migration to the United States became, under these conditions, a more attractive option. For many in these years, such as the middle classes negatively affected by the Revolution, migration to the United States became a permanent option.

Given the instability of the years from 1910 to 1930 and an open land frontier, it is perhaps surprising that many more people did not migrate from Mexico to the United States. As we have seen, much higher proportions of the European population moved to the United States at the beginning of the twentieth century when faced with domestic conditions that, on the surface at least, were less difficult than those facing the Mexican peasantry. Mexico had, of course, a less developed agrarian structure than did the European countries, and its peasantry, some 70 percent of the population in 1920, was probably more inured to penury and had a more locally focused world view than did the peasantries of Ireland or Italy. From 1930 onwards, however, Mexico's agrarian structure stabilized with the emergence of a strong central government and in the context of an agrarian reform that destroyed the old *hacienda* system there. The new arrangements still permitted private farming but imposed an individual size limit on holdings. The *ejido* was created, partly out of property taken from *haciendas*, as a form of social property to which peasants and their families had individual farming rights, but could not legally sell or lease these rights to others. Agrarian reform was never fully completed. By the time of its effective end with the 1992 laws permitting the sale of *ejidal* lands, there were still many unsettled cases in which peasant communities claimed land from nearby landowners. Despite its limitations, agrarian reform was successful in restoring the social and economic viability of Mexico's agrarian structure. From the 1930s to the 1960s, the Mexican peasantry, mainly through the *ejidal* system and rain-fed agriculture, produced the food needed to feed an expanding urban population. Commercial, private agriculture, making extensive use of peasant migrant labor, and some *ejidos* provided a large part of the export revenues that helped finance Mexico's industrialization.

After the 1930s, the survival strategies of the Mexican peasantry were similar to what they had been during the *Porfiriato*, but at a higher level of economic development. Family labor was used to farm *ejidal* plots, care for animals, create craft work, and often engage in some trade. The developing road network intensified trade in agricultural products with the cities, creating many commercial opportunities at the village level. Savings from migrant labor played an important part in village economies by generating the cash needed to make small investments in farming or housing. The scarcity of government credits to support *ejidal* farming made migrant earnings even more necessary. Migration to the United States was attractive because the wages were many times higher than what could be obtained through migrant labor in Mexico. Migration also tended to concentrate in areas where agriculture was highly market-oriented and thus the need for cash greater and the contacts with the outside more intense. These were primarily the areas of the Center-West of

Mexico, Guanajuato, Jalisco, and Michoacán, which already had long-established migrant links with California and the Southwest of the United States. Areas of mainly subsistence farming, particularly in geographically remote regions, such as Chiapas and Oaxaca, had few international migrants until the 1970s, though villagers worked seasonally in Mexican plantation agriculture.

The vitality of the Mexican agrarian structure from the 1930s to the 1960s helped ensure that international migration was mainly temporary in nature. It was a strategy that enabled young heads of family or prospective heads of family to acquire some savings to set up their own households and to sustain their village-based families. Migrants returned because they had something to return to. There was, of course, a large-scale permanent out-migration of villagers in these years, but this flow went to Mexico's expanding cities. Population increase in Mexico was rapid after 1930 as a result of sharp declines in mortality and, in the rural areas, constantly high levels of fertility. The village economies, despite their growth, could not sustain this population expansion. And there were more peasant farmers in Mexico in 1960 than there were in 1910. However, the urban economies, particularly those of Mexico City, Guadalajara, and Monterrey, were demanding labor from the 1930s onward, as Mexico undertook a rapid program of import-substituting industrialization.

Though the issue of peasants flooding into cities evoked some government and media concern in Mexico during the period of rapid urbanization from 1930 to 1970, it was overshadowed by the evident need that urban industries had for labor, particularly in construction, other services, and manufacturing. These were also years of intense nationalist sentiment at official levels. Thus, official attitudes toward migration to the United States tended to emphasize the undesirability of permanent migration, which was seen as depriving Mexico of valued skills. Temporary labor migration, however, was officially encouraged since it provided cash inflows to the rural economy, thus easing the pressure on government to inject more funds into the *ejidal* sector. The *Bracero* agreement with the United States, while responding to the needs of U.S. growers, was also very much in the interest of the Mexican government.

Until the 1970s, there was very little in Mexican migration to the U.S. or in Mexican government attitudes toward it that made Mexican migration a difficult policy issue for the United States. The United States had other policy concerns about Mexico in these years, but migration was one of the least controversial. More difficult issues for U.S.-Mexican relations were the nationalization of the oil industry in the 1930s, Mexico's nationalistic stance on foreign policy, and the country's support of Castro-led Cuba. The United States context was also one that made Mexican migration a relatively secondary issue for U.S. policy The first quota restriction on immigration in 1921 responded to concerns over further large increases in the foreign-born population and, in particular, to increases that would change the ethnic composition of the U.S. population. Mexican immigration was not, at that time, a specific concern of the policy debates and was not limited by quotas. One reason for this lack of restriction was that Mexican migrants were perceived by officials, employers, and by the non-Mexican-ancestry public as essentially sojourners who were not part of U.S. society. These perceptions of Mexicans were reinforced by the concentration of Mexican migration and settlement in the Southwest, close to the border with Mexico (Taylor, 1970 [1932]; Gamio, 1930; Romo, 1983). Even in places such as Los Angeles, which had 90,000 Mexican-origin residents by 1930, the local press and Chamber of Commerce ignored the role of Mexicans in the settlement of the city, categorizing the Mexicans in the city as casual laborers who would return to Mexico. Likewise, the Californian Development Association argued that Mexicans were mostly temporary migrants, partly to avoid having a quota placed on the entry of Mexican labor (Romo, 1983).

As Paul Taylor (1970 [1930]) pointed out, Mexican migrant communities in rural and urban areas were spatially and socially isolated from native-born populations, particularly those who were not of Mexican ancestry. Thus, the visibility of these migrant workers to the general U.S. population was low. Since the migrant workers filled a niche in agricultural production that few native-born workers desired—that of seasonal and temporary workers—there was, for much of the time, little competition between migrant and native-born. When U.S. workers did compete for the same jobs, in the late 1920s and 1930s, then Mexican migrant workers were removed on a massive scale, deportations that were made easier by the concentrated and isolated nature of Mexican migrant settlement. By 1935, it was estimated that as many as 500,000 Mexican migrant workers had returned to Mexico through forced or voluntary repatriation (Hoffman, 1972). The temporary character of Mexican migration, though based on conditions in Mexico, was undoubtedly reinforced by U.S. actions and attitudes. And from the 1920s onward, U.S. immigration policy fostered the development of truly temporary migration from Mexico, through programs such as the *Bracero* program and its predecessors. After the ending of the *Bracero* program in 1964, U.S. immigration policy with respect to Mexico operated mainly by default.

## The Contemporary Situation

By the 1970s, changes in the U.S. economy were altering the demand side of the migrant flow. The demand for migrant labor in agriculture continued even though mechanization reduced demand in some areas. The expansion of fruit and vegetable production in California and in new areas, such as the Northwest and Florida, increased demand. The change in demand occurred principally in urban jobs. Some Mexican migrants had, from the turn of the century, taken jobs in cities such as Los Angeles and Chicago, but the massive migrant entry into such jobs dates from the 1970s, when the number of Mexican migrants begins to exceed by substantial numbers the amount that could be absorbed by the demand for temporary agricultural work.

Part of the reason for the increase in the numbers of Mexican migrants are conditions in Mexico, particularly the economic crises of the 1980s and the stagnation of the Mexican peasant economy, but part is based on the long-term shift in the pattern of demand in the United States labor market as employment in the U.S. economy became more service based. This shift had both a spatial and an occupational component, both of which created job opportunities for Mexican migrants. The economic expansion of the 1970s onwards disproportionately took place in the states that had traditionally received Mexican migrants—the Sunbelt states of the Southwest, particularly California. Some of the occupational shift in demand was toward skilled, white-collar jobs and away from skilled and semi-skilled manual jobs. There was, however, also an increase in demand for relatively unskilled jobs in service, retail, and construction activities to build the cities and the suburbs and to provide inexpensive consumer services for their inhabitants. These jobs required little in the way of language proficiency, and in times of high employment, there was not a ready supply of native born willing to work for low pay and, often, poor working conditions.

Though these jobs were insecure, they were not seasonal, unlike agricultural work. Thus, they offered Mexican migrants the possibility of year-round work and thus a basis for settling with their families. The crisis of the Mexican peasant economy meant that migrants were less likely than before to see themselves as returning to agriculture in Mexico; while the crisis of the Mexican urban economy made that a less attractive alternative. Building upon networks that usually were still based on villages of origin, but included migrants who had already made the transition from agricultural to urban work, increasing numbers of Mexican migrants found their way to urban areas and urban jobs in the 1970s and 1980s.

## The Contribution of This Volume

The chapters in this volume address some of the key issues raised for policy by this history of Mexican migration, from both the United States and Mexican perspective. The themes addressed can be divided into five main categories. First is the question of the history of U.S. immigration policy toward Mexico. Second is the question of the social and economic changes in Mexico that have altered the pattern of migration to the United States. Related to this issue is that of the changes in U.S. labor markets that have affected Mexican migrants. Third is the issue of the impact of Mexican immigration on U.S. society. What do we know about the demographic impact of Mexican immigration, its consequences for labor markets, and its costs and benefits in terms of taxes paid and services used? Fourth are the political implications of Mexican migration for Mexico and for the United States. Fifth are the implications of Mexican migration for U.S.-Mexico relations and foreign policy. In a concluding section, the editors explore the broader policy questions concerning immigration raised by the Mexican case.

## The History of U.S. Immigration Policy Toward Mexico

Freeman and Bean take up the issue of how the United States has treated Mexico in its past immigration policies. They describe the evolution of U.S. immigration policy from early in this century, concentrating on those unresolved policy tensions that have particular consequences for Mexico. They enumerate three: the tension between a policy that treats immigrants equally irrespective of their national origins and one that takes account of special relations with particular countries; the tension between the felt need to control and diminish immigration and the continuing demand for foreign labor to meet employers' needs in the United States; and the tension between the desire to act as a sovereign state in full control of its borders and the recognition that, in an interdependent world, multilateral negotiations may be required to resolve even immigration control issues.

They show that attempts to resolve these tensions account for many of the fluctuations in U.S. immigration policy that continue to the present. Thus, Freeman and Bean describe how the numerical limitations on Mexican and Latin American immigration were slow to be implemented, and their practical impact was vitiated by the combined effect of exempting family reunification from quota restrictions and of offering amnesty under IRCA to substantial numbers of undocumented migrants. Though IRCA had an immediate effect, they argue, in reducing undocumented immigration, this reduction was only temporary, probably because the employer sanctions proved ineffective in controlling immigration. They review the hardening of attitudes toward immigration in recent years that has begun to result in tighter border control and even to changes in policy over legal immigration. Finally, they discuss the policy options open to the United States with respect to Mexican immigration, drawing on experience from other parts of the world. These include a common labor market as part of NAFTA, temporary labor migration agreements, and special quotas for Mexican immigration. They conclude that none of these options are likely in the present political climate, though some combination of these measures taking effect over time is more probable.

## Social and Economic Changes in Mexico and the United States

Agustin Escobar and Bryan Roberts seek to explain why Mexican migration to the United States changed its character in the last two decades, becoming more permanent and family-based. They argue that until the 1970s, rapid urbanization and industrialization in Mexico absorbed the surplus rural population. Migration to Mexican cities, not international migration, was the preferred alternative for those who thought of abandoning permanently the rural sector. Escobar and Roberts view Mexican migration to the United States before the 1970s as essentially a temporary labor migration that was one, among several, income strategies, that Mexican farm families used as a complement to agriculture. They see the situation as changing in the 1970s as the economic and population growth of Mexican cities slowed so that the urban sector was less successful than in the past in absorbing permanently rural migrants.

Urban-to-urban migration increases as economic restructuring leads to new spatial patterns of urban growth, particularly along the northern border, and to labor market instability and worsening labor conditions. This inter-urban migration becomes linked to international migration as both rural and urban migrants move toward the cities of the north of Mexico. The changes in migration patterns are related only indirectly, they argue, to government policy. Certainly there was an urban bias in Mexican government economic and social policies that made cities attractive at the expense of the rural sector. Also, current free trade policies and the elimination of many subsidies are responsible for some of the instability in urban labor markets and for the spatial reorientation of the urban system. However, Escobar and Roberts can find no evidence of any systematic migration policy in the pattern of Mexican government expenditures, whether to slow down out-migration by investing in regions that expel population or to provide extra resources to regions that are capable of absorbing population from elsewhere. They advocate more systematic attention being given to improving living conditions in those cities, such as those along Mexico's northern border, that can potentially absorb migration and thus act as a buffer reducing the pressures to migrate to the United States.

Philip Martin looks at the impact of the pattern of agricultural development in Mexico and the United States on Mexico-U.S. migration. He argues that Mexican rural migration to the United States is currently being driven by an agricultural revolution in Mexico that is destroying the traditional pattern of *ejido*-based peasant agriculture. Small-scale farmers are likely, he argues, to be increasingly driven out of agricultural work by the competitive pressures deriving from a series of policy measures: the removal of price support for agricultural products; the reduction of tariff protection; and the Agrarian Law of 1992 that permits the sale of *ejidal* lands, eases restrictions on foreign ownership of agricultural enterprises, and, in effect, ends further land distribution. These processes may, of course, help generate jobs in agriculture or, at least, stem job losses by making Mexican agriculture more competitive internationally, particularly in labor-intensive sectors such as fruit and vegetables. However, Martin warns of the difficulties facing Mexican agriculture as it is forced to restructure in an economic context in which credit is limited, interest rates high, and investment cautious. Also, grower opposition in the United States and the use of non-tariff barriers limits the potential for increasing Mexican agricultural exports to the United States.

Martin examines the factors in the organization of U.S. agriculture that have created a demand for Mexican migrant labor. He points out that U.S. agriculture, particularly the labor-intensive sectors of fruit and vegetables, has a continuing demand for Mexican labor because of the high turnover among agricultural workers. This demand, he argues, is a conditional one since the U.S. growers are likely to mechanize either if the supply of labor is cut off or if labor costs rise. Martin's main recommendations concentrate on the need to recognize that agricultural reform in any developing country will have migration consequences, and these require of the receiving country understanding, patience, and some short-term measures to alleviate the immediate pressures. In the U.S. context, he warns, these are unlikely to be ideal and are likely to include a combination of more effective immigration control measures and aid or guest-worker programs aimed to enlist Mexican co-operation.

## The Impact of Mexican Migration
## on U.S. Society

Alene Gelbard and Marion Carter outline the demographic context of Mexican immigration. They remind us of the continuing importance of immigration to U.S. population growth. While the foreign born are not as high a percentage of the U.S. population as they were earlier in the century, new immigrants and the U.S.-born children of immigrants account for about half of U.S. population growth. In the last two decades, Mexicans have become the largest national immigrant group, accounting by 1994 for an estimated 28 percent of the total U.S. foreign-born. Predicting that population momentum as well as further immigration will continue the growth of the Mexican-origin population, Gelbard and Carter document the major demographic characteristics of this population. They show that the Mexican-origin population, reflecting the recency of large-scale Mexican immigration, is younger than the total population, contains more males than females, and has a higher fertility level. The Mexican-origin population is also more likely to marry and less likely to divorce than the U.S. population as a whole, though the second and third generations have increased rates of marital break-up and single-parent households. The educational levels of the Mexican-origin population are lower than those of the U.S. population as a whole and their rates of poverty higher. Other important characteristics of Mexican immigration, highlighted by Gelbard and Carter, are that it contains an unusually high proportion of undocumented migrants and of legal immigrants admitted under the family reunification provisions of immigration law. It is also geographically concentrated in relatively few states and metropolitan areas. In California, in particular, they show how the demography of the state has been shaped by Mexican immigration.

Public debate about immigration and about Mexican immigration has been fueled by concerns over the fiscal impacts of immigration. Immigrants are, from one perspective, viewed as a fiscal burden since they contribute less in taxes than they receive in health, educational, and welfare services. Additionally, there have been fears that immigrants take away jobs from natives and, thus, indirectly add to the fiscal burden through unemployment and welfare dependency among the native-born population. From an opposing perspective, immigrants make a valuable contribution to the U.S. economy through the skills and work they contribute. The taxes they pay exceed the services they receive, it is argued, once the total amount of direct and indirect taxes are considered. According to this perspective, immigrants do not displace U.S. born workers, but take jobs that the native-born do not want and, by helping the economy expand, actually help create jobs.

In their review, Susan Gonzalez Baker, Robert Cushing, and Charles Haynes look carefully at the various studies that have examined the fiscal burden of immigration. They argue that it is not possible to arrive at a definitive answer to the issue of the fiscal burden of Mexican immigration because of the absence of reliable and representative data. Moreover, there is no agreement among researchers about the best way to estimate the fiscal burden. The result, as the three authors show, is that the widely different estimates coming from the two opposing perspectives are mainly artifacts of what individual researchers have chosen to include or exclude in the fiscal balance sheet. Gonzalez Baker, Cushing, and Haynes find that to the extent a fiscal burden exists, it falls heaviest on states and localities rather than on the federal government.

However, they argue that the poverty and fiscal burden issues associated with immigration reflect the broader issue of poverty and inequality in the United States. Even if immigration stopped, there would still be poverty in the United States simply because the economy does not generate enough high-wage, stable jobs. Solutions to the low-wage and poverty problems, from their perspective, rest not in stopping immigration but in improving the employability and productivity of all workers, whether immigrant or native-born.

Michael Rosenfeld and Marta Tienda use a case-study approach to argue that Mexican migrants make a considerable, but often overlooked, entrepreneurial contribution to the U.S. economy. Arguing from a perspective that sees positive returns to scale, they view the increasing numbers of immigrants as expanding the pools of knowledge, innovation, and entrepreneurial spirit in a society. Mexican immigration does not, at first sight, appear to make an important contribution to expanding these pools, since it has mainly been composed of low-skilled workers and has included few professionals or entrepreneurs. Rosenfeld and Tienda argue, however, that Mexican immigrants, irrespective of their formal skills, are likely to be self selected for innate skill and motivation. Using data from the Mexican Little Village community in Chicago, they document the various ways in which Mexican immigrants, often starting through the informal economy, have contributed to the economic growth of their communities. Even when businesses began as informal ones, and thus contributed few taxes, their cases show that, over time, their fiscal contribution grew as they formalized through, for example, buying a store. Even the informants with little or no education had demonstrated significant entrepreneurial skills, building up businesses within the Mexican American community. The immigrant influx has, in Chicago, helped consolidate a substantial ethnic economy catering to the tastes and lifestyles of the Mexican-American community. In turn, the dynamism of this economy contributes to that of the wider economy.

## Political Implications
## of Mexican Migration

International migration usually has significant political implications in both the sending and in the receiving country. In the sending country, emigration may be overtly political, as in the case of political refugees. Even when political refugees are an insignificant proportion of the total, as in the case of Mexico, emigration can still have important political overtones that influence national policy-making. Rodolfo de la Garza and Gabriel Szekely remind us that emigration from Mexico has always had a political component that is as important as the economic one. It has suited successive Mexican governments, they argue, to have high levels of emigration, which have served as both political and economic safety valves. Mexicans fled the political instability of Mexico from 1910 to 1930, and, in the rural sector, they emigrated, often temporarily but repeatedly, because of the constantly broken promises of agrarian reform.

Despite the relative lack of overt Mexican policies toward emigration, Mexican governments have, in practice, encouraged high levels of legal emigration through programs such as the *Bracero* agreement and through arguing for the continuation of special quotas for Mexican immigrants to the United States. Also, De la Garza and Szekely point out that there are Mexican government policy stances that implicitly encourage undocumented migration, such as those supporting the rights of Mexican undocumented migrants in the United States or providing protection services on the border for returning migrants. This implicit encouragement is particularly significant, it can be argued, in the absence of any official words or actions discouraging undocumented migration.

Finally, they stress the substantial and significant impact that dissatisfaction with the nation's political processes and governmental corruption have on emigration. Additionally, they review the possible role that Mexican emigrants will play in Mexico's efforts to democratize. Emigrants will shortly have the right to vote in presidential elections. Since 1988, emigrant communities have become targets for Mexican communities seeking moral and financial support. Also, programs sponsored by federal and state governments have sought to involve emigrant groups in the development of their communities of origin. The political attitudes of emigrants are, however, little known, leaving unanswered questions regarding whether the government or opposition parties will benefit from emigrant support. Even less is known about the extent to which political rather than economic concerns influenced the decision to emigrate.

The political implications of Mexican migration to the United States are evident in the widespread support among voters for immigration control measures, such as California's Proposition 187. Thomas Espenshade and Maryann Belanger review U.S. public perceptions and reactions to Mexican migration. They remind us that the resident U.S. population has seldom been in favor of new immigration, particularly where it meant the arrival of people of different ethnic and language background to themselves. Opinion polls show that respondents are more hostile to illegal immigrants than to legal immigrants, but since those surveyed believe (incorrectly) that most immigrants are illegal, sentiments against current levels of immigration are at historic highs. The negative political implications of these sentiments for Mexican migration are reinforced by the preferences that respondents have for immigrant groups. They favor European immigrants over Asians and Asian over Hispanic immigrants. Though immigration is currently a major preoccupation among voters, their opinions carry an ambiguous message for policy-makers. Polls show, Espenshade and Berger argue, that while the public feels that government should be doing more to control the flow of undocumented migrants, they are reluctant to support the harsh measures that are more likely to be effective.

## Consequences for U.S.-Mexico Relations

The political implications of Mexican migration are nowhere more evident than in the recent history of U.S.-Mexico relations. Though NAFTA gave little attention to the flow of labor between Canada, the United States, and Mexico, the migration issue figured prominently in the arguments for and against the agreement. The virtual ignoring of labor migration in NAFTA indicates, argues Peter Smith in his paper, the contradictions between U.S. trade policy with Mexico and its immigration policy. Labor migration was too controversial a political and economic issue to include in NAFTA; but NAFTA was promoted in the United States as offering a solution to Mexican migration to the United States through an economic development in Mexico that would retain potential migrants. Opponents of NAFTA argued, in contrast, that the agreement would destroy jobs in Mexico, particularly in agriculture, thus increasing migration to the United States.

It is virtually impossible to determine which of these expectations is correct, as Smith points out, because it is too early to estimate the impact of NAFTA on migration. Moreover, it is difficult to disentangle the effect of NAFTA from that of other economic and political factors that impact the flow of Mexican migration to the United States. These include, for example, the cycles of growth and stagnation in the Mexican and in the U.S. economies, and the efficiency of immigration control measures. Debates over whether NAFTA diminishes or increases Mexican migration are, Smith argues, beside the point. Effective immigration controls, particularly employer sanctions, are likely to reduce migration, but so long as Mexican wage levels are substantially below those of the United States, and U.S. employers want to take advantage of this labor pool, there will be continuing pressures leading Mexicans to migrate.

Smith emphasizes the desirability of making immigration policy with Mexico more compatible with trade policy, since closer economic links are unlikely to thrive in the climate of political suspicion and hostility that the immigration issue is creates between the United States and Mexico. He advocates policies that combine deterrence, particularly employer sanctions, with those that give special attention to Mexico through bilateral consultations over issues such as a guest-worker program, the apprehension of those who traffic in migrants (the *coyotes*) and the targeting of development aid to traditional sending areas. Above all, he emphasizes the importance of sticking with NAFTA as a means of sustained development in Mexico and thus the basis for resolving the migration issue.

Mexico and the United States have had a long and often troubled historical relationship. In his chapter, Sidney Weintraub places Mexican migration within the context of this relationship. He sees Mexican immigration as essentially an intractable issue. A common border, a history of conflict and conquest that left a strong residue of ethnic prejudice against Mexicans in the United States, the many kinship relationships between Mexicans in the United States and in Mexico, and the economics of supply and demand all ensure that Mexican migrants come to the United States and are likely to be a main target when anti-immigrant fervor rises.

He emphasizes that the relationship between Mexico and the United States is complicated by regional and sectoral issues as well as by national foreign policy issues. Thus, in the United States, employers who have special needs for Mexican immigrants are concentrated in certain states and in certain sectors of agriculture. Their interests have often been in conflict with those of others in their own states or elsewhere in the United States who see immigrants only as a fiscal burden. Likewise, alliances are often cross-national as enterprises in the United States seek links with agricultural workers in Mexico or combine in joint production with Mexican growers.

U.S. policy, as Weintraub points out, has had repeated turnabouts, alternatively welcoming and rejecting Mexican immigrants depending on the need of the U.S. economy for labor. The Mexican authorities have, in turn, used the U.S. demand for Mexican labor to define Mexican migration to the United States as essentially a market issue of supply and demand that involves the Mexican government only insofar as the rights of Mexican subjects abroad are abused. A situation has thus been created, Weintraub argues, in which Mexican policy-makers tend to react to U.S. policies rather than suggesting initiatives of their own. Weintraub warns of the problems this situation is creating for U.S.-Mexico relations, especially since the economic crisis in Mexico has made NAFTA look less attractive to Mexicans, while the passage of Proposition 187 in California and the incidents in Riverside County have embittered Mexican attitudes to the United States.

The chapter concludes with a strong plea to commentators on both sides not to overreact to immigration issues and to understand the constraints that policy-makers in both countries face. The immigration issue, Weintraub points out, will not go away since, as he puts it, the rural exodus in Mexico is inexorable. But immigration should not be allowed to dominate the policy agenda between the two countries.

## Implications for Immigration Policy

Before closing, it is worth noting that there are some topics that we have not been able to cover here in depth that clearly have implications for immigration policy and for U.S.-Mexico relations. Temporal and financial constraints kept us from being able to cover everything we would like to have included. In particular, we do not have a chapter that looks specifically at changes in U.S. urban labor markets that are attracting Mexican migrants. Gelbard and Carter provide some information on employment characteristics of Mexican migrants, showing that by 1990 only 13 percent of the Mexican foreign-born population was employed in agriculture. And Martin, as well as Freeman and Bean, provide some discussion illustrating the influence of U.S. labor demand on Mexican migration flows. But in general we do not treat this subject at length. Nor were we able to include chapters on the U.S. labor market impact of Mexican migration or on how the continued growth of the Mexican origin population will affect U.S. politics, especially in view of recent dramatic increases in the number of immigrants who are becoming American citizens.

These limitations notwithstanding, the collection of chapters presented here illustrate that the debate over Mexican migration raises a broader set of issues that confront U.S. policy makers. These include the continuing demand on the part of some U.S. employers for an unskilled, temporary labor pool. This demand exists alongside a large potential supply of migrants from the developing world attracted by the sharp contrasts in wage levels between the United States and the developing world. A substantial undocumented migrant presence means, however, that large numbers of U.S. residents occupy a no-man's land in terms of their legal rights. This situation not only subjects them to exploitation, but could substantially informalize U.S. society and economy. More positively, there is also the issue of the extent to which migration policy can serve as a form of development aid through migrant remittances, through imparting skills to migrants which they can take back to their countries of origin, and through fostering migrant-based transnational economic enterprises and infra structural projects. In addition, there is the general question of what role U.S. immigration policy can play in fostering further integration between the United States and Mexico. These and other policy issues are examined in the concluding chapter.

## References

Bean, Frank D., and Michael Fix. 1992. The Significance of Recent Immigration Policy Reforms in the United States. In G. Freeman and J. Jupp, eds. *Nations of Immigrants: Australia, the United States, and International Migration*. Melbourne: Oxford University Press, pp. 41-55.

Bean, Frank D., G. Vernez, and C. B. Kelly. 1989. *Opening and Closing the Doors: Evaluating Immigration Reform and Control.* Washington, D.C.: The Urban Institute Press.

Beck, Roy. 1996. *The Case Against Immigration: The Moral, Economic, Social, and Environmental Reasons for Reducing U.S. Immigration Back to Traditional Levels.* New York: W. W. Norton and Company.

Brimelow, Peter. 1995. *Alien Nation: Common Sense About America's Immigration Disaster.* New York: Random House.

Cardoso, Lawrence A. 1980. *Mexican Emigration to the United States 1897-1931.* Tucson: The University of Arizona Press.

Castañeda, Jorge G. 1995. *The Mexican Shock: Its Meaning for the U.S.* New York: The New Press.

Fuentes, Carlos. 1996. *A New Time for Mexico.* New York: Farrar, Straus and Giroux.

Gamio, Manuel. 1930. *Mexican Immigration to the United States.* Chicago: University of Chicago Press.

Hoffman, Abraham. 1972. Mexican Repatriation Statistics: Some Suggested Alternatives to Carey McWilliams. *Western Historical Quarterly* 3: 391-404.

Jasso, Guillermina, and Mark R. Rosenzweig. 1990. *The New Chosen People: Immigrants in the United States.* New York: Russell Sage Foundation.

Katz, Friederich (ed.). 1988. *Riot, Rebellion, and Revolution: Rural Social Conflict in Mexico.* Princeton: Princeton University Press.

Knight, Alan, 1986. *The Mexican Revolution.* 2 vols. Cambridge: Cambridge University Press.

Oppenheimer, Andres. 1995. *Bordering on Chaos: Guerillas, Stockbrokers, Politicians, and Mexico's Road to Prosperity.* Boston: Little, Brown and Company.

Romo, Ricardo, 1983. *East Los Angeles: History of a Barrio.* Austin: University of Texas Press.

Taylor, Paul, 1970 [1932]. *Mexican Labor in the United States, Vols I and II.* New York: Arno Press.

Teitelbaum, Michael S., and Myron Weiner (eds.). 1995. *Threatened Peoples, Threatened Borders.* New York: W. W. Norton and Company.

# 1.
# Mexico and U.S. Worldwide Immigration Policy

*Gary P. Freeman and Frank D. Bean*

A number of circumstances—the size of Mexico's population (about 95 million) in 1996, the 1900-mile border it shares with the United States, and a sizeable Mexican-origin population in the United States (over 15 million)—point to the increasing importance of Mexico for U.S. worldwide immigration policy. Currently, the movement of people across the U.S.-Mexico border is the subject of intense interest and controversy. The U.S. approach to cross-border flows, legal and illegal, is in flux; the economic and political climate in Mexico is uncertain; and relations between the two neighbors have entered a new stage with the launching of the North American Free Trade Agreement. This chapter seeks to provide background and context for examining how Mexico has fit into U.S. immigration law and practice in the past and rethinking what the U.S.-Mexico relationship might be in the future.

Our survey will address three chronic tensions in overall U.S. immigration policy that have particular consequences for Mexico. The first is strain between the idea that our national immigration law should be founded on the fundamental equality of persons versus the idea that policy should take into account the needs or interests of particular countries and/or regions within the United States that appear to warrant exceptions to general policies. Universalism is consistent with the doctrine of human rights as enunciated in the Declaration of Independence and more recently in instruments promulgated by the United Nations. Commitment to equal treatment has recently turned U.S. policy away from considerations of race and national origins toward a color-blind system which, in principle, gives persons in every country in the world an equal opportunity to receive a visa to the United States. Equal treatment is also behind the effort to establish a unified worldwide policy. On the other hand, special circumstances lead policy makers to exempt some countries from general rules, often in response to the demands of influential regional interests in the United States. This has been a persistent characteristic of policy toward Mexico, leading some to claim that it has been accorded *de facto* status as a "most-favored nation" for purposes of migration (Corwin, 1978).

The second tension in U.S. policy is between the mounting desire for control of population movements across national borders and the perennial if cyclical demand for access to Mexican (and other foreign) labor to meet employers' needs in agriculture and industry. The effects of this conflict are especially evident in the frequent disparity between the formal rules of the immigration system and the way those rules are enforced. The gap between the two is often sufficiently large to suggest it is a deliberate attempt to reconcile apparently irreconcilable objectives of policies that fail to satisfy the diverse interests of important sectors of American society.

Third, the impulse to treat control of national borders as a core element of the prerogatives of national sovereignty conflicts with the recognition that immigration policy often raises multilateral issues between sending and receiving states that require negotiation. U.S. policy has typically been implemented unilaterally, often precipitating protests from Mexican authorities caught unawares. In recent years, however, there has been growing willingness to inform, if not consult, on immigration and border issues, both at the national and at the regional, state, and local levels.

We address the particular role of Mexico within an analysis of general policy developments that illustrates these dualities. U.S. decision makers have at various times perceived Mexico (1) as a pool of cheap, unskilled, seasonal labor; (2) as a source of illegal migration that threatens, periodically, to undermine the ability of the U.S. to control its borders; (3) and as an ally whose dependability is often in question due to economic and political instability and for whom migration represents an indispensable safety valve against social unrest. These competing perspectives have produced inconsistent and contradictory policies.

Our review will stress several specific aspects of U.S. policy. First, the salience of Mexico for U.S. immigration decision makers varies considerably over time.

Always important to dominant economic interests and their political representatives in the Southwest, Mexico was seldom central to the preoccupations of national elites until the twentieth century. Even then, interest in Mexico has tended to wax and wane with fluctuations in the American economy and political events in Mexico. Second, U.S. immigration policy has dealt with Mexico with a combination of *formal* exemptions from general rules and a pervasive pattern of *informal* concessions through desultory and often deliberate non-enforcement of the law. Finally, Mexico has been incorporated within a unified worldwide immigration policy only since 1978, and during this brief period there have been repeated efforts to reintroduce elements of the exceptionalism that has long characterized U.S. policy.

## The Evolution of Policy

Mexicans never constituted as much as one percent of total migration to the United States until 1910 (see Table 1.1). Nevertheless, migration has been central to the history of the Southwest. Although today the dominant movement is from south to north, American settlement in northern Mexico led to the secession of the Texas Republic and to its admission into the United States in 1845.[1] The Treaty of Guadalupe Hidalgo in 1848, which brought the war over Texas to a close, rearranged the boundaries between the two countries and made parts of the Southwest previously open to Mexicans technically off limits.

Migration from Mexico to the United States in the second half of the nineteenth century was, in fact, almost wholly unrestricted. Mexicans moved easily across the border to help build the railroads in the region, to work in seasonal agriculture, and to create such bi-national cities as Juarez-El Paso. As U.S. national immigration policy began to develop, it made special accommodation for Mexico either by limiting the law's scope to the Eastern Hemisphere or by taking steps to exempt Mexican migrant workers from specific provisions applying in the West. One of the first important examples of the tendency toward Mexican exceptionalism in U.S. immigration law was prompted by the passage, over Woodrow Wilson's veto, of the Immigration Act of 1917. Responding to an outcry among Southwestern growers, the Secretary of Labor used his powers under the act to waive two of its provisions, the literacy test and the head tax, for Mexican farm workers. During World War I, President Wilson authorized the Food Administration and the U.S. Employment Service to act as employers and contractors with Mexican workers as they crossed the border.[2]

Mexican migration rose significantly after the Revolution in 1910. Concern over this influx came to a head during the fight over immigration restriction in the twenties, even though that episode was focused largely on European migrants.

Table 1.1
**Legal Mexican Immigration to the United States, 1881–1994**

| Decade or Year | Number (in thousands) | As Percent of Total Immigration |
|---|---|---|
| 1881–1890 | 2 | 0.0 |
| 1891–1900 | 1 | 0.0 |
| 1901–1910 | 50 | 0.6 |
| 1911–1920 | 219 | 3.8 |
| 1921–1930 | 459 | 11.2 |
| 1931–1940 | 22 | 4.2 |
| 1941–1950 | 61 | 5.9 |
| 1951–1960 | 300 | 11.9 |
| 1961–1970 | 454 | 13.7 |
| 1971–1980 | 637 | 14.2 |
| 1981–1980 | 1651 | 22.5 |
| 1981 | 101 | 17.0 |
| 1982 | 54 | 9.1 |
| 1983 | 59 | 10.6 |
| 1984 | 58 | 10.6 |
| 1985 | 61 | 10.7 |
| 1986 | 67 | 11.1 |
| 1987 | 72 | 12.0 |
| 1988 | 95 | 14.8 |
| 1989 | 405 | 37.1 |
| 1990 | 679 | 44.2 |
| 1991–1994 | 1398 | 31.0 |
| 1991 | 946 | 51.8 |
| 1992 | 214 | 22.0 |
| 1993 | 127 | 14.0 |
| 1994 | 111 | 13.9 |

SOURCE: U.S. Immigration and Naturalization Service, Statistical Yearbooks (1981–1994), Portes and Bach, 1985, table 10, p. 79.

There was a significant effort to restrict migration from Mexico through the National Origins Quota Act of 1924. A coalition led by southern members of Congress, especially Representative Box of Texas, rallied behind the call for "closing the back door" to immigration (LeMay, 1987, p. 89). That door remained open, however, in the face of concerted opposition from Southwestern farmers, cattlemen, mining, sugar, and railroad interests (p. 90; cf. Reimers, 1982, p. 13). The State Department opposed restrictions as well, articulating a strong interest in pan-Americanism. Later, in 1929, when Senator Harris of Georgia introduced an amendment to the quota law to limit Mexican entries, President Hoover threatened a veto.

Despite the absence of hemispheric or country ceilings, officials had the authority to limit immigration from the region under the "qualitative" exclusions incorporated in U.S. law, such as the literacy test and the health and public charge provisions. These measures were not effective in the early years. Between 1918 and 1921, less that 0.5 percent of prospective immigrants were excluded because of inability to read (Rico, 1992, p. 243). About 1.5 million persons immigrated to the U.S. from the Western Hemisphere in the twenties (459,000 from Mexico); perhaps another half-million Mexicans came illegally (Portes and Bach, 1985, pp. 76-83; Reimers, 1982, p. 13). No agency with responsibility for controlling the land borders existed until 1924, when Congress created the Border Patrol.[3] The Great Depression succeeded, however, where law had not. Legal entries from Mexico in the thirties fell by 95 percent (see Table 1.1). The decade also witnessed a good deal of voluntary and involuntary repatriation of Mexicans from the southwest; perhaps as many as 400,000 went home (Hoffman,1974, p. ix; Hoffman, 1978).

With the outbreak of World War II, however, labor shortages again became an issue. Growers in the southwest demanded access to temporary Mexican labor. Congress responded with the *Bracero* program (1942-1964), which had enormous implications for subsequent Mexican migration to the U.S. as it fostered a parallel illegal migration and re-established the practice of seasonal agricultural work that had declined significantly during the Depression.[4] The *Bracero* agreement illustrated the continuing effort to shape U.S. policy to address simultaneously pressure emanating from the eastern industrial region to eliminate illegal entry, while maintaining access to Mexican labor in the southwest (Bach, 1985, pp. 92-96). Fatefully, the U.S. unilaterally ended the program in 1964 just as it was about to impose a ceiling on Western Hemisphere immigration for the first time.

The 1952 McCarran-Walter Act retained the principles of the National Origins Quota Act of 1924 but created a preference system for the allocation of visas. The act formally linked immigration policy to labor market considerations by favoring persons with special skills in short supply in the United States. McCarran-Walter did not extend the quota system to the Western Hemisphere. Nor was the debate over the act much concerned with the *Bracero* program or illegal immigration. As Reimers notes, the McCarran subcommittee supported temporary labor programs and tighter border controls, but "in general these were not pressing issues surrounding the 1952 act and were seldom discussed" (p. 28). The law also included the so-called "Texas Proviso," which criminalized "the willful importation, transportation or harboring of illegal aliens" while holding harmless any employer (Rico, 1992, p. 246). According to the Bilateral Commission on the Future of United States-Mexican Relations, "this provision exemplifies the main source of tension and misunderstanding between the two countries. Even in the face of anti-foreign public sentiment, the Texas Proviso implicitly acknowledged that some U.S. employers strongly desired Mexican labor" (1989, p. 102).[5]

One indicator of the marginality of Mexican migration to worldwide policy in this era is the report of the President's Commission on Immigration and Naturalization, *Whom We Shall Welcome* (1953), produced in the wake of the passage of the McCarran-Walter Act over Truman's veto. The report recommended the abolition of the national origins quota system and the adoption of a unified annual quota system equal to one-sixth of one percent of the total population of the United States at the latest census (p. 118). Admission would be without regard to national origin, but the annual quota would not apply to countries in the Western Hemisphere. The commission's report devotes only one sentence to illegal migration from Mexico (p. 31).

In fact, illegal migration from Mexico, which had declined considerably in the thirties, had begun to rise again in the forties and fifties, either as an accompaniment to the *Bracero* program or in place of it. A bi-lateral agreement between Mexico and the U.S. in 1949 legalized many undocumented farm workers and in 1951 the President's Commission on Migratory Labor complained that more *braceros* were being regularized than directly recruited. In June 1954 "Operation Wetback" was launched. According to Reimers, "the success of the INS in 1954 in removing illegals was so dramatic that the question of illegal immigration remained unimportant throughout the 1960s" (p. 46).

The 1965 amendments to the Immigration and Nationality Act finally eliminated the national origins quota system. They raised the ceiling for Eastern Hemisphere migrants to 170,000 and established an annual limit of 20,000 visas for any one country. The law also modified the preference system to the advantage of persons with relatives already in the United States. Insofar as the Western Hemisphere was concerned, an overall ceiling of 120,000 visas per year was adopted for the first time, but no limits were placed on specific countries. Even this limited step was resisted by the Kennedy and Johnson administrations.[6] The bill drafted by the Kennedy White House had retained the traditional unlimited entry from the Western Hemisphere. During the congressional stage, however, Senators Everett Dirksen (R-Ill) and Sam Ervin (D-NC) forced the (now Johnson) administration to accept a ceiling as the price of passage.[7] It was the *quid pro quo* for the abolition of the national origins quota system.[8]

The extent of resistance to numerical limitations on Mexican and Latin American migration is suggested by the provision in the 1965 amendments creating the Select Commission on Western Hemisphere Immigration. If, on the recommendation of the commission, legislation was enacted prior to July 1, 1968, the ceiling would not go into effect. In that event, the commission report reached no consensus on a recommendation to Congress. Instead, it suggested that implementation be delayed one year.[9] Congress allowed the ceiling to go into effect on schedule, but without per country limits.

The 1965 amendments excluded the entry of spouses, unmarried minor children, and parents of U.S. citizens from the hemispheric ceilings. The imposition of the ceiling led, nonetheless, to a growing backlog of visa applications from Latin American countries, especially Mexico. These were lodged by persons related to previous immigrants but who were in categories falling under the numerical ceiling. By 1976 there was a waiting period of more than two years for eligible new applicants from the region. Briggs notes that "the backlog gave credence to earlier arguments that population pressures in Latin America were so strong that, if restrictions were not imposed, a massive migration from these nations to the United States would eventually take place" (1992, p. 113; Briggs and Moore, p. 18).

In an effort to regulate admissions and avoid imposing hardships on families, in 1976 Congress finally imposed the 20,000 annual limit on countries in the region, as well as the seven-category preference system and labor certification process. These moves, while dictated by the desire that "people of all nations should be treated equally in terms of their opportunity to immigrate to the United States" (Briggs, 1992, p. 114), had the effect of exacerbating the backlog of Mexican visa applications that had prompted concern in the first place. When the 20,000-per-year limit went into effect, Mexico was already supplying over three times that number of legal immigrants annually. One outcome of the new country limits was that the number of non-quota immigrants from Mexico rose considerably after 1976 (see Table 1.2), keeping it a major sending country (Rico, 1992, pp. 232-233; Bilateral Commission, 1989, p. 83).

The State Department had been opposed to limits on annual migration from Mexico, but the pressure to enact them was apparently irresistible. In 1975, State and Justice had issued a joint statement endorsing uniform quotas for all countries and noting that even if there were no limit on Mexican migration there would still be problems with illegal immigration (cited in Reimers, 1982, p. 43). President Gerald Ford nonetheless criticized the provision when he signed the bill and promised to submit legislation in the next Congress "to increase the immigration quotas for Mexicans desiring to come to the United States" (cited in Reimers, p. 43). A presidential election intervened.

**Table 1.2**
**Legal Mexican Immigrants Admitted by Type of Admission**
**(Selected Years 1947 to 1994)**

| | Quota | | Non-Quota | |
|---|---|---|---|---|
| | Number | % of Total | Number | % of Total |
| 1947 | 286 | 3.8 | 7,272 | 96.2 |
| 1950 | 174 | 2.6 | 6,570 | 97.4 |
| 1955 | 88 | 0.2 | 43,614 | 99.8 |
| 1960 | 150 | 0.5 | 32,558 | 99.5 |
| 1965 | 168 | 0.4 | 40,518 | 99.6 |
| 1970 | 27,267 | 60.8 | 17,554 | 39.2 |
| 1975 | 42,218 | 67.5 | 20,334 | 32.5 |
| 1980 | 24,831 | 43.8 | 31,849 | 56.2 |
| 1985 | 20,633 | 33.8 | 40,444 | 66.2 |
| 1986 | 20,369 | 30.6 | 46,164 | 69.4 |
| 1987 | 21,558 | 29.8 | 50,793 | 70.2 |
| 1988 | 20,341 | 21.4 | 74,698 | 67.6 |
| 1989 | 20,922 | 5.2 | 384,250 | 94.8 |
| 1990 | 20,134 | 3.0 | 658,934 | 97.0 |
| 1991 | 19,683 | 2.1 | 926,484 | 97.90 |
| 1992 | 36,587 | 17.1 | 177,215 | 82.9 |
| 1993 | 36,754 | 29.0 | 89,807 | 71.0 |
| 1994 | 42,392 | 38.1 | 69,006 | 62.0 |

SOURCE: U.S. Immigration and Naturalization Service, Statistical Yearbooks (1986-1994); Report of the Bilateral Commission on the Future of United States-Mexican Relations, 1989, Table 3-2, p. 83.

In 1978 another amendment to the 1965 act combined the two hemispheric ceilings so that there was one worldwide numerical limitation (290,000 visas) for the first time. The imposition of the ceiling and the country limits, along with the unilateral cessation of the Bracero program in 1964, contributed directly to the rise in illegal migration from Mexico and from Latin America more generally (Briggs, 1992, p. 152). It also meant that after 1976 there were no non-preference visas available to anyone under the U.S. program. As Briggs argues, "the only channel available for people determined to immigrate but who did not meet the preference requirements was to enter illegally" (p. 152).

The United States had no truly "worldwide" immigration policy until 1978. A *country-neutral* immigration policy, at least formally, has been in place for only eighteen years. The main force driving the adoption of a world-wide country-neutral policy was the desire to remove all vestiges of the national origins quota system from American immigration law. The elimination of any consideration of national origins was a victory on the part of those advocating civil rights and non-discrimination and was consistent with developments in international human rights and refugee law (the United States also ratified the U.N. Protocol on Refugees in 1967). Once the need to place numerical limits on Western Hemisphere migration was conceded, country-neutral quotas followed logically.

Even so, there was resistance to submitting Mexico to the same visa limits as other countries when the Western Hemisphere ceiling was adopted, and efforts to alter the law in Mexico's favor have continued. In August 1977 the Carter administration offered an immigration bill dealing mostly with illegal immigration, but including a provision that would have raised the annual quotas for Canada and Mexico from 20,000 to a combined 50,000 based on demand. This would have meant that about 42,000 would have gone to Mexicans, as Canadians were using only about 8,000 per year at the time (Briggs, 1992, p. 154). The bill died, but the idea did not go away.

The Contiguous Neighbors Act of 1978, sponsored by Senator Edward Kennedy, incorporated the Carter proposal (Teitelbaum, 1985, p. 41). It was unsuccessful, but its main provisions were later included in various versions of the Simpson-Mazzoli bills, only to be deleted before final passage in 1986 (Rico, 1992, p. 262). Both the Kennedy and Simpson-Mazzoli versions, as with the earlier Carter proposal, anticipated that Canada would underutilize its quota and that Mexico would claim the balance. In other words, the apparent parity between Canada and Mexico was a transparent effort to inflate the number of visas going to Mexicans.

Having ignored the Carter administration's suggestions for immigration reform, in October 1978 Congress established the Select Commission on Immigration and Refugee Policy and ordered it to report by March 1980. Certain interest groups, such as the Hispanic Task Force, urged that Mexico be given larger quotas than other countries and the commission staff considered both special quotas for Mexico and Canada and a worldwide scheme for different ceilings based on each country's particular situation (Herschkowitz, 1994, pp. 134, 136). Nonetheless, a slim majority of the commission recommended adopting a fixed percentage quota applicable to all countries (Select Commission, 1981, pp. 140-141).[10]

## IRCA and Its Aftermath

The Select Commission's recommendations set the agenda for major immigration legislation in 1986. The Immigration Reform and Control Act (IRCA) focused most directly on illegal immigration, understood to be primarily from Latin America and Mexico. While the law imposed civil and criminal penalties on employers who knowingly hired undocumented workers, it also granted legalization to all undocumented persons living continuously in the United States since before January 1, 1982, and to persons who had been engaged in seasonal agricultural work for at least 90 days during the years immediately preceding passage of the legislation (the so-called SAWs legalization). IRCA was the first piece of immigration legislation seeking to regulate flows by dealing with the "demand" for immigrants as opposed to its "supply" (Bilateral Commission, 1989, p. 100).

Because IRCA has been the central legislative response to illegal migration to date and because conflict over illegal migration (over half of which comes from Mexico) continues to dominate the debate over immigration policy reform, it is useful to consider IRCA's impact closely. One major criterion by which the law's effectiveness can be judged is the extent to which the law reduced the flow of illegal immigrants into the country and the size of the resident illegal alien population (beyond the reduction brought about by the legalization programs). Certainly IRCA reduced the number of illegal residents by virtue of its legalization program. The SAWs program also legalized substantial numbers of temporary migrants. But was the flow of migrants coming into the country reduced? That is, apart from changes in the size of the undocumented population already here, did IRCA reduce the numbers of illegal entrants coming to the United States, especially in the years immediately after its passage?

An answer to this question can be obtained by examining INS apprehensions data, one of the most frequently cited sources of information about undocumented immigration to the United States. Apprehensions statistics come from monthly tallies of the number of times persons entering the country illegally are apprehended by the U.S. Border Patrol or by other INS enforcement personnel. Over 95 percent of apprehensions (97 percent in fiscal years 1987 through 1993) are made by the Border Patrol, and of these, more than 99 percent consist of persons who "enter without inspection" (EWIs) as opposed to persons who enter on tourist, student, or work visas and then overstay the term of the visa (overstayers). Most Border Patrol apprehensions occur at the U.S.-Mexico border (e.g., 97 percent in 1987) and most of these involve entrants from Mexico (98 percent in 1987) (Espenshade, White, and Bean 1990). The number of apprehensions of illegal entrants has averaged over 1.2 million a year since 1980. These numbers seem to imply an illegal population of enormous size in the United States. But such apprehensions include not only various types of migrants, they also include persons who have been apprehended several times. Also, many persons apprehended during a given year return to Mexico before the end of the year. Thus, the number of apprehensions, which peaked at 1,767,400 in fiscal year 1986 (U.S. Immigration and Naturalization Service, 1996), substantially overstates the size of the illegal population that enters and remains in the country within any year.

Apprehension statistics are particularly useful for inferring changes from one time period to another in the flow of undocumented entrants (Bean et al, 1990; Espenshade, 1990; Espenshade, 1995). Data on apprehensions are virtually the only large data base from which to gauge, however roughly, flows from Mexico. In fact, total Border Patrol apprehensions declined in the three years after the passage of IRCA, dropping from 1,767,400 in FY 1986 to 1,190,488 in FY 1987, to 1,008,145 in FY 1988, and to 954,253 in FY 1989. However, the number of apprehensions of illegals along the U.S.-Mexican border reflects in part the level and vigor of the INS effort to intercept the flow. For example, the number of hours devoted to patrolling the border has fluctuated over the years. To make apprehensions a better indicator of changes in the undocumented flow, it is important to remove this source of variation. To minimize the influence of changes in enforcement strategies that occur away from the border that can influence apprehensions independently of the number of illegal crossings, it is useful to focus attention on so-called line-watch apprehensions, or those apprehensions which result from the direct patrolling of the border.

Table 1.3 includes data on the number of line-watch apprehensions, line-watch hours, and line-watch apprehensions per hour for fiscal years 1977-95. These years encompass five distinct periods. The first is 1977-82 (a period of relative boom in the Mexican economy) during which line-watch apprehensions were relatively stable (even slightly lower, at times) and the number of apprehensions per hour declined slightly. The second period is 1983-86 (after the slowdown in the Mexican economy but before the passage of IRCA) during which line-watch apprehensions jumped sharply (by almost 46 percent from FY 1982 to FY 1983). After a lag, line-watch hours also increased, and importantly, line-watch apprehensions per hour climbed substantially (by more than 47 percent compared to the 1977-82 years).

The third period includes 1987-1989 (the fiscal years immediately after the passage of IRCA) during which line-watch apprehensions declined, as did line-watch apprehensions per hour. A comparison of the average number of apprehensions per line-watch hour for 1987, 1988, and 1989, with the average for 1983-86, shows a decline from 0.355 to 0.268, or a drop of about 24 percent. Even with this reduction, line-watch apprehensions did not fall to their 1977-82 levels. The extent to which IRCA itself was responsible for this decline after 1986 is an issue we return to below.

**Table 1.3**
**Yearly Line-Watch Apprehensions and Hours, FY 1977–1995**

| Fiscal Year | Line-Watch Apprehensions | Line-Watch Hours | LWAs per Hour |
|---|---|---|---|
| 1977 | 441,265 | 1,740,446 | 0.254 |
| 1978 | 481,612 | 1,762,616 | 0.273 |
| 1979 | 488,941 | 1,935,926 | 0.253 |
| 1980 | 428,966 | 1,815,797 | 0.236 |
| 1981 | 452,821 | 1,929,448 | 0.235 |
| 1982 | 443,437 | 1,871,173 | 0.237 |
| 1983 | 646,311 | 1,976,126 | 0.327 |
| 1984 | 623,944 | 1,843,179 | 0.339 |
| 1985 | 666,402 | 1,912,895 | 0.348 |
| 1986 | 946,341 | 2,401,575 | 0.394 |
| 1987 | 750,954 | 2,546,397 | 0.295 |
| 1988 | 614,653 | 2,069,498 | 0.297 |
| 1989 | 521,899 | 2,436,788 | 0.214 |
| 1990 | 668,282 | 2,549,137 | 0.262 |
| 1991 | 711,808 | 2,390,500 | 0.298 |
| 1992 | 814,290 | 2,386,888 | 0.341 |
| 1993 | 840,326 | 2,713,024 | 0.310 |
| 1994 | 687,163 | 3,074,060 | 0.224 |
| 1995* | 480,580 | 1,891,413 | 0.254 |

| | Mean | Mean | LWAs per Hour |
|---|---|---|---|
| 1977–82 | 456,174 | 1,842,568 | 0.248 |
| 1983–86 | 720,750 | 2,033,444 | 0.354 |
| 1987–89 | 629,169 | 2,350,894 | 0.268 |
| 1990–93 | 758,677 | 2,509,887 | 0.302 |
| 1994–95* | 699,247 | 2,973,337 | 0.235 |

SOURCE: INS Statistical Yearbooks and special INS tabulations.
NOTE: *FY-95 only includes September1994–April 1995.

The fourth period is the years 1990-1993 (the "late" IRCA but pre-NAFTA period) during which apprehensions again moved upward closer to pre-IRCA levels, indicating that any deterrent effects of IRCA had seemingly dissipated. The fifth period is fiscal years 1994 and 1995, which are the post-NAFTA and (in the case of 1995) the post-peso-devaluation years. It is difficult to interpret apprehensions data during this time unless new and specially targeted enforcement efforts during the period (e.g., those involved in Operations Hold-the-Line and Gatekeeper) are explicitly and carefully taken into account. After carefully considering the impact of such factors, one recent study argued that the apparent increases in the flows from Mexico during 1995 are at least as much the result of conditions in the United States as they are the consequence of conditions in Mexico (Bean and Cushing, 1994). This being the case, the recent increases in flows much discusssed in the press would not appear to be attributable solely to the negative economic consequences following the Mexican peso devaluation.

Other studies about IRCA's effects present evidence that is more relevant to stock than flow assessments. Woodrow and Passel (1990) examined 1980 Census data and a series of CPS (Current Population Survey) data sources from the 1980s (including the June 1988 CPS) in order to estimate the size of the illegal population included in these data sources and its change over time. They found that the undocumented population of the United States declined after IRCA to the point where the total number in 1988 may have been smaller than the number in the country in 1980 (estimated by Passel [1986] to be in the range of 2.5 to 3.5 million). Although they did not find evidence for a decrease in the overall net flow of illegal migrants, their results indicated the possibility of a decline in the flow of undocumented immigrants from Mexico (thus supporting the evidence reported above from apprehensions data regarding flows across the U.S.-Mexico border).

In sum, the evidence from a wide variety of research studies is generally consistent in indicating that IRCA brought about a reduction in illegal Mexican immigration to the United States during the three years immediately after the legislation was passed (Espenshade, 1995; Bean et al, 1990; Donato, Durand and Massey, 1992). After 1989, research results suggest that undocumented immigration was again on the rise. An important further question from a policy point of view concerns the extent to which the reduction that occurred was due to IRCA, and explicitly due to the deterrent effects of employer sanctions. While IRCA's legalization programs clearly accounted for a substantial part of the reduction, they did not account for all of it, suggesting that sanctions might explain the remainder (Bean, Passel, and Edmonston, 1990). However, the fact that the implementation of sanctions occurred gradually over a three-year period (1987-89), with the INS not fully enforcing sanctions compliance until 1989, the third year after the law was passed, suggests that sanctions may *not* have accounted for the decline. The greatest reductions took place in the first and second years of the legislation, not in subsequent years when sanctions were more strongly enforced. Thus, the decrease in flows during 1987-89 appear to have owed less to the deterrent effects of sanctions than to some other factors, perhaps generalized patterns of anxiety and rumor, especially in Mexico, about what the effects of the law might be on migrants who moved to the United States. Once it was learned that the legislation was not going to lead to draconian outcomes (such as undocumenteds being thrown in jail), the process of undocumented labor migration resumed unabated.

After IRCA was passed, it was unclear whether the legislation signaled a new restrictive phase in American immigration policy (Bean, Vernez, and Keely, 1989). If we consider IRCA's features in combination with those of the Immigration Act of 1990, which substantially increased overall legal admissions, it is hard to argue that the last ten years represent a new restrictionism. But IRCA and the 1990 Act may again reflect an uneasy compromise involving the tolerance of increased legal and illegal entrants as long as the perception of control remains in place. The central control mechanism in IRCA, employer sanctions, appears to be more symbolic than real in its effects. The chief control mechanism in the 1990 Act, the ceiling on legal admissions, also is more symbolic than real because the ceiling is "pierceable" and because overall the act increased immigration. Thus, both pieces of legislation give the appearance of control while either not changing illegal immigration very much (in the case of IRCA) nor holding the line on legal immigration (in the case of the Immigration Act of 1990). Thus, U.S. policy toward Mexican undocumented migration as represented by IRCA has maintained its curiously contradictory character, emphasizing the appearance of control while in fact failing to stop substantial undocumented flows (Bean and Fix, 1992).

## Recent Developments

By the time Congress got around to passing legislation on legal immigration in the early nineties, there was growing concern that new entries were coming predominantly from Latin America and Asia and there was interest in the difficulty potential migrants from traditional European sending countries faced acquiring visas. These new realities were the combined effect of the family reunion and country-neutral features of the law, as amended in 1965. By the late 1980s about 85 percent of all legal immigrants were coming from Asian and Latin American countries; only about 10 percent from Europe.[11]

One of IRCA's major legacies is the roughly 2.7 million successful applicants for legalization, over 70 percent of whom were from Mexico (U.S. Department of Justice, 1992). The legalization entrants continue to be a major contributor to legal immigration because of subsequent decisions to admit dependents of those legalized. Legalization also probably contributes to illegal immigration as dependents come to the U.S. illegally while waiting to be granted entry visas. Thus, without giving Mexico any explicit preference in law, and without changing the country quotas, IRCA had the effect of vastly increasing the Mexican share of official immigration in the years 1989-1992 (see Table 1.1).

These considerations appear to have pushed aside, momentarily, the argument that Mexico should be given even more visas. Senator Kennedy had been behind earlier changes that took immigration law away from its emphasis on national origins, but during hearings in 1987 he said: "One of the issues . . . that I am particularly concerned about is . . . how we correct the unexpected imbalances stemming from the 1965 Act—the inadvertent restriction on immigration from the 'old seed' sources of our heritage" (cited in Briggs, p. 169). The Kennedy-Simpson bill that passed the Senate on March 15, 1988, provided for 50,000 visas for independent migrants, those who could qualify neither under the family or occupational categories. Applicants were to be selected by a points system, some of the criteria for which were training, age, occupational demand, and English proficiency. Originally, applicants could earn points if they came from a list of 34 countries that had been "adversely affected" by the Immigration Act of 1965 (mostly European countries). Criticized for reintroducing aspects of the national origins system, this particular provision was dropped and the bill as a whole failed to pass the Senate. When the 1990 Immigration Act was adopted it included no independent category, but it had a diversity category that provided 55,000 visas for countries adversely affected by the 1965 law (Bean and Fix, 1992, p. 50). The significance of this episode for our purposes is twofold. First, it demonstrates that there is sentiment within the Congress and country to redress, at least in part, the shift in immigration source countries of the last thirty years. Such a move, assuming the overall ceiling did not rise, would bode ill for Mexican migration prospects. On the other hand, the diversity provision is undeniably a step back from universalism and, as such, opens the door to further exceptionalism that could, as in the past, benefit Mexicans.

Moreover, the 1990 Immigration Act included several features involving the family preference system and treatment of family relations of aliens legalized under IRCA that may be construed as partially designed to give special consideration to Mexico. Even though other countries are also advantaged, migrants from Mexico constitute a major share of those likely to benefit from the provisions that create a framework within which Mexico obtains visas far in excess of the new per country limits on legal annual immigration to 25,620 visas a year for any country. Immediate relatives of U.S. citizens, who are entitled to first preference visas, are exempt from these ceilings, as in previous law. The second preference category, which includes family members sponsored by lawful permanent residents (LPRs), fell under the overall ceiling an per country limits under previous law and there were consequently large backlogs of applicants from some countries, most prominently Mexico. Just prior to the passage of IMMACT, for example, there were 414,045 persons on the waiting list for second preference visas, mostly from Mexico, the Philippines, and the Dominican Republic. The 1990 act introduced changes that sought to ease these backlogs.

Congress doubled the number of visas under the second preference to 114,200, plus any unused visas from the first preference numbers. In addition, it created a special sub-allocation process for second preference visas. A minimum of 77 percent of these must go to spouses and *minor* children of lawful permanent residents. Moreover, 75 percent of these are to be distributed in the order in which the applications were filed and do not count against a country's numerical limitation. A maximum of 23 percent of the visas in this category may go to the unmarried adult sons and daughters of LPRs. These latter visas will continue to be subject to the country ceilings.

The 1990 act also created a transition program during FYs 1992-94 during which an additional 55,000 visas per year were available for the spouses and children of LPRs legalized under IRCA. Over half of those admitted under this program in 1992 were from Mexico. In 1995 and thereafter family immigration is set at 480,000, minus the number of "immediate relatives" admitted during the previous fiscal year, plus any unused numbers under the employment-based preference. If the resulting number drops below 226,000, the "cap" is simply waived. Finally, the law included a Family Unity provision that gave work authorization and relief from deportation to the spouses and unmarried children of aliens legalized under IRCA who were in the U.S. illegally as of May 5, 1988. Each of these measures had the effect of making concessions to Mexican migrants even if they were not exclusively or explicitly labeled as such. They help account for the fact that Mexico was the leading immigration source country in 1991 (946, 167), 1992 (213,802), 1993 (126,561), and 1994 (111,398) (see Table 1.2).

Currently, U.S. responses to illegal Mexican migration may be coming to a critical juncture. Since the demise of the *Bracero* program, the United States has allowed large and increasing numbers of illegal migrants into the United States while, at the same time, deploying a policy of limited but highly visible border enforcement which provided political gains but was essentially ineffective (i.e., it *de facto* allowed many migrants to enter the United States illegally). First-time illegal migrants from Mexico continued to come to the Mexican northern border from the interior, and there was little indication that IRCA or any other legal or enforcement action had permanently slowed much of the flow (Bean et al., 1990;

Bean et al., 1994). Starting in 1994, however, additional personnel and resources, new technologies, and a tougher attitude on the U.S. side of the border seemed to bring about new levels of difficulty for migrants trying to enter the United States illegally. This modification in enforcement may eventually produce changes in the level of the actual flow, in the geography of illegal immigration, and in the actors and their strategies. Furthermore, it may have effects on employers and their lobbying efforts. Farm lobbies once again have become very active in Washington. Enforcement may be at the critical point where migrants are effectively deterred and U.S. demand for migrant labor begins to exceed supply. Conflicting interest-group resolutions of this problem may be less and less acceptable as increasing bilateral cooperation between Mexico and the United States, which itself occurs within a legal framework, increases pressure to put migration flows between the two countries on a more legal footing.[12]

Will the apparently hardening U.S. attitude toward illegal Mexican migration affect policy regulating legal flows? What directions might U.S. policy toward legal Mexican migration take, either as part of a comprehensive overhaul of immigration law or as more limited and specific changes dealing exclusively with Mexico? Recent discussions of changes in the legal immigration program have focused on the scale of entries and their composition.

Discussion of the appropriate ceiling on overall immigration is highly contentious. A bill introduced in the Congress in June 1995 would have reduced annual entries from 675,000 to 535,000. Determining a reasonable ceiling is difficult in the absence of consensus about the economic, fiscal, cultural, and political consequences of immigration. Mexican immigration is inevitably central to this evolving debate. Any reduction in the annual ceiling would work to the disadvantage of Mexico, the leading sending country in recent years. Large recent flows, connected to and amplified by the IRCA legalizations, raised the U.S. foreign-born population of Mexican origin at the 1990 Census to 4.3 million, or 21.7 percent of the total foreign-born population. Mexico contributes over four times as many foreign-born U.S. residents as any other country (Center for Immigration Studies, 1994, pp. 3-4).

The concentration of this population in a handful of Southwestern states gives it a potential impact that could eventually approach that of Cuban settlement in south Florida. Traditionally, Mexican immigrants have exhibited low rates of naturalization, but there is at least anecdotal evidence that this is changing. Continued high levels of Mexican migration into the region, especially if it is legal, could have dramatic effects on political dynamics in a number of states. Any increase in levels of legal migration, and especially any concession of extra visas to Mexicans, would certainly accelerate the ethnic transformation of the southwest and likely trigger political resistance (Bouvier and Poston, 1993;

Bouvier, 1991). The disproportionate share of total migration that is made up of persons of Mexican origin makes it likely that any discussion of overall ceilings or special arrangements for Mexico will raise once again sensitive ethnic issues that the 1965 amendments sought to lay to rest.

Apart from questions of the scale of immigration, there is concern that the existing preference system, with its emphasis on family reunification, produces a flow of migrants whose human capital endowments are inadequate. Any concerted effort to reinforce the skill component of U.S. immigration has direct implications for Mexico. Restructuring the admissions and selection system to favor the highly skilled at the expense of the unskilled and persons with family relations in the United States, moves endorsed by the U.S. Commission on Immigration Reform,[13] is inconsistent with sustained high levels of immigration from Mexico. To the extent that U.S. immigration policy is on a trajectory to make it more supportive of the international competitiveness of the economy, that policy would seem to dictate against simultaneous steps to increase the numbers of unskilled Mexicans coming to the United States.

One conceivable scenario is gradual progress toward free movement of labor for Canadians, Americans, and Mexicans within NAFTA, along the lines of developments in the European Union. If this sounds farfetched, it should be remembered that free movement in the EU has only been imperfectly achieved since 1993, after a transition period of over thirty years (Miles and Thranhardt, 1995). The obstacles to the European Union as a model for North America are, nonetheless, imposing. The vast differential in living standards between the U.S. and Mexico, quite apart from the cultural and linguistic divide, militates against serious consideration of free movement. Indeed, neither free nor even liberalized movement was on the table during negotiations preceding NAFTA. The trade agreement shares few of the compelling historical and cultural antecedents that have made the far more ambitious program of European unity plausible (Weintraub, 1992).

If freer movement within the context of free trade is problematic, specific bilateral concessions to Mexico may not be. Our historical review uncovered two perennial proposals: special annual quotas for legal immigration from Mexico, and a formal guest worker program for agricultural workers. Giving Mexico additional visas, though frequently advanced, would be inconsistent with the thrust of non-discrimination and universalism inherent in the decision in 1965 to eliminate national origins quotas. On the other hand, the unique American preference system dominated by family reunion means that setting some limits on per-country entries is unavoidable.[14] Moreover, there are precedents in the immigration laws of other Western nations for preferential bilateral treatment of particular sending countries where there are special historical or cultural circumstances.

The most pertinent for our purposes may be those affecting Britain-Ireland and Australia-New Zealand. In both cases there is free movement between the two countries. The relationship between Britain and Ireland grants the broadest possible rights of movement and settlement to the citizens of each country, although it is not the direct result of bilateral negotiations. Since 1949 the British government has simply refused to treat the Irish Republic as a foreign country. Irish citizens have been treated since then as if Commonwealth citizens: They can vote, stand for office, work in the public service, and so on in Britain. If they wish to become British citizens they can do so by the same means as Commonwealth citizens. They are not aliens (Dummett and Nicol, 1990, p. 129). In 1984 British citizens were accorded national voting rights in Ireland (they had local rights along with other foreign residents since 1985), so that full reciprocity between the two countries was achieved (Layton-Henry, 1992, p. 4).

The free movement of people between Australia and New Zealand has been a constant during all the variations in the legal relationships between the two entities. The Trans-Tasman Travel Arrangement, which governs movement of New Zealand and Australian passport holders, has been in place since the 1920s (Poot, 1993, p. 396; Nana and Poot, 1995; Trlin, 1993). The Australian-New Zealand Closer Economic Relations Trade Agreement, adopted in 1983 and strengthened in 1988, goes much farther than the North American Free Trade Agreement in that it virtually eliminates all barriers to trade in goods between the two countries, involves free movement of persons, and has made real progress on services (Holmes, 1990).

Key elements in the cases of both Britain-Ireland and Australia-New Zealand cast doubt on their utility as models for the U.S. and Mexico. The affected countries are similar in terms of ethnicity, language, culture, and economic development. Granted that although in both cases one of the countries is relatively poorer than the other, the gap in living standards between the two is not so large as to generate mass influxes. It does, however, ensure that the flows are mostly unidirectional.[15] Finally, these agreements are reciprocal, although in the case of the British Isles, reciprocity was only lately achieved.

Special annual quotas for Mexico would raise the specter of a political struggle in Congress by partisans of other countries seeking similar treatment. Proponents of such a measure would also have to deal with the suspicion that it was a means of legalizing what would otherwise be an unimpeded illegal flow rather than an adjustment of the legal flow after illegal entries had been significantly deterred. If recent initiatives at the border are seen as dramatically successful, however, the chances for passage of special concessions for Mexico would probably increase.

Support for a new guest worker program among agricultural interest groups and their political representatives increases as the effectiveness of border controls rises and as U.S. labor demand grows. An effort to insert such a program into a recent House bill was barely defeated. Nonetheless, the evidence from the *Bracero* program, as well as that of European states managing temporary labor schemes in the postwar era, demonstrate that such programs tend to lead to permanent settlement, increased illegal entry and work, and the establishment of social networks and migration patterns that are difficult if not impossible to shut down when the programs are ended (Miller and Martin, 1982; Martin, 1995). As a consequence, the U.S. Commission on Immigration Reform unanimously concluded recently that "such a program would be a grievous mistake" (1995, p. 172). But the fact that in the United States proposals for such programs can coexist with support for total clampdowns on undocumented labor crossings at the U.S./Mexico border indicates that the complex forces out of which U.S. immigration policy emerges are still very much in effect.

# Notes

1. Ironically, the Mexican government tried to prevent the loss of Texas to the U.S. by banning immigration from the United States through the so-called Mexican Decree of April 6, 1830. Garrisons were sent to enforce the policy, but the U.S. settlers already in Texas ignored its provisions.

2. See Bach (1990, p. 127). The program admitted 72,862 Mexican workers (Rico, 1992, p. 243). The importation of foreign contract workers had been illegal since the Foran Act of 1885, but the law had never been taken seriously in the southwest (Archdeacon, 1983, p. 129).

3. Although Portes and Bach argue that the Border Patrol was not intended primarily to control movement across the Mexican border (1985, p. 78), Carlos Rico suggests that "the numbers of Mexican immigrants were growing fast during the twenties. The perceived need for greater control over land borders that resulted from this realization led to the establishment of the Border Patrol in 1924" (1992, pp. 243-44). The numbers in Table 1.1 support the latter interpretation.

4. *Braceros* were also recruited from the Bahamas, Barbados, Canada, Jamaica, and Newfoundland, but the bulk were from Mexico (cf. Craig, 1971; Galarza, 1964; and Calavita, 1992).

5. This provision of the 1952 law got its name because it was the handiwork of Senator Lyndon B. Johnson from Texas (Miller, 1992, p. 58).

6. The Johnson administration worried that the move would damage relations with countries in the region, and the State Department voiced strong opposition (Morris, 1985, p. 53).

7. The 120,000 annual figure had no particular significance as it was based on the actual flow of immigrants in the years immediately preceding passage (LeMay, 1987, p. 112; 1994, p. 13).

8. According to Briggs, "Congress feared that the absence of such a limit, combined with the extraordinarily high population-growth rates in Latin America, would lead to an uncontrolled influx of immigrants in the near future" (1992, p. 108).

9. The commission was split. The majority wished to delay implementation of the ceiling, hoping Congress would write new legislation substituting Department of Labor certification (or qualitative limits) for quantitative numerical restrictions. Furthermore, they recommended that if the ceiling went into effect, Congress should establish per country quotas of 40,000 rather than the 20,000 in effect in the East. As the majority put it: "the Commission believes that recognition must be given, and allowance made, for differences inherent in the relationship of the United States with its sister hemispheric republics . . . the annual 20,000 limitation per country. . . would be unnecessarily disruptive to the traditional patterns of Western Hemisphere immigration" (p. 12). Three members from the Senate (Eastland, Dirksen, and Hruska) wrote a spirited dissent which pointed out that in passing the 1965 amendments Congress had made clear its support for a ceiling on Western Hemisphere immigration. They pointed out that unless per country quotas were imposed a handful of countries in the region would dominate the flows. Finally, they objected to relying entirely on the labor certification procedure as it would place in the hands of an executive agency ultimate control over the numbers of immigrants entering each year, a traditional prerogative of Congress (pp. 15-18).

10. The proposal was never adopted by Congress. Four options rejected by the commission included (1) imposing no per-country ceilings on independent immigration; (2) imposing no per-country ceilings on independent immigration, but barring independent migration from any country where the family reunification category exceeded 50,000 in the previous year; (3) continuing the 20,000 per country limit but reducing the number of visas available to natives of a country by the number used by that country in the numerically limited family reunification category; and (4) establishing a fixed, uniform numerical ceiling on independent on independent immigration from any one country.

11. It is often said that these changes were wholly unanticipated, and certainly legislative proponents of the 1965 act assured the public that there would be no change in the ethnic composition of the migration streams (see the comments of Emanuel Celler [D-NY]), quoted in Briggs [1992, p. 111]). Nevertheless, immigration from Asia and Latin America had been growing discernibly at least since 1961 and it is difficult to believe that no one foresaw the direction, if not the amplitude, of the changes about to take place.

12. Bilateral approaches to the southern border have a long but troubled history. In 1909 Presidents Diaz and Taft authorized contracts for a thousand Mexican workers for the sugar beet fields of Colorado and Nebraska (Rico, 1992, p. 222). The pact that created the *Bracero* program was a model of cooperation, but its elimination came over Mexican objections (Craig, 1971, pp. 185-188). Mexican officials tend to believe that the United States is obligated to receive large numbers of migrants and any effort to cut the flow is perceived as an unwarranted attack (Bach, 1990, p. 124). However, domestic politicization of immigration policy leaves U.S. decision makers with limited margin for taking Mexican views into account (Mitchell, 1992, p. 288). The Report of the Bilateral Commission

on the Future of United States-Mexican Relations (1989), an independent group funded by the Ford Foundation, criticized the process by which IRCA was passed for failing to provide genuine consultation with Mexico (p. 104; cf. Rico, 1992, pp. 265-66). The commission, unwittingly, illustrates the problems of a bilateral process undertaken by two unequal "partners." The burden of their major recommendations falls almost entirely on the U.S. (1989, pp. 110-12).

13. The commission recommends reducing the annual ceiling of legal immigrants to 550,000, restructuring the preference system to enhance the position of skilled migration, and eliminating unskilled migration altogether (1995).

14. No other country operates a preference and quota system like that of the United States. Canada, Australia, and New Zealand, the other major countries of immigration for settlement, employ a points system for selecting potential migrants that allows them to avoid setting any per country limits (Jenks, 1992).

15. The net flows of permanent and long-term migrants across the Tasman fluctuate annually. There is considerable evidence that absent legal regulations the flows reflect contingent economic conditions and do so more directly than do flows between New Zealand and other countries more heavily regulated (Holmes, 1990, p. 6). The flows are primarily a matter of the movement of New Zealanders between the two parts of Australia. This is because the destination of between 50 and 60 percent of permanent or long-term departures from New Zealand is Australia. More than two-thirds of the opposite flow, on the other hand, is made up of New Zealanders returning after an absence of twelve months or more (Poot, 1993, p. 403).

# References

Archdeacon, Thomas. 1990. Immigration and U.S. Foreign Policy in Latin America and the Caribbean. In Robert W. Tucker, Charles B. Keely, and Linda Wrigley, eds. *Immigration and U.S. Foreign Policy.* Boulder, CO: Westview, pp. 123-149.
———.1983. *Becoming American: An Ethnic History.* New York: The Free Press.
Bach, Robert L. 1985. Western Hemispheric Immigration to the United States: A Review of Selected Research Trends. Hemispheric Migration Project. Center for Immigration Policy and Refuge Assistance, Georgetown University.
Bean, Frank D., R. Chanove, R. Cushing, C. Haynes, G. Freeman, and D. Spencer. 1994. *Illegal Mexican Migration and the United States/Mexico Border: The Effects of Operation Hold-the-Line on El Paso/Juarez.* Washington, D.C.: U.S. Commission on Immigration Reform, 1994, 132 pp.
Bean, Frank D., Thomas Espenshade, M. White, and R. Dymowski. 1990. Post-IRCA Changes in the Volume and Composition of Undocumented Migration to the United States: An Assessment Based on Apprehensions Data, pp. 111-158 in F. Bean, B. Edmonston and J. Passel (eds.), *Undocumented Migration to the United States: IRCA and the Experience of the 1980s.* Washington, D.C.: The Urban Institute Press.
Bean, Frank D., and Michael Fix. 1992. The Significance of Recent Immigration Policy Reforms in the United States. In Gary P. Freeman and James Jupp, eds. *Nations of*

*Immigrants: Australia, the United States, and International Migration.* New York and Melbourne: Oxford University Press, pp. 41-55.

Bean, Frank D., Jeffrey Passel, and Barry Edmonston. 1990. *Undocumented Migration to the United States: IRCA and the Experience of the 1980s.* Washington, D.C.: The Urban Institute Press.

Bean, Frank D., Georges Verney, and Charles B. Keely. 1989. *Opening and Closing the Doors: Evaluating Immigration Reform and Control.* Washington, D.C.: The Urban Institute Press. 142 pp.

Bilateral Commission on the Future of United States-Mexican Relations. 1989. *The Challenge of Interdependence: Mexico and the United States.* New York: University Press of America.

Bouvier, Leon F. 1991. *Fifty Million Californians?* Washington, D.C.: Center for Immigration Studies.

Bouvier, Leon F., and Dudley L. Poston, Jr. 1993. *Thirty Million Texans?* Washington, D.C.: Center for Immigration Studies.

Briggs, Vernon M. Jr. 1992. *Mass Immigration and the National Interest.* Armonk, N.Y.: M. E. Sharpe.

Briggs, Vernon M., Jr., and Stephen Moore. 1994. *Still an Open Door?: U.S. Immigration Policy and the American Economy.* Washington, D.C.: The American University Press.

Calavita, Kitty. 1992. *Inside the State: The Bracero Program, Immigration, and the I.N.S.* New York: Routledge.

Center for Immigration Studies. 1994. *Immigration-Related Statistics—1994.* Washington, D.C.

Corwin, Arthur F. 1978. A Story of Ad Hoc Exemptions: American Immigration Policy toward Mexico. In Arthur F. Corwin, ed. *Immigrants—and Immigrants: Perspectives on Mexican Labor Migration to the United States.* Westport, Conn.: Greenwood Press.

Craig, Richard B. 1971. *The Bracero Program: Interest Groups and Foreign Policy.* Austin: University of Texas Press.

Donato, Katharine M., Jorge Durand, and Douglas S. Massey. 1992. Stemming the Tide? Assessing the Deterrent effects of the Immigration Reform and Control Act. *Demography* 29 (2): 3-42.

Dummett, Ann, and Andrew Nicol. 1990. *Subjects, Citizens, Aliens and Others: Nationality and Immigration Law.* London: Weidenfeld and Nicolson.

Espenshade, Thomas J. Unauthorized Immigration to the United States, *Annual Review of Sociology.* 1995, 21: 195-216.

———. Using INS Border Apprehension Data to Ensure the Flow of Undocumented Migrants Crossing the U.S.-Mexico Frontier, *International Migration Review.* Summer 1995, 29 (2): 545-565.

———. Undocumented Migration to the United States: Evidence from a Repeated Trials Model, pp. 1599-181 in the Bean, Edmonston, and Passel. Urban Institute volume, 1990.

Espenshade, Thomas J., Michael J. White, and Frank D. Bean. 1991. Patterns of Recent and Illegal Migration to the United States, pp. 301-336 in Wolfgang Lutz (ed.), *Future Demographic Trends in Europe and North America.* New York: Academic Press.

Galarza, Ernesto. 1964. *Merchants of Labor: The Mexican Bracero Story*. Santa Barbara: McNally & Loftin.

Herschkowitz, Andrew J. 1994. *American Political Institutions and Policymaking: The Select Commission on Immigration and Refugee Policy*. Doctoral dissertation, Department of Government, University of Texas, Austin.

Holmes, Frank. 1990. CER, The Free Movement of People and Immigration Policies. Paper delivered at the National Immigration Outlook Conference, November 14-16, Melbourne.

Hoffman, Abraham. 1978. Mexican Repatriation During the Great Depression. In Arthur F. Corwin, ed. *Immigrants—and Immigrants: Perspectives on Mexican Labor Migration to the United States*. Westport: Greenwood Press, pp. 225-247.

————. 1974. *Unwanted Mexican Americans in the Great Depression: Repatriation Pressures, 1929-1939*. Tucson: University of Arizona Press.

Jenks, Rosemary E. ed. 1992. *Immigration and Nationality Policies of Leading Migration Nations*. Washington, D.C.: Center for Immigration Studies.

Layton-Henry, Zig. 1992. *The Politics of Immigration*. Oxford: Blackwell.

LeMay, Michael C. 1994. *Anatomy of A Public Policy: The Reform of Contemporary American Immigration Law*. Westport, Conn.: Praeger.

————. 1987. *From Open Door to Dutch Door: An Analysis of U.S. Immigration Policy Since 1820*. Westport, Conn.: Praeger.

Martin, Philip. 1995. Guest Worker Policies: An International Survey. Paper presented for the Workshop on Migration and Migration Policies: The International Experience. Massachusetts Institute of Technology, February 23-24.

Miles, Robert, and Dietrich Thranhardt, eds. 1995. *Migration and European Integration: The Dynamics of Inclusion and Exclusion*. London: Pinter Publishers.

Miller, Mark J. 1992. Never Ending Story: The U.S. Debate over Illegal Immigration. In Gary P. Freeman and James Jupp, eds. *Nations of Immigrants: Australia, the United States, and International Migration*. New York and Melbourne: Oxford University Press, pp. 56-71.

Miller, Mark J., and Philip L. Martin. 1982. *Administering Foreign Worker Programs: Lessons for the United States*. Lexington, Mass.: Lexington Books.

Mitchell, Christopher. 1992. Reviewing the Case Studies: Implications for Understanding and for Policy Choice. In Christopher Mitchell, ed. *Western Hemisphere Immigration and United States Foreign Policy*. University Park, Penn.: Pennsylvania State University Press, pp. 285-300.

Morris, Milton. 1985. *Immigration: The Beleaguered Bureaucracy*. Washington, D.C.: The Brookings Institution.

Nana, Ganesh, and Jacques Poot. 1995. Trans-Tasman Migration and Closer Economic Relations in Australasia. Paper presented at a Conference on International Trade and Migration in the APEC Region, University of Melbourne, 10-11 July.

Passel, Jeffrey. 1986. Undocumented Immigration. In *Annals, American Academy for Political and Social Sciences* 487 (Sept.): 181-200.

Poot, Jacques. 1993. The Role of Trans-Tasman Migration in Forecasting the New Zealand Population. *Asian and Pacific Migration Journal* 2/4:395-416.

Portes, Alejandro, and Robert L. Bach. 1985. *Latin Journey: Cuban and Mexican Immigrants in the United States*. Berkeley: University of California Press.

President's Commission on Immigration and Naturalization. 1953. *Whom We Shall Welcome*. Washington, D.C.: U.S.G.P.O.

Reimers, David M. 1982. Recent Immigration Policy: An Analysis. In Barry R. Chiswick, ed. *The Gateway: U.S. Immigration Issues and Policies*. Washington, D.C.: American Enterprise Institute, pp. 13-53.

Rico, Carlos. 1992. Migration and U.S.-Mexican Relations, 1966-1986. In Christopher Mitchell, ed. *Western Hemisphere Immigration and United States Foreign Policy*. University Park, Penn.: Penn State University Press, pp. 221-284.

Select Commission on Immigration and Refugee Policy. 1981. *U.S. Immigration Policy and the National Interest*. Washington, D.C.: USGPO.

Teitelbaum, Michael S. 1985. *Latin Migration North: The Problem for U.S. Foreign Policy*. New York: Council on Foreign Relations.

Trlin, Andrew. 1993. The Social Effects and Institutional Structure of Immigration in New Zealand in the 1980s. *Asian and Pacific Migration Journal* 2/1: 1-26.

U.S. Commission on Immigration Reform. 1995. *Legal Immigration: Setting Priorities*. Washington, D.C.: USGPO.

U.S. Immigration and Naturalization Service. 1995. *Statistical Yearbook of the Immigration and Naturalization Service*. Washington, D.C.: U.S. Government Printing Office.

———. 1992. *Immigration Reform and Control Act: Report on the Legalized Alien Population*. Washington, D.C.

Weintraub, Sidney. 1992. North American Free Trade and the European Situation Compared. *International Migration Review* 26/2: 506-523.

Woodrow-Lafield, Karen, and Jeffrey Passel. 1990. Post-IRCA Undocumented Immigration to the United States: An Assessment Based on the June 1988 CPS. In Frank D. Bean, Barry Edmonston, and Jeffrey S. Passel, eds. *Undocumented Migration to the United States: IRCA and the Experience of the 1980s*. Washington, D.C.: The Urban Institute Press, pp. 33-75.

# 2.

# Mexican Social and Economic Policy and Emigration

*Bryan R. Roberts and Agustin Escobar Latapi*

I n this chapter, we will examine the general impact of Mexican social and
economic policies on international migration. While international migration
from Mexico to the United States is the focus of increasingly intense debate
within the United States, that process is only one effect of the drastic
redistribution of the Mexican population during this century. The social and
economic policies that shaped internal migration during Mexico's period of rapid
urbanization and industrialization also affected international migration. Likewise,
current social and economic policies are changing the character of both internal
and international migration.

Social and economic policies affect migration, whether national or international, by changing the relative living and working advantages of places of origin
and destination. Sometimes this change does not by itself produce migration, as
employers actively hire workers from areas of lower wages and living standards. In
other instances, workers themselves build the networks that allow them to move
from place to place or to exploit the different social and economic conditions of two
places at once. In other words, migration is an outcome of both contextual changes

and behavioral changes. Growing gaps in social and economic conditions do not by themselves produce migration; people must act for change to occur. The changes observed after 1975 in Mexican emigration are due, in our view, not only to growing gaps in socioeconomic conditions, but also to direct actions of Mexican migrants and U.S. employers and to actions or "omissions" of both governments, both as they relate directly and indirectly to migration via regional differences in employment opportunities, wages, social conditions and promotion. In this chapter, we limit ourselves to the implications of Mexican social and economic policies for migration, particularly in terms of their spatial biases. These biases are closely related to the changing character of population mobility in Mexico.

Mexican emigration has shifted in size and character. Before 1940, it was closely related to outbreaks of violence and political insecurity or to specific periods of U.S. demand for labor. From 1940 to around 1977, a small proportion of the Mexican workforce emigrated, in our view, in response to U.S. demand. After 1975-1980, emigration grows steadily and part of it becomes permanent. Trends during this last period are unprecedented. Events in Mexico play the most significant role among many complex factors. While the constant in Mexican history since 1930 has been rural emigration, this constant is not useful for understanding the latest developments in emigration from Mexico. We contend that, while Mexican cities successfully attracted and retained rural migrants during Import Substitution Industrialization, the capacity of cities to support migrants fails after 1980. This development is responsible for the growth of international migration and the change in character of the internal and international migrants themselves.

The factors driving national and international migration patterns become starkly visible when the Mexican city is viewed as the convergent point of social and economic policy effects. Mexico's social and economic policies, either through positive intervention or neglect, have affected a city's attractiveness to labor and have favored certain locations over others, thus determining the direction of migration and the degree to which it is of a temporary or permanent nature. This urban emphasis does not belittle changes in the rural sector in Mexico. On the contrary, economic and institutional changes had significant effects on the rural sector, particularly after 1988 (Escobar, Bean, and Weintraub 1996). But we argue that international migration would not have changed as it did had Mexican cities retained their ability to absorb labor.

## Social and Economic Policies

Though migration from Mexico to the United States has a long history, with substantial flows beginning in the last quarter of the nineteenth century, this international migration did little to alter the basic social and economic patterns of Mexican rural or urban life. It was mainly temporary in character. Migrant earnings maintained an embattled peasant agricultural system. In contrast, the large-scale rural-to-urban internal migrations of the 1930s onwards involved a more fundamental transformation of Mexican society and, thus, more policy debate. Until the 1980s, official concern with migration was overwhelmingly focused on the nature of internal migration flows and on labor and price support policies that were aimed to facilitate urbanization and industrialization.

There were exceptions to this preoccupation with internal migration, one of the most important of which was the *Bracero* agreements between the U.S. and Mexican governments beginning in 1942. Until 1964, these agreements provided for the seasonal migration of more than 200,000 agricultural workers a year. The termination of the program in 1964 was the reason for the initiation of the Border Industrialization Program, designed to offset the loss of temporary work opportunities in the United States by creating jobs along the border. In recent years, the Mexican government has launched several programs designed to protect migrants as they cross the border as well as when they work and live in the United States. Through the *Solidaridad* program, the government has also created programs providing incentives for migrants to use their savings and remittances in community development projects.

An important aim of Mexican social and economic policy has been to create a stable modern labor force through the gradual extension of an employment-related social security system financed by employers, workers, and, to a lesser extent, the federal government. The system was first extended to groups of workers that played a key role in Mexico's industrialization—oil industry workers, railroad workers, government employees, and workers in large-scale industry (Mesa Lago 1978). Rural workers were among the last to be included in the system, and were the least protected by it.

The social security system comprises health coverage, disability payments, pensions, housing (beginning in 1972[1]), and the limited provision of child care facilities. It is managed by various federal agencies, such as the *Instituto Mexicano del Seguro Social* (IMSS), *Instituto de Seguridad Social al Servicio de los Trabajadores del Estado* (ISSSTE), and the *Instituto del Fondo Nacional para la Vivienda de los Trabajadores* (INFONAVIT). The system, extremely limited at its inception in 1942, expanded to cover some 50 percent of the labor force by 1992. Coverage has always had geographical biases, with urban areas receiving higher coverage than rural ones. The extent of benefits also has been restricted. Crucial aspects of social policy have therefore, paradoxically, remained the privilege of those in formal and stable employment, with the unemployed left unprotected. Also, inflation has caused pensions, which rarely amount to more than one minimum salary, consistently to lose value. Housing benefits have been available to only a small minority of those eligible, usually the most stable and best paid workers. There is also an open-coverage health system, available regardless of employment status, which is fairly effective in providing preventive and primary health care—vaccination, hygienic training, first aid, birth control—to the population at large. But only a small proportion of the major medical needs of the "unprotected" population are covered.[2]

A second arm of social policy has been the provision of price subsidies of various kinds. Subsidies guaranteeing the price of corn, sugar cane, and other staples were intended to sustain agricultural production while reducing the costs of basic foodstuffs to the consumer. Subsidies for electricity, gasoline, and other fuels and for urban transport were also intended to reduce subsistence costs. In practice, the subsidies were directly aimed at urban rather than rural areas. Subsidy structures worked better at the receiving, market end: in the country, for example, peasants and *ejidatarios* were rarely paid the full, subsidized price for their crops, while most urban consumers benefited from the official low price for most staples. The subsidies created an urban bias in development and contributed to the rural population's relocation to urban areas.

Despite their limitations in coverage, the above social policies were important factors in enabling Mexico to make a relatively untroubled, rapid transition from a rural to an urban society. From the 1930s onwards, Mexico pursued an explicit policy of import-substituting industrialization based on tariff protection and state control and development of key industrial sectors. Revenues from primary sector exports, mainly generated by a commercial agricultural sector, paid for needed industrial inputs, while the domestic food supply was mainly provided by small-scale, rain-fed, peasant farming. In the context of declining mortality and high fertility rates, industrialization led to rapid urbanization. Import-substituting industrialization expanded rapidly through basic goods industries that catered to the internal market.

As these industries and the distributive services associated with them generated income opportunities in cities, rural areas became increasingly bound to rural-urban commercial relationships. The small scale of peasant farming and its limited access to modern technology meant there were few local income opportunities to retain the growing rural population. In this situation, a variety of migration patterns emerged. Foremost was a permanent rural-urban migration in which the young and able-bodied moved to the city, often to be followed by other family members. Some of this rural-urban migration began as an experiment: villagers would go to the city on a trial basis, intending to return if things did not work out.

Temporary labor migration took three main forms: rural-to-rural migrations, as in the case of villagers from the south of Mexico who moved seasonally to the commercial harvests of the Northwest or Southwest; rural-to-urban migration of peasants working in construction or unskilled services in the cities; and rural-to-U.S. migration that, until recently, was heavily concentrated in the states of the Center-West of Mexico. The rural areas from which these international migrants were drawn were not the poorest in Mexico, but had long been involved in cash-crop production and trading networks. Temporary migration complemented village economies: it provided cash to supplement income from farming and, to some extent, enabled small-scale farmers to purchase animals or other inputs. Anthropologists reporting at this time showed how, although migration was the mechanism allowing some peasants to exit dying communities, in other cases it provided one of the bases for the continuing viability of rural settlements (Arizpe 1975).

The National Minimum Wage Commission was established in 1942 in order to improve base wages, a mandate both social and economic in conception and implementation. The commission's wage and income policy defined general, regional, and "professional" (mostly craft and technical) wage levels, which have been increasingly implemented throughout the country since 1942. The government's favorable attitude towards wages can be seen in the consistent gains of wages and salaries in the public sector (education, health, and public administration) as well as in government-controlled industries, including oil, steel, sugar, paper manufacturing and a growing constellation of enterprises and manufacturing corporations in which the government acquired controlling interests over the lifetime of import substitution industrialization (ISI).[3] The government's wages played a role in raising wage levels throughout the modern economy. Again, however, wages were better controlled, and their increases more consistent, in urban rather than rural areas and in corporations rather than in small and dispersed economic units.

In this period, therefore, Mexico's social and economic policies could be said to have an "urban bias" and thus directly or indirectly promoted rural to urban migration. The concentration of resources and subsidies in Mexico City best illustrates the effects of this bias. Gustavo Garza (1985) calculated that the subsidization of transport, housing, and food attracted entrepreneurs to the capital city. Since businesses in Mexico City did not have to pay the full costs of their workers' subsistence, then wage levels remained competitive with those of less congested locations. Of course, Mexico City's central location, access to communications and transportation networks, and availability of workers were added advantages to industrial location there.

The mostly urban wage and salary bias had a significant effect on the distribution of income in its urban and rural components: from 1957 to 1977, the lowest 10 percent of the income distribution reduced its share of income from 2.4 to 1.1 percent, while the middle deciles gained considerable ground and the top decile also declined (Reyes Heroles 1985, Escobar and Roberts 1991). Rural laborers (the bottom 10 percent) and urban professionals, managers, and employers (the top ten percent) lost income relative to the middle of the distribution (employees, technicians, teachers, urban workers). In absolute terms, however, all incomes improved as the economy grew rapidly and steadily.

These social and economic policies, combined with sustained growth, also had a significant effect on poverty, which dropped systematically from the 1950s through the 1970s (Hernandez Laos 1992, Boltvinik 1994). Since policies were pro-urban and centers of growth urban, this meant most poverty was and remained rural. As we have written elsewhere, by 1976 the mean real manufacturing wages were such that, for the first time in Mexican history, a single earner could afford to purchase the "basic needs basket" of an urban family (Escobar and Roberts 1991 ). This was by no means the case for the unskilled laborer, nor for the average *ejidatario*.

As the major market for basic goods was Mexico City, it was cost effective to locate near that market and use the rail and road network to distribute to the rest of the country. From 1940 to 1980, during Mexico's rapid urbanization, Mexico City so maintained dominance that the index of primacy (Mexico City's size ratio to the next two largest cities) changed from 3.9 in 1930 to 3.3 in 1980. State employment was an important component of this population concentration. Between 1970 and 1980, central government employment in Mexico grew by 12.5 percent annually, reaching 3.2 million persons, or 17 percent of total employment by 1980 (Oliveira and Roberts, 1994: 285). While Mexico City attracted the lion's share of this employment, regional capitals also benefited from this expansion.

A counterpoint to the provision of subsidies to the cities was the relative neglect of the rural sector. Despite government emphasis on the importance of agrarian reform and on the centrality of the *ejido* to Mexico's development, relatively few resources were devoted to promoting a broad-based, job-oriented agrarian development in agriculture, linked industries, and services. The weakness of rural development continued as returning international migrants often invested their savings in urban economies rather than the traditional sending areas' development. Advances were made in providing educational services and health clinics, but the quantity and quality of these lagged behind those of the cities.

Government policy, particularly in the 1970s, began to emphasize regional development as a counterweight to excessive urban growth. Some large-scale regional development programs, such as the Papaloapan Basin project and irrigation projects in the Northwest, were intended to generate employment and retain local population. Other programs, such as the Sistema Alimentario Mexicano (SAM), during the administration of Lopez Portillo (1976-1982), aimed to revitalize peasant farming by providing modern inputs. Some programs deliberately sought to offset concentration in Mexico City by promoting regional industrial development. All of these programs failed due to inadequate investments in the rural sector, the growth of capital-intensive commercial farming in certain regions, and the continuing economic advantages to entrepreneurs and to governments of centralizing production in Mexico City (Barkin 1975).

Throughout this period, and in spite of the massive population flows from rural areas, the Mexican urban system successfully absorbed the surplus rural population. This success has been somewhat overlooked in the appraisal of ISI. Before 1980, Mexico's urban labor markets, particularly those of the three major cities, Mexico City, Guadalajara, and Monterrey, showed a striking capacity to generate enough *formal* jobs to absorb a labor force that increased at rates of four to five percent a year. In this period of massive in-migration to the cities, real wages increased and "informal" urban employment, particularly self-employment, declined (Gregory 1985, Oliveira and Roberts 1994, Garcia, 1988). In this context, the push factors generating permanent international migration were minimal, since urbanization and the social and economic policies supporting it provided an effective alternative to emigration.[4] People on the lowest tiers of the income structure did migrate, but they found jobs in larger Mexican cities. The majority of Mexican international emigration arose from regions of previous intensive international recruitment (the Center-West and Center-North), which were not the poorest regions.

## Migration and Social and Economic Policies since 1980

This situation changed during the 1980s because, we argue, the Mexican urban system became less capable of providing job opportunities for the growing population. The import-substituting model of development was replaced by greater openness to external trade. Increased need for external finance prompted Mexican governments to open the internal market to competition and outside investment. Fiscal austerity policies were adopted as part of debt restructuring, which affected wages and employment mostly through uncompensated inflation. Most wages, particularly the minimum wage, were cut in half. The combined effect of these policy initiatives reduced the state's direct role in the economy through privatization, which reduced direct and indirect state employment. General subsidies for transport, fuel, food, electricity, and urban infrastructure were ended and only a few (milk, corn, and tortillas) replaced by targeted subsidies. The net effect was a substantial reduction of state subsidies to urban economies.

The changes in the macro-economic context affected migration both through its direct impact on employment and through the rural-urban and interregional distribution of growth. The most notable features of the distribution of growth after 1980 are the dynamism of regions and cities associated with export-oriented production and with tourism, the relative stagnation of Mexico City, and the continuing impoverishment of most of the South-Southeast region of Mexico.

The changes in the spatial distribution of growth came at a time when the previous patterns of migration were undergoing fundamental change. Rural-urban migration became a smaller component of Mexican urban growth as the relative size of the rural population declined. At the same time, urban-to-urban migration increased as the primacy of Mexico's urban system declined and intermediate cities, often linked to export-oriented industrialization, grew in importance.

There was a notable outmigration from Mexico City to other urban centers. This outmigration was received mostly by states in the Center, West and Center North, where Mexico City emigrants amounted to more than 33 percent of immigrant flows. Only an average eleven percent of the immigration flows of states in the Border North came from the capital city (Escobar 1996, Browning and Corona 1995).

Rural-based, temporary migration patterns also changed. By the 1980s, the economies of many rural areas had altered in ways that made temporary labor migration an inadequate subsistence strategy for small-scale farmers. Increasingly, younger people saw permanent outmigration as the only solution to inadequate farm incomes, unavailability of land, and depleted natural resources. In addition, the end of subsidies for urban consumers were matched with the end of subsidized crop prices, credit and inputs for peasants (Escobar, Bean, and Weintraub 1996)[5]. Thus, international migration ceased to be a temporary migration strategy and became, like rural-urban migration, more permanent. Those who, for various reasons, saw the need to leave for good had to shift their outlook from Mexican cities to the U.S. International migration, therefore, included more whole families and not simply the migrant laborer who left his family to subsist at home. International migration became permanently linked with rural-urban and urban-urban migration patterns that prevailed in Mexico in the 1980s and 1990s.

We can gauge the extent of the change by referring to Corona's analysis of the shift in migration patterns from 1970 to 1990. In 1970, of the 16.3 percent of the Mexican population who had left their state of birth, 1.5 percent had moved to the United States and 14.8 percent had migrated internally. In 1990, 23.2 percent of the population were living outside their state of birth. Of these, 18 percent had moved to another Mexican state and an estimated 5.2 percent had moved to the United States. Relative to the total population in each date, total interstate and international migration increased 42 percent, interstate migration only by 21 percent, and international migration 247 percent. The relative and absolute importance of international migration as part of the total migration flows rises enormously.

Working from the 1990 Census, Lozano et al. (1996) document a net shift of Mexican migration northwards between 1985 and 1990, particularly to the border cities. Using the Mexican National Survey of Demographic Dynamics (ENADID), the same authors show that most internal migration was inter-urban: the majority (55.5 percent) of the population who had migrated internally during the five-year period of 1987-1992 moved among cities with more than 20,000 inhabitants. Among the international migrants surveyed by ENADID in Mexico, approximately a third had also migrated within Mexico (Lozano et al. 1996). This internal migration was mainly to cities and was least common among those international migrants born and residing in the traditional sending areas (Durango, Nayarit, Colima, Jalisco, Aguascalientes, Michoacan, Guanajuato, San Luis Potosi, and Zacatecas).[6]

Regional reorientation in economic growth clearly affects the distribution of urban growth. De Oliveira and Roberts (1996: Table 8.2) show how the "urban boom" peaked during the 1960s. Rates of growth fell consistently after this, indicating Mexico's process of urbanization probably reached a point of stabilization, due in part to falling population growth rates but mostly to the urban system's failure to absorb the growing population. Mexico City's growth halted almost completely, the urban fringe around it (the rest of the Center region) was among the fastest growing, the growth of the border cities was the second most dynamic, and "the cities of the interior with outward looking economies" were the most dynamic.

The intercity variation is considerable. Thus, the census reports Mexico City as growing at only 1 percent annually between 1980 to 1990, whereas the fastest-growing city of its size in 1980, Tijuana, increased at an annual rate of 5.4 percent in these years[7]. Cancún, Tlaxcala, and Puerto Vallarta (all housing less than 100,000 inhabitants in 1980) were all above nine percent. The considerable intercity variation in growth rates indicates the importance of inter-urban migration in Mexico in the 1980s. This was the first decade in which Mexico City showed net population loss through outmigration and in which those born in the Federal District are, relative to previous censuses, more likely to appear as residents in cities throughout the country.

Urban growth is a sign of a growing economy. However, it simultaneously places pressure on local governments to increase the provision of urban infrastructure, housing, and services. Table 2.1 depicts the quality of housing in the main Mexican cities in 1990. Our classification of housing quality reflects significant differences in housing quality and urban services, particularly between the border cities and Guadalajara and Monterrey. That the quality of housing is good in slow-growth cities is not surprising, especially in Mexico City, Guadalajara, and Monterrey: these cities received privileged levels of expenditure in the past, and have the second highest per worker earnings after the border.

**Table 2.1**
**Housing Quality in the Main Mexican Cities**

| City Grouping | Very Poor Housing[A] | Poor to Moderate Housing[B] | Good Standard Housing[C] |
|---|---|---|---|
| Border cities | 36.3 | 37.4 | 26.3 |
| Export-oriented cities | 20.4 | 24.4 | 55.2 |
| Gulf Cities | 22.6 | 22.1 | 55.3 |
| Traditional Cities | 22.5 | 19.4 | 58.1 |
| Guadalajara & Monterrey | 10.3 | 19.3 | 70.4 |
| City Fringe of Mexico City | 19.3 | 26.5 | 54.2 |
| Mexico City | 17.4 | 24.8 | 57.8 |

SOURCE: One percent sample of 1990 Mexican Census.

[A]Very poor housing is categorized as housing without piped water and with non-solid construction materials used for the walls, roof, and floor.

[B]Poor to moderate housing has piped water, and most of the materials used for walls, roof or floor are not solid construction materials.

[C]Good standard housing has piped water, and the construction materials are solid.

In our view, the significance of this table lies in the poor quality of housing along the border and in the reasonable quality of housing in the Gulf and export-oriented cities. This is significant on two levels. First, because incomes were lower in the Gulf and export-oriented cities than on the border, the reasonable quality of housing when compared to the border was not due to higher income. Second, because the Gulf and export-oriented cities grew as rapidly as the border, a slower growth is not the explanation for reasonable housing either. The border cities, where international migration is an option—offer the least attractive living conditions. In our view, in order to more successfully retain population, the border cities would have to significantly improve housing, urban infrastructure, and services.

Paradoxically, during the period of import-substituting industrialization in Mexico, when federal investment might have enabled rural areas to retain a greater part of their increasing population, the bulk of government subsidies were aimed at the major metropolitan areas. From 1980 to 1988, when the major urban areas were unable to absorb their growing labor force, there was a tendency for social expenditures to increase in the most impoverished rural states which had little potential for absorbing population growth. In contrast, as we will see, there was a relative neglect of fast-growing areas along the border and in the Center-North of the country. In terms of general considerations of equity and social justice, there is, of course, a strong argument for targeting the most impoverished rural areas. Our point, however, is that the urban areas, not the rural, hold the key to providing the job opportunities and living conditions that will sustain Mexico's population growth. Thus, more policy attention needs to be given to improving living and working conditions in Mexican cities. In the next section, we examine the changes in Mexican urban labor markets that took place during economic liberalization from 1987 to 1994. We will then look at the regional pattern of Mexican government investment, including the social expenditures associated with the Solidaridad program.

## Income and Employment

The basic employment-related economic policies that have prevailed in Mexico since the early eighties, but more radically since 1988, are various: wage controls were one means of reducing inflation and stimulating industrial expansion; deregulation aimed at increasing flexibility in work organization and providing incentives to employers to restructure enterprises; privatization of former state enterprises somewhat reduced the state's payroll; and tariff reductions, until the devaluation of December 1994, fostered imports and increased competition for domestic producers. The overall result of these policies was a freer internal market in goods and labor. What were the specific impacts of these economic policies on incomes and employment conditions? To obtain an indication of what was happening in the urban labor markets that traditionally absorbed most internal migrants, we use data from the Mexican Urban Employment Surveys of the second quarter of 1987 and the second quarter of 1994. This period covers the initiation of economic restructuring policies under President Miguel de la Madrid and almost all of the presidency of Carlos Salinas de Gortari, when these policies were fully implemented.[8]

In general, this was a period of both population and economic growth for middle-sized cities. From 1980 to 1990, census figures indicate a slowing of urbanization compared to previous decades, but Mexican cities of 100,000 continued to absorb populations migrating from smaller places. Thus the cities of over 100,000 grew at an annual rate of 2.1 percent between 1980 and 1990, whereas Mexican population growth in this period was 1.9 percent annually.

## Table 2.2
## Changes in Income and Labor Market Conditions
## 16 Mexican Cities, 1987-1994

|  | Men | | | Women | | |
|---|---|---|---|---|---|---|
|  | 1987 | 1994 | % Change 1987-94 | 1987 | 1994 | % Change 1987-94 |
| Average real income[A] | 432.7 | 595.4 | 37.6 | 313.4 | 423.5 | 35.1 |
| Real Income at the 40th percentile[B] | 293.4 | 334.6 | 14.0 | 244.5 | 255.5 | 4.5 |
| Real Income at the 90th percentile[B] | 763.4 | 1167.4 | 52.9 | 537.9 | 778.2 | 44.7 |
| Income ratio of top 10% to bottom 40% | 1.6 | 2.8 | 75.0 | 1.6 | 2.2 | 37.5 |
| Percent informally employed[C] | 38.3 | 40.5 | 5.7 | 42.5 | 43.8 | 3.1 |
| Percent covered by social security[D] | 51.6 | 49.6 | -3.9 | 54.8 | 50.8 | -7.3 |

[A] Income is monthly income in pesos (thousands) of the second quarter of 1988 adjusted through the monthly Consumer Price Index (exchange rate approximately 2990 to the US dollar).

[B] This is the monthly income earned by the person who is at the 40th or 90th percentile of the income distribution respectively.

[C] The categorization of "informal" employment includes owners of firms with less than five employees, employees of firms with less than five workers, the self-employed, and unpaid family workers.

[D] Social security coverage is defined as having state coverage, through IMSS or ISSTE, or private coverage.

Table 2.2 shows the labor market performance of the largest and middle-sized Mexican cities from 1987 to 1994, a period during which economic growth resumed in Mexico after the recession of the early 1980s. From 1987 to 1994, the aggregate figures for income growth in the sixteen cities are positive. In this period, labor force growth was more than three percent per year, but average real income still managed to increase by 37.6 percent for men and 35.1 percent for women. The achievement of real income growth was hindered, however, by increasing income inequality. Growth in real income was slow for the bottom 40 percent of the income distribution, whereas the top 10 percent showed rapid growth resulting in a widening ratio of income inequality by 1994. The other employment indicators in the table suggest urban labor markets are highly differentiated. Thus, the proportion of men and women working "informally" slightly increased in these years and the proportion covered by social security slightly declined. The decline is related to the falling proportion of waged workers in the workforce (self-employed and unpaid family workers could be, but in fact are not, covered by Social Security). The worsening, however, is modest.

These indicators of worsening labor market conditions do not support the most negative prognoses of the impact of free trade policies. In light of the growth in employment and the impact of economic restructuring, the Mexican urban labor market did remarkably well to maintain, with only slight declines, its levels of formal employment and social security coverage, and achieve modest real income gains even for low-income earners. However, it is also clear that this period of economic opening did not bring substantial labor market gains for the majority of the urban population.

Certainly, however, these trends do not suggest that urban labor markets became more capable of absorbing and stabilizing labor through substantially increased income and benefits. On the contrary, from 1980 to 1988, according to ECLAC, the proportion of the Mexican labor force working informally grew from 24 to 33 percent of the total, and in absolute terms by 80 percent, since the labor force was growing rapidly as younger workers and women tried to earn a living. Women's entry into the labor force was marked by high levels of intermittent employment and instability. At the same time, employment became less secure and stable for men (see Escobar's [1996] depiction of changes in the three main Mexican labor markets, and the rise in insecurity of men's employment). Women's role in household income earning became more and more vital (Gonzalez de la Rocha 1994), but the basis of employment stability was gone for urban working-class households in general.

Also, at the same time as income rose, the proportions of the self-employed increased by 24.8 percent in Mexico City, by 31 percent in Monterrey, and by 42.5 percent in Guadalajara (Escobar 1996). And, while the income provided by self-employed jobs had at times been higher than wage income in these cities up to 1982, after 1982 that income is clearly lower. The persons moving towards self-employment did so mostly because waged jobs were scarce, not because self-employment was particularly attractive.[9] We therefore see fundamental problems not with income levels, but with labor absorption, with employment instability, and with income inequality.

We can explore this issue further by looking at what happened to individual cities in these years. Labor market differences between cities are, we suggest, some of the key factors in promoting inter-urban migration and, by extension, international migration. We group the sixteen cities into five categories. First are four cities on the U.S. Mexico border: Tijuana, Ciudad Juarez, Nuevo Laredo, and Matamoros. These cities had some of highest population growth rates from 1980 to 1990 as industrialization linked to the *maquiladora* in-bond industry attracted migrants from nearby rural areas and from other cities, including Mexico City. Mexico City is a category of its own because of its economic predominance and large population. Although it appears to have lost the most population through outmigration, Mexico City remains the dominant urban economy of Mexico and is the center of the service industries that have profited from economic opening.

The third grouping are the two next largest metropolitan areas in Mexico— Guadalajara and Monterrey. Both cities are the dominant service and production centers of their regions and have attracted migrants from rural areas and small towns, Guadalajara in particular. Both cities are also major sources of international migration to the U.S.[10] The fourth grouping consists of three cities of the Gulf coast of Mexico—Tampico, Veracruz, and Merida. We group these cities together because all three of them are likely to have benefited economically by the economic opening in the period from 1987 to 1994. Tampico and Veracruz are Mexico's principal ports for imports, as well as centers of the oil industry. Merida has become an important organizing center for the tourist industry of the Yucatan peninsula and has port facilities close by. The fifth category is made up of six cities of the interior of Mexico, Puebla, San Luis Potosi, Leon, Torreon, Chihuahua, and Orizaba. Though these cities differ in size and in economic structure, they are similar in that they are less likely than the other groupings to have benefited directly from economic opening. They are not centers of services tied to international trade (as are the three major metropolitan centers), or locations of in-bond industry, or major recipients of the trade or tourist flows that occurred with economic opening.

A more detailed analysis of the data reported in Table 2.2 shows that the labor markets of these sixteen cities responded in very different ways to the economic opening of the 1987-1994 period. The border cities began with the highest average income but showed relatively slow growth. It was during this time that a favorable exchange rate for the peso against the dollar stimulated Mexican purchases of U.S. goods, but probably discouraged U.S. cross-border tourism. However, the income growth that does occur in the border cities is relatively equitable, and for males there are clear gains in formal employment and in social security coverage.

In 1987, the border cities had the lowest percentage of men working in firms of five or more workers, but by 1994 the border cities outranked the other city groupings in this category. In these years, men entered the *maquiladora* labor force in greater relative numbers than women. The border's equitable income growth contrasts with Mexico City, where real income growth is relatively high and heavily concentrated in the top 10 percent of the income distribution. Both men and women lose ground in terms of formal employment and social security coverage. This pattern is repeated for Guadalajara and Monterrey and for the three Gulf coast cities.

Rodriguez's (1996) detailed analysis of the transformation of Veracruz's labor market from 1987 to 1994 provides insight into the processes producing these aggregate outcomes. Veracruz lost jobs in large-scale manufacturing plants in the 1980s as state enterprises were restructured or privatized. Using occupational histories, Rodriguez shows that the workers who lost jobs became self-employed or worked in microenterprises, mainly in the services. There was, however, some expansion in better-paying jobs, particularly in professional services and in the tourist industry, providing for a remarkable growth of income in this bracket. The overall effect, Rodriguez concludes, was to make Veracruz's labor market less attractive to migrants from within the state since, in the past, they had mainly worked in manufacturing. Also, housing conditions in Veracruz worsened, forcing migrants and those who are unemployed or in insecure jobs to seek rudimentary shelter on the edges of the city. Based on his interviews with residents, Rodriguez sees housing and labor market conditions in Veracruz pushing residents to seek work elsewhere in Mexico and in the United States, the latter a previously uncommon destination for people from this state.

The six interior cities, in contrast, fall between the border cities and the Gulf or major metropolitan areas showing moderate income growth, a moderate increase in income inequity, and little change in the proportions employed in formal enterprises and covered by social security. There is the suggestion, then, that the increased trade and service activity associated with economic opening led, in the cities most affected, to increases in real income, particularly at the top of the income distribution, but a worsening of income inequality and of labor market conditions for the semi-skilled and unskilled workers at the bottom. On the border, economic opening translated mainly into more production jobs. The income gains of these years were more widely dispersed.

These different patterns of labor growth undoubtedly affected internal migration. Mexico City, the traditional magnet of internal migration became, in these years, not only a less attractive labor market for migrants with relatively low levels of education, but a less stable work environment for those already in the city. The same is likely true of Guadalajara, Monterrey, and the Gulf cities. In contrast, the northern border cities offered more stable work opportunities for those without the education and skills to profit from entrepreneurial opportunities in sectors such as producer services and distribution. Even the border cities, however, did not have labor markets likely to stabilize their working populations. Jobs in large-scale industry, mainly the *maquiladoras*, are heavily concentrated among young, unmarried men and women, and turnover rates are high. Older workers who are heads of households are more likely to be self-employed or work in small-scale enterprises. Though on the border, workers in this "informal" sector can often earn incomes that are higher than the *maquiladora* sector, income opportunities are unstable, prompting many to seek work on the other side of the border.

In summary, Mexico's economic policies from 1987-1994 had ambivalent consequences for emigration. The opening of markets and the increase in trade was associated with economic growth and real income growth. The job opportunities created by this growth acted as an alternative to international migration for both rural and urban migrants. However, this growth seems to have increasingly differentiated and destabilized urban labor markets, encouraging inter-urban migration. As a consequence, there is a shift towards northern border cities whose markets, while absorbing labor flows, likely encouraged movement across the international boundary.

## The Pattern of State Investment

In this section, we will analyze federal allotments to states, federal investment patterns and social investment under the National Solidarity Program, which attempts to relate government policy to the territorial reorganization of the Mexican economy and migration. Our analysis explores whether or not a pattern can be observed in the relationship between federal expenditure and the relative economic dynamism of states, including their rates of in- or out-migration. Is there evidence, for instance, of the targeting of poor states with high levels of out-migration? Do the states that are growing fastest economically and could, consequently, absorb outmigration from poorer regions, benefit from federal expenditures?

The first type of federal expenditure, federal *participaciones* or allotments to individual states, amounts to 61 percent of the states' total income. In principle, allotments are based on those states' value added taxes, PEMEX reimbursements and some aspects of external trade, all of which are collected by the federal government. If this were always the case, allotments would simply reflect changes in economic activity, but they are also a powerful policy instrument. These transfers are used to foster investment (as in Quintana Roo, during the development of Cancun during the 1970s) or to compensate for extreme levels of poverty. Additionally, the states do not always have the means to control federal taxes within their territory, which means negotiations with the federal government can lead to diverse outcomes.

In the past, the states complained that federal expenditures had a pro-central, pro-metropolitan bias. Here we analyze whether this bias remained during the eighties, when a number of economic and demographic trends changed.[11] Two-thirds of the total list of states show coinciding patterns of GNP growth and federal allotments as either growth-growth or loss-loss. However, there are large variations in the evolution of each variable: some states grew slightly and received large increases in federal allotments, while the reverse is true for others. In other cases, participation in GNP dropped, there was a negative migration balance and federal allotments increased, suggesting a counterbalancing role of federal expenditure.

It would seem migration balances played no role in defining federal allotments. Among the northern states on the border, only Baja California showed growth, a positive migration index, and a favorable trend in allotments exceeding growth in relative GNP. Baja California Sur, although not on the border, could be considered a similar case. Sonora's federal payments grew to the same extent as its GNP, in spite of its population attraction. Chihuahua's participation dropped in spite of growth and positive migration balances. In the cases of Sinaloa and Tamaulipas, federal payments followed opposite trends in GNP irrespective of positive migration flows. Nuevo Leon is unfavorably treated by federal payments, in spite of growth and a positive migration balance. In general, the North's share of federal allotments is far below its growing economic power and increase in migrants. From documents provided by the government of Nuevo Leon, however, it could be said this state regarded its lower dependence on federal funds as a sign of autonomy. This could be the case of other northern states, where other revenue sources grew.

The Center-North differed from the North mostly because of its negative migration balances. Durango, San Luis Potosi and Zacatecas, all of which gained in relative GNP, witnessed their allotments grow more than their economies. Aguascalientes, the only state in this region that had a positive migration balance, resembled Queretaro in all respects, except that its positive migration balance was more modest. As in Queretaro, its federal allotments grew less than its economy. Guanajuato grew, lost population, and its allotments remained stable relative to GNP.

In the South-Southeast, federal allotments for Guerrero, Michoacan, Oaxaca, and Yucatan grew far beyond their importance in GNP, in spite of extremely negative population flows. Campeche, Chiapas, and Veracruz were also favorably treated, although their economies lagged behind, in one case markedly, and they lost population. In the region, only Quintana Roo, a "new" state which grew at a rapid pace on the basis of tourism and attracted population, showed federal allotments which grew less than its relative GNP. Tabasco, which had prospered thanks to its large oil fields but later suffered a fall in PEMEX payments and relative GNP, did receive fewer allotments by 1988, but its trend was still better than the state's economic performance. Tabasco also exhibited a negative migration balance by 1990. In the South-Southeast, therefore, the trend in allotments was in general favorable, although migration was in general negative and economic performance negative or modestly positive. The negative side to this was that these states depended largely on allotments to finance expenditures, with other sources contributing minor shares. Dependence of these states on allotments was much greater than the national average of 61 percent.

The Center followed more varied paths than the regions discussed above. The Federal District, which became the largest population expeller during the last decade, suffered a slight drop in Federal allotments, in accordance with economic performance but not migration. The state of Mexico showed perhaps the most contradictory performance: its relative GNP grew modestly, its population rose rapidly as a result of deconcentration, and its relative federal allotments diminished. A similar pattern is visible in Queretaro, a dynamic economy which attracted population with only modest growth in federal allotments. The rest of the perimetropolitan states in the region attracted federal allotments beyond their economic performance. Of these, all showed positive migration balances with the exception of Puebla. This region, therefore, was still favored by federal allotments, the state of Mexico and Queretaro excepted. Those most favored were the ones which had previously been very poor and rural in the region (Hidalgo, Tlaxcala and, to a lesser extent, Morelos). Lastly, in the West, Jalisco and Colima grew and attracted population, but only Colima's share of federal allotments grew. Nayarit was negative on both counts, but its share grew.

The second type of federal expenditure, federal investment, is based on government perceptions of need and opportunity for development of specific projects. It was mostly aimed at infrastructure, and in this case also included PEMEX investments, which should have clear consequences in terms of a state' s contribution to GNP. The main differences between the changes in the distribution of allotments and the changes in the distribution of investment were: that the Center region increased its share of federal investment and the Federal District, especially, received an increase substantial enough to reduce levels of investment elsewhere; and that the South-Southeast, which housed the largest poor populations, also dropped in importance.

Since federal investment varied from one year to the next, we have averaged the two years at the beginning of the crisis and two years in the "transition" from adjustment to restructuring in order to more reliably assess the changes taking place between these two moments. While the biases in allotment changes can be seen to some extent as counteracting the undesirable consequences of restructuring (as poor states in the Center and the South-Southeast increased their shares), investment seemed to have a logic independent of either growth or poverty. The substantial pro-central bias evident in the trends in federal investment from 1982 to 1989 leads one to question the state's ability or interest in coordinating its action with the observed geographical redistribution of the economy.

The third type of federal expenditure that we consider, social spending, entered an entire new period in terms of the levels and forms of organization in 1988. Social spending rose from 5.76 percent of total government expenditure in 1988 to 9.1 percent in 1993. This was a time of substantial growth in income and expenditure for the government, which made this increase still more substantial. Within social spending, however, the National Solidarity Program played an increasing and vital role. Spending on infrastructure in health, education and rural development was channeled through this program. It was innovative in several significant respects. It bypassed many federal and state governments and bureaucracies and associated instead with local governments and grassroots organizations; it required (and was intended to respond to) local participation, either through labor or through partial funding of the investment. It promoted subsistence agriculture, small enterprises in general and women's in particular, and sports fields; improved shanty towns, introduced piped water and sewage, and supplied electricity to dispersed communities. It promoted various production schemes, specific programs in indigenous communities, subsistence grants for poor schoolchildren, direct grants, subsidies, refinancing of unpaid debts and interest-free loans to poor peasants, and many other programs. The variety reflects one of the program's idiosyncrasies: support of the priorities chosen by local communities and organizations.

The complexity and breadth of the Solidarity program would require a detailed discussion beyond the scope of this chapter.[12] However, we relate the investments carried out by this program to this chapter by asking these two questions: What is the relationship between income and Solidarity investment? What is the relationship between the overall marginality of each state and its reception of Solidarity investment? These two questions address the nature of Solidarity as an anti-poverty program. And finally, is there a relationship between the biases of this program and international emigration?

At first glance, Table 2.3 reveals a significant mismatch. A gross measure indicates that sixteen states received a share compensating for their income (higher

## Table 2.3
### GNP Per Capita, Marginality Index and Social Investment in Solidarity, Per State and Region (1989-91 Total)

| Region | GNP P/C Ratio to Mean | Marginality Index | Investment P/C Ration to Mean |
|---|---|---|---|
| **Border** | **1.37** | **low** | **1.07** |
| B Cal. Norte | 1.42 | very low | 1.48 |
| B Cal. Sur | 1.37 | low | 2.29 |
| Coahuila | 1.41 | low | 1.27 |
| Chihuahua | 1.24 | low | 1.02 |
| Nuevo Leon | 1.90 | very low | 0.87 |
| Sinaloa | 0.94 | average | 0.83 |
| Sonora | 1.40 | low | 1.11 |
| Tamaulipas | 1.13 | low | 0.92 |
| **Center North** | **0.82** | **high** | **1.07** |
| Aguascalientes | 0.94 | low | 2.31 |
| Durango | 0.91 | high | 1.47 |
| Guanajuato | 0.77 | high | 0.57 |
| S. Luis Potosi | 0.86 | high | 0.75 |
| Zacatecas | 0.75 | high | 2.00 |
| **Cent er** | **0.95** | **low** | **0.68** |
| D. Federal | n/a | very low | 1.09 |
| Hidalgo | 0.84 | very high | 1.09 |
| Mexico | 1.08 | low | 0.46 |
| Morelos | 0.99 | low | 1.19 |
| Puebla | 0.70 | very high | 0.60 |
| Queretaro | 1.16 | high | 0.96 |
| Tlaxcala | 0.70 | average | 1.60 |
| **South- S. East** | **0.81** | **high-v. high** | **1.29** |
| Campeche | 3.87 | high | 2.50 |
| Chiapas | 0.56 | very high | 1.76 |
| Guerrero | 0.67 | very high | 0.98 |
| Michoacan | 0.66 | high | 1.00 |
| Oaxaca | 0.53 | very high | 1.79 |
| Quintana Roo | 1.36 | average | 2.10 |
| Tabasco | 1.15 | high | 0.62 |
| Veracruz | 0.85 | very high | 0.78 |
| Yucatan | 0.80 | high | 2.66 |
| **West** | **1.14** | **low** | **0.68** |
| Colima | 1.15 | low | 2.35 |
| Jalisco | 1.19 | low | 0.44 |
| Nayarit | 0.82 | average | 1.36 |

SOURCE: BANAMEX-ACCIVAL. *Mexico Social 1992-1993. Indicadores seleccionados.* 1993: 295, 312. GNP P/C and Invest P/C are both states' ratios to Mexico's mean GNP P/C and Solidarity Investment P/C. The marginality index combines ratios to the mean of illiteracy rates, unschooled population, overcrowding, population in dispersed rural settlements and population earning under two minimum wages.

than average income with lower than average investment or vice versa), while fifteen did not. While the two poorest states nationally did receive privileged amounts of per capita funds, regionally there were serious mismatches. The poorest state in the North (Sinaloa) received less than average, and significantly less than the regional average. In the Center North, the poorest received a large amount, but the second poorest (Guanajuato) received the lowest PC Solidarity investment in that region. In the Center, one of the two poorest (Tlaxcala) was privileged, but a state with the same mean GDP (Puebla) received one of the lowest per capita shares. In the South-Southeast, Chiapas and Oaxaca benefited significantly, but Michoacan, Guerrero, and Veracruz, all below average levels of PC GDP, did not. A similar mismatch can be observed in the West.

The marginality index reveals a still more problematic relationship. Twelve states exhibit a "match," while nineteen do not. It is necessary to conclude that this program's investments were not dictated by states' income nor to their levels of marginality. While some of the poorest states did benefit from this program substantially, others did not. On the other hand, many states with above average incomes or low marginality did.

The third (and main) issue needs further consideration. From 1989 to 1991, the regions with the highest international emigration rates were: the West, with 5.86 individuals per thousand per year; the Border North, with 4.27; and the Center North, with 3.17[13]. The Border North and the West as a whole did benefit from Solidarity, but parts of the West did not, particularly Jalisco, which was one of the two most important origins of international emigrants (Colima had a higher emigration rate, but due to its relatively small population counts little in the region's total balance). A similar problem is evident with Guanajuato, in the Center North, which also showed high emigration rates. Guanajuato was the source of a large part of the total emigration flows, and received very little support from Solidaridad. The South-Southeast was the region whose international emigration rates grew most rapidly. Within this region, Oaxaca, a strong participant in these flows, received support, but Guerrero and Michoacan did not.

Did states with high immigration rates receive particular attention under this program? We have argued that, in the eighties, international emigration stemmed from a crisis in the urban system in Mexico. The argument in this case is that the population flowing into high-growth cities may find jobs, but places pressure on local infrastructure and social services, which could be met through the program. The relative privilege of the North under Solidarity could be explained by this argument. Within the region, the state with the second-highest per capita Solidarity investment (Baja California Norte) was also among the top immigration states. But the highest per capita investment went to a state undergoing tourist development (Baja California Sur), but with lower immigration rates. Nuevo Leon, on the other hand, was still an immigration state, in spite of slowing urban growth, but received very little investment per capita.

In the Center North, Aguascalientes was the only state to have reversed its negative population balance through migration. It received the top per capita budget. But Zacatecas was a high emigration state and it also received an above average share. In the Center, the highest immigration state (Estado de Mexico) received the lowest per capita investment. Morelos was among those with the highest immigration rates and highest urban growth rates and received 19 percent more than average. But Queretaro was also a high immigration state and its two major cities were growing rapidly (Queretaro, the capital, grew at 6.6 percent per annum, and San Juan del Rio at 8.5), in spite of which it received little support. In the South-Southeast, the high immigration states of Campeche and Quintana Roo received above average investment, more so than the poorest states, indicating that perhaps this is a better gauge of their importance for social spending. In the West, Colima had the highest immigration rate of the three states, and it received above average funds, but Jalisco also had a positive balance and did not.

In summary, then, from 1980 to 1988 allotments and federal investments paid attention to poor states and the Center (the Federal District particularly), and very little to states with dynamic populations and economies away from the Center, particularly but not exclusively in the North. Starting in 1988, when the Solidarity program led the way for social expenditure and investment, the panorama was much more complex. Particular attention was paid to states along the Northern border, but not to all. The Center North also received particular attention, but this attention was not distributed within that region according to emigration. The Center seemed to be the least privileged region, except that the Federal District did not figure in Solidarity investment reports, leaving the extent and forms of social investment there to other sources. In the South-Southeast, both extreme poverty and extreme levels of growth and immigration seemed to attract social investment, bypassing seriously poor states.

## Conclusion

In attempting to answer the question of how social and economic policies encourage international migration, we have ruled out a number of apparently obvious answers. More importantly, we have assumed that a large number of analyses are correct in saying that, during the 1980s and the beginning of the 1990s, Mexican emigration rose to unprecedented levels in absolute terms (Bean, Edmonton, and Passel 1990, Cornelius 1991, Corona 1993, Massey et al. 1994, Escobar, Bean, and Weintraub 1996). Since we agree with these analyses, the question is then whether Mexican socioeconomic policy played a role in increasing emigration.

The role played by these policies should be understood in the context of larger bilateral forces leading to increased competition in all factors: markets, lower wages, lower labor absorption rate and greater flexibility in labor management. In other words, policies operated in the context of growing "push" and "pull" forces; but social relationships gave workers access to labor markets throughout Mexico and the United States.

We would argue that social conditions and social policies, in the specific sense of education, health, and infrastructure, did not contribute to increased emigration. During the eighties and contrary to expectations, social welfare, as expressed in life expectancy, mortality, schooling, and housing did not deteriorate substantially throughout Mexico. Mexico's performance *in social terms* during the 1980s is illustrated in the following national figures:

a) Education: in academic year 1992-93, there were 25.6 million students enrolled in the Mexican education system, up from 11.5 million in 1970. Growth is approximately 6.6 percent from 1970 to 1983, but only 0.8 percent since 1983. This reduction is mostly due to a drop in growth of the school-age cohort. In 1990, the 6-11-year-old cohort was growing at 0.34 percent annually, and the 12-14 cohort at 0.87. By 1995, their estimated growth rates are 0.13 and 0.27 percent (CONAPO 1995b). The growth of teaching positions in the federal system is just under 2 percent per year since 1983. A slightly faster growth of teaching positions than enrollment has brought down the number of students per teacher. Similarly, the number of pupils per schools also fell (Banamex 1993:241-2). The illiteracy rate among the population 15 years of age and older dropped from 17.0 to 12.4 percent from 1980 to 1990 (INEGI 1985 and INEGI 1992).

b) Health: From 1980 to 1990, men's life expectancy rose from 63.7 to 66.4 years. Women's rose more, from 69.9 to 73.0. This was a significant slowdown in the rate of improvement for men, but only a marginal slowdown for women (Ibid: 188). Both figures are five years below life expectancy in the U.S., but better than those of Argentina, Brazil, and Colombia. Infant mortality rates were 30/1000 in 1991, one third of their 1960 level, but still three times the comparable rate in the U.S. Expenditure per beneficiary was $120 in 1991 at the Social Security Institute. In the open coverage system, it stood at less than one-third that amount ($33).

c) Housing: In 1980, 28.4 percent of all Mexican dwellings lacked a piped water supply. By 1990, this was down to 19.8. The percentage of housing without sewage connections also dropped, from 42.8 to 34.6 percent. Lastly, housing lacking electricity fell from 21.8 to 12.4 percent (INEGI 1985 and INEGI 1992).

These improvements are noteworthy, especially since the government's programmable spending and investment fell between 60 and 80 percent after 1981 and only began to recover in 1988. However, there are significant differences between regions. Rising life expectancy and falling mortality levels were concentrated both in urban areas and in the north of the country. Poor regions witnessed no improvement, in fact suffered a rise in poverty-related diseases (Langer et al. 1991). Improvement in housing was concentrated in the major cities and in cities of the interior. But improvement in urban living standards did not mean that the rural poor could migrate and settle there. Far fewer rural migrants arrived in the largest cities in the eighties than before, because these labor markets could not absorb them. When regional and rural-urban differences are taken into account, however, the fact remains that there were marked improvements in some areas, while others remained largely stagnant in their social indicators. Perhaps the tendency is best summed up in statements made both by Langer et al. (1991) and Boltvinik (1994): social conditions slowed their rate of improvement, but did not worsen.

Furthermore, there is little evidence that negative trends in real income were significant push factors making for emigration. On the contrary, these levels rose, more so, as we have noted, in the old centers and in interior cities than in the border. But the policies leading to substantial adjustment and restructuring did accelerate, or shift the course of, events in Mexico's urbanization and employment structures. During this period, waged employment grew slowly, while informal, self- and unpaid employment grew rapidly. Labor markets destabilized throughout the country and, most significantly, the capacity of the urban system to absorb labor was substantially diminished. As the centers of the previous model of development suffered, manufacturing employment dropped and other cities did not fully compensate for this change. Income inequality rose significantly, especially in the three main metropolitan areas, but access to high-paying occupations was more restricted than ever.

In addition, the large- and medium-sized cities which grew during restructuring did not consistently receive government support in the form of allotments, federal investment, or social investment. This in spite of the fact that Mexico City stagnated almost completely, and the resources traditionally concentrated there could have been used elsewhere. Other cities were left to their own resources in order to cope with significant population inflows. As a result, living conditions deteriorated or remained unsatisfactory. For workers, this meant poor housing, urban infrastructure, and services. For the middle classes and small and medium entrepreneurs it meant urban disorder and high local taxes needed to compensate for federal neglect. This was most evident along the border, the region in which we found the worst housing conditions. Along the border, also, the income structure was relatively flat, with large numbers of workers in the lower-middle income brackets, but very few above.

We therefore tend to view the rise in emigration as related, or responding to, this greater instability caused by the rise in income inequality and segmentation. Regional restructuring sends the population looking for new opportunities, but the urban system can neither absorb labor in waged occupations nor attract and retain internal migrants.

Additionally, there may be other connections. In the past, urban labor markets, and the significant urban expansion which accompanied their growth, provided not only significant employment opportunities, but also gave urban dwellers, and rural seasonal migrants, the resources to fund their independence and relative security in old age—in small firms, shops, a house for themselves or for rental in a shanty town or barrio, or in their fields. As urbanization progressed, their investment in urban property paid off reasonably. The new economics of migration (Taylor 1987 and 1992) shows that the formation of capital among lower class rural Mexicans was a significant result of international emigration. We believe rural-urban migration within Mexico provided such capital too. However, from the 1980s onwards, migration to Mexican cities may have become a less successful way of accumulating capital and providing long-term welfare, making international migration the most effective option for those wishing to accumulate savings[14].

We believe social policy in Mexico need not address emigration as its primary concern. But the ability of the urban system to absorb Mexico's working population and provide it with long term security needs to be addressed as a fundamental issue in Mexico's future. We therefore see a substantial reorientation in Mexico's urban labor markets, and a far more forceful effort in ensuring the success and viability of Mexico's growing cities of the border and the interior, as necessary changes both for Mexico's future and the future of Mexican emigration.

## Notes

1. The labor law of 1931 placed the responsibility for workers' education, health and housing (in places where housing did not exist or was insufficient) squarely on the firms when they employed more than a given number of workers. These provisions did

not, however, work adequately, leading to the creation of specialized Social Security Institutions, which were directly managed by the public administration. Wage policy underwent a similar institutional evolution, with initial general provisions in the law, and government confidence in the ability of unions to enforce labor-management agreements. In 1942, due to the insufficiency of these bilateral agreements, the government set up a specialized Minimum Wage Commission. The housing provision in the 1931 law remained unenforced, except in the case of the most powerful unions and in a few cities, such as Monterrey. The government therefore set up a centralized worker housing fund to control the provision of housing. In many areas of economic and social life, government centralization of regulation and control functions proceeded likewise.

2. The open coverage system of the Ministry of Health also includes several major hospitals and highly specialized medical centers, staffed by some of Mexico's most prestigious physicians. This system, however, is extremely insufficient and highly centralized in Mexico City.

3. In Mexico, it has become fashionable to say that these pro-wage policies are partly to blame for the marked inefficiency of Mexican manufacturing. We disagree. Higher wages, as a rule, forced management to implement more efficient ways to use labor. The main obstacle to growing efficiency lay rather in the pricing policies (i.e., government price subsidies to other industries and consumers), which reduced the ability of these firms to produce and reinvest earnings, as well as in union power and corruption. The price these firms paid for the political loyalty of the unions was a lack of control over worker selection and the management of labor, both because of bureaucratically established mechanisms which granted significant power to these unions and because of the significant corruption in management-union and worker-union relations.

4. Consider the counterfactual argument that, had a country with an economic structure like that of Ireland bordered the United States in these years, the pressures to emigration would have been enormous. In that case, there would not have been industrialization to provide alternatives to the inhabitants of a stagnant rural sector.

5. This is a justifiable oversimplification. In 1990, corn prices were left to the market, together with the prices of most crops. In 1991, however, corn prices were again regulated, in an attempt to protect poor corn farmers. However, it was large-scale commercial agriculturalists that seemed to reap the gains from re-guaranteed corn prices (Escobar, Bean, and Weintraub 1996). There were new subsidy programs for poor farmers: those qualifying received a "loan" equivalent to 1 ton of maize per hectare provided they worked the land. The repayment of the loan was not enforceable. Again, prosperous agriculturalists took advantage of these no-interest loans. On the other hand, farmers growing other crops (sugar, rice, sorghum, wheat) were subject both to free, international market prices for their crops, and to real-cost, unsubsidized credit and inputs. They argued, to no avail, that the prices of imported crops reflected subsidies received by farmers in the United States and Europe. A large percentage of Mexican cash agricultural and dairy farmers are today insolvent as a result of these policies.

6. Since, by definition, the international migrants surveyed in Mexico are temporary migrants, they are more likely to reflect the older type of international migration in

which people moved directly from villages to the United States. We suspect that among recent cohorts of Mexican migrants in the United States, greater proportions than in the past will have migrated internally in Mexico.

7. Tijuana was the fastest growing among the cities with more than 400,000 inhabitants in 1980. Cancun, Tlaxcala, Puerto Vallarta, Acapulco, Queretaro, Toluca, and Cuernavaca all grew faster than Tijuana, however.

8. The surveys cover sixteen of Mexico's largest cities, including Mexico City, that contain some 36 percent of Mexico's total population and 73 percent of the urban population in cities of over 100,000.

9. There are nevertheless reasons why workers may prefer self-employment, ranging from independence to the ability to work at home, part-time or irregular hours.

10. Guadalajara has been a major reception center for U.S. remittances also.

11. The allotment and investment data used in this analysis are drawn from INEGI, *Estadisticas Historicas de Mexico*, 1990 and the on-line *Banco de datos de INEGI*, October, 1995. The migration calculations are taken from the 1990 Census of Mexico.

12. The reader is referred to Denise Dresser's (1991) account of the political biases in the Solidarity Program.

13. The rates are derived from Corona (1993), weighted and recalculated by the authors, according to our own regional classification.

14. We refer to welfare as well-being, not to institutional welfare. Also, we see institutional welfare in the United States as irrelevant to Mexico-U.S. migration. Mexican migrants improve their long-term well-being in Mexico by employment and by savings from their U.S. jobs, not by using welfare services in the United States. When their employment strategy fails, some use welfare, but this is not a factor driving migration.

# References

Arizpe, Lourdes. 1975. *Indigenas en la Ciudad de Mexico: el Caso de las Marias*. Mexico City: Sepsetentas.

Arroyo Alejandre, Jesus. 1980. Migracion y Formacion de Mercados de Trabajo en Mexico y en Jalisco, *Revista Jalisco* 3: 27-38.

BANAMEX-ACCIVAL. 1993. *Mexico Social 1992-1993*. Mexico City: Grupo Financiero Banamex/Accival.

Barkin, David. 1975. Regional Development and Inter Regional Equity: A Mexican Case Study. In W. Cornelius and Felicity M. Trueblood, eds. *Latin American Urban Research 5*. Beverly Hills and London: Sage.

BDI, Banco de Datos del Instituto Nacional de Estadistica, Geografia e Informatica. 1994. August (online).

Boltvinik, Julio. 1994. La Satisfaccion de las Necesidades Esenciales en Mexico en los Setenta y Ochenta. In P. P. Moncayo and J. Woldenberg, eds. *Desarrollo, Desigualdad y Medio Ambiente*. Mexico City: Cal y Arena.

Browning, Harley, and Rodolfo Corona. 1995. Migracion: La Migracion Inesperada de los Chilangos. *Demos* 8:16-17

Carrillo, Jorge. 1991. *Mercados de Trabajo en la Industria Maquiladora de Exportacion: Sintesis del Reporte de Investigacion.* Mexico: Secretaria del Trabajo y Prevision Social and El Colegio de la Frontera Norte, COLEF.

———. 1989. Transformaciones en la Industria Maquiladora de Exportacion. In B. Gonzalez Arechiga and R. Barajas Escamilla, eds. *Las Maquiladoras: Aiuste Estructural y Desarrollo Regional.* Mexico: El Colegio de la Frontera Norte, COLEF, and F. Friedrich Ebert.

Carrillo, Jorge, and Alfredo Hualde. 1992. Mercados Internos de Trabajo ante la Flexibilidad: Analisis de las Maquiladoras. In COLEF *1 Industria Maquiladora y Mercados Laborales. Vol. II.* Ciudad Juarez: El Colegio de la Frontera Norte, COLEF and Universidad Autonoma de Ciudad Juarez.

Carrillo, Jorge, and Jorge Santibailez. 1993. Deterrninantes de la Rotacion de Personal en las Maquiladoras de Tijuana. Tijuana: El Colegio de la Frontera Norte, COLEF.

CEPAL / INEGI. 1993a. *La Pobreza en Mexico.* Aguascalientes: Author.

———. 1993b. *La Pobreza en Mexico. Apendice Metodologico.* Aguascalientes: Author.

Cerrutti, Marcela, and Bryan Roberts. 1994. Entradas y Salidas de la Fuerza de Trabajo: La Intermitencia del Empleo Femenino en Mexico. Austin: Population Research Center, University of Texas at Austin.

CONAPO, Consejo Nacional de Poblacion. 1995a. *Programa Nacional de Poblacion.* Mexico City: Author.

———.1995b. *Estimaciones de la Poblacion Base y Proyecciones de Poblacion 1990-2030.* Mexico City: Consejo Nacional de Poblacion.

COPLAMAR. 1983. *Macroeconomia de las Necesidades Esenciales.* Mexico City: Siglo XXI.

———. 1982. Vivienda. Vol. 111 in *Necesidades esenciales de Mexico.* Mexico City: Siglo XXI.

Corona, Rodolfo. 1993. Migracion Permanente Interestatal e Internacional, 1950-1990. *Comercio Exterior* 43(8): 749-761.

Cordera, Rolando, and E. Gonzalez Tiburcio. 1991. Crisis and Transition in the Mexican Economy. In M. Gonzalez de la Rocha and A. Escobar Latapi, eds. *Social Responses to Mexico's Economic Crisis of the 1980's.* La Jolla: Center for U.S.- Mexican Studies, University of California, San Diego.

Cortes, Fernando. 1994. La Evolucion en la Desigualdad del Ingreso Familiar durante la Decada de los Ochenta. Mexico City: Centro de Estudios Sociologicos, El Colegio de Mexico.

———. 1992. Cambio Estructural y Concentracion: Un Analisis de la Distribucion del Ingreso Familiar en Mexico, 1984-1989. Paper delivered at the conference "Sociodemographic Impact of Restructuring in Mexico," Austin, The University of Texas at Austin, April.

De la Pena, Guillermo. 1986. Mercados de Trabajo y Articulacion Regional: Apuntes sobre el Caso de Guadalajara y el Occidente Mexicano. In G. De la Pena and A. Escobar, eds. *Cambio Regional, Mercado de Trabaio y Vida Obrera en Jalisco.* Guadalajara: El Colegio de Jalisco.

de Oliveira, Orladina, Bryan Roberts and Richard Tardanico. 1996. Changing Employment Patterns in the Cities of the U.S.-Mexico Gulf Region. Austin: Population Research Center, The University of Texas at Austin.

Diaz Briquets, Sergio, and Sidney Weintraub, eds. 1991. *Determinants of Emigration from Mexico, Central America, and the Caribbean.* Boulder: Westview Press.

Diez-Canedo, Ruiz. 1984. *La Migracion Indocumentada de Mexico a los Estados Unidos. Un nuevo enfoque.* Mexico City: Fondo de Cultura Economica.

Dresser, Denise. 1991. *Neopopulist Solutions to Neoliberal Problems.* La Jolla: Center for U.S.-Mexico Studies, University of California, San Diego.

Escobar Latapi, Agustin. 1996a. Politics and Academic Disciplines: Poverty Research in Mexico. In E. Oyen, et al., eds. *Poverty: A Global Review.* Copenhagen: Scandinavian University Press.

————. 1996b. Restructuring, Social Inequality and State Action in Mexico. Paper delivered at the conference "Variation in Societal Adjustment in a Period of Neo-Liberal Economic Policies in Latin America," Austin, Department of Sociology, The University of Texas at Austin, April.

————. 1995. Reestructuracion, Movilidad y Clases Sociales. *Estudios Sociologicos* 38: 231-259.

————. 1993. The Connection at its Source: Socioeconomic Conditions and Migration Patterns. In A. Lowenthal and K. Burgess, eds. *The California Mexico Connection.* Stanford: Stanford University Press.

————. 1988. The Rise and Fall of an Urban Labour Market: Economic Crisis and the Fate of Small Workshops in Guadalajara, Mexico. *Bulletin of Latin American Research* 7 (2): 183-205.

————. 1986. *Con el Sudor de tu Frente: Mercado de Trabajo y Clase Obrera en Guadalajara.* Guadalajara: El Colegio de Jalisco.

Escobar Latapi, Agustin, Frank D. Bean, and Sidney Weintraub. 1996. *The Dynamics of Mexican Emigration.* IOM Monograph.

Escobar Latapi, Agustin, and Mercedes Gonzalez de la Rocha. 1995. Crisis, Restructuring and Urban Poverty in Mexico. *Environment and Urbanization,* 7(1)l: 57-75.

Escobar Latapi, Agustin, Mercedes Gonzalez de la Rocha, and Bryan Roberts. 1987. Migration, Labour Markets and the International Economy: Jalisco, Mexico and the United States. In J. Eades, ed. *Migrants, Workers, and the Social Order.* London: Tavistock (ASA Monographs 26).

Escobar Latapi, Agustin, and Bryan Roberts. 1991. Urban Stratification, the Middle Classes, and Economic Change in Mexico. In M. Gonzalez de la Rocha and A. Escobar Latapi, eds. *Social Responses to Mexico's Economic Crisis of the 1980s.* La Jolla: Center for U.S.-Mexican Studies, University of California, San Diego.

Garcia, Brigida. 1988. *Desarrollo Economico y Absorcion de Fuerza de Trabajo en Mexico: 1950-1980.* Mexico City: El Colegio de Mexico.

Garcia, Brigida, and Orlandina de Oliveira. 1994. *Trabajo y Vida Familiar en Mexico.* Mexico City: El Colegio de Mexico.

Garza, Gustavo. 1992. Crisis del Sector Servicios en la Ciudad de Mexico. Paper delivered at the conference "Sociodemographic Effects of the Mexican Economic Crisis," Austin, The University of Texas at Austin, April.

———. 1985. Dinamica Industrial y Perspectivas de Descentralizacion. *Dialogos*, 21(11).

———. 1980. *Industrializacion de las Principales Ciudades de Mexico*. Mexico City: El Colegio de Mexico.

Garza, Gustavo, and Departamento del Distrito Federal. 1987. *Atlas de la Ciudad de Mexico*. Mexico City: Departamento del Distrito Federal and El Colegio de Mexico.

Gonzalez de la Rocha, Mercedes. 1994a. *The Resources of Poverty: Women and Survival in a Mexican City*. Oxford and New York: Blackwell Publishers.

———. 1994b. Reestructuracion Social en Dos Ciudades Mexicanas: Un Analisis de Grupos Domesticos en Guadalajara y Monterrey. Paper delivered at XVIII meeting of the Latin American Studies Association, LASA.

Gonzalez de la Rocha, Mercedes, Agustin Escobar Latapi, and Maria de la O Martinez. 1991. Estrategias versus Conflicto: Reflexiones para el Estudio del Grupo Domestico en Epoca de Crisis. In De la Pena, Guillermo, et al., *Crisis: Conflicto y Sobrevivencia. Estudios sobre la Sociedad Urbana en Mexico*. Guadalajara: CIESAS-Universidad de Guadalajara.

Gregory, Peter. 1985. *The Myth of Market Marginality*. Baltimore: Johns Hopkins Press.

Harvey, Neil. 1994. *Rebellion in Chiapas*. La Jolla: Center for U.S.-Mexican Studies, University of California, San Diego (Mexican Agrarian Studies Series 5).

Hernandez Laos, Enrique. 1992. La Pobreza en Mexico. *Comercio Exterior* 42 (4).

INEGI, Instituto Nacional de Estadistica, Geografia e Informatica (Various dates). *Encuesta Nacional de Ingresos y Gastos de los Hogares*. Mexico City and Aguascalientes: Author.

———. 1995a. *Encuesta Nacional de la Dinamica Demografica*. CD-ROM. Aguascalientes: Author.

———. 1995b. *Encuesta Nacional de Ingresos y Gastos de los Hogares*. 2 vols. CD-ROM. Aguascalientes: Author.

———. 1994a. *El ingreso y Gasto Publico en Mexico*. Aguascalientes: Author.

———. 1994b. Encuesta Nacional de Empleo Urbano. Diskette version from the 4th quarter of 1992, and various other dates.

———. 1993. Migracion. Tabulados Tematicos. *XI Censo General de Poblacion y Vivienda. 1990*. 2 vols. Aguascalientes:Author.

———. 1992a. *El Ingreso y Gasto Publico en Mexico*. Aguascalientes: Author.

———. 1992b. Areas Metropolitanas de la Republica Mexicana. Xl Censo General de Poblacion y Vivienda: Resultados Preliminares. Aguascalientes: Author.

———. 1990. *Estadisticas Historicas de Mexico*. Aguascalientes: Author.

———. 1986. *Sistema de Cuentas Nacionales*. Aguascalientes: Author.

———. 1985. *X Censo Nacional de Poblacion y Vivienda: 1980*. Mexico City: Author.

Iszaevich, Abraham. 1988. Migracion Campesina en el Valle de Oaxaca. In G. Lopez Castro, and S. Pardo, eds. *Migracion en el Occidente de Mexico*. Zamora: El Colegio de Michoacan.

Langer, Ana, Rafael Lozano, and Jose Luis Bobadilla. 1991. Effects of Mexico's Economic Crisis on the Health of Women and Children. In M. Gonzalez de la Rocha and A. Escobar Latapi, eds. *Social Responses to Mexico's Economic Crisis of the 1980's.* La Jolla: Center for U.S.-Mexican Studies, Universitiy of California, San Diego.

Lozano Asencio, Femando, Bryan R. Roberts, and Frank D. Bean. Forthcoming. The Interconnectedness of Internal and International Migration: The Case of the United States and Mexico. *Soziale Welt.*

Massey, Douglas S., et al. 1993. Theories of International Migration: A Review and Appraisal, *Population and Development Review* 19: 431-466.

Mesa Lago, Carmelo. 1978. *Social Security in Latin America: Pressure Groups. Stratification and Inequality.* Pittsburgh: University of Pittsburgh Press.

Munoz, Humberto, and Orlandina de Oliveira. 1989. Concentration or Deconcentration? Mexico City and Its Region. In M. Edel and R. G. Hellman, eds. *Cities in Crisis. The Urban Challenge in the Americas.* New York: Bildner Center, City University of New York.

Oliveira, Orlandina, and Bryan R. Roberts.1996. Urban Development and Social Inequality in Latin America. In J. Gugler, *The Urban Transformation of the Developing World.* Oxford: Oxford University Press.

———. 1994. Urban Growth and Social Structure in Latin America, 1930-1990. In L. Bethell, *Cambridge History of Latin America, Vol VI.* Cambridge: Cambridge University Press.

Passel, Jeffrey S., Frank D. Bean, and Thomas J. Espenshade, eds. 1990. *Undocumented Migration to the United States: IRCA and the Experience of the 1980s.* Washington, D.C.: The Urban Institute Press.

Portes, Alejandro, Jose Itzingsohn, and Carlos Dore-Cabral. 1994. Urbanization in the Caribbean Basin: Social Change during the Years of the Crisis. *Latin American Research Review* 29(2):3-38.

Pozas, Maria de los Angeles. 1993. *Industrial Restructuring in Mexico. Corporate Adaptation, Technological Innovation and Changing Patterns of Industrial Relations in Monterrey.* La Jolla: Center for U.S.-Mexican Studies, University of California, San Diego.

Rendon, Teresa, and Carlos Salas. 1993. El Empleo en Mexico en los Ochenta: Tendencias y Cambios, *Comercio Exterior* 43 (8): 719-731.

Reyes Heroles G. G., Jesus. 1985. Politica Economica y Desigualdad Social: Elementos de una Estrategia para Redistribuir el Ingreso en Mexico. In *Encuentro Hispano Mexicano de Cientificos Sociales Igualdad, Desigualdad y Equidad en Espana y Mexico.* Madrid: Instituto de Cooperacion Economica and Mexico City: El Colegio de Mexico.

Rodriguez, Hipolito. 1996. Movilidad Social y Espacio Urbano en dos Ciudades del Golfo de Mexico. Ph.D. dissertation. Guadalajara: CIESAS Occidente.

Taylor, J. Edward.1992. Remittances and Inequality Reconsidered: Direct, Indirect and Intertemporal Effects. *Journal of Police Modeling* 14:187-208.

————. 1987. Undocumented Mexico-U.S. Rural Migration and the Returns to Households in Rural Mexico, *American Journal of Agricultural Economics* 69: 616-638.

Unikel, Luis. 1976. *El Desarrollo Urbano de Mexico. Diagnostico e Implicaciones Futuras.* 2a. ed. Mexico: El Colegio de Mexico.

# 3.

# Do Mexican Agricultural Policies Stimulate Emigration?

*Philip Martin*

Mexico today is on the verge of its "Great Migration," analogous to the net one million Americans who moved from U.S. farms to cities each year in the 1950s and 1960s. The number of people living in rural Mexico is likely to be reduced sharply from the current 24 to 27 million over the next two decades—some 3 to 4 million rural households that now depend on farming are likely to have to find nonfarm jobs within commuting distance of their current residences, migrate to Mexican cities for nonfarm jobs, or migrate to the United States. The "promised land" for many of the Mexicans leaving agriculture in the 1990s is, ironically, the same as for the small farmers and farm workers leaving U.S. fields in the 1950s—large U.S. cities.[1]

Mexico undertook four agricultural reforms in the early 1990s to reduce the costs of the food system to the government and to encourage investments in labor-intensive fruit and vegetable production in which Mexico may have a long-run comparative advantage. These changes in farm policy, the economic crisis, and the slow transition from corn and grains to alternative crops will compress the period of rural-urban migration in Mexico.

The Mexican-U.S. case in the 1990s illustrates what happens when there is an agricultural revolution in one country that has a pre-existing migration relationship with a richer neighbor. As a result of the Mexican agricultural revolution, up to one million of the 24 to 27 million rural Mexicans[2] living in places of 2,500 residents or less are leaving their homes at least temporarily each year.

## Mexican Agricultural Policies

Mexico's farming system is a creature of government and, for most of the twentieth century, Mexican agricultural policies had the dual objectives of supporting rural incomes by offering high government-guaranteed prices to farmers, and then providing consumers with basic foods at low prices. The Mexican government was involved in all aspects of agriculture, from the distribution of land, to the provision of inputs such as fertilizer and credit, to the marketing and processing of commodities, to the distribution of food to consumers. Beginning in the mid-1980s, and especially in the early 1990s, the government began to withdraw from agriculture, accelerating what is likely to be a massive movement off the land in Mexico.

The government's withdrawal from agriculture in the 1990s was motivated primarily by the failure of the Mexican agricultural system to produce enough food at world prices. During the 1950s and 1960s, government intervention in the form of guaranteed high prices, the development of irrigation systems, and the adoption of high-yielding wheat and other grains was associated with rising farm output—up an average 6.6 percent per year (Yates, 1981). In the mid-1960s, Mexico declared itself to be self-sufficient in food. During this period of rapid growth, Mexico was also able to reduce informal employment in the urban economy centered in Mexico City and reduce economic inequality (Escobar, 1995).

The growth in farm output slowed to 2.2 percent per year from 1966 through 1979—about the same as the rate of population growth. In 1980, flush with oil-generated monies, Mexico launched the Sistema Alimentario Mexicano (SAM) policy to make Mexico self-sufficient in basic grains, including corn and beans, by encouraging small farmers to expand their output of these staples. After the economic crisis of 1982-83, SAM was abandoned, and the remainder of the 1980s are widely considered a "lost decade" in Mexican agriculture. The growth of farm output was only 1.3 percent annually, despite a sharp reduction in the value of the peso, which should have accelerated farm exports.

By the early 1990s, the agricultural system was in crisis. Production was not increasing, raising the bill for imported food, rural poverty was widespread despite costly subsidies, and the government did not have the funds to re-capitalize agriculture. The Mexican government decided to phase out some subsidies for agriculture, change the way that remaining subsidies are provided to farmers, and simultaneously change the land tenure system and free up trade in farm commodities.

These changes mean that many of the institutions that have evolved over decades are being reformed or eliminated. Institutions that provide subsidized water, credit, and fertilizer to farmers are being shrunk and privatized, and the major institution involved in Mexican agricultural policy, Conasupo (Compania National de Subsistencias Populares), is being drastically changed.[3]

The Mexican farm crisis seems to have reached a peak in 1996. Mexico is facing its largest-ever food import bill[4] as a result of drought and the inability of farmers to find the money to buy fertilizer, thereby lowering yields.

## Table 3.1
## Milestones in Mexican Agricultural Policy

1983–1993—Gradual removal of input subsidies, price guarantees reduced or eliminated for all commodities except corn and beans

mid-1980s—Productivity falls in rain-fed agriculture; real wages fall by 50 percent, and the government imports cheaper food to keep down food costs for urban workers

1986—Mexico joins GATT, and sets maximum tariff on food imports at 20 percent; government reduces the number of imported commodities requiring licenses, and permits private firms to import food

1991-92—Constitution amended January 7, 1992; agrarian law effective February 27, 1992; *ejido* land can be rented or sold; foreigners may own land; no more expropriation of "excess land"

1993—*Procampo*—decoupling of commodity production and price support; El Barzon protests farm indebtedness, lack of credit

1994—Zapatista uprising on January 1; complaints included opposition to land reform—women could lose their land if husband decides to sell— and fear that pending unresolved "excess land seizures" cases would be dropped. March—retail price controls dropped on all commodities except tortillas and milk.

1995-96—Fruit and vegetable exports increase with peso devaluation; Florida growers complain. Drought and lack of fertilizer reduce Mexican yields and increase imports, government begins removal of price controls on food, including tortillas.

Mexico today has 24 to 27 million residents in rural places with less than 2500 residents. In the 1990 Census, 7.8 million of Mexico's 29 million workers were farmers or farm workers. However, agriculture in Mexico generated only 8 percent of the country's $377 billion GDP in 1994, and rural incomes were less than one-third of Mexico's $4,180 per capita GDP.[5] From 1987 to 1992, per capita income among farmers declined by 32 percent.

Some 40 to 50 percent of all Mexicans are considered to be poor, and two-thirds of Mexico's poor people live in rural areas, as do three-fourths of the very poor (Levy and Van Wijnbergen, 1992, 498).[6] Although most of Mexico's population and rural poor are mestizos, the rate of poverty is highest among indigenous peoples in rural areas.[7]

Mexican agriculture in the mid-1990s is adjusting to a new era with a different role for government, and fewer human resources in agriculture. About the only agreement among those who are examining how Mexican agriculture adjusts to this new era is that there will be fewer people who depend on farming for their livelihood after 2000.

The key question is what will happen to ex-farmers. The Mexican government hopes that many farmers remain will remain in rural areas and switch from corn and beans to fruits and vegetables. However, most reports from rural Mexico are dominated by discussion of a lack of credit and other obstacles that make it hard for farmers to switch crops and remain in agriculture.[8]

## Mexican Farm Structure

The Mexican Revolution was led by Emiliano Zapata's call for land for the peasants, "Tierra y Libertad," and the *ejido* system was the land tenure system that came out of that struggle. Before the Revolution, less than 5 percent of Mexicans owned more than 90 percent of the land.

Under Article 27 of the Mexican Constitution of 1917, peasants could petition Mexico's agrarian reform ministry to redistribute large private land holdings to *ejidos*, and then to grant *ejidatario* members and their heirs rights to the land as long as they actively worked and lived on it. In this manner, *ejidos* accommodated population growth by fragmenting land holdings, resulting in ever-smaller plots of land as the rural population increased.

Land reform proceeded slowly. In 1919, Zapata was assassinated, and in 1923, 2 percent of landowners still owned 82 percent of the land. According to the Mexican Census of 1933, of 325 million acres of land, 93 percent was owned by private landowners. By the end of the Cardenas presidency in 1940, *ejidos* controlled about 50 percent of Mexico's cultivated land. According to the World Bank, by 1970 about 43 percent of all farm land and 51 percent of crop land was in *ejidos*, and 66 percent of the rural population were *ejidatarios*. Mexico today has a farm structure that consists of at least four distinct elements: commercial farms, family farmers, subsistence farmers, and landless workers. The most important type of farm for job creation and the production of export commodities are the large commercial farmers. There are perhaps 400,000 commercial farmers that hire at least one laborer for one month or more—they represent about 10 percent of Mexico's 4 million farms. Commercial farms cultivate about half of Mexico's farm land; many are in Mexico's northwestern states, where they grow most of Mexico's fruits and vegetables destined for export, as well as wheat and corn. Other commercial farms grow rice, sugar, tobacco, and coffee.

Commercial farmers were until 1992 limited by Article 27 of Mexico's constitution to a maximum 100 hectares (247 acres) of irrigated land to grow

### Table 3.2
### Mexican Farm Structure in Early 1990s

| Type of Farm Operator or Worker | Number | Amount of Land (percent) | Source of Income | Farm Output |
|---|---|---|---|---|
| Commercial | 400,000; half in *ejidos* | 50 | Farm sales | Produce most export fruits and vegetables; sugarcane; cotton and rice |
| Family | 1,000,000; 75 percent in *ejidos* migration | 40 | Farm sales; some | Corn, beans, coffee, rice, forage |
| Subsistence | 1,500,000; 66 percent in *ejidos* | 10 | Subsistence production and migration | Corn and beans |
| Landless | 600,000 to 700,000 | – | Local labor markets and migration | |

SOURCE: Philip L. Martin 1993. *Trade and Migration: NAFTA in Agriculture.* Institute for International Economics. Washington.

grains and corn, 300 (741 acres) hectares of irrigated land for orchards, or enough land to maintain 500 head of cattle. However, commercial farmers routinely evaded these restrictions on land ownership by having each family member own the maximum number of acres, and farming or operating the land as a single unit. Such extended land holdings were not secure; the Mexican Constitution permitted until 1992 the expropriation of "excess land" and its redistribution to the landless families who sometimes occupied it. There are still unresolved occupations of land in parts of Mexico, especially in southern Mexican states such as Chiapas.

This threat of expropriation is one reason cited frequently to explain why there is so little private investment in agriculture: investment in Mexican agriculture in the early 1990s was equivalent to just 2 percent of farm output, versus 15 percent of output for the entire economy. A farmer with 1,000 hectares of land used to graze cattle risked having his land expropriated if he installed an irrigation system, since a maximum of 100 hectares of irrigated land was permitted. A January 1992 amendment to Article 27 of the Mexican constitution ended the right of landless persons to claim excess private lands for themselves, and permitted both foreigners and corporations to buy land in Mexico.

The second type of Mexican farm are family farms that use family labor to produce food for their families, and an excess that is sold to the government and in local markets. There are about 1 million such small farms, and they control about 40 percent of Mexico's farm land. Many of these family farmers cultivate *ejido* or communal land, on which they grow corn and beans.

The largest of these family farms operate like commercial farms—if they have access to credit, technology, and markets, they switch between corn and other crops on the basis of which crop promises the highest return. The smaller family farms aim to produce some of what the family consumes, so that their planting decisions are influenced by both family needs and market considerations. Members of small family farm households often supplement their farm earnings by working for wages in local or distant labor markets.

The largest group of farmers are subsistence farmers, sometimes known as *minifundists* or *milpa*. The 1.5 million subsistence farmers, concentrated in the north central and southern states, many on *ejido* land, produce primarily the corn and beans on which their families depend.[9] Many do not produce a surplus to sell to the government agency—CONASUPO—that buys crops from Mexican farmers at higher-than-world-market prices, so they do not benefit from government price guarantees for corn and beans; many subsistence farmers are poor. The productivity of subsistence farmers varies enormously.

Subsistence farmers are about 40 percent of Mexico's farmers, but they control only about 10 percent of the farm land. Their main source of cash income has been and remains off-farm work: many are migrant workers who shuttle in and out of the United States from home bases in low-cost-of-living rural areas of Mexico. Much of the migration research done in rural Mexico over the past two decades has explained how these subsistence households rationally allocate their labor between local and distant labor markets sending, for example, young women to jobs in urban Mexico, and young men to U.S. jobs (Taylor, 1984; Grindle, 1988).

The fourth group in rural Mexico are landless workers. There are about 700,000 such workers, although estimates of their number range as high as 3 million. Households headed by landless workers survive by working in local and distant labor markets for wages. These households are most likely to be in extreme poverty, defined in one study as an income of less than $232 annually in the early 1990s. Landless workers are distributed in a fashion similar to *ejidatarios*, i.e., they are everywhere except the Pacific Northwest.

Escobar notes that, during the 1970s and 1980s, *ejido* and other "rural" labor markets were urbanized by better transportation links, the development of factories in some urban areas, and increased internal migration. Seasonal farm labor markets became less attractive—the supply of farm workers increased faster than the demand for them, putting downward pressure on rural wages, and increasing seasonality. According to one estimate, only about 20 percent of the rural residents in the labor force have steady work (Leya, Vazquez, and Solano, 1990, 5).

## *Ejidos*, Corn, and Farm Policy

A distinguishing feature of the Mexican agricultural system are its *ejido* and communal farms. *Ejidatarios* or farmer-members of ejidos can use their *ejido* land, pass it on to their children, but not sell it or rent it. *Ejidos* control about 50 percent of Mexico's farm land, and half of its irrigated land. In the early 1990s, there were about 28,000 *ejidos* and indigenous communities, involving about 3 million *ejidatarios* and communal farmers, each of whom had an average 6 acres of *ejido* land. Rural families tend to be large, so that *ejido* agriculture involves 15 to 18 million people.

In 1991-92, Mexico amended its constitution to permit *ejido* land to be sold, rented, or used as collateral for loans. This change—"the most radical, and yet the most necessary, of Salinas's economic reforms" (Smith, 1992)—was motivated by the belief that a new regime of property rights was needed to lay the basis for increases in agricultural production efficiency.

One review noted that the *ejido* reform "opens up the possibility for 48 percent of the country (95 million hectares) to enter the free market" (Banamex, 1992, 339). President Salinas in his 1991 State of the Nation address said that: "The land distribution established more than fifty years ago . . . brought justice to the countryside. But to attempt in the present circumstances to continue along [this] path, no longer signifies prosperity for the country or justice for the campesinos. In the past, land distribution was a path of justice; today it is unproductive and impoverishing."

Under the Agrarian Law that went into effect on February 27, 1992, individuals are still limited to 100 irrigated hectares (247 acres) or its dryland and grazing equivalents, but Mexican majority corporations are also allowed to own up to 25 times the individual allotment, and up to 12 of the 25 shareholders who own T-shares representing land ownership may be foreigners. Foreigners can own 100 percent of food processing and distribution operations. In addition:

- The Mexican government no longer has an obligation to redistribute land

- Land disputes are to be settled by new and autonomous Agrarian Tribunals rather than the agrarian reform ministry

- *Ejidatarios* can decide by majority vote to privatize *ejido* land, and by a two-thirds majority vote to sell land to outsiders

- *Ejidatarios* are no longer required to personally work on their *ejido* land.

The Salinas government trumpeted these reforms as a reasonable compromise between complete elimination of *ejidos*, and maintaining the status quo (Cornelius, 1992a, 4).

There was relatively little reaction in Mexico at the time to what was considered a revolutionary change, although there is now considerable research underway to determine how freeing up market in *ejido* land will affect agricultural production, farm structure, and migration patterns. The major conclusion so far is that *ejido* reform will have evolutionary rather than revolutionary impacts in rural Mexico, for several reasons. First, there was already a considerable amount of illegal and quasi-legal land selling and renting before 1992, especially by the families of workers who migrated to the United States, and *ejido* land in tourist development zones, at the edges of expanding urban areas, and where the land was of especially good quality.

Second, the government has been very slow to organize meetings and distribute titles to *ejido* land to *ejidatarios* and communal farmers, so that *ejido* land can be rented and sold.[10] Third, foreigners have not rushed in to take advantage of the opportunity to invest in Mexican farm land: even in the United States, there is an increasing separation in the low-inflation 1990s between land owners an farm operators (Shwedel, 1992).

In addition to land reform, Mexico in the late 1980s and early 1990s reduced the prices that it guarantees to farmers, bringing them in line with world prices, and in 1993 changed its system for subsidizing farmers of corn and other basic crops—subsidies in 1993 cost the Mexican government $3 billion. Until 1993, Mexico supported the price of corn, beans, and other basic grains by offering to buy all of the commodity delivered to *Conasupo* at a price that was often 50 to 75 percent above the world price. The Producer Subsidy Equivalent is a measure of the gain in farm incomes that result from higher-than-market prices, expressed as a percentage of farm sales, and the PSE for Mexican corn and grains was often 50 to 75 percent of the price received by the farmer.

On October 4, 1993, the PROCAMPO (Programa de Apoyos Directos al Campo) program "decoupled" farm production from income support, substituting income transfers for 3 to 4 million producers of corn and basic grains for price guarantees. PROCAMPO promises to make direct payments for the next 15 years to producers of corn and seven other field crops—sorghum, wheat, soybeans, cotton, rice, barley, safflower, and dry beans—who keep their land in productive use.

Payments are based on farmers' production histories over the past 15 years, but farmers no longer have to grow corn or other grains to qualify for PROCAMPO payments.[11] The PROCAMPO income transfer system, the argument runs, will allow Mexico to more effectively assist the subsistence farmers who have often been hurt rather than helped by the old price support system,[12] and will save the government money by ending the purchase and storage operations of CONASUPO. Procampo payments to Mexico's 2.2 million corn farmers were estimated to be about $43 per acre, or $430 for a 10-acre plot in 1994.

Corn occupies a special place in the Mexican diet and agriculture—about half of Mexico's crop land is used to grow corn—7 to 8 million hectares in the early 1990s, including 25 percent of Mexico's irrigated land, produced about 14 to 16 million tons of corn each year. Three in four Mexican farmers produce some corn, and corn is the principal crop for almost half of Mexico's farmers (Valdes, 1994, 34). An estimated 90 percent of the 2.3 million Mexican farmers who planted corn in 1993 planted it on plots of land of less than eleven acres, and 40 percent planted on plots of less than two acres.

Corn production uses half of Mexico's land, water, and human resources because of the high government price offered for corn, and Mexicans consume a great deal of corn in tortillas because the price of tortillas is heavily subsidized by the government. Mexico for decades intervened in the corn market, offering to buy corn from farmers at about twice world prices, and then selling corn to tortilla makers at a low price. This $2 billion per year corn policy was a "de facto rural employment and anti-poverty program," since it encouraged many farmers to grow corn. However, most of the benefits of high corn prices go to the largest producers, who dominate corn production for sale to CONASUPO.

In the early 1990s, it was estimated that about 40 percent of Mexico's corn was produced on non-irrigated land by subsistence and small family farmers, 30 percent by family farmers on irrigated land, and 30 percent by commercial farmers on irrigated land. Mexican production costs are estimated to be about 30 percent higher than U.S. production costs, and yields are low. In the early 1990s, Mexican yields averaged less than two tons per hectare on non-irrigated land, and just over three tons on irrigated land, or 30 bushels per acre, while the U.S. average is 134 bushels per acre.

As with many other aspects of Mexican agriculture, there is great variation in Mexican corn yields. Some Mexican farmers obtain U.S.-style 150-bushel-per-acre yields, and some are able to produce two crops of corn on a plot of land in one year. However, the United States produces most of North America's corn—of the 220 million metric tons of corn produced in North America in 1990, over 90 percent was produced in the United States, 6 percent was produced in Mexico, and 4 percent was produced in Canada.

PROCAMPO is expected to reduce producer prices for most basic grains, which should encourage farmers to switch to other crops or get out of agriculture. According to a 1991 government survey of corn producers, only about 10 percent would be competitive at world market prices, and almost half could be made competitive with special assistance. However, the Mexican agriculture department, SARH, concluded that 1 million corn producers would not be competitive at world market prices for corn. Calva (1991) was far more pessimistic about the competitiveness of Mexican corn and bean farmers—he concluded that free trade in corn and beans would reduce corn acreage by 95 percent, and completely eliminate Mexican bean production.

It is clear that most predictions are that there will be fewer corn and grain producers in rural Mexico in the 1990s than there were in the 1980s. The question is, what will ex-corn farmers do? Will they remain in agriculture, and change crops, or will they migrate? If they leave the land, will they go to nearby Mexican cities, to distant Mexican cities and regions, or to the United States?

Many farmers have tried to stay in agriculture, but found it very hard to obtain the capital needed to restructure their operations. During the summer of 1993, well before the peso crisis, the farm sector was considered to be in "crisis," as banks foreclosed on loans that many farmers had taken to buy new equipment for the "new era in Mexican agriculture." Estimates of the amount of farm loans in default in September 1993 ranged from $1 billion to $4 billion, and farmers called for a moratorium on bank foreclosures (Solis, 1993). Without easy access to capital, it will be hard to convert the land now used to produce corn in Mexico to grow fruits and vegetables.

Luis Tellez, former Mexican undersecretary of agriculture and architect of the agricultural policy reforms, predicted an average annual exit of one million farmers each year for ten years from Mexican agriculture. Levy and van Wijnbergen predicted that 700,000 farmers would will be displaced in nine years, while Robinson and Hinojosa projected that 800,000 farmers would be displaced over the next six years, and that 600,000 of those displaced would migrate to the United States.

Regardless of who is right about the number of Mexican farmers who abandon agriculture, no one argues that agricultural policy reforms will make Mexicans less likely to migrate to the United States.[13] There is a "revisionist" literature that emphasizes that many corn producers grow corn only for their own consumption—and thus are not affected directly by reductions in the guaranteed price of corn—but even these rural households realize that rural Mexico is changing in a manner that does not promise a future growing basic crops such as corn.[14]

## NAFTA, Trade, and Migration

The North American Free Trade Agreement (NAFTA) went into effect on January 1, 1994. NAFTA requires Canada, Mexico, and the United States to convert non-tariff agricultural trade barriers into "tariff-rate quotas," or monetary tariffs, and then to phase them out within 15 years. Half of the agricultural trade between the United States and Mexico became duty-free on January 1, 1994, and, as free trade is extended to more commodities, there is expected to be an increased flow of agricultural goods across North American borders.

For example, Mexico used to require Mexian importers of corn to obtain licenses, and thus limited corn imports by limiting licenses. Under NAFTA, Mexico agreed to import tariff free at least 2.5 million metric tons (98.5 million bushels) of U.S. corn each year, and to permit the amount of duty-free corn to grow by 3 percent per year[15] until there is free trade in corn in 2009.[16]

During the first ten years of NAFTA, i.e., until 2004, NAFTA includes a "snap back" provision that permits each country to monitor the volume of imports and, if a "trigger" level of imports is reached, the tariff on the commodity can "snap back" to its pre-NAFTA levels.

## From Mexican Corn to Mexican Vegetables?

Many observers in both the United States and Mexico assume that Mexican farmers who today grow corn and beans for the Mexican market will soon be growing tomatoes and avocados for U.S. consumers. NAFTA was expected to accelerate the shift of North American fruit and vegetable production to Mexico and, in 1995-96, allegations from Florida vegetable growers that Mexican producers were dumping tomatoes and other vegetables make it seem that stiff Mexican competition has already arrived.

However, a careful analysis of trends in the North American horticultural industry suggests that most labor intensive agriculture will remain in the United States (Cook et al. 1991). Mexico's primary competitive advantage in producing fruits and vegetables for the U.S. market is its climate; Mexico can produce fresh vegetables during the winter months when most U.S. production areas except Florida are not producing. Even if Mexico were to completely displace winter vegetable production in Florida, most fruit and vegetable production would remain in the United States, because two-thirds of North American fruit and vegetable production occurs in the summer and fall, when Mexico is not producing significant quantities.[17]

Mexico is not likely to completely displace Florida as the source of most winter fruits and vegetables because, in many cases, low yields and low labor productivity make vegetable production more expensive in Mexico than in Florida. Florida producers have also been adept at using the U.S. government to limit Mexican imports.

Florida grows most of its vegetables from October through June, and historically accounted for 40 percent of the roughly 4 billion pounds of six major fresh vegetables—tomatoes, bell peppers, cucumbers, eggplant, snap beans, and squash—sold in the United States during these months. Florida produced 2.5 billion pounds of these six fresh vegetables in 1995, other states produced 3.8 billion pounds, and 2.6 billion pounds were imported—about three-fourths of these fresh vegetable imports were from Mexico. The farm value of these winter fresh vegetables is about $2 billion each year.

Before NAFTA went into effect in 1994, Mexico was exporting to the United States fruit and vegetables worth about $1.4 billion per year, and importing from the United States produce worth about $350 million per year. Fruits and vegetables were about half of the value of Mexican agricultural exports to the United States, and about 10 percent of value of U.S. farm exports to Mexico.

## Florida Winter Vegetables

Most of the year-to-year fluctuation in Florida and Mexico shares of the winter vegetable market has been due to weather, but in December 1994, the Mexican peso was devalued. Mexican fruit and vegetable exports surged in 1995-96, due to both the peso devaluation and to cold weather in Florida (Love and

Lucier, 1996, 20). Florida has filed two separate actions against Mexican winter vegetables, has lost one, and is likely to win the other.

Florida growers argue that they need to get at least $8 per 25-pound box of tomatoes that they sell—they estimate their cost of production to be about 32 cents per pound. In February 1996, Mexican tomatoes were selling in the United States for $5 per box, roughly the estimated cost of production in Mexico, before jumping, in mid-March, 1996, to $25 per carton.

NAFTA permits governments to protect industries that are hurt by import surges, and Florida growers argued that a Mexican import surge in 1995-96 was hurting the U.S. tomato industry. But Florida growers lost this case because most U.S. tomatoes are not produced in Florida—tomatoes are produced in California, South Carolina, and other states, and the "injury" clause of NAFTA does not single out one seasonal component of an entire industry. In response, Florida proposed, and the Clinton administration supports, the re-definintion of the Florida tomato industry as an "industry" for the purpose of invoking the NAFTA import-surge clause.

Under the current definition of the fresh vegetable industry, on July 2, 1996, the International Trade Commission ruled in a 4 to 1 decision that U.S. tomato and pepper farmers were not being economically injured by tomato and pepper imports from Mexico, Canada, and the Netherlands. If the ITC had agreed that U.S. producers were being "substantially" hurt by increased imports, President Clinton could have imposed increased tariffs or taken other steps to limit imports under Section 201 of the Trade Act.

Florida producers filed a separate petition on April 1, 1996, that alleges that Mexico dumped tomatoes in the United States at less than their cost of production. Many observers expect Florida to win the dumping case, largely because the Clinton administration permitted the Florida growers to mix two marketing years in providing data on Florida and Mexican costs and prices. The International Trade Commission in May 1996 voted 5-0 to have the Commerce Department determine whether Mexico "dumped" tomatoes in the United States in 1996, and a Commerce Department decision is expected in September 1996.

Tomatoes and other winter vegetables are produced by a handful of large growers who rely on migrant Mexican workers in both Florida and Mexico. In Florida, four "family" farms dominate the Florida tomato industry—DeMare, Gargiulo, Heller, and Esformes—together they account for half of Florida's $400 million in annual tomato sales.

Mexico's export-oriented winter vegetable industry is centered in Sinaloa, about 600 miles south of the U.S. border. Large farms there employ about 170,000 Mexican workers for four to five months. Most of these seasonal workers are migrants: three-fourths migrate to Sinaloa from other parts of Mexico. In 1996, typical wages for tomato picking in Sinaloa were reported to be about $3 -$5 per day, and children often join their parents in the fields.[18]

The 1996 tomato war does not hinge on tariffs—U.S. tariffs on Mexican tomatoes are low and falling. The tariff averaged about 4 percent of the wholesale price in recent years during the winter period (November 15 to the end of February), and fell from $0.014 per pound before NAFTA to $0.01 per pound on January 1, 1994. Tariffs on tomatoes will be phased out by 2004—the tariff is $0.01 on the $0.30 per pound that farmers typically receive for winter tomatoes.

However, the 1996 tomato war indicates that Mexican producers will not gain easy access to the U.S. market simply because NAFTA is in place. Even though most U.S. observers are not very sympathetic to the Florida growers—a recent story in the Wall Street Journal was headlined, "With little evidence, Florida growers blame tomato woes on NAFTA"[19]—U.S. producers can wage effective campaigns to retard imports despite, in the tomato case, Mexico making correct technological choices.

## Mexican Vegetable Exports

Tomatoes originated in Mexico, and tomatoes are now Mexico's most important horticultural export. A record 593,000 metric tons of tomatoes worth $406 million were imported into the United States from Mexico in 1995—up sharply from the usual $200 million of Mexican tomato imports. Mexico exports about 25 percent of the fresh vegetables it produces, while the U.S. exports 10 percent of the fresh vegetables it produces.

Many of Mexico's tomatoes bound for the United States are produced in cooperation with California and Florida growers who want to supply tomatoes to U.S. retailers year round. Over 75 percent of Mexico's tomato exports come from two Mexican states—Sinaloa, about 600 miles south of the U.S. border, where 50 percent of the tomatoes from the 67,000 acres grown are exported, and Baja California, where about 75 percent of the tomatoes grown on 12,500 acres are exported. In both areas of Mexico, producers import from the U.S. inputs such as seeds, fertilizers, drip irrigation tubes, and even boxes in which to put tomatoes—many Mexican production costs are in dollars.

Most Mexican tomatoes are so-called "Extended Shelf Life" (ESL) varieties developed in Israel that are picked "vine-ripe" every day and carefully laid in eggshell-type flats inside 20-pound cartons for transport. ESL varieties grow well in Mexico but not in Florida.[20] In Florida, most tomatoes are mature greens, which means that the tomatoes are picked every seven to ten days while entirely green, sorted and packed loosely into 25-pound cartons, and then turned red in "gassing chambers" before being shipped to market. Florida tomatoes are preferred for slicing in many foodservice operations, while Mexican "vine-ripe" tomato varieties that can be picked pink reportedly taste better than mature green tomatoes, and seem to be preferred by consumers.[21]

Tomatoes seem to provide a clear example of the relationship between trade and migration expressed by ex-President Salinas, who said, "When it becomes easier to export tomatoes, fewer Mexican tomato pickers will migrate to the U.S." However, surveys of workers employed in Mexico's winter vegetable industry in Sinaloa during the 1980s suggest that Salinas's assertion of the trade off between Mexican tomatoes and Mexican tomato pickers is too simple.

Most of the tomato pickers in the Mexican export-oriented tomato industry are migrants. A survey in 1974 found that 56 percent of 180,000 peak seasonal workers were migrants. By 1985, an estimated 80 percent of 170,000 peak workers were migrants, and most of the migrants had come from far away to Sinaloa (Thompson and Martin 1989, 14). In 1985, about 27 percent of the Mexican migrants in Sinaloa intended to continue migrating north to Baja California or the United States. These continuing migrants tended to be single, young, and landless men; migrant families with small farms were more likely to return to southern Mexico.

As Mexican migrants move north, they are more likely to enter the United States. For example, In Baja California's San Quintin Valley, the ten largest tomato growers have peak migrant work forces of 2,000 or more mostly Mixtec Indians from the southern Mexican state of Oaxaca. In the late 1980s, U.S. foremen and labor contractors recruited Mixtec workers for U.S. farm jobs, setting in motion a migration network that now brings southern Mexican workers directly to the United States. Surveys of these Mixtec workers in California and Oregon in the early 1990s reveal that two-thirds had worked in Baja California before coming to the United States (Zabin et al. 1993).

## Florida versus Mexico

Does comparative advantage in winter vegetables lie in Mexico or Florida? Although wages are lower in Mexico than in Florida, labor productivity is also lower in Mexico, and Mexican producers often have to pay recruitment fees, and to provide housing, to attract migrant workers.

In Florida, by contrast, most workers pay their own transportation to the area, and arrange for their own housing and transportation to the fields. In addition, Florida producers have the advantage of publicly funded agricultural research, while Mexican producers rely on a private organization, CAADES (Confederation of Agricultural Associations of the State of Sinaloa), to conduct yield-increasing and disease-fighting research.

It appears that selecting the preferred type of tomato played a more important role in giving Mexico a competitive advantage in the winter vegetable market than lower labor costs. Indeed, the mature green tomato was developed in Florida in the early 1970s in the expectation of labor shortages—Florida researchers developed mature green tomatoes so that winter tomatoes could be harvested mechanically. One professor in 1992 asserted that mature green tomatoes could be harvested mechanically "with no more damage than harvesting by hand. But growers weren't interested in . . . machines as long as they could find labor to harvest crops" (UF Impact, Spring 1992, 18). Mexican workers moved into Florida in large numbers in the early 1970s.

The tomato war of 1996 illustrates how U.S. producers with higher costs and the "wrong" technological choice can still mount potent protests to imports. If the Florida tomato growers are successful, they may encourage other U.S. commodity groups also to complain of unfair Mexican competition.

For example, when USDA in July 1995 proposed that avocados from approved orchards in Michoacan could be shipped to 19 northeastern U.S. states beginning in November 1995 during the winter months, California avocado growers protested that the Mexican avocados would introduce diseases that would ruin U.S. avocado growers. Mexico exports avocados to 20 countries, and Mexican producers pointed out that they have been shipping avocados to Japan since 1992 without any detected pests.[22] Mexico produces about 45 percent of the world's avocados, some 800,000 tons per year—85 percent in Michoacan—but Mexican avocados have been banned from the U.S. since 1914. Some 100,000 workers are employed on 8,000 avocado farms in Michoacan, one of the major states of origin for Mexican migrants headed to the United States. Canadians pay $0.50 to $0.60 per Mexican avocado in retail stores, while United States consumers often pay $1 each for California avocados.

Even if Mexico wins the "tomato wars," and there is freer trade in labor-intensive commodities, much of North America's fruit and vegetable production will remain in the United States. The movement of even competitive production to Mexico has been slowed by problems in Mexico: higher transportation costs, less research on disease and other factors that reduce yields,[23] and lower worker productivity. Mexican growers in 1992 even complained of labor shortages, arguing that "the best farm workers are in the U.S." A 1990 review of the potential to generate employment in rural areas by growing fruits and vegetables concluded that the "main problem . . . is marketing, i.e., where to sell [so Mexican policy] should concentrate on" helping Mexican farmers to develop export markets (Leyva, Vazuez, and Solano, 1990, 34).

These Mexican disadvantages in labor-intensive agriculture can be overcome, but the period before there will be in Mexico a labor-intensive agriculture employing millions of Mexicans to produce fresh fruits and vegetables for the United States is likely to be measured in decades rather than years. In the meantime, there may be an increase in U.S. fruit and vegetable production under freer trade that draws Mexicans into the United States. U.S. fruit and vegetable exports to Mexico rose sharply in 1994, the first year of NAFTA, meaning that some Mexican workers picked crops in the United States that were exported to Mexico.

Some analysts expect U.S. fresh fruit and vegetable exports to Mexico to increase rapidly, as the Mexican retailing industry changes to a U.S.-style system of chain stores that want standardized produce supplies year-round; because Mexico has a young and fast-growing population, which increases the demand for fruits and vegetables; and as north-south trucking costs fall. For example, California's agricultural exports to Mexico doubled between 1993 and 1994 to $1 billion, and included 2.25 million 25-pound cartons of tomatoes.[24] U.S. produce exports to Mexico jumped from $193 million in 1993 to $209 million in 1994, while Mexican produce exports to the United States were $1.2 billion in 1994.

It should be noted that the Bajio region of north-central Mexico, as well as Sinaloa, are areas in which fruits and vegetables such as strawberries and broccoli are grown, processed in Mexico, and exported to the United States. In some cases, U.S. companies that used to process frozen vegetables in California closed operations there and opened or expanded operations in central Mexico.

## U.S. Agriculture and Mexican Migration

Agriculture has traditionally been the port of entry for many of the Mexican workers arriving in the United States. U.S. agriculture employs about 2.5 million workers for wages sometime during a typical year—high turnover ensures that there are openings for at least 250,000 new workers each year. Since two-thirds of all farm workers, and 99 percent of the new entrants, are immigrants, rural and urban Mexicans arriving in the United States for the first time often find farm jobs.

The binational labor market linking especially rural Mexico and rural America has evolved over the past 100 years into such a sophisticated institution that information about new jobs flows far more freely back and forth across the border than it does within the United States. An Oregon strawberry farmer needing additional farm workers is more likely to get them from Oaxaca than from south Texas. However, Mexicans are relative latecomers to a farm labor market that has long depended on immigrants who were willing to accommodate themselves to seasonality—they are the most recent "wave of immigrants" to the southwestern United States that began with Chinese workers in the 1860s.

The key reason why immigrant workers came to dominate the seasonal farm labor force in the Southwest is because they were willing to wait to go to work at their own expense, and then work when needed for relatively low wages. This held down labor costs, encouraging the southwestern agricultural industry to expand, raising land prices and, allegedly, slowing the internal migration of whites westward.[25] The southwestern states expanded their production of labor-intensive crops for distant markets—predictable weather, extensive irrigation systems, and flat land turned California and Arizona valleys into "open-air greenhouses" or "factories in the fields."[26]

Farmers were always worried about too little labor, and they were among the first U.S. employers to band together in overlapping regional, commodity, and other associations to lobby local, state, and federal governments to preserve their access to an immigrant work force. When one group of immigrants was no longer available, another group was found, so that the Chinese were followed by the Japanese as the mainstays of the seasonal fruit and vegetable labor force in California at the turn of the century, and then by immigrants from present-day India and Pakistan, and then by Filipinos and Mexicans in the 1920s.

Farmers did not discriminate by race or ethnicity—their only requirement was that seasonal farm workers should accommodate themselves to the farmers' need for labor, and accept piece-rate wages that reflected each worker's productivity. Farmers recognized that diverse farm workers shared one goal—the hope that, next year, the worker would find a nonfarm job.

One farmer in the 1920s summarized the reasons why immigrants must keep coming into rural America. "The trouble with the idea of importing any class of laborers into the United States as 'cheap labor' and keeping them here any length of time . . . is that . . . [the United States] is not conducive to servility . . . [because] laboring men, whether white, black, or yellow, are soon inoculated with the spirit of independence to be farmers in their own right or to seek year-round jobs in cities" (quoted in Fuller 1942, 19842).

## Pre-Bracero Migration—1917-1942

For most of the twentieth century, Mexicans have been the mainstay of the seasonal farm work force in the southwestern United States. Mexican workers began to cross the Mexico-U.S. border in large numbers in response to the civil war in Mexico and U.S. recruitment efforts after World War I. U.S. policies, however, have not been consistent as to whether the Mexicans recruited to work in the United States should be legal and temporary sojourners, illegal workers, or legal or illegal settlers.

The U.S. typically "admitted" Mexicans as farm workers by making "exceptions" to immigration policies. The first exceptions came near the end of World War I—in 1917 the United States exempted Western Hemisphere nationals coming to the United States to perform seasonal farm work from literacy tests and head taxes imposed on European immigrants.[27] The 1917-22 "first Mexican farm worker program" was a labor certification program, in the sense that U.S. farmers and railroads could not legally employ Mexican workers until the Department of Labor certified that U.S. workers were not available. Many Mexican guest workers admitted under this program ran up debts—they had to repay growers for their transportation, so many arrived in debt, and piled up more debt at company stores.

The Mexican workers were supposed to be non-immigrants, meaning that they were expected to return to Mexico when their seasonal jobs ended. However, many remained in the United States. Federal immigration laws in 1921 and 1924 that restricted immigration from Europe and other Eastern Hemisphere nations did not apply to Mexico, and the U.S. Border Patrol, established in 1924 as part of the U.S. Department of Labor, did little to impede Mexican sojourners who migrated north to be seasonal farm workers.

Development patterns in Mexico contributed to the willingness of Mexicans to emigrate seasonally to the United States. The seven central states of Mexico—Nuevo Leon, Tamaulipas, Zacatecas, San Luis Potosi, Guanajuato, Jalisco, and Michoacan—contributed over half of all migrants to the United States for most of the twentieth century (Cross and Sandos 1981, xvi). During the Mexican Revolution (1913-1920), these states became the battleground between the central government in Mexico City and revolutionaries from Mexican states near the U.S. border, and the fighting led most haciendas to reduce their employment. As a result, many Mexicans left. Between 1910 and 1930, by one estimate, 20 percent of the residents of north-central Mexico left the region, including 1.5 million, or 10 percent of Mexico's entire population, who migrated to the United States (Cross and Sandos 1981, 9-10).

The Mexican-born population in California tripled from 120,000 in 1920 to 368,000 in 1930, and additional Mexican workers came to the United States seasonally.[28] However, only about one-fifth of the farm workers in California were Mexican nationals. By one estimate, there were 200,000 hired laborers in California agriculture in 1930, and 43 percent were native-born whites, 17 percent were foreign-born whites, 21 percent were Mexican nationals, 8 percent were Filipinos, and 7 percent were Japanese (Fuller 1942, 19859). However, Mexicans dominated the seasonal work force, which offered the lowest wage and least secure jobs. A 1928 estimate held that Mexicans were 70 to 80 percent of the 72,000 casual and seasonal workers (Fuller 1942, 19871).[29]

The economic depression and U.S. deportations of Mexicans during the 1930s practically stopped Mexican immigration. One result was that the 1930s produced a high-water mark in literature on the plight of the farm worker since, it was said, writers and journalists could easily communicate with the relatively large number of U.S.-born farm workers. However, the resulting plight-of-the-farmworker literature, highlighted by John Steinbeck's *The Grapes of Wrath* in 1939, brought about no significant changes in the farm labor market.

More academic books in the 1930s demonstrated why especially California land owners, and their processing and banking and transportation allies, wanted a continuing influx of immigrants to keep land prices high. A 1939 book by Carey McWilliams, *Factories in the Fields*, and a 1939 doctoral dissertation by Varden Fuller, "The Supply of Agricultural Labor as a Factor in the Evolution of Farm Organization in California," demonstrated that land prices had been bid up as a result of having seasonal farm workers available at relatively low wages when they were needed, and the capitalized value of the immigrant wage subsidy explained why landowners so strenuously resisted the extension of labor law coverage to their farms.

The 1930s literature convinced many Americans that the seasonal immigrant farm labor system was "un-American" and should be reformed, but World War II prevented the extension of labor laws to such farms, and gave farmers another chance to obtain Mexican workers on their terms. A series of so-called *Bracero* programs institutionalized the dependence of farmers on Mexican workers. Many rural Mexicans and their families, in turn, became dependent on the U.S. labor market.

## *Braceros* 1942-1964

For 22 years, the United States imported about 4.6 million Mexican farm workers under a series of unilateral and bilateral agreements. Like many guest worker programs, the *Bracero* program was rife with contradictions:

- Begun to deal with "wartime labor shortages," the number of *Braceros* was ten times larger during the mid-1950s than during the "World War II emergency."

- Justified as a means to produce "Food to win the war," most *Braceros* hand-picked cotton, a surplus crop bought by the government and stored.

- *Braceros* were joined in the fields by prisoners of war, Japanese residents who were interned, and inmates from state and local jails, sending unmistakable signals about the place of farm work in the U.S. job hierarchy.

In Mexico, the *Bracero* program encouraged many residents of the Central

Highlands to orient themselves northward for opportunity. Many moved their families to the Mexican side of the U.S. border.

The *Bracero* program was controversial on both sides of the border. In the spring of 1942, California farmers predicted that there would be labor shortages in the fall, and they called for the importation of between 40,000 and 100,000 Mexican farm workers for the September harvest. Unions complained bitterly that there was no shortage of workers, only, "a mere repetition of the age-old obsession of all farmers for a surplus labor supply" (Quoted in Craig, 1971, 38-39). However, farmers won the right to import *Braceros* by arguing that crop losses caused by labor shortages would hamper the war effort.

The Mexican government, sensitive about the conditions under which some of its nationals had previously worked in the United States,[30] and doubtful that there was a real labor shortage in U.S. agriculture, insisted that the U.S. government guarantee the contracts that farmers provided to wartime Mexican workers, including round-trip transportation and the payment of wages equal to those of similar American workers (Craig, 1971, 41). The U.S. government agreed to guarantee the contracts that U.S. farmers provided to Mexican *Braceros*, and Mexican workers were admitted by establishing an exception to immigration laws for "native-born residents of North America, South America, and Central America, and the islands adjacent thereto, desiring to perform agricultural labor in the United States." Wartime admissions peaked at 62,000 in 1944, less than 2 percent of nation's 4 million hired farm workers.

The *Bracero* program with the U.S. government as the contractor of Mexican workers lapsed on December 31, 1947, and there followed several years of informal and private U.S. employer recruitment of Mexican workers. Illegal immigration increased as *Braceros* learned they did not have to pay bribes to local Mexican officials to get on recruitment lists, and then pay additional bribes at Mexican recruitment centers in order to work in the United States.

U.S. farmers were pleased because they could employ Mexican workers without government "red tape," such as having their housing for *Braceros* inspected and being required to offer them the minimum or government-calculated prevailing wage, whichever was higher. American workers protested that *Braceros* were being used to break their strikes, as occurred during the 1947 strike of table grape harvesters at DiGiorgio farms (Pollit, 1971, 67).[31]

When the official *Bracero* program ended in 1947, many Mexican workers migrated illegally. Their illegal entry was tolerated by the United States. After an illegal Mexican worker found a U.S. job, the worker was legalized by granting him a work permit, a process that came to be termed, even in official U.S. government publications, "drying out the wetbacks" (President's Commission, 1951). The number of aliens who were legalized after arriving and finding employment illegally far exceeded the number of Mexican workers that U.S. employers contracted legally in the interior of Mexico.[32] Farmers saved the cost of transportation for these so-called wetbacks, who arrived on their own.

## PL-78

A President's Commission on Migratory Labor was established in 1951 to determine whether U.S. agriculture needed Mexican immigrants. It recommended that "no special measures be adopted to increase the number of alien contract workers beyond the number admitted in 1950," which was 67,500 (President's Commission, 1951, 178).

The Commission's *Bracero* recommendations were not adopted. Growers tied their request for a new *Bracero* program to the nation's ability to win the Korean War and, in 1951, Congress enacted PL-78, the Mexican Farm Labor Program (Craig, 1971). This is the program that is usually meant when describing "the" *Bracero* program.

The PL-78 *Bracero* program permitted U.S. agriculture to expand without raising farm worker wages. As U.S. workers learned that they did not face *Bracero* competition in non-farm labor markets, they abandoned the farm labor market, and the *Bracero* share of the work force harvesting citrus, tomatoes, and lettuce soon passed 50 percent. Farm wages as a percent of manufacturing wages fell in California during the 1950s. The ratio of U.S. farm wages to machinery costs fell sharply in the late 1940s, and then remained flat throughout the 1950s (farmers have an incentive to mechanize when this ratio is rising).

There was considerable illegal immigration alongside legal *Bracero* entries. Between 1942 and 1964, there were 4.6 million *Braceros* admitted, and 4.9 million Mexicans were apprehended in the United States. Apprehensions peaked at 1.1 million in 1954, during what was then a July 1953-June 1954 fiscal year. Most of these "Operation Wetback" apprehensions occurred at the border— there were only 80,000 apprehensions during the height of the June-August 1954 interior sweeps. Stepping up border controls, and making it easier to employ *Braceros* legally, increased *Bracero* entries and reduced apprehensions, explaining why apprehensions fell sharply in 1955-56, while *Bracero* entries rose.

The availability of *Braceros* permitted the southwestern states to become the garden states of the United States. In California, fruit and nut production rose 15 percent during the 1950s, and vegetable production rose 50 percent. New irrigation facilities expanded the acreage available to grow fruits and vegetables, the interstate highway system allowed produce to be shipped cheaply to eastern markets, and new plant varieties and packing technologies made California produce preferred to locally grown fruits and vegetables in the eastern United States, where most Americans lived.

This expansion of farm production in California was not accompanied by higher farm wages. The U.S. Department of Agriculture's estimate of average hourly farm earnings rose 41 percent—slightly more than the 35 percent increase in consumer prices—from $0.85 in 1950 to $1.20 in 1960. In contrast, average factory wages in California rose 63 percent, from $1.60 per hour in 1950 to $2.60 in 1960. Slowly rising farm wages and faster-rising factory wages drew American workers to factory jobs, where there were no *Braceros*.

By the early 1960s, *Braceros* were essential to harvest only a few crops. As cotton and other geographically dispersed crops were mechanized, the *Bracero* program became a non-immigrant program for a handful of farmers, and political support in the United States for its continuation weakened. As unions and ethnic groups called for the end of the *Bracero* program, growers made familiar arguments to maintain the program: American workers were not available; without the immigrants crops would rot and food prices would rise; and the admission of *Braceros* has no adverse effects on U.S. workers (California Senate, 1961).

The Mexican government publicly did not oppose an end to the *Bracero* program. Even though most Mexican statements acknowledged that there would be adjustment costs if Mexicans could no longer work in the United States, stories of the abuse Mexicans had endured in U.S. fields convinced many Mexicans that the program should be ended. Behind the scenes, however, the Mexican government lobbied for the continuation of the program, and Mexican pressure permitted the program to continue until 1964.

### *The* Bracero *Legacy*

After the *Bracero* program ended, foreign workers could still be imported under the H-2 section of the Immigration and Nationality Act of 1952, which allowed the Attorney General "after consultation with appropriate agencies of the Government" to import needed workers. Employers seeking H-2 workers to fill vacant jobs had to satisfy a double temporary provision—(1) the alien worker was coming temporarily to the United States to perform temporary services or labor and (2) unemployed persons capable of performing such services cannot be found in this country (Congressional Research Service, 1980, p. 59).

Many farmers expected to import Mexican workers under the H-2 provisions of the INA. However, the secretary of labor published regulations in December 1964 that had the effect of making it much more expensive and difficult to import Mexican farm workers under the H-2 program than it had been to import Braceros.[33] Many U.S. senators were outraged, and an effort to transfer the authority to certify the need for H-2 alien farm workers from the Department of Labor to the Department of Agriculture failed in the Senate only because the vice-president cast the deciding vote (Congressional Research Service, 1979, p. 42).

The number of migrant farm workers—most of whom were U.S. citizens— reached a postwar peak of 466,000 in 1965, and grower interest in mechanization increased so much that a major study predicted that, by 1975, if a fruit or vegetable could not be harvested mechanically, it would not be grown in the United States (Cargill and Rossmiller, 1970).

In anticipation of farm mechanization, the federal government in the mid-1960s launched a series of programs to help farm workers who were considered to be trapped in the farm labor market to find non-farm jobs before they were displaced by machines (Martin and Martin, 1994, chapter 2). There as also another mid-1960s development: in 1965, a community organizer named Cesar Chavez joined a strike called by Filipino grape pickers in California to obtain a wage increase. In 1966, what became the United Farm Workers union won a 40-percent wage increase.

About 60 percent of the *Braceros* employed in California in the early 1960s picked processing tomatoes, and *Braceros* were 80 percent of the harvest workers in California's processing tomato industry. Tomato growers argued that "the use of Braceros is absolutely essential to the survival of the tomato industry." (California Senate, 1961, 105).

What happened when *Braceros* disappeared? The termination of the *Bracero* program accelerated the mechanization of the harvest in a manner that quadrupled production to 12 million tons between 1960 and 1995.[34] Cheaper tomatoes permitted the price of ketchup and similar products to drop, helping to fuel the expansion of the fast food industry (Martin and Olmstead, 1985). In this case, the demand for unskilled farm labor dropped sharply when the supply of labor shrank and wages rose.

The United States continued to import unskilled foreign workers to fill vacant U.S. jobs under the H-2A (farm) and H-2B (nonfarm) programs. Under the H-2A program, about 3,000 U.S. farmers requested 17,000 nonimmigrant aliens to perform agricultural labor of a temporary or seasonal nature—usually less than 12 months—in 1995.[35]

Farm employers wishing to employ H-2A foreign workers must follow an application procedure set out in law and regulation that is similar to the rules governing the *Bracero* program. The application process requires U.S. employers to complete a job order seeking U.S. workers at least 60 days before the anticipated need for H-2A farm workers. Both the farmer and the Department of Labor use the next 40 days to search for U.S. workers.

If U.S. workers cannot be found, DOL "certifies" the farmer's need for H-2A workers, and this DOL certification is attached to the farmer's request to INS, the agency that transmits the names of the workers the farmer has found to the U.S. consulate in their country of origin, and to the U.S. port through which the foreign workers will enter the U.S.

The H-2A program was expected to expand from about 20,000 jobs certified and workers admitted annually in the mid-1980s to 200,000 or more after IRCA's employer sanctions took full effect in U.S. agriculture in 1989. Farmers were certified to import H-2A workers to fill 26,600 jobs in 1989, but since then the number of certifications has fallen to less than 17,000 annually.[36]

## Current Guest Worker Proposals

The key issue in U.S. guest worker programs is whether individual employers or the U.S. government should have the power to open the border gate to Mexican and other foreign workers. The *Bracero* and H-2A programs were and are certification and contract programs, which means that the border gate to foreign workers is not opened unless a government agency certifies that the U.S. employer faces a legitimate labor shortage. After the farmer is certified to need foreign workers, the foreign workers are given contracts that spell out their wages and benefits and housing and transportation arrangements.

Certification means that government control over entry and wages and working conditions is up front—the border gates stay shut until the government opens them. Written contracts give aggrieved U.S. and foreign workers a means to enforce employer promises.

The alternative is an attestation and free agent program. This means that the employer's assertion that he faces a labor shortage is enough to open the border gate to foreign workers, and the foreign workers who enter are free to work for any farmer who has filed an attestation. Governmental control comes at the back end of the process. If there are complaints, the government investigates, and a grower or worker can be barred from participating in the program.[37]

On March 5, 1996, the House Agriculture Committee approved as the "Alternative Agricultural Temporary Worker Program . . . to provide a less bureaucratic alternative for the admission of temporary agricultural workers." As approved by the Agriculture Committee, up to 250,000 foreign farm workers could be admitted to the United States each year after employers attested that they were needed, with the ceiling to be reduced by 25,000 each year.

The Clinton administration opposed the attestation program for fear that it would increase illegal immigration, reduce job opportunities for U.S. workers, and depress wage and work standards for U.S. workers. In March 1996, Secretary of Labor Robert Reich and U.S. Attorney General Janet Reno said that that they would "strongly recommend" a veto of 1996 immigration legislation if it included temporary foreign farm worker provisions for agriculture. The House on March 21,1996, rejected the Alternative Agricultural Temporary Worker Program in a 242-180 vote.

Under the proposal considered by the House in 1996, growers, labor contractors, or associations wanting to employ foreign farm workers would file at least 25 days before the job was to begin a one-page labor condition attestation (LCA) with their state Employment Service office, and post it at the work place.[38] Local ES offices would review these LCAs "only for completeness and obvious inaccuracies" within seven days after they are filed. Employers violating their attestations or program rules could be assessed civil money penalties, and be debarred from the program.

To encourage workers to leave the United States, 25 percent of the foreign workers' wages would be placed into a federal trust fund, which foreign workers could reclaim with interest in their country of origin. Program costs were to be financed by contributions equivalent to social security and unemployment insurance taxes that would not be paid by growers.

There is no doubt that a significant percentage of the U.S. hired farm workforce of some 2.5 million are unauthorized workers, primarily from Mexico and Guatemala. In evaluating policy responses to the fact that 20 to 25 percent of U.S. farm workers are not authorized to work in the United States, it is important to clarify the distinction between supply and demand adjustments to fewer unauthorized workers.

Farmers typically frame the argument for a new guest worker program in supply terms. If there are currently 100 workers employed and 20 are unauthorized, and effective immigration controls eliminate these 20 from the work force then, farmers assert, a mechanism must be developed to obtain 20 legal worker replacements, because currently unemployed or underemployed U.S. workers are not likely to go to the fields.

Economists, by contrast, typically look for demand adjustments to fewer workers and higher wages. When the *Bracero* program ended, for example, the harvesting of tomatoes was mechanized. This is not new; most of the adjustments to fewer and more expensive workers in agriculture tend to occur on the demand, not the supply side, of the labor market. In other words, in the face of immigration reforms, lasting farm labor adjustments are more likely to be found by accelerating labor-saving mechanization, or changing the way farm work is done, or letting the production of some commodity production shift overseas, not in launching new efforts to recruit U.S. workers, to build housing for migrant workers, or to provide government services to farm workers that raise their effective incomes.

## Implications for Policy

The United States and Mexico created a binational labor market that links parts of rural Mexico with parts of rural America by permitting U.S. employers to recruit Mexican workers. As network and other factors have become more important, and U.S.-sanctioned guest worker recruitment in rural Mexico less important, this binational labor market has become less subject to government control.

Within the United States, one clear lesson for policy makers is that, after a job or labor market has been dominated by foreign workers for decades, it is virtually impossible to re-attract nationals back into that job unless jobs and labor markets are significantly changed by technology, work organization, or wages and benefits. In other words, simply stopping the immigration of foreign workers and assuming that the "market" will push and pull nationals back into "foreigner" jobs is a pipe dream. Adjustments in the U.S. farm labor market to fewer immigrant workers and higher wages are likely to be on the demand, not the supply side of the labor market.

Five policy recommendations that flow from this analysis are:

1. Agricultural policy reforms can have migration spillover consequences. Just as trade negotiators worry about how, e.g., NAFTA might affect sugar imports from the Caribbean, so we may be in an era when one country's agricultural policies should be scrutinized for the migration externalities they generate. Some 1.1 billion of the 2.1 billion workers in the developing world are farmers, many in emigration nations such as Mexico, the Philippines, and Turkey, and agricultural policy decisions made within these countries can have migration consequences in destination countries.

2. Mexico is reforming its agricultural policies in a time of economic recession and crisis, so that, for example, yields are down in 1996 because of a drought and lack of inputs such as credit to buy fertilizers, which reduces the attractiveness of farming in Mexico, raises the cost to the Mexican government and Mexican consumers of imported food, and increases the desirability of emigration. To the extent that the United States is negatively affected by this migration, there may be an argument for U.S. assistance in supplying inputs, or concessionary food exports, etc.

3. The United States has tried to deal with the migration spillover from
the Mexican agricultural revolution unilaterally—primarily by increasing border control efforts. However, U.S. immigration control efforts
are complicated by past and current U.S. policies that legalized many
rural Mexicans and permit these Mexican immigrants to unify their
families in the United States.

4. As the United States considers how to reform its farm labor market,
the traditional port of entry for rural Mexicans to the United States, it
is important to remember that most adjustments in farm labor markets
to fewer workers and higher wages occur on the demand side of the
market, not the supply side. This means that the United States should
look to mechanization, trade, and other changes that reduce the demand
for immigrant workers, not an influx of ex-welfare recipients or other
U.S. residents into the fields in the event immigration from Mexico is
slowed.

5. The options under consideration to deal with the current "migration
hump" from rural Mexico include even more U.S. immigration controls, a guest worker program to better regulate an "inevitable" flow,
and "Mexican cooperation" to slow border crossings. All are problematic, but in the second-best world in which immigration policies
are made, some combination of these is likely to be implemented.

## Notes

1. Many Mexicans who leave the land will also migrate to Mexican cities, especially provincial growth centers, to the border regions of northern Mexico, and to rural
areas of the United States.

2. Mexico's rural population grows by about 600,000 per year.

3. CONASUPO in the past bought all corn delivered to it at the government guaranteed price. In 1992, CONASUPO bought 30 percent of Mexico's corn production at a
price of NP750 per ton, versus a world price of NP450 per ton. Conasupo then sold the
corn to corn processors, who in turn sold corn dough to tortilla makers, who sold tortillas to consumers at a fixed government price. Tortilla subsidies cost 8.5 billion pesos
($1.2 billion) in 1995.

One company, Maseca or Mission Foods in the U.S., receives much of this tortilla
subsidy, allegedly by using its close ties to the government to force a switch in the way
tortillas are made. Instead of boiling corn kernels in water and lime, and then grinding
the pulp into dough (*nixtamal*), Maseca supplies tortilla makers with corn flour.

The tortilla subsidies benefit mostly urban Mexican residents who can buy subsidized tortillas. Mexico's rural poor usually do not buy ready-made tortillas. Anthony

DePalma, "How a Tortilla Empire Was Built on Favoritism," *New York Times*, February 15, 1996.

4. Mexico is expected to import 11 to 12 million tons of corn, wheat, and sorghum in 1996, at a cost of $2 billion (Reuters, May 6, 1996).

5. The 23 million rural Mexicans shared the $30 billion rural GDP in 1994, giving them an average $1,311 each, while the 67 million urban Mexicans who shared the remaining $347 billion GDP had an average $5,179 GDP each. Mexico's economy shrank by about 7 percent in 1995.

6. According to a Mexican proposal to the World Bank in 1995, 41 percent of Mexicans live in rural areas, and 84 percent of the extremely poor Mexican residents are in rural areas. Mexico Agricultural Development and Rural Poverty Project, MXPA7711.

7. At the other end of the spectrum, Mexico includes the fourth largest number of billionaire families—24—after the United States, Japan, and Germany. The wealthiest Mexicans in 1994 included Carlos Slim Helu ($6.6 billion in assets, Telmex), Emilio Azcarraga ($5.4 billion, Grupo Televisa), Lorenzo Zambrano ($3.1 billion, Cemex), and Aleko Peralta ($2.5 billion, Grup IUSA)

8. For example, a Mexican peasants organization, the National Union of Autonomous Regional Campesino Organizations (UNORCA), in April 1996 asserted that more than 80 percent of what it said were Mexico's 3 million *ejidatarios* and 2.5 million small farmers were vulnerable to bankruptcy. In late April 1996, the Mexican government announced a plan to provide $1 billion in credit and technical assistance to 600,000 producers of grains on 11.5 million acres.

9. The Mexican government in 1995 estimated that there were 1.9 million farmers in seven of the poorest states in the south and center regions of Mexico (Chiapas, Guerrero, Hidalgo, Michoacan, Oaxaca, Puebla, and Veracruz), that two-thirds of these farmers had less than five hectares of cultivable land, and that the corn that was grown on 60 percent of these poor farmers' land yielded one ton per hectare. Mexico-Agricultural Development and Rural Poverty Project, MXPA7711.

10. Cornelius (1992a) reports that 2,000 to 3,000 of the 28,000 *ejidos* in 1992 had legally demarcated individual *ejidatario* land plots. Foreign investment is trickling in to rural Mexico—at least one foreign firm had by 1996 invested $1.8 billion in an *ejido* forestry project covering 300,000 hectares in the states of Tabasco, Campeche, and Chiapas.

11. During the about fall-winter 1993/94 crop cycle, each producer received a government payment of 330 pesos per hectare (about $45 dollars per acre)—a payment that reflects past average yields and the difference between the current support price of corn and the world price—the Mexican support price is to be reduced to the world price in 1996.

Farmers report their production, but payments may be adjusted at the district level because payments are capped district by district.

12. Subsistence farmers and landless workers are hurt by high corn prices if they (1) do not produce a surplus to sell and (2) do not have access to subsidized tortillas. In

such cases, which Taylor (1993) believes to be common, the rural poor are hurt because any surplus corn is drained as farmers sell to the government, but subsidized corn does not return to the area's consumers.

13. If migration decisions are the result of wage differences, and if the PROCAMPO payment is viewed as a wages subsidy for farmers, then PROCAMPO payments might discourage emigration. However, if the payment is viewed as a lump-sum gift, and if farmers who receive payments decide to look for wage work rather than plant crops, local wages might decline, increasing the incentive to migrate.

14. A survey in west-central Mexico by de Janvry, Sadoulet, and Anda (1994) found that a majority of corn producers did not sell corn in 1990. The government estimated in 1993 that only 30 percent of Mexican corn growers benefited from the old system of price supports.

There are many reasons why most of the benefits of the old corn price support system went to a handful of large producers, including the fact that the corn producer must have been close to a CONASUPO (the National Commission for Distribution of Basic Food) outlet to deliver the corn and take advantage of the high government corn price.

15. In April 1996, Mexico raised the duty-free corn import quota to 4.9 million tons. About 2.6 million tons of corn were imported in 1995.

16. Mexican farmers typically produce white corn, and U.S. farmers produce yellow corn, but the two types of corn are substitutes, which is why Mexico protected its corn market from imports.

17. There are a few commodities that can be produced cheaper in Mexico, including avocados. However, when the USDA held hearings on whether Mexican avocados could be imported into the American northeast, where the pests common in Michoacan could not survive the winter, California producers called for keeping trade barriers in place until there was much more study and information available on the possible risks to U.S. avocados and citrus. California has 60,000 acres of avocados, and California avocado sales in 1995 were about $225 million.

18. Most Mexican vegetable exporters provide housing in 125 camps in the Culican Valley at no charge to their harvest workers, often 150 square feet for each family, which can range from six to ten family members. Government doctors visit the camps to dispense basic medicines and to teach techniques of birth control; however, the schools in the camps teach from 5 to 8 PM, so that children can help their parents in the fields

19. Helene Cooper and Bruce Ingersoll, "With little evidence, Florida growers blame tomato woes on NAFTA," *Wall Street Journal*, April 3, 1996.

20. ESL tomatoes can be left on the vine several days longer, until 90 percent of the fruit is pink and red. If they reach the supermarket or wholesaler within five to seven days, ESL tomatoes last about two to three weeks on the shelf—a week longer than a mature green tomato (picked just before it turns pink). Tomato growers in Sinaloa and Baja converted to ESL varieties since 1993. A 1992 University of Florida economist noted that 30 percent of Mexico's tomato exports in 1992 were mature greens, and predicted wrongly that Mexico would imitate Florida.

21. Florida in 1995 proposed that all tomatoes sold in the U.S. market in winter

months be shipped in 25-pound loose cartons, which would damage Mexican tomatoes.

22. If allowed, the Mexican avocados would have to be shipped between November and February in trucks that would have to follow prescribed routes, and would not pass through California. Mexican avocado producers would pay for any costs incurred by USDA to monitor the presence of pests.

23. By 1992, the Mexican government's experiment station in Sinaloa was effectively closed, according to Florida researchers.

24. NAFTA was, according to the California Farm Bureau, the top agricultural story of 1993. The summary report of the California Farm Bureau noted that tree fruit, nut, and dairy farmers expected to benefit immediately from easier access to Mexico, and that vegetable farmers did not think that competition from Mexico would stiffen for years. (*Ag Alert*, January 5, 1995, 9)

25. "Hitherto the one great objection to an increase of the unskilled white labor population in California has been, that necessary as it was to have more help during the summer and harvest, the manner of husbandry in this state was such as to assure those who labor for others, work only for three, or at the highest, five or six months during the year. It was admitted to be an unnatural condition of affairs, and one that should be remedied, but which, under prevailing circumstances, could not be changed, especially as long as Chinamen in sufficient numbers could be hired during the busiest seasons of the year." (California Labor Commissioner John Enos, quoted in Fuller 1967, 433-4)

26. Varden Fuller argued that the structure of California agriculture—its system of large farms dependent on seasonal workers—developed because (immigrant) workers without other U.S. job options were usually available. In his words, the assumption was "that with no particular effort on the part of the employer, a farm labor force would emerge when needed, do its work, and then disappear—accepting the terms and conditions offered, without question. (Fuller 1991, vii)

27. This exemption from the 1917 Immigration Law was extended from agriculture to railroad maintenance workers and coal miners in June 1918. Between May 1917 and June 1920, some 51,000 Mexicans entered the United States under these exemptions, and 80 percent were farm workers (Fuller 1942, 19853). Mexican workers had contracts that required them to remain in the employ of the farmer or railroad who recruited them or face deportation.

28. According to one estimate, only about one in three Mexicans who migrated to the United States between 1910 and 1930 settled here (Garcia y Griego, 1981, 4).

29. Farm wages averaged about $3.60 daily without board in 1928, or $0.36 per hour for a 10-hour day.

30. The Mexican government did not permit *Braceros* to be employed legally in Texas during World War II years because of past abuses.

31. Despite explicit regulations prohibiting *Braceros* from being used to break strikes, DiGiorgio was able to use them for six weeks of the strike, until the federal government stopped their employment.

32. In 1949, for example, about 20,000 Mexicans received contracts from U.S. employers at recruitment centers in Mexico and legally entered the United States as

contract workers, while over 87,000 arrived illegally in the United States and then had their status legalized after they found jobs (President's Commission 1951, p. 53).

33. Secretary of Labor Wirtz interpreted the decision to terminate the Bracero program as signifying congressional intent to reduce or eliminate the presence of temporary foreign workers in U.S. agriculture. Under December 19, 1964, DOL regulations, U.S. employers wishing to receive DOL certification to import H-2 workers had to attempt to recruit U.S. workers at a DOL-established Adverse Effect Wage Rate (AEWR), and to offer such workers free housing, round-trip transportation, and then receive certification to employ H-2 workers for a maximum of 120 days, because "the only justification for bringing in labor is to meet the peak conditions the highly seasonal agricultural industry" (Congressional Research Service 1980, p. 65).

34. The largest acreage vegetable in California is processing tomatoes, the small round tomatoes that were developed in the 1960s to be harvested mechanically after the end of the *Bracero* program—some 330,000 acres were planted in 1995, and they yielded an average 33 tons per acre. In 1995, there were a record almost 12 million short tons of processing tomatoes produced. Americans each consumed a record 80 pounds of fresh-weight equivalent processing tomatoes in 1995, and the total 20 billion pounds was five times the four million pounds of fresh tomatoes consumed.

35. There is one exception: 1100 H-2A sheepherders (one-third of whom are employed in California) must have their need recertified each year, but they are allowed to remain in the United States as H-2A workers for up to 36 months.

. 36. DOL certified labor shortages for 25,700 farm jobs in 1991, but the number fell to less than 19,000 in 1992 and 1993, largely because the Florida sugarcane harvest, for which 8,000 H-2A workers were admitted in 1991, has largely been mechanized, so that only 2,000 H-2A workers are expected in 1993-94, and none in 1995-96. Conversation with John Hancock, January 4, 1994 and Vick, 1993.

37. The United States uses an attestation procedure to admit up to 65,000 foreign professionals each year under the so-called H-1B program; each foreign worker can stay in the United States up to six years. The theory behind this program is that U.S. high-tech companies should have easy access to the world's best engineers and programmers, and that U.S. professionals could and would complain if high-tech companies abuse the attestation privilege.

38. Employer LCAs would have to promise to pay the higher of the local prevailing wage or the minimum wage; spell out working conditions, housing and transportation arrangements that do not adversely affect local workers; and promise to give preference to U.S. workers who apply for jobs until five days before work begins.

Farmers, labor contractors, or employer associations could apply for workers, and the workers who could be employed under the program could be in the United States or abroad. If the workers were outside the United States, growers would submit their names to INS and consulates abroad, and these named workers would be given H-2B visas to enter the United States at the consulates or at a port of entry. Foreign workers would have to leave the United States when their jobs end or be subject to deportation, unless another employer promises to hire them within 14 days.

# References

Abowd, John M., and Richard B. Freeman (Eds). 1991. *Immigration, Trade and the Labor Market.* Chicago: University of Chicago Press.

Acevedo, Dolores, and Thomas Espenshade. 1992. Implications of a NAFTA for Mexican Migration into the United States. *Population and Development Review* Vol. 18, No. 4, December, 729-744.

Alarcon, Rafael. 1992. Norteizacion: Self-Perpetuating Migration from a Mexican Town, In Jorge Bustamante, Clark Reynolds, and Raul Hinojosa-Cjeda (Eds). *U.S. Mexican Relations: Labor Market Interdependence.* Stanford, CA: Stanford University Press.

Alba, Francisco. 1992. Migrant Labor Supply and Demand in Mexico and the United States: A Global Perspective. In Jorge Bustamante, Clark Reynolds, and Raul Hinojosa-Ojeda (Eds). *U.S. Mexican Relations: Labor Market Interdependence.* Stanford, CA: Stanford University Press.

Appleyard, Reginald. 1994. IOM/UNFPA Project on Emigration Dynamics in Developing Countries. *International Migration* Vol.32, No.2.

———. 1991. *International Migration: Challenge for the 1990s.* Geneva: International Organization for Migration.

Ascencio, Fernando. 1993. *Bringing it Back Home: Remittances to Mexico from Migrant Workers in the United States.* La Jolla: UCSD Center for U.S.-Mexican Studies.

Asch, Beth J. (Ed). 1994. *Emigration and its Effects on the Sending Country.* Santa Monica, CA: Rand.

Austin, James, and Gustavo Esteva (Eds). 1987. *Food Policy in Mexico: The Search for Self-Sufficiency.* Ithaca, NY: Cornell.

Banamex. 1992. A Diagnosis of Rural Areas. *Review of the Economic Situation in Mexico.* July vol. 68. 339-346.

Barkin, David. 1990. *Distorted Development: Mexico in the World Economy.* Boulder, CO: Westview.

Bean, Frank, Barry Edmonston, and Jeffrey Passel (Eds). 1990. *Undocumented Migration to the United States: IRCA and the Experience of the 1980s.* Washington: The Urban Institute Press.

Borjas, George J. 1990. *Friends or Strangers: The Impact of Immigrants on the U.S. Economy.* New York: Basic Books.

Borjas, George J., and Marta Tienda. 1987. The Economic Consequences of Immigration. *Science*, February, 645-651.

California Senate. 1961. *California's Farm Labor Problems: Part 1.* Sacramento. Senate Fact Finding Committee on Labor and Welfare.

Calva, Jose Luis. 1991. *Probables Efectos de un Tratado de Libre Comercio en el Campo Mexicano.* Mexico City: Fontamara.

———. 1988. *Crisis agricola y alimentaria en Mexico, 1982-1988.* Mexico: Fontamara.

Cargill, B. F., and G. E. Rossmiller (Eds). 1970. *Fruit and Vegetable Harvest Mechanization: Policy Implications.* East Lansing: Rural Manpower Center, Michigan State University.

Calva Tellez, Jose Luis, and Gerardo Gomez Gonzalez. 1992. *La Agricultura Mexicana*

*Frente al Tratado Trilateral de Libre Comercio.* Mexico: Juan Pablos/Chapingo.

Castles, Stephen, and Mark Miller. 1993. *The Age of Migration.* New York: Guilford Press.

CEPAL. 1989. *Magnitude de Pobreza en America Latina en los Años Ochenta.* Santiago: LC/L533.

Chiswick, Barry (Ed). 1982. *The Gateway: U.S. Immigration Issues and Policies.* Washington: American Enterprise Institute.

Coleman, Gail S. 1989. Overcoming Mootness in the H-2A Temporary Foreign Farm Worker Program. *Georgetown Law Journal,* 78 October.

Commission on Agricultural Workers. 1993. *Commission on Agricultural Workers Report, Appendix II.* Washington, DC: Commission on Agricultural Workers.

Congressional Research Service. 1980. *Temporary Worker Programs: Background and Issues.* Prepared for the Senate Committee on the Judiciary. February. Washington, DC.

Cornelius, Wayne. 1992a. The Politics and Economics of Reforming the Ejido Sector in Mexico: An Overview and Research Agenda. *Latin American Studies Association Forum.* Vol. 23. No. 3. 3-10.

————. 1992b. From Sojourners to Settlers: The Changing Profile of Mexican Immigration to the United States. In Jorge Bustamante, Clark Reynolds, and Raul Hinojosa-Ojeda (Eds). *U.S. Mexican Relations: Labor Market Interdependence.* Stanford, CA: Stanford University Press.

Cornelius, Wayne, and David Myhre. 1996. *The Transformation of Rural Mexico: Reforming the Ejido Sector.* La Jolla: Center for U.S.-Mexican Studies

Craig, Richard B. 1971. *The Bracero Program: Interest Groups and Foreign Policy.* Austin: University of Texas Press.

Cross, Harry, and James Sandos. 1981. *Across the Border: Rural Development in Mexican and Recent Migration to the United States.* Berkeley: Institute of Governmental Studies, University of California.

de la Rocha, Mercedes Gonzalez, and Augustin Escobar Latapi. 1991. *Social Respones to Mexico's Economic Crisis of the 1980s.* La Jolla: Center for U.S.-Mexican Studies.

de Janvry, Alain, Elisabeth Sadoulet, and Gustavo Anda. 1994. *NAFTA and Mexico's Corn Producers.* Berkeley: UC ARE Working Paper 275. July.

de Janvry, Alain, Elisabeth Sadoulet, and Gustavo Gordillo. 1996. *Re-orienting Mexico's Agrarian Reform: Household and Community Responses, 1990-94.* La Jolla: Center for U.S.-Mexican Studies

Durand, Jorge, and Douglas S. Massey. 1992. Mexican Migration to the United States. *Latin American Research Review* 27(2): 3-42.

Escobar Latapi, Agustin. 1995. Restructuring, Social Inequality, and State Action in Mexico: A Labor Systems Approach. mimeo.

Escobar Latapi, Agustin, and Bryan Roberts. 1996. Mexican Social and Economic Policy and Emigration. June. mimeo.

Fisher, Lloyd. 1953. *The Harvest Labor Market in California.* Cambridge, MA: Harvard University Press.

Fix, Michael. 1991. *The Paper Curtain: Employer Sanctions' Implementation, Impact, and Reform*. Washington: Urban Institute Press.

Fix, Michael, and Paul Hill. 1990. *Enforcing Employer Sanctions: Challenges and Strategies*. Washington: Urban Institute Press.

Fleck, Susan, and Constance Sorrentino. 1994. Employment and Unemployment in Mexico's Labor Force. *Monthly Labor Review*. November. 3-31.

Fox, Jonathan. 1992. T*he Political Dynamics of Reform: State Power and Food Policy in Mexico*. Ithaca, NY: Cornell.

Fuller, Varden. 1942. The Supply of Agricultural Labor as a Factor in the Evolution of Farm Organization in California. Unpublished Ph.D. dissertation, UC Berkeley, 1939. Reprinted in Violations of Free Speech and the Rights of Labor Education and Labor Committee, [The LaFollette Committee]. Washington: Senate Education and Labor Committee. 19778-19894.

————. 1989. The Mexican Labor Supply, 1990-2010, in Wayne Cornelius and Jorge A. Bustamante (Eds.), *Mexican Migration to the United States: Origins, Consequences and Policy Options*. La Jolla: UCSD Center for U.S.-Mexican Studies.

Garcia y Griego, Manuel. 1981. The Importation of Mexican Contract Laborers to the United States, 1942-1964: Antecedents, Operation, and Legacy. La Jolla: Program in U.S.-Mexican Studies, UCSD, Working Paper 11.

Greenwood, Michael. 1994, Potential Channels of Immigrant Influence on the Economy of the Receiving Country. *Papers in Regional Science*, 73(3): 211-240

Heimpel, Gretchen. 1981. Mexico: Agricultural and Trade Policies. USDA: FAS-306.

Hinojosa, Raul. 1994. *The North American Free Trade Agreement and Migration. Migration and Development New Partnerships for Cooperation*. Paris, France: OECD, 229-239.

Hinojosa-Ojeda, Raul, and Sherman Robinson. 1992. Labor Issues in a North American Free Trade Area. In Nora Lustig, Barry Bosworth, and Robert Lawrence (Eds.), *North American Free Trade: Assessing the Impact*. Washington, D.C.: The Brookings Institution. 69-108.

Huerta, Mario M. Carillo. 1990. Maquiladoras Y Migracion en Mexico. Puebla: Asesoria y Consultoria Economica.

Hufbauer, Gary, and Jeffrey Schott. 1992. *North American Free Trade: Issues and Recommendations*. Washington: Institute for International Economics.

Johnson, William B. 1987. *Workforce 2000: Work and Workers for the 21st Century. Report to the U.S. Department of Labor.* Indianapolis, Indiana: Hudson Institute.

Leya, Amado, Marcos Vazquez, amd Celia Solano. 1990. Mexican Agriculture: The Potential for Export Prodcution and Employment Generation in Rural Areas. U.S. Commission for the Study of International Migration and Cooperative Economic Development. Working Paper 49. July.

Levy, Santiago, and Sweder van Wijnbergen. Mexico and the Free Trade Agreement between Mexico and the United States, *The World Bank Economic Review*, Vol. 4, No 3, 1992, pp. 481-502.

Lira, Enrique, and Simon Commander. 1989. Agricultual Commercialization and the growth of a migrant labor market in Mexico. *International Labor Review*, Vol 128, No 6,

769-789.

Lopez, Ramon, John Nash, and Julie Stanton. 1995. Adjustment and Poverty in Mexican Agriculture: How Farmers' Wealth Affects Supply Response. Working Paper 1494,

Lustig, Nora. 1992. *Mexico: The Remaking of an Economy*. Washington: Brookings Institution.

Mamer, John, and Donald Rosedale. 1980. *The Management of Seasonal Farmworkers under Collective Bargaining*. Berkeley: DANR Leaflet 21147. March.

Martin, Philip. 1994. Collective Bargaining in Agriculture, in Paula Voos (Ed). *Contemporary Collective Bargaining in the Private Sector*. Madison: Industrial Relations Research Association.

———. 1993. *Trade and Migration: NAFTA and Agriculture*. Washington: DC: Institute for International Economics. October.

———. 1990. The Outlook for Agricultural Labor in the 1990s, *UC Davis Law Review*, 23, 3: 499-523.

Martin, Philip, and David Martin. 1993. *The Endless Quest: Helping America's Farmworkers*. Boulder, CO: Westview Press

Martin, Philip, and Alan Olmstead. 1985. The Agricultural Mechanization Controversy, *Science*, Vol. 227, No. 4687, February 8, pp. 601-606

Massey, Douglas S. 1988. Economic Development and International Migration in Comparative Perspective. *Population and Development Review*, Vol. 14, No. 3 (September): 383-413.

Massey, Douglas, Rafael Alarcon, Jorge Durand, and Humberto Gonzales. 1987. *Return to Aztlan: The Social Process of International Migration from Western Mexico*. Berkeley, CA: University of California Press, 1987.

Massey, Douglas S., Joaquin Arango, Grame Hugo, Ali Kouaouci, Adela Pelligrino, and J. Edward Taylor. 1994. Theories of International Migration: A Review and Appraisal. *Population and Development Review*, pp. 431-466.

Massey, Douglas, Katherine Donato, and Zai Liang. 1990. Effects of the Immigration Reform and Control Act of 1986: Preliminary Data from Mexico, in Bean, Frank, Barry Edmonston, and Jeffrey Passel (Eds). 1990. *Undocumented Migration to the United States: IRCA and the Experience of the 1980s*. Washington: The Urban Institute Press, 183-210.

McWilliams, Carey. 1939. *Factories in the Fields*. Boston: Little, Brown.

Muller, Thomas, and Thomas Espenshade. 1985. *The Fourth Wave: California's Newest Immigrants*. Washington: The Urban Institute Press.

Myers, Norman, and Jennifer Kent. 1995. *Environmental Exodus: An Emergent Crisis in the Global Arena*. Washington: The Climate Institute. May

North, David, and Marion Houstoun. 1976. *The Characteristics and Role of Illegal Aliens in the U.S. Labor Market: An Exploratory Study*. Washington: New Transcentury.

Oliveira, Victor, Anne Effland, Jack Runyan, and Shannon Hamm. 1993. *Hired Farm Labor Use on Fruit, Vegetable, and Horticultural Specialty Farms*. Washington: U.S. Department of Agriculture, Economic Research Service, Agricultural Economics Report 676. December.

Piore, Michael J. 1979. Birds of Passage: *Migrant Labor and Industrial Societies*. New York: Cambridge University Press.

Pollitt, Daniel. 1971. History of the Farm Labor Movement in the 20th Century. Seminar of Farm Labor Problems. U.S. Congress, House of Representatives, Committee on Education and Labor, Subcommittee on Agricultural Labor. (June 2, 3, 10).

President's Commission on Migratory Labor. 1991. *Migratory Labor In American Agriculture*. Washington: U.S. Government Printing Office.

Randall, Laura (Ed.). 1996. *Changing Structure of Mexico: Political, Social, and Economic Aspects*. Armonk, NY: M. E. Sharpe.

––––––. 1996. *Reforming Mexico's Agrarian Reform*. Armonk, NY: M. E. Sharpe.

Reynolds, Clark. 1992. Will a Free Trade Agreement Lead to Wage Convergence? Implications for Mexico and the United States, in Jorge Bustamante, Clark Reynolds, and Raul Hinojosa-Ojeda (Eds.). *U.S. Mexican Relations: Labor Market Interdependence*. Stanford, CA: Stanford University Press.

Sanderson, Steven. 1986. *The Transformation of Mexican Agriculture*. Princeton: Princeton University Press.

Russell, Sharon Stanton, and Michael Teitelbaum. 1992. *International Migration and International Trade*. Washington, D.C.: World Bank

SARH-CEPAL Proyecto. 1992. Primer Informe Nacional Sobre Tipologia de Productores del Sector Social. Mexico: SARH (Subsecretaria de Politica Sectorial y Concertacion), June SARH. 1993. Mexican Agricultural Sector: An Overview. May.

Schlichter, Sumner. 1929. The Current Labor Policies of American Industries. *Quarterly Journal of Economics*, May, 393-435.

Schwartz, Michelle, and Jessica Notini. 1994. *Desertification and Migration: Mexico and the United States*. Washington: Commission on Immigration Reform.

Select Commission on Immigration and Refugee Policy (SCIRP). 1981. Final Report. Washington: SCIRP.

Shwedel, Kenneth. 1992. Agricultural Investment Slows in the Wake of Ejido Reform. *Business Mexico*. December, 4-7.

Smith, Wesley. 1992. Salinas Prepares Mexican Agriculture for Free Trade. October 1.

Solis, Dianne. 1993. Agricultural Crisis in Mexico Deepens, *Wall Street Journal*, September 13.

Stalker, Peter. 1994. *The Work of Strangers: A Survey of International Labour Migration*. Geneva: International Labour Office.

Stark, Oded. 1991. *The Migration of Labor*. Cambridge: Basil Blackwell.

Taylor, J. Edward. 1995. *Micro Economywide Models for Migration and Policy Analysis. An Application to Rural Mexico*. Paris: OECD.

––––––. 1992 .Remittances and Inequality Reconsidered: Direct, Indirect and Intertemporal Effects. *Journal of Policy Modelling*, 14(2):187-208

––––––. 1987. Undocumented Mexico-U.S. Migration and the Returns to Households in Rural Mexico. *American Journal of Agricultural Economics* 69, 626-638.

––––––. 1986. Differential Migration, Networks, Information and Risk, in Research in Human Capital and Development, Vol. 4, Migration, Human Capital, and Development.

Oded Stark (Ed). Greenwich, CT: JAI Press. 147-71.

Thomas, Robert. 1985. *Citizenship, Gender, and Work: Social Organization of Industrial Agriculture*. New York: Cambridge University Press.

U.S. Commission for the Study of International Migration and Cooperative Economic Development. 1990. *Unauthorized Migration: An Economic Development Response.* Washington, D.C.

U.S. Commission on Agricultural Workers. 1992. *Final Report.* Washington: U.S. Government Printing Office

U.S. Council of Economic Advisors. 1986. *The Economic Effects of Immigration, Economic Report of the President.* Washington: Council of Economic Advisors. 213-234.

U.S. Department of Agriculture. 1996. Vegetables and Specialties. Part 5. April 30.

U.S. Department of Labor, International Labor Affairs Bureau. 1989. The Effects of Immigration on the U.S. Economy.

U. S. House of Representatives, Committee on Government Operations. 1993. Mexican Agriculture Policies: An Immigration Generator? Subcommittee on Employment, Housing, and Aviation. October 28

U.S. Immigration and Naturalization Service. Annual. *Statistical Yearbook of the Immigration and Naturalization Service.* Washington, D.C.

U.S. Industrial Commission. 1901. Reports, *U.S. Industrial Commission.* Washington: Government Printing Office.

Valdes, Constanza. 1994. Mexico. Western Hemisphere. WRS-94-2. June. 31-37. Mexico.

Yates, Paul L. 1981. *Mexico's Agricultural Dilemma.* Tucson, Arizona: University of Arizona Press.

Zabin, Carol, Michael Kearney, David Runsten, and Ana Garcia. 1993. *A New Cycle of Rural Poverty: Mixtec Migrants in California Agriculture.* Davis: California Institute for Rural Studies.

# 4.
# Mexican Immigration and the U.S. Population

*Alene H. Gelbard and Marion Carter*

More people immigrate to the United States from Mexico than from any other country. In recent years, Mexican immigrants have accounted for about 14 percent of all legal immigrants per year. They comprise a larger percentage of undocumented immigrants. In 1992, estimates indicate that nearly 40 percent of all undocumented immigrants residing in the United States were from Mexico.

This chapter looks at how Mexican immigration affects the demographic profile of the United States. It focuses on characteristics relevant to public policy and looks at the particular case of California to examine the implications of Mexican immigration at the sub-national level.

The Mexican immigrant population is less educated, poorer and younger than the U.S. population. More recent immigrants are less educated than earlier immigrants. Mexican immigrants comprise just over a third (37 percent) of the Mexican-American population. The latter are also younger, poorer and less educated than the U.S. population as a whole, but older, more educated and more financially well-off than Mexican immigrants.

Findings on the socioeconomic characteristics of the Mexican immigrant and Mexican-origin populations are mixed. The percentage of children living in poverty appears to be declining with succeeding generations, although the percentage of children living in single-parent families, a condition often linked to poverty, appears to be increasing. Education levels are lower for third- and higher-generation Mexican Americans, in contrast to trends in levels of educational attainment for non-Hispanic whites that rise over time. Findings such as these raise important questions about the nature of assimilation of Mexican immigrants into U.S. society and call for more detailed analysis of the factors that may explain them.

The impact of Mexican immigration is most keenly felt in a small number of states and metropolitan areas. The majority of Mexican immigrants live in California, Texas and Illinois. In California, one in five individuals is of Mexican origin compared to one in twenty for the United States as a whole. Mexican immigration will continue to contribute to the size of the Mexican-origin population. However, even if Mexican immigration were to cease tomorrow, the Mexican-origin population will continue to increase as a percentage of total U.S. population. Its younger age structure and the higher average number of children for women of Mexican origin compared to other U.S. women are the major factors contributing to the future growth of this group.

The United States is one of the fastest growing industrialized countries in the world as a result of its relatively high birth rate and immigration. Immigration is estimated to account for a third to one-half of current population increases, depending upon whether the U.S.-born children of immigrants are counted. Mexico contributes the largest number of immigrants to the United States, both legal and illegal. In fiscal year 1994, Mexican immigrants accounted for about 14 percent of all legal immigration (INS February 1996). While it is difficult to estimate the contribution of Mexicans to illegal immigration, it is estimated that over a third of the new undocumented immigrants each year are from Mexico (Warren 1994).

The impact of immigration on U.S. population is an increasingly controversial public policy issue. Difficulties in measuring immigration contribute to the controversy. The complexity of categories of immigration, a lack of data which distinguish immigrants from the native born, the difficulties in estimating illegal immigration, and the differences of opinion about who should be included in estimates of immigration are examples of issues that confound the measurement of immigration and its impact on the size and nature of the U.S. population.

In this chapter, we look at Mexican immigration and its effects on the demographic and socio-economic profile of the U.S. population, highlighting characteristics relevant for public policy. We try to differentiate between legal and illegal Mexican immigration where possible and include information on immigration overall to put Mexican immigration into context. We include a discussion of the specific case of California, the nation's most populous state and the recipient of the largest number of immigrants from Mexico. We also discuss the implications of Mexican immigration for the future of the U.S. population. The paper ends with a summary and a few conclusions about the status of current Mexican migration to the United States as it affects the U.S. demographic profile.

## The U.S. Population

A recent assessment of the U.S. population at mid-decade sums it up in three words: large, diverse and growing (De Vita 1996). With a 1996 population of 265 million, the United States is the third largest country in the world (PRB 1996). The United States has gradually shifted from a predominantly white, European population to an increasingly mixed society, racially and ethnically. The shift has become more pronounced since 1970 as a result of increasing immigration from Asia and Latin America and relatively low birth rates among white non-Hispanics (ibid.). Immigration from Asia and Latin America accounted for 85 percent of all immigration during the 1980s (Martin and Midgley 1994).

The U.S. population is growing at a rate of about 1 percent per year. In 1995, an additional 2.4 million people were added to the U.S. population as a result of both its birth rate and immigration. The birth rate reflects "fertility," which is measured by the average number of births a woman has in her lifetime or her total fertility rate (TFR). For the United States as a whole, this rate is 2.0, though there are variations between ethnic and racial groups.

## Immigration and the U.S. Population

Immigration to the United States has been estimated at approximately 1 million people per year over the last few years (Martin and Midgley 1994). This total is a combination of legal immigration, emigration, and illegal immigration. Most recent estimates show a slightly lower total. In fiscal year 1995, the Immigration and Naturalization Service (INS) estimated that about 720,000 people became legal immigrants (INS, March 1996). Although statistics are not kept on emigration, the most recent official estimate is that 222,000 legal residents emigrate each year (U.S. Bureau of the Census 1996), resulting in a net legal immigration of about 498,000. Undocumented immigration is estimated at about 225,000 per year (ibid.), suggesting a net immigration of about 723,000 for fiscal year 1995. This represents slightly under a third of the annual absolute increase in the U.S. population.

Immigration has both a direct and indirect impact on the growth of the U.S. population. Immigrants contribute directly through their absolute numbers. They contribute indirectly through their childbearing and, to a much smaller extent, their mortality. When U.S.-born children of immigrants are included in the estimates, immigration may contribute about half of total U.S. population growth (Martin 1995).

More recent levels of immigration are down from the all-time high in 1991 of 1.8 million immigrants who were granted legal status, largely the result of the 1986 Immigration Reform and Control Act, or IRCA[1]. As seen in Figure 4.1, the number of legal immigrants has been steadily increasing since the 1940s. With the exception of 1991, current levels remain lower than the legal immigration levels found in the earlier part of this century. In 1995, the foreign-born population of about 23 million represented nearly 9 percent of the total population, much less than the 15 percent recorded in the 1910 census (De Vita 1996).

**Figure 4.1**
**Immigrants Admitted to the United States, 1890-1995**

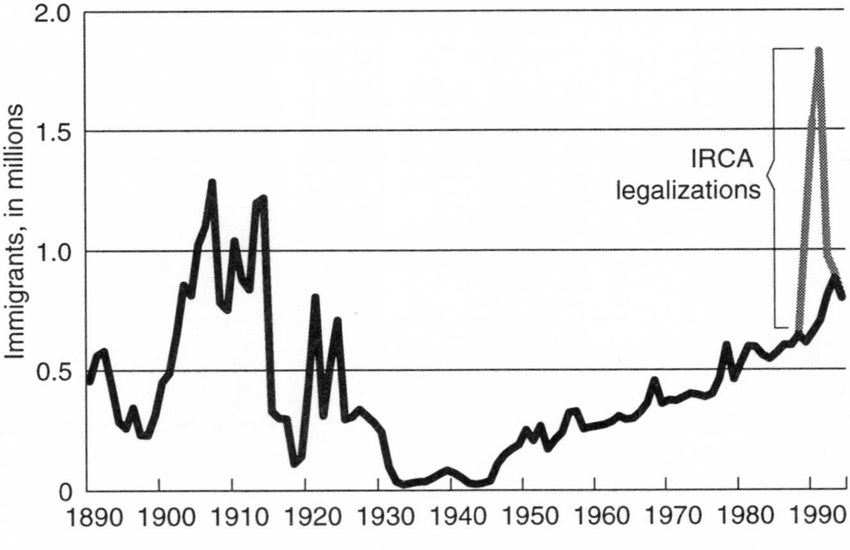

Note: Totals for 1988–1995 include persons legalized under the Immigration Reform and Control Act (IRCA).

Source: 1994 Statistical Yearbook of the INS.

## Mexican Immigration and the U.S. Population

To look at Mexican immigration and the U.S. population, we rely primarily on census data and data from the INS. The U.S. Bureau of the Census provides information on two population subgroups that come closest to reflecting Mexican immigration, the *Mexican-origin* population and the *Mexican foreign-born*.[2]

The Mexican-origin population includes all people who identify themselves as having origins in Mexico, whether born there (i.e., foreign-born) or in the U.S. (i.e., Mexican-Americans). The Mexican foreign-born population is a subset of the Mexican-origin population and includes all people born in Mexico who are in the United States legally or illegally. Table 4.1 compares the size and citizenship status of these population groups in 1994. The Mexican-origin population totaled 17.1 million in 1994, or about 7 percent of the total U.S. population. Sixty-two percent were native-born Americans. The foreign-born component of the Mexican-origin population totaled 6.3 million in 1994. Only 14 percent of this group were naturalized citizens.

Data from the INS (Table 4.2) show that since 1950 legal Mexican immigration has stayed relatively stable as a percent of total immigration, with the exception of the late 1980s and early 1990s when IRCA legalizations were in effect. Between 1986 and 1995, over 2 million Mexicans received permanent resident status through IRCA, accounting for about three-quarters of all immigrants legalized under IRCA

### Table 4.1
### Mexican-Origin Population and Mexican
### Foreign-Born Population, 1994

| | |
|---|---|
| **Mexican-Origin Population** | **17, 090, 000** |
| % Native-Born | 62% |
| % Foreign-Born | 37% |
| **Of the Foreign-Born** | **6,264,000** |
| % Naturalized Citizen | 14% |
| % Not a citizen | 86% |
| % Arrived After 1990 | 20% |
| % Arrived between 1980 and 1990 | 39% |

Source: CPS 1994

### Table 4.2
### Legal Immigrants from Mexico,
### by Decade and Fiscal Year, 1951-1995

| Period/Year | Number | % of Total Immigrants |
|---|---|---|
| 1951-60 | 299,811 | 12 |
| 1961-70 | 453,937 | 14 |
| 1971-80 | 637,161 | 14 |
| 1981 | 101,268 | 17 |
| 1982 | 56,106 | 9 |
| 1983 | 59,079 | 11 |
| 1984 | 57,557 | 11 |
| 1985 | 61,077 | 11 |
| 1986 | 66,533 | 11 |
| 1987 | 72,351 | 12 |
| 1988 | 95,039 | 15 |
| 1989 | 405,172 | 37 |
| 1990 | 679,068 | 44 |
| 1991 | 946,167 | 52 |
| 1992 | 213,802 | 22 |
| 1993 | 126,561 | 14 |
| 1994 | 111,398 | 14 |
| 1995 | 89,932 | 13 |

Sources: 1986, 1970, 1968 INS Yearbooks; INS February and March 1996

(De Vita 1996). Legal Mexican immigration peaked in 1991 when it comprised 52 percent of all legal immigration.

The annual number of legal Mexican immigrants has increased since the 1950s, although the increases did not become substantial until the late 1980s, again reflecting IRCA legalizations. Since 1993, the numbers have declined each year. It is important to note that data on legal immigration do not include Mexican temporary legal migration. Between 1942 and 1964 nearly 5 million migrants from Mexico, called Braceros, entered the United States to fill temporary agricultural labor jobs (Martin and Midgley 1994).

Most Mexicans receiving legal immigrant status in recent years have done so as family members. In fiscal year 1994, 92 percent received legal immigrant

**Table 4.3**
**Proportion of Legal Immigration by Type of Admission:**
**All Immigrants and Immigrants Born in Mexico, Fiscal Year 1994**

| Type of Admission | % of All Immigrants | % of Total Mexican Immigrants |
|---|---|---|
| Family-sponsored preferences | 26% | 35.1% |
| Employment based | 15% | 2.9% |
| **Total** | 100% (804, 416) | 100% (111, 398) |
| Immediate relatives of US citizens | | |
| spouses | 18% | 17.8% |
| children | 6% | 4.8% |
| parents       7% | 4.4% | |
| Refugee/Asylee adjustments | 15% | 0.01% |
| Diversity | 5% | — |
| IRCA | 0.8% | 3.9% |
| Legalization dependents | 4% | 29.7% |
| Other | 2% | 1.2% |
| **Total** | 31% | 27.1% |

Source: INS, February 1996

status as immediate relatives of permanent resident aliens (family sponsored preferences), immediate relatives of U.S. citizens, or as "legalization dependents" (children of legalized immigrants) (See Table 4.3).

Mexico is also the country of origin of the largest number of undocumented immigrants and migrants in the United States. According to the INS, in 1992, there were an estimated 3.4 million undocumented immigrants living in the United States, of which approximately 1.3 million, or 39 percent, were Mexican (Warren 1994). These numbers may underestimate the total number and total contribution of undocumented Mexican immigrants to the United States because so many became legalized through IRCA in the few years preceding the survey (ibid., Martin and Midgley 1994).

Undocumented *immigrants* are distinct from undocumented *migrants*, i.e., the millions of Mexicans who illegally come to the United States on a temporary basis. These migrants comprise the vast majority of illegal entries into the United

States from Mexico, and their movement sustains a significant circular flow of people between the United States and Mexico (Massey and Espinosa 1996). One recent study suggests that in a given year, about 85 percent of new entries are offset by departures (NICHD 1996). Many of these migrants are farm workers. Mexican farm workers comprise at least 60 percent of seasonal agricultural workers in the United States (Kissam 1992).

Figure 4.2 shows the trend in the absolute numbers of foreign-born (including both legal and undocumented immigrants) from Mexico since the beginning of the century. Figure 4.3 shows the trend for the Mexican foreign-born population as a percentage of the total foreign-born population for the same period. As can be seen, both the numbers of Mexican-foreign born and their contribution as a percentage of the total U.S. foreign-born population increased dramatically after 1970.

## Geographic Distribution of Mexican Immigrants

Nearly three-fourths of the foreign-born population are concentrated in just six states: California, New York, Texas, Florida, Illinois and New Jersey. California is the largest receiving state, with one third of the foreign-born population in 1990 (Martin and Midgley 1994).

**Figure 4.2**
**Foreign-Born Mexicans in the United States, 1900-1994**

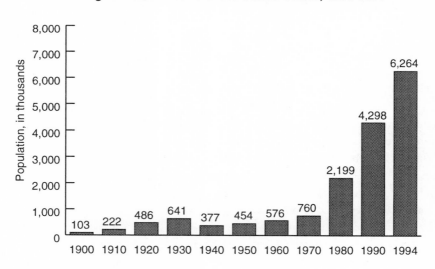

Sources: CPS 1994, Lapham 1993.

Legal immigration is largely an urban phenomenon. Over 90 percent of new immigrants migrate to urban areas first (De Vita 1996) and over two-thirds of all U.S. immigrant growth from 1985 to 1995 occurred in 10 metropolitan areas: Los Angeles, New York, San Francisco, Chicago, Miami, Washington, D.C., Houston, San Diego, Boston and Dallas (Frey 1996). As shown in Table 4.4, the Los Angeles metropolitan area received the largest number of immigrants during this time, followed closely by New York.

A recent study of over 200,000 immigrants legalized by the IRCA program showed that 87 percent of undocumented immigrants arriving in California stayed there, while other states receiving undocumented immigrants experienced more turnover (Neuman and Tienda 1994). Texas and Florida had a net loss of one-third of their undocumented entrants, while Illinois, New York and New Jersey experienced an increase in the size of their undocumented immigrant population by one-third due to secondary migration after entry.

An examination of immigrant settlement patterns and domestic migration trends from 1985 to 1995 suggests that metropolitan areas and states with the highest concentration of immigrants are also experiencing outflows of domestic migrants to destinations that do not attract immigrants (Frey 1996). Outmigration tends to be concentrated among less-educated and lower-skilled long-term residents. It is also more pronounced among non-Latino whites (ibid.).

**Figure 4.3**
**Mexican Foreign-Born as a Percentage of Total U.S. Foreign-Born**

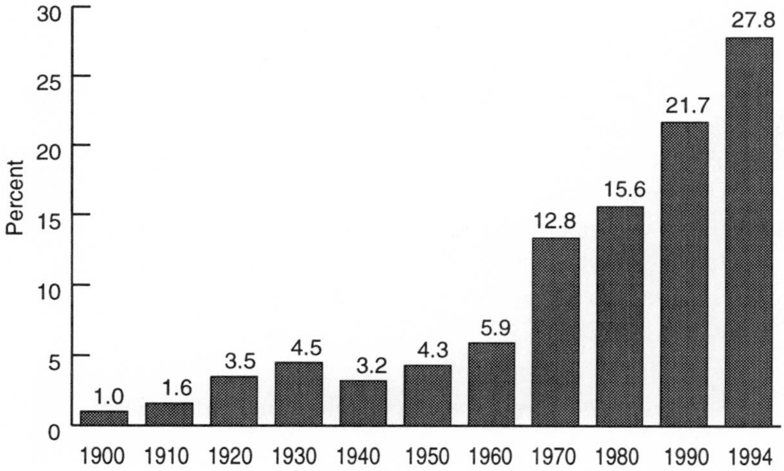

Sources: Lapham 1993.

## Table 4.4
### High Immigration Metro Areas, 1985-1995

| Metropolitan Area | Immigration, 1985-90 | Immigration 1990-95 |
| --- | --- | --- |
| Los Angeles | 842,675 | 792,712 |
| New York | 714,346 | 705,939 |
| San Francisco | 262,185 | 262,519 |
| Chicago | 160,760 | 216,309 |
| Miami | 194,491 | 157,059 |
| Washington, DC | 163,696 | 125,479 |
| Houston | 82,964 | 110,323 |
| San Diego | 96,350 | 85,025 |
| Boston | 123,958 | 74,316 |
| Dallas | 63,289 | 72,246 |

Source: Frey 1996

Immigrants often follow the paths of friends and family. Mexican immigrant distribution mirrors that of the Mexican-origin population. The Mexican-origin population is concentrated in California, Texas, and Illinois, although during the 1970s and 1980s other states began to emerge as growing centers of Mexican immigration, namely New York, Nevada, and Florida (Montaño and Smith 1994). In 1995, 7 percent of all legal Mexican immigrants stated their intent to live in California, Texas or Illinois (INS, March 1996). The INS estimated that in 1992, 83 percent of all undocumented immigrants from Mexico lived in these three states: 60 percent in California, 17 percent in Texas, and 6 percent in Illinois (Warren 1994).

These figures might give the impression that California's immigrant population is predominantly Mexican, but the percentage of the total foreign-born population that is Mexican (Figure 4) is higher in Arizona, Texas and Illinois than in California (CPS 1994).

## Sex and Age Distribution of Mexican Immigrants

The sex and age distribution of a population has direct implications for a number of public policy areas: employment, education, health, and social services. Both also affect future population changes through their impact on childbearing.

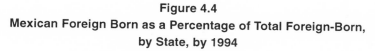

**Figure 4.4**
**Mexican Foreign Born as a Percentage of Total Foreign-Born,**
**by State, by 1994**

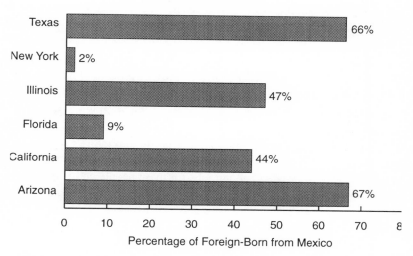

Sources: CPS 1994.

The Mexican-origin population and Mexican foreign-born population today is more male than the general U.S. population. In 1994, 54 percent of the Mexican foreign-born were male (CPS 1994). Nearly 60 percent of petitioners who applied under the pre-1982 provision of IRCA were male, as were over 80 percent of those who applied under the special agricultural worker provision (INS 1990).

This gender imbalance is beginning to change both through legal and illegal immigration. In fiscal year 1994, 56 percent of legal immigrants from Mexico were female (INS, February 1996). Through IRCA, a substantial number of Mexicans, many of whom were males separated from their families, became eligible to apply to bring their families to the U.S. through family reunification policies. Studies of illegal migration suggest similar shifting in the gender balance of Mexican migration. Since IRCA, the proportion of migrants from Mexico who are women and children has been increasing, though most undocumented immigrants and migrants are still male (Bean et al. 1990, Donato and Kanaiapuni 1994).

In general, immigrants tend to be younger than the native-born population and to be concentrated in the most economically active and reproductive age groups. This is the case for Mexican immigrants. Figure 4.5 compares the age structure of the Mexican-origin population with that of the total U.S. population and shows the higher percentage of the Mexican-origin population in the younger age groups. In 1994, the median age of the Mexican-origin population was about 24 years old—2 years younger than the average for all Hispanics and a full 10 years younger than the U.S. median (CPS 1994). The median age for recent Mexican immigrants is even younger; in fiscal year 1994, it was 21.3 (19 for males, 24.4 for females). Undocumented immigrants are most likely to be young as well.

The pattern of young immigrants from Mexico reflects Mexico's own age structure (*see* Mexico: A Demographic Snapshot boxed at the end of this chapter). Like many developing countries, Mexico's population is weighted heavily in the younger ages. The large number of people entering early adulthood, and the greater likelihood for people at that stage in life to migrate suggest that this youthful migration stream will probably continue, especially if the Mexican economy is unable to provide enough jobs for these people and U.S. employers continue to hire them. U.S. immigration policies that encourage family reunification for both citizens and legal immigrants are also likely to sustain the young age structure of the Mexican foreign-born population.

**Figure 4.5**
**Age Structure of the U.S. Population**
**and the Mexican-Origin Population, 1994**

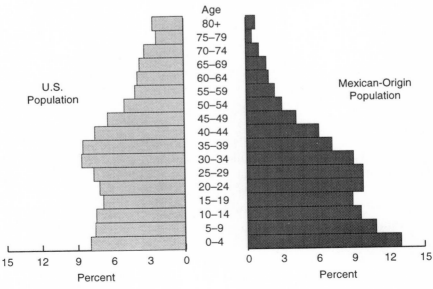

Sources: CPS 1994.

Immigrants do not account for most of the children of Mexican origin in the United States. The vast majority of children and adolescents in the Mexican-origin population are native-born—85 percent in 1994—the offspring of immigrants and Mexican-Americans (CPS 1994).

## Fertility and Mortality

Women of Mexican origin have more children than other racial or ethnic groups in the United States, averaging 3.2 children per woman in 1993 (Frisbie and Bean 1995, NCHS 1995). In California, studies show that in 1993, Mexican foreign-born women had the highest fertility level of all foreign-born women, and nearly twice the fertility levels of European foreign-born women (Heim and Austin 1995). The teen pregnancy level for the Mexican-origin population (18 percent of all births were to teens in 1993) was higher than the national average (12 percent), but other racial and ethnic groups had larger shares of births to teens (NCHS 1995). A similar pattern was seen for births to unmarried mothers (ibid.). The higher fertility rates seen among the Mexican foreign-born and Mexican-origin populations are linked to a variety of factors, including the pattern of higher fertility in Mexico (Mexico: A Demographic Snapshot), education levels, and traditional cultural norms. The higher fertility levels factor significantly in the demographic impact of these population groups.

The mortality rates of the Mexican-origin population are similar to those of the U.S. population as a whole, though the causes of death differ (Bradshaw and Frisbie 1992). Mexican immigrants actually show lower death rates than the Mexican-origin or native population (Frisbie, pers. comm., 1996). Research on infant mortality indicates that despite indicators that would imply higher infant mortality compared to the United States as a whole—such as less prenatal care and shorter birth intervals (NCHS 1995)—infant mortality rates for the Mexican foreign-born population are the same or somewhat lower than rates for white Americans and the Mexican-origin population (Guendelman 1994). Underreporting of infant deaths may be a factor, but healthier behaviors (e.g., less use of cigarettes, drugs, and alcohol) and strong family support are also thought to play a role (ibid.).

## Socioeconomic Characteristics of Mexican Immigrants

Several social and economic characteristics of Mexican immigrants have important implications for the demographic profile of the U.S. population and its links to public policies, e.g., on schools, the labor market and social services as well as on political participation.

## Family and Household Composition

The Mexican-origin population shows a higher propensity to marry and lower rates of divorce than many other ethnic and racial groups (Frisbie and Bean 1995, CPS 1994). This population also has the largest average family size among Hispanic groups; 4.5 members per family, compared to 3.2 for non-Latino white families and 3.7 for non-Latino black families (Frisbie and Bean 1995). Their families are more likely to include the elderly than non-Latino white or black families, though not as likely as some other Latino groups (ibid.). A study of teen mothers among different ethnic groups indicates a higher percentage of adolescents of Mexican origin live with their parents compared to other teen mothers (Berkowitz 1996).

The increasing percentage of children living in single-parent households over time suggests that the stability of the Mexican-American family may be changing. In 1990, 39 percent of third- and higher-generation children of Mexican origin were living in single-parent households compared with only 19 percent and 23 percent for first- and second-generation children, respectively. This is also more than twice the percentage of non-Hispanic white children in single-parent households (Turner 1996). Other immigrant groups were experiencing similar patterns (Figure 4.6).

## Education

The Mexican-origin population has less education than the total U.S. population. The percentage of the Mexican-origin population over 25 years old completing at least high school (47 percent) is significantly higher than the Mexican foreign-born population (29 percent) (Table 4.5). Data on educational levels of Mexican immigrants arriving between 1960 and 1988 show declining levels for more recent immigrants (Bean et al. 1994). A comparison of education levels by generation for more recent birth cohorts indicates that contrary to patterns for non-Hispanic whites that rise over time, later generations of Mexican Americans have lower levels of education than the second generation (ibid.).

## Language

In 1990, over 32 million people, or 14 percent of the U.S. population ages 5 and over, reported speaking a language other than English at home. This is an increase of nearly 40 percent since 1980. Over half who reported speaking a language other than English speak Spanish (De Vita 1996). Most Mexican

**Figure 4.6**

**Share of Children Living in Single-Parent Households
by Generation and Ethnic Group, 1990**

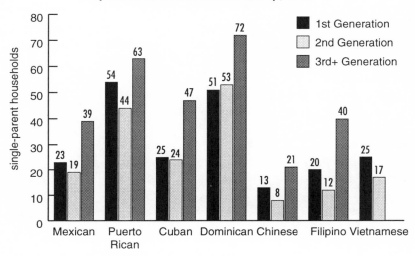

U.S. Average=21%; Non-Hispanic white average=17%

Source: Turner 1996

foreign-born residents speak Spanish at home, but nearly two-thirds of the Mexican-origin population use English at home (Martin and Midgley 1994).

## Income

On both the individual and family level, a higher percentage of the Mexican-origin population lives in poverty compared with the U.S. population (Table 4.5). Within the Mexican-origin population, the foreign-born fare worse. In 1993, the percentage of individuals in both groups living in poverty was more than twice the U.S. population percentage, 36 percent and 30 percent for the Mexican foreign-born and Mexican-origin populations respectively, compared with 14 percent for the U.S. population.

Trend data indicate that the Mexican-origin population has not enjoyed the same level of economic gains that other groups have since the 1960s (Bean et al. 1994), however, a study of poverty and family structure indicates that poverty rates decline for succeeding generations within the Mexican-origin population. In 1990, 44 percent of first-generation children of Mexican origin lived in poverty, compared with 32 percent of second- and 28 percent of third-generation (Turner 1996). This is despite the trends for higher percentages of children of

**Table 4.5**

**Socio-economic Indicators of the U.S. Population, Mexican-Origin Population, and Mexican Foreign-Born Population**

| Indicator | Total U.S. Population | Mexican-Origin Population | Mexican Foreign- Born Population |
|---|---|---|---|
| **Education, 1994*** | | | |
| % Less than High School | 19% | 53% | 71% |
| % with at least high school | 81% | 47% | 29% |
| **Income, 1989** | | | |
| % Families in Poverty | 10% | 23% | 27% |
| Median Family Income | $34,213 | $24,119 | $21,585 |
| **Income, 1993** | | | |
| % Individuals in Poverty | 14% | 30% | 36% |
| **Labor Force, 1990** | | | |
| *Employment by Type* | | | |
| Managerial | 26% | 12% | 6% |
| Technical, Sales, | | | |
| Administrative Assist. | 32% | 24% | 13% |
| Service | 13% | 19% | 21% |
| Production, Craft, Repair | 11% | 14% | 16% |
| Operators, Laborers | 15% | 25% | 32% |
| Farming, Fishing, Forestry | 2% | 7% | 13% |
| **Labor Force, 1994** | | | |
| % Unemployed | 6% | 10% | 11% |
| % of Persons over 16 not | | | |
| in Labor Force | 33% | 32% | 34% |
| *Participation Rate by Sex* | | | |
| Male | 75% | 59% | 82% |
| Female | 53% | – | – |

*Attainment levels for the population 25 years and older.

Sources: U.S. Bureau of the Census: CPH-L-150; C-PHL-148; CP-2-1; Statistical
        Abstract 1993, 1995; CPS 1994

subsequent generations to be living in single-parent households, a condition linked strongly to poverty.

## Employment Status

Unemployment among the Mexican foreign-born was 11 percent in 1994, almost twice the national rate of 6 percent (Table 4.5). For the Mexican-origin population, the unemployment rate was 10 percent. The percentage of persons over age 16 not in the labor force was about the same for all three groups. Higher labor force participation rates were found for men in the Mexican-origin population compared with the total for all U.S. men, 82 percent vs. 75 percent, while lower rates were found for Mexican-origin women compared to all U.S. women, 53 percent vs. 59 percent (Table 4.5).

Much higher percentages of Mexican foreign-born are concentrated in blue-collar and agricultural occupations and much lower percentages are found in managerial positions compared to the total U.S. population (Table 4.5). The Mexican-origin population falls in between: a higher percentage in managerial positions and lower percentage in blue-collar occupations compared to the Mexican foreign-born.

## Political Participation

To be able to vote, immigrants must become naturalized citizens. Both the number of people being naturalized and the number of immigrants applying for citizenship has increased dramatically in the past few years. Applications nearly doubled between 1991 and 1993 and may increase by as much again, exceeding 1 million by the end of fiscal year 1996 (De Vita 1996). Naturalization rates are low for citizens from countries that are historically and geographically closest to the United States (Martin and Midgley 1994). As seen in Figure 4.7, after Canada, Mexico has the lowest percentage of legal immigrants who arrived during the 1970s and were subsequently naturalized (19 percent). Naturalization records suggest that Mexican immigrants arriving later have relatively low naturalization rates as well (INS, February 1996). Although the rates are low, Mexico was the country of birth of the largest number (39,310) of naturalized citizens in 1994 (ibid.).

## The Case of California

With such a strong concentration of Mexican immigrants and Mexican-Americans, California serves as a good example of how Mexican migration can affect the demographic landscape in the United States at the state and local levels.

**Figure 4.7**

**Immigrants Admitted, Calendar Year 1970-79 by Selected Country of Birth and Naturalizations of Those Immigrants, PV 1970-94**

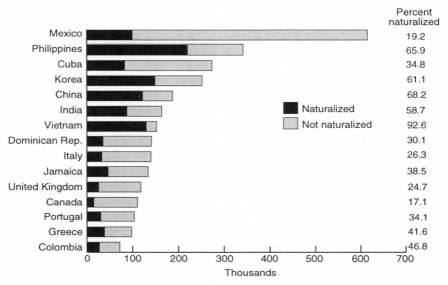

| | Percent naturalized |
|---|---|
| Mexico | 19.2 |
| Philippines | 65.9 |
| Cuba | 34.8 |
| Korea | 61.1 |
| China | 68.2 |
| India | 58.7 |
| Vietnam | 92.6 |
| Dominican Rep. | 30.1 |
| Italy | 26.3 |
| Jamaica | 38.5 |
| United Kingdom | 24.7 |
| Canada | 17.1 |
| Portugal | 34.1 |
| Greece | 41.6 |
| Colombia | 46.8 |

Note: China includes mainland China and Taiwan.

Source: INSF February 1996.

Between 1970 and 1990, immigrants and their native-born children accounted for nearly 70 percent of the state's total growth (McCarthy 1996). Mexicans have played a significant part in this process. For decades, California has been the major receiving area for Mexican migrants. In fiscal year 1993, half (52,848) of all legal Mexican immigrants to the United States went to California (State of California, October 1995).

A comparison of the total state population and the Mexican-origin population within the state (Table 4.6) suggests that Mexican immigration is having, and will continue to have, a significant impact on California's demographic profile:

• In 1990, 1 in 5 Californians was of Mexican origin. Nationally, 1 in 20 people was of Mexican origin (CCSCE 1992).

• Over half (53 percent) of the Mexican-origin population is under age 25 compared with 37 percent of the state as a whole. The average number of children ever born to Mexican-origin women is higher than for women overall in California (3 and 2 respectively). The younger age

## Table 4.6
## Comparison of the Total Population of California and
## the Mexican-Origin Population of California, 1990

| Indicator | Total Population of California | Mexican-Origin Population |
|---|---|---|
| % Foreign-born | 22% | 43% |
| % Under 25 years old | 37% | 53% |
| Median age | 31.7 years | 23.6 years |
| % of Population 25 or older with a high school degree or higher | 76% | 41% |
| % of Families living in poverty | 9% | 19% |
| Median family income, 1989 | $40, 559 | $27,411 |
| Average family size | 3.3 persons | 4.3 persons |
| Children ever-born to ever-married women | 2.07 | 3.05 |
| % Unemployed | 6.6% | 10.8% |
| % of the population 5 years and older reporting that they do not speak English "very well" | 16% | 43% |

Source: U.S. Bureau of the Census  CP-2-6

structure and high fertility of the Mexican-origin population is contributing to a California that is not aging as fast as the rest of the United
States (CCSCE 1992, State of California, April 1995).

- The Mexican-origin population is less educated and poorer than the
state population as a whole. It also suffers from higher unemployment.
The percentage reporting that they do not speak English very well is
about 2-1/2 times higher than for the state population as a whole (43
vs. 16 percent).

The state will continue to experience strong growth in total numbers, and
in the size of the Hispanic population, 80 percent of which is of Mexican origin

(CCSCE 1992). Demographers project that by the year 2020, the Hispanic and non-Hispanic white populations will converge, each accounting for 42 percent of the total population (State of California 1993). Hispanics are likely to account for nearly 30 percent of the state's labor force by 2000 (CCSCE 1992). Both natural increase (births minus deaths) and immigration factor significantly into California's growth. As already noted, immigration of Mexicans to California is strong. However, in 1993, the number of births to women of Mexican origin in California (221, 905) was four times the number of legal immigrants from Mexico who came to California (52, 858) (NCHS 1995; State of California, January 1995). This comparison indicates that presently, fertility is having an especially strong impact on the growth of the Mexican-origin and Hispanic population in California.[3]

California's school system will continue to experience large inflows of children of Mexican origin. By 2003, Hispanic children are expected to account for 50 percent of all students in California's public elementary and secondary schools, up from 38 percent today (State of California 1995; CCSCE 1992). Most of these Hispanic children will be of Mexican origin, given current immigration and fertility patterns.

The Mexican-origin population in California is more widely distributed across the state than many other immigrant groups, but in general tends to be more concentrated in the southern region of the state (State of California, October 1995; CCSCE 1992). Recent Mexican immigrants conform to this same distribution pattern (ibid.). However, the distribution pattern in Los Angeles suggests a tendency for the Mexican-origin population to be fairly segregated from other racial and ethnic groups within communities (Allen and Turner 1996).

Many of California's rural communities have undergone significant demographic changes over the past few decades through the influx and flow of Mexican farm workers and their families. Some experts even talk of the "Mexicanization"—not mechanization—of California farm labor (Palerm 1992). Mexican farm workers are overwhelmingly male, relatively young, and have low levels of formal education (Howenstine 1996, Kissam 1992, Pellet 1994), though there is some indication that farm workers are becoming more diverse. More women, older workers, and people from non-traditional sending communities in Mexico are joining the farm worker labor force (Palerm 1994).

## Future Trends

While it is difficult to quantify the extent to which Mexican immigration will have an impact on the U.S. population in the future, a few trends are certain.

- The Mexican-origin population in the United States will grow more rapidly than the United States population as a whole. The Census Bureau estimates that it is growing at a rate five times faster than the U.S. population (U.S. Bureau of the Census 1992).

- Barring dramatic changes in U.S. policies, immigration will remain strong at least in the short term. U.S. immigration policy increases the likelihood of continued immigration from Mexico. As more Mexican foreign-born people in the United States become citizens, they will be able to reunite their families more easily through legal immigration mechanisms. Many experts assume illegal immigration will continue at high levels as long as the Mexican economy is unable to absorb the growing Mexican labor force, and the wage gaps between the two countries remain wide. NAFTA and other economic measures are expected to increase illegal immigration in the short term, but lead to declines in the long term (Massey and Espinosa 1996, Heppel and Torres 1995, Martin 1994, Dumas 1994, Cornelius and Martin 1993).

- The effects of the increase in the Mexican-origin population will be felt most strongly at the local and community levels in a few states and metropolitan areas. It will continue to alter the ethnic and racial composition of these areas if current patterns and trends persist.

- Growth of the Mexican work force in the United States will continue. Some experts estimate that it will increase annually by 114,000–138,000 workers over the 1990s (Dumas 1994). Such increases are likely to have a significant effect on the absolute increases in numbers of the U.S. labor force, but not on the size of the labor force as a whole as shown in Figure 8 (Arriaga 1994).

As discussed in this chapter, a myriad of demographic, economic, social, political, and cultural factors affect the size, composition and distribution of the Mexican-origin population that is now part of the U.S. population. It is difficult to predict how these factors will interact to affect the future of this population, based on available information. How we measure race and ethnicity will make a difference. For example, because of inter-ethnic marriage and for other reasons, it will become increasingly difficult to predict how people with at least part of their ancestry from Mexico will identify themselves (Fix and Passel 1994) or even what "Hispanic" may mean in the future.

**Figure 4.8**

**Projected Population Ages 15-64 in the United States,
With or Without Migration, 1990-2020**

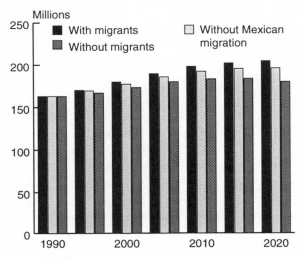

Source: Arriaga 1994

## Conclusion

This chapter has examined the demographic and socioeconomic characteristics of the Mexican-origin and Mexican foreign-born population in the United States and their implications for the demographic profile of the U.S. population. This review suggests that:

- Mexican immigration is playing an important role in the growth, distribution, and composition of the U.S. population; however, its impact is strongest in a small number of states and cities.

- Today, the majority of legal Mexican immigrants are granted permanent resident status as family members.

- Legal Mexican immigrants have comprised about 14 percent of all legal immigrants per year in recent years. Mexicans account for a much larger percentage of undocumented immigrants; in 1992, it was estimated that they accounted for nearly 40 percent of undocumented immigrants residing in the United States.

- The Mexican-origin population within the United States will continue to grow more rapidly than the U.S. population as a result of its age structure, childbearing patterns and immigration.

- The Mexican foreign-born population has a lower level of education, higher level of poverty and lower level of English proficiency compared with the Mexican-origin population as a whole, and the education levels of more recent immigrants are lower than for earlier immigrants.

- Research findings on the educational and socio-economic situation of the Mexican-origin population are mixed. The percentage of children of Mexican origin living in poverty is declining by each generation, although a greater number live in single-parent families. Educational attainment is also lower for third and higher generation Mexican-origin children compared to second generation children.

Immigration policies have had an important impact on the volume and characteristics of Mexican immigration to the United States and the effects of these policies on the U.S. population will continue regardless of policy changes. For example, even if policy changes were instituted tomorrow to slow the flow of immigration from Mexico, the Mexican-origin population will continue to grow much more rapidly than the U.S. population as a result of population momentum. Thus, this group will represent an increasingly larger percentage of the U.S. population in the future.

The impact of Mexican immigration, as with other immigration to the United States, is most keenly felt at present in a small number of states and metropolitan areas. California, Texas and Illinois are home to the majority of Mexican immigrants and their descendants. The impact on California is especially striking. It is the destination of half of all legal Mexican immigrants and more than half (60 percent) of undocumented immigrants live there. Further, it continues to be the destination of the majority of undocumented farm workers, who add to the overall presence of the Mexican-origin population.

There is a serious shortage of data on the demography of immigrants to the United States. We have made some general observations about the links between Mexican immigrant and U.S. population profiles, but have refrained from drawing more specific conclusions given the nature of available data. There is a need for information that can better distinguish legal from undocumented immigrants and migrants, and their respective social, demographic, and economic characteristics in greater detail and over time. Such data are essential for designing policies that can facilitate the effective adaptation of legal immigrants to this country and this country's ability to adapt effectively to its immigrant populations.

---

### Mexico: A Demographic Snapshot

Mexico's population is a third the size of the U.S. population, but Mexico's rate of natural increase is about triple that of the U.S. population. At the current growth rate, the Mexican population will double in 32 years. Though its rate is likely to slow in the future, the Mexican population is still expected to keep growing rapidly in the coming decades, as the country continues to go through a demographic transition.

In 1996, the Mexican population was estimated to be about 94.8 million. Like many developing countries, Mexico's population is very young, with about 36 percent of the population under age 15, and 4 percent over age 65 (PRB 1996).

The average fertility rate is about 3.1 children per woman, down from an average of 5.9 in the mid-1970s (Dumas 1994). Within the population, this average varies widely. Among indigenous ethnic groups, women have an average of 5.4 children, while non-indigenous women average 2.6. Women without schooling average 5.4 children, while women with more than an elementary education average 2 children (Gutierrez 1994).

Mexican women and men marry earlier than Americans and typically start working earlier as well; 12 is the official minimum age of the working population (16 in the United States). The combination of labor force participation, a large cohort of young people, and a high population growth rate is expected to lead to increasing numbers of people entering the labor force each year (Dumas 1994). These numbers challenge the Mexican economy's ability to meet employment needs. For example, between 1988 and 1994, the total number of paid jobs rose by only 1.6 million, while the economically active population rose by nearly 7 million (*Migration News* 1995, NAFTA and *Inter-American Monitor* 1995).

---

## Notes

1. IRCA granted legal status to 3.1 million undocumented immigrants who had either been living in the United States prior to 1982 or had worked in agriculture in the United States for three months in the previous year. The program is now in its final stages.

2. The three principal sources of data on U.S. immigration are the U.S. Bureau of the Census, the Immigration and Naturalization Service (INS) and special surveys. Each

has its advantages and disadvantages. Census data provide information on a variety of population and socioeconomic characteristics of the U.S. population over time. The data distinguish citizens from non-citizens, but do not distinguish between legal and illegal immigrants. The INS provides information on the immigration status of individuals, their age, sex, country of origin and intended place of residence in the United States for each fiscal year. Data from border control efforts, such as apprehension data, provide some information on illegal immigration flows, but are limited. INS information is perhaps most useful for examining the characteristics of, and changes in, immigration flows, as opposed to the characteristics of individual immigrants. Finally, special surveys can provide much more detailed information on the characteristics of particular groups of immigrants, but not on the populations of immigrants as a whole. It can be difficult to generalize to the total immigrant population from these surveys.

3. This is not to suggest that each year there are four times more Mexican-Americans born in California than Mexican foreign-born coming in. The number of immigrants given here only accounts for legal immigrants, and does not include the substantial number of undocumented immigrants and migrants who come to California each year.

# References

Allen, James P., and Eugene Turner. 1996. Ethnic Diversity and Segregation in the New Los Angeles. In *EthniCity: Geographic Perspectives on Ethnic Change in Modern Cities*. Eds. Curtis C. Rossman, Hans Dieter Laux, and Gunter Thieme. Boston, MA: Rowman and Littlefield Publishers, pp. 130.

Arriaga, Eduardo E. 1994. Past Demographic Characteristics and Current Population Implications of NAFTA Countnes. U.S. Bureau of the Census. Paper presented at the Population Association of America Conference, 1994.

Acevedo, Dolores, and Thomas J. Espenshade. 1992. Implications of a North American Free Trade Agreement for Mexican Migration into the United States. *Population and Development Review*. Vol. 18, no. 4. December, pp. 729-744.

Bean, Frank D., et al. 1994. Educational and Sociodemographic Incorporation Among Hispanic Immigrants to the United States. In *Immigration and Ethnicity: The Integration of America's Newest Arrivals*. Eds. Barry Edmonston and Jeffrey S. Passel. Washington, DC: The Urban Institute Press, pp. 73-95.

Bean, Frank D., et. al. 1990. Post-IRCA Changes in the Volume and Composition of Undocumented Migration to the United States: An Assessment Based on Apprehensions Data. In *Undocumented Migration to the United States: IRCA and the Experience of the 1980s*. Eds. Frank D. Bean, Barry Edmonston, and Jeffrey S. Passel. Washington, DC: The Urban Institute Press, pp. 111-158.

Berkowitz, Rosalind E. 1996. Family Strategies and the High School Completion of Young Latina Mothers. Paper Presented at the Annual PAA meeting, Miami, May.

Bradshaw, Benjamin S., and W. Parker Frisbie. 1992. Mortality of Mexican Americans and Mexican Immigrants: Comparisons with Mexico. In *Demographic Dynamics of the U.S.-Mexico Border*. Eds. John R. Weeks and Roberto Ham-Chande. El Paso,

142 ALENE H. GELBARD AND MARION CARTER

Tex.: Texas Western Press, pp. 125-150.

CPS. 1994. Current Population Survey. See V.S. Bureau of the Census.

Center for Continuing Studies of the California Economy (CCSCE). 1992. *California Population Characteristics—1992 Edition.* Palo Alto, Calif.: Center for Continuing Study of the California Economy.

Cornelius, Wayne A., and Phillip L. Martin. Fall 1993. The Uncertain Connection: Free Trade and Rural Mexican Migration to the United States. *International Migration Review.* Vol. 27, pp. 484512.

De Vita, Carol. March 1996. The U.S. at Mid-Decade. *Population Bulletin,* Vol. 50, no. 4. Washington, DC: Population Reference Bureau, Inc.

Donato, Katherine M. and Shawn Malia Kanaiapuni. October 1994. Poverty, Demographic Change, and the Migration of Mexican Women to the United States. In the published papers of the IUSSP Committee on Gender and Population's seminar: Women, Poverty, and Demographic Change. Oaxaca, Mexico.

Dumas, Jean. March 1994. The Demographic Situation of Mexico at the Signing of NAFTA. In *Report on the Demographic Situation of Canada 1993.* Statistics Canada Ottawa, Ontario, pp. 109*217.*

Edmonston, Barry, Jeffrey S. Passel, and Frank D. Bean. 1990. Perceptions and Estimates of the Undocumented Migration to the United States. In *Undocumented Migration to the United States: IRCA and the Experience of the 1980s.* Eds. Frank D. Bean, Barry Edmonston, and Jeffrey S. Passel. Washington, DC: The Urban Institute Press, pp. 11-31.

Fix, Michael, and Jeffrey Passel. 1994. *Immigration and Immigrants: Setting the Record Straight.* Washington, DC: The Urban Institute Press.

Frey, William. April 1996. Immigration, Internal Out-Movement, and Demographic Balkanization in America: New Evidence for the 1990s. Population Studies Center, University of Michigan. Research Report No. 96-364.

Frisbie, W. Parker. May 6, 1996. Personal Communication.

Frisbie, W. Parker, and Frank D. Bean. 1995. The Latino Family in Comparative Perspective: Trends and Current Conditions. In *American Families: Issues in Race and Ethnicity.* Ed. Cardell K. Jacobson. New York: Garland Publishing, pp. 29-71.

Guendelman, Sylvia. August 6, 1994. Mexican Women in the United States. *The Lancet.* Vol. 334 , p. 352.

Gutierrez, Francisco Javier. 1994. The Demographic Impact in Mexico of the North American Free Trade Agreement. National Institute of Statistics of Mexico. Paper presented at the Population Association of America Meeting. Denver, April.

Hansen, Kristin, and Arnara Bachu. August 1995. The Foreign-Born Population: 1994. U.S. Bureau of the Census. Current Population Reports, p. 20-486.

Heim, Mary, and Nancy Austin. Fertility of Immigrant Women in California. Prepared for the Annual PAA Meeting, San Francisco, April 1995.

Heppel, Monica L., and Luis R. Torres. 1995. Migration in the Post-NAFTA Era: Policy Issues for the United States and Mexico. Hemispheric Migration Project. Center for Inter-Cultural Education and Development, Georgetown University, September.

Howenstine, Erick. 1996. Expectations and Reality: Mexican Migration to Washington State. *MigrationWorld*. Vol. 24, No. 1/2, pp. 16-19.

Immigration and Naturalization Service. August 27, 1990. Provisional Legalization Application Statistics. Statistics Division, Office of Plans and Analysis. Washington, DC.

———. *Statistical Yearbook 1994*. February 1996, and various years.

———. Immigration to the United States in the Fiscal Year 1995. March 1996.

Kissam, Ed. An Outline of the Situation of Migrant Farmworkers in the United States. *Migration World*. Vol. 20, No. 4, 1992, pp. 31-33.

Lapham, Susan. From Melting Pot to Mosaic: The U.S. Foreign-Born Population: What the Census Tells Us. U.S. Bureau of the Census. Presented at the Population Reference Bureau, March 17, 1993.

Martin, John. Immigration Contributes Over Half of U.S. Population Growth. *Immigration Review*, Center for Immigration Studies. No. 23, Fall 1995.

Martin, Philip and Elizabeth Midgley. 1994. Immigration to the United States. *Population Bulletin*. Vol. 49, No. 2. Washington, DC: Population Reference Bureau, Inc., September.

Massey, Doug, and Kristin E. Espinosa. What's Driving Mexico-U.S. Migration? A Theoretical, Empirical, and Policy Analysis. Paper presented at America Becoming/Becoming American: International Migration to the United States. Conference organized by the Social Science Research Council, Committee on International Migration, Sanibel Island, Florida, January 18-21, 1996.

McCarthy, Kevin F. Immigration: Problem to Solve or Issue to Manage? RAND Corporation, Internet Homepage, 1996.

Migration News. Mexico: Immigration and NAFTA.. University of California, Davis, November 1995.

Montafio, Luz Maria Valdez de, and Robert Smith. Mexican Migration to the New York City Metropolitan Area: An Analysis of Selected Socio-Demographic Traits and the Links Being Formed between a Mexican Sending Region and New York. Tinker Foundation report. January 1994.

NAFTA and Inter-Am Monitor. Unemployment Pushes Workers North. October 20, 1995.

National Center for Health Statistics (NCHS). Monthly Vital Statistics Report, Vol. 44, No. 3 (5). September 21, 1995.

National Institute of Child Health and Human Development (NICHD). Social and Economic Factors Affecting Undocumented Migration from Mexico. In *T.I.: NICHD Research on Today's Issues*. May 1996.

Newnan, Kristin E., and Marta Tienda. 1994. The Settlement and Secondary Migration Patterns of Legalized Immigrants: Insights from Administrative Records. In *Immigration and Ethnicity: The Integration of America's Newest Arrivals*. Eds. Barry Edmonston and Jeffrey S. Passel. Washington, DC: The Urban Institute Press. pp. 187-226.

Palerm. Juan Vicente. A Season in the Life of a Migrant Farrn Worker in California In Crosscultural Medicine—A Decade Later [Special Issue]. *The Western Journal of Medicine*. Vol. 157, No. 3, September 1992, pp. 362-366.

Immigrant and Migrant Farm Workers in the Santa Maria Valley, California Center for Chicano Studies and the Department of Anthropology, University of California, Santa Barbara, California, September 1994.

Pellet, Lea B. Still Sons of the Shaking Earth: Mexican and Guatemalans in the East Coast Migrant Labor Stream. *Migration World.* Vol. 22, Nos. 2/3. 1994, pp. 28-31.

Population Reference Bureau. 1996 World Population Data Sheet.

State of California, Department of Finance. Population Projections By Race/Ethnicity for California and Its Counties, 1990-2040, Report 93 P-1. Sacramento, Calif., April 1993.

———. K-12 Graded Public School Enrollment by Ethnicity, History and Projection — 1995 Series.

———. Legal Foreign Immigration to Califomia: Size and Characteristics of the Flow According to the INS Statistics for 1993. October 1995.

Tumer, Scott. Single Parenthood Hurts Immigrants' Economic Gains. *Population Today,* Population Reference Bureau, Inc. Vol. 24, No. 5, May 1996, pp. 4-5.

U.S. Bureau of the Census. 1990 Census of Population and Housing, United States. CP-2-1.

———. 1990 Census of Population and Housing, California CP-2-6.

———. 1990 Profiles of the Foreign-Born Population: Selected Characteristics by Place of Birth. CPH-L-148.

———. 1990 Profiles of the Hispanic Population: Selected Characteristics by Hispanic Origin. CPH-L-150.

———. Current Population Survey (CPS), March 1994. Various tables. Census Bureau Internet Homepage.

———. Ethnic and Hispanic Branch. 1990 CPH-L-90, 1990 Census Special Tabulations. 1992.

———. *Statistical Abstract of the United States,* 1995.

———. Current population statistics. Internet Homepage. 1996.

U.S. Commission on Immigration Reform. U.S. Immigration Policy: Restoring Credibility. 1994 Report to Congress, September 1994.

U.S. Department of State, Immigrant Visa Control and Reporting Division. Personal Communication, May 20, 1996.

Warren, Robert. Annual Estimates of Nonimmigrant Overstays in the United States: 1985 to 1988. In *Undocunented Migration to the United States: IRCA and the Experience of the 1980s.* Eds. Frank D. Bean, Barry Edmonston, and Jeffrey S. Passel. Washington, DC: The Urban Institute Press, 1990, pp. 77-110.

———. Estimates of the Unauthorized Immigrant Population Residing in the United States, by Country of Origin and State of Residence: Oct. 1992. Immigration and Naturalization Service, 1994.

# 5.
# Fiscal Impacts of Mexican Migration to the United States

*Susan Gonzalez Baker, Robert G. Cushing, and Charles W. Haynes*

T his chapter critically assesses the methodology and findings of 15 recent studies of the fiscal impact of immigration to the United States. With important exceptions, the literature concludes that the net effect of immigrants and immigration is negative. Yet, wide disparities exist among estimates of the magnitude of the impact. These disparities are often the result of controversy about population measurement, about quantifying costs and benefits, and about choosing which costs and benefits to include in the analysis in the first place. Some studies deal with only undocumented immigrants, some with only legal immigrants, and others with both. As analyses move from state/local to national aggregates, the complexity of the estimation problem increases and the accumulation of error escalates, yielding substantially different results. At one end of the spectrum is Huddle's (1993) study, which concludes that immigrants imposed a net cost of $42.5 billion on U.S. taxpayers in 1992. At the other extreme, Passel's (1994) rebuttal argues that Huddle's revenue estimates are erroneous and egregiously low while his cost estimates are inflated, concluding that "today's immigrants generate a surplus of at least $25-30 billion," a $70-billion disparity between two researchers looking at the same data.

The remaining studies generally show that immigrants use more in social services than they pay for through taxes. This is particularly true of studies targeting undocumented immigrants, and particularly true when the comparison is drawn at the state or local level. None of the studies provide detailed information on the fiscal impact of specific national-origin populations. County/metropolitan and state data, drawn primarily from Los Angeles and San Diego Counties and from the states of California and Texas, give some indication of the fiscal impact of Mexican migration, but methodological issues compromise the utility of these estimates for anything more than the broadest interpretation. We conclude this assessment with a review of six persistent challenges that bear attention in any attempt to establish a serious basis for policymaking or theory-building on questions of fiscal costs and benefits associated with U.S. immigration.

## The Fiscal Impact of Immigration: What We Think We Know

Fiscal effects of immigration are a subset of the economic effects that have interested researchers and policymakers throughout U.S. history. Indeed, many of the earliest restrictionist measures adopted by Congress excluded persons likely to become dependent on the state or otherwise drain the public purse.[1] However, little seems to have been said about illegal immigration as a peculiar problem, and Mexican immigration was of relatively minor concern. What concern did exist is evidenced by the references to Mexican migration in the 1911 report of the Dillingham Commission, a federal body dedicated to overhauling the immigration system in keeping with U.S. interests.

> While the Mexicans are not easily assimilated, this is of no very great importance as long as most of them return to their native land after a short time. They give rise to little race friction, but do impose upon the community a large number of dependents, misdemeanants, and petty criminals where they settle in considerable number. (as quoted in Bustamante, 1978)

> In the case of the Mexican, he is less desirable as a citizen than as a laborer. (U.S. Congress, *Senate Immigration Commission Report*, Document No. 747, 61st Congress, 3rd Session, 1911: 690-91, as quoted in Calavita, 1994)

Thus, the concern then, as now, was on how to limit the fiscal impact of welfare dependency and social costs imposed by some types of immigrants.

That a numerical calculation can actually be attached to the costs and benefits of any particular immigrant group is a contemporary notion and a derivative of the economic cost-benefit analysis that has dominated the entire domestic policy agenda in recent decades. The attraction is due, in part, to the apparent simplicity of totaling up the social costs of immigrants, for example, as measured by public services consumed and by subtracting that sum from the tax revenue they generate. But, there are serious problems to overcome in this effort. Although indicators of public expenditures and revenues are readily available, they must be selected from a potpourri of possible candidates at local, state, and federal levels. No clear standard on what to include is yet apparent, although more consensus appears on the cost than on the revenue side in the studies we have encountered.

Furthermore, any calculation focusing on undocumented immigrants is especially problematic given the difficulty in estimating the size of the target population. Many of the estimates we encountered in our review were imputations or best guesses, sometimes founded on a plausible argument, but far from serious estimates in a statistical sense. Thus, if research results are ideologically rather than theoretically driven, almost any result is possible. In a recent study, for example, Huddle (1993) "estimated" a net cost of $42.5 billion annually from all immigrants, legal and undocumented, residing in the United States in 1992. Looking at the same data, in a challenge to Huddle, Passel (1994) estimated a net surplus as high as $30 billion—leaving a $72.5 billion difference for policymakers to ponder. The two studies probably mark the upper and lower bounds of fiscal impact, but, combined, they provide a window large enough to justify almost any immigration policy imaginable. Academic support weighs in on Passel's side, for reasons discussed below, but Huddle's work is more often cited among influential policymakers. Rather than accepting the two figures as marking extrema, one extreme or the other is taken as a real-life estimate.

If this task is an exercise in futility, why do social scientists direct attention to it? First, although the methodological problems are considerable, they are not insurmountable. Second, although the intellectual roots of the research question often take a back seat to things political, important theoretical issues, nonetheless, lie at the core of the research question—questions about how U.S. society distributes its resources and its responsibilities across its diverse constituencies. Finally, the policy matter is important. Containing government expenditure is a real problem in an era of mounting deficits, and it is yet unclear how immigration will affect that situation.

With these points in mind, we have focused on 15 studies, 13 of which have tried to generate a net figure for the fiscal impact of immigrants upon the United States (see Table 5.1 for a general profile of each study according to its

**Table 5.1**
**Profile of Studies Reviewed**

| Study | Methodology | Primary Data Sources | Level of Analysis (Scope) | Immigrant Status |
|---|---|---|---|---|
| Huddle (1985) | static | federal government cost-benefit analysis | national data, Census | legal undocumented |
| Huddle (1993) | static | federal government cost-benefit analysis | national data, Census | legal undocumented legalized |
| Passel (1994) | critical review of Huddle (1993) | Los Angeles County, federal government data legalized | national undocumented | legal |
| Clark et al. (1994) | static cost-benefit analysis | INS, Census, state government data | state and local (7 states) | undocumented |
| GAO (1994) | static cost-benefit analysis | California state data, Urban Institute report | state (California) | undocumented |
| Romero et al. (1994) | static cost-benefit analysis | California Finance Dept., California Office of Planning and Research, INS | state (California) | undocumented |
| Huddle (1994) | static cost-benefit analysis | Census, federal government data, Texas state data | state (Texas) | legal undocumented legalized |
| Paral (1996) | static cost analysis analysis | Latino Institute Illinois Immigrant Policy Project | state (Illinois) | all |
| Passel & Clark (1996) | static benefit analysis analysis | Urban institute Illinois Immigrant Policy Project | state (Illinois) | all |
| Espenshade & King (1996) | static cost-benefit analysis | Census, local/state federal government data | state (New Jersey) | all |

**Table 5.1** (Continued)

| Study | Methodology | Primary Data Sources | Level of Analysis (Scope) | Immigrant Status |
|-------|-------------|----------------------|---------------------------|------------------|
| Gumbleton et al. (1996) | static cost-benefit analysis | state government data | state (California) | all |
| LA County ISD (1992) | static cost-benefit analysis | INS, Census, California state records, non-profit surveys | county (Los Angeles) | post-1979 legal, undocumented, legalized, citizen children of undocumented immigrants |
| Parker and Rea (1993) | static cost-benefit analysis | interviews, state and local government records, INS data | county (San Diego) | undocumented |
| Borjas and Hilton (1996) | regression model (longitudinal) | Survey of Income and Program Participation | households (national) | all |
| Van Hook, Glick, & Bean (1996) | algebraic calculation (longitudinal) | 1980 & 1990 PUMS, March CPS 1994 & 1995 | households, families, individuals (national) | all |

methodology, data sources, level of analysis and geographic scope, and immigration status of the target population). Thirteen of the studies were carried out in approximately the same time period and give an indication of the variation in results that are possible. To simplify comparisons across space and time, where possible we summarize the estimated net cost-benefit per immigrant and per capita for each study (see the bottom two rows of Tables 5.3-5.5, which present the estimated net dollar costs-benefits per immigrant and per capita). Four studies are not included in the comparison tables. The methodology used in the study by Gumbleton et al. (1996), on California immigrants is sufficiently unclear to make inclusion in the comparison tables difficult. The study by Espenshade and King (1996) presents some interesting comparisons between native-born and immigrant populations in New Jersey in 1980 but is not included in the comparison tables since its methodology differed substantially from other studies by focusing on household costs and benefits rather than on individuals'. Two other studies, Borjas and Hilton (1996) and Van Hook et al. (1996), also take a different approach from the others by focusing on household data drawn from national surveys to examine differential welfare participation rates and do not pretend to be cost-benefit analyses of the fiscal effects of immigration.

Two of the fiscal impact studies reviewed here focus on the county/metropolitan level. Both center on southern California, where high levels of Mexican immigration, legal and undocumented, are evident. Eight of the studies examine state data. Four studies include data from California, Texas, and Arizona, states in which the immigrant population is heavily Hispanic, primarily Mexican in origin. Florida, Illinois, New Jersey, and New York are represented in other studies. The national studies are frequently cited in the public debate about Mexican immigration, even though they are intended to estimate total immigration impact. None of the studies provides a detailed analysis of immigrants by country of origin or ethnic group. Hence, none of the studies provides direct evidence about Mexican migrants. With the exception of the household studies by Borjas and Hilton (1996) and Van Hook et al. (1996) and possibly the Gumbleton et al. (1996) study's attempt to look at life-cycle effects, none of the studies is longitudinal. Indeed, most are descriptive and do not attempt theory-driven hypothesis testing. Few provide a clear reference point for comparative purposes.[2]

## Cost-Benefit Studies at the National Level

Huddle (1985) begins with a 1983 Immigration and Naturalization Service (INS) report in an attempt to measure economic costs of immigration by including fiscal considerations. Huddle's use of the INS report is indicative of the methodological problems and distortions that can creep into fiscal impact analysis if assumptions are not carefully checked by independent empirical evidence. (A corrected and amended version of Huddle's main table is present as Table 5.2[3]).

The received wisdom at the time of the INS report was that 6 million undocumented immigrants were in the United States. Huddle inflated that estimate to 9 million. Since that time the effect of the amnesty provisions of the Immigration and Control Act of 1986 have provided a basis for more realistic estimates, and Huddle's figures and the early INS estimates have been roundly criticized as overstatements.[4] The INS now estimates that 3.4 million undocumented immigrants were living in the United States in 1992, and the U.S. Census Bureau weighed in with an estimate of 3.5 to 4.0 million in 1994. Huddle's job displacement costs are based on an undocumented labor force as large as 5.5 million,

## Table 5.2
## Estimated Costs of Illegal Immigration to U.S. Taxpayers

| Cost Categories | 1 million illegal aliens | 3 million illegal aliens | 6 million* illegal aliens | 9 million illegal aliens | 12 million illegal aliens |
|---|---|---|---|---|---|
| Job displacement | 1,500.0 | 4,500.0 | 9,000.0 | 13,500.0 | 18,000.0 |
| Education (public) | 262.2 | 816.6 | 1,600.0 | 2,400.0 | 3,300.0 |
| Unemployment benefits | 181.4 | 544.2 | 1,100.0 | 1,600.0 | 2,200.0 |
| Welfare | 115.0 | 345.0 | 690.0 | 1,000.0 | 1,400.0 |
| Health care | 92.9 | 278.7 | 557.4 | 836.1 | 1,100.0 |
| Law enforcement (Federal, State, Local) | 91.6 | 274.8 | 549.6 | 824.4 | 1100.0 |
| Total in millions of dollars | *2,243.1* | *6,759.3* | *1,3497.0* | *20,160.5* | *27,100.0* |
| Tax contributions | 995.0 | 2,985.0 | 5970.0 | 8,955.0 | 11,940.0 |
| Net (millions of dollars) | *-1,248.1* | *-3,774.3* | *-7,527.0* | *-11,205.5* | *-15,160.0* |
| Net less job displacement costs (millions of dollars) | *251.90* | *725.70* | *1,473.00* | *2,294.50* | *2,840.00* |

*Assumption of Simpson and Mazzoli immigration bills: 6 million illegal aliens

Illegal aliens include workers and dependents; cell entries are in millions of dollars.

"Source: Central Office, U.S. Immigration and Naturalization Service, Washington, D.C., Fall 1983"

Cited in Huddle 1985: 10 (the changes and corrections to the table cited by Huddle are in italics)

well above the estimates for the entire population (working-age and dependent) a decade later.

The 1992 INS estimates for Mexican undocumented immigrants were about 38 percent of the undocumented total, or 1.3 million Mexicans. Huddle's figures, in keeping with estimates of the day, set the Mexican share at approximately half of the total, with considerable implications for the bottom line in estimating the "Mexican" share of the total job displacement effect.

Job displacement costs were critical to Huddle's assessment of immigration costs. Job displacement is an economic, rather than a strictly fiscal, measure. When used alone, it ignores the positive economic consequences of undocumented immigration cited by other authors. Furthermore, Huddle's figures are extrapolated from a 1980 San Diego County study, where 20 percent of the population is of Latino origin, to the nation as a whole. It strains credulity to imagine that California, with 19.2 percent Latino residents in 1980 is comparable to Illinois, with 5.6 percent Latino-origin residents, or New York, New Jersey, and Florida, all of which had Latino populations smaller than 10 percent of their state totals.

Removing the job displacement figures from consideration to get at fiscal impact alone yields a net of revenues over costs in the INS table (see bottom row of Table 5.2). Yet even this reversal of Huddle's trend should be subject to considerable scrutiny. Each of the social cost indicators appears based on relationships asserted, not empirically demonstrated. It is unclear how the education figures are constructed, since the estimation technique for the number of undocumented schoolchildren is not presented. Although the U.S. Department of Education is identified as the source, no citation is provided. The unemployment benefits "estimates" are extrapolated to the total United States from an Illinois study in 1982. The welfare costs are extrapolated from an AFDC study in San Diego County; health care from figures for Los Angeles and San Diego counties; and law enforcement costs from Los Angeles County data. The taxes paid are extrapolated from the weighted averages of five estimates in 1980 and 1982, apparently drawn from Los Angeles and San Diego counties. Indicators for the nation as a whole are generated from this hodgepodge, but no truly national figures are available to assess immigration drain on public expenditure or contribution to public revenues.

Huddle used these figures as a basis for generating his own net cost estimates based on his own population imputations. He uses, without reasoned argument, a higher job displacement factor than anyone else at the time (65 percent, meaning 3.5 million legal workers were displaced by the "estimated" 5.5 million undocumented workers in the country at the time). By exaggerating the social costs and underestimating the revenues received from undocumented workers, Huddle came up with an estimate of $35 billion in costs and a net loss of $26 billion to the national treasury in 1982, nearly 2.5 times the $11 billion net loss estimated by the INS for an "estimated" 9 million-strong undocumented total population. This study may be far from the hard, empirical evidence that characterizes good scholarship, but it has been an attention-getter, and has set a standard of sorts. At best, the research depicts the upper bound of fiscal costs, but the political life of the research has exceeded its academic longevity and a non-fact has become part of the conventional wisdom.

Huddle (1993) examined the 1992 net costs of providing public assistance to immigrants who settled in the United States between 1970 and 1992. The author, funded by the Carrying Capacity Network, estimated the costs of 23 major federal, state, and local government assistance programs, including public education, county health care and social services, Medicaid, public higher education, bilingual/

limited-English programs, Supplemental Security Income, food stamps, housing, criminal justice/corrections, Aid to Families with Dependent Children, Earned Income Tax Credit, and unemployment compensation. Revenues included those from federal and excise taxes; state sales and excise taxes; the state lottery; and county sales and property taxes. Costs and contributions the author specifically identified as not being addressed were Social Security and Medicare, fraud and misrepresentation, administration, specialized city programs and revenues, indivisible government services (public goods), non-immigrants, commuter immigrants, lost revenues (foregone because of displaced workers), and costs to the environment.

This national-level study used data from 1991 government sources, including the U.S. Census, data from Los Angeles County, an article by Borjas and Jensen, and the *1992 Statistical Abstract* (for tax revenues). Huddle first calculated the annual nationwide cost of public assistance per beneficiary (for both citizens and immigrants) for each program. He then determined the probability of immigrant recipiency in each program by ascertaining the overall national recipiency rate and estimating the extent of variation in immigrant recipiency rates from the overall rate. Finally, he multiplied the probability of immigrant recipiency by the number of immigrants in the population to determine the number of immigrants receiving assistance.

The study encompassed legal, legalized (through amnesty), and undocumented immigrants. Huddle found that the poverty rate among immigrants is now 42.8 percent higher than that among natives and that immigrants are 13.5 percent more likely than natives to receive public assistance. According to Huddle, over 19 million immigrants settled, legally and illegally, in the United States between 1970 and 1992 and consumed $62.7 billion in public assistance, while paying $20.2 billion in taxes. Thus, Huddle concluded that the net cost of immigration to the United States in 1992 was $42.5 billion, a figure which he contended would only grow in the future. Included in that figure was $11.9 billion for costs of assistance to U.S. residents who became and/or remain unemployed because of the immigrant presence.

Passel (1994) reviewed and disputed the methodology used by Huddle. Passel argued that Huddle erred in estimating tax revenues generated by immigrants and inflated cost estimates. Passel then developed new revenue estimates from Los Angeles County and federal income tax data. He used Huddle's population estimates to ensure comparability between the two sets of estimates and concluded that Huddle (1993) overestimated fiscal costs by as much as $20 billion and underestimated revenues by approximately $50 billion. Thus, Passel concluded, immigrants actually contribute a net $25-to-$30-billion benefit to the country, or $1,055 per immigrant compared to Huddle's estimated cost of $1,589

Table 5.3

## Fiscal Cost-Benefit Studies at the National Level

| Author Year of estimates Immigrant population | INS 1983 Undoc. | Huddle 1983a Undoc. | Huddle 1992 Legal | New Legal | Undoc. | Amnest. | Total | Passel 1992b Legal | Undoc. | Amnest. | Total |
|---|---|---|---|---|---|---|---|---|---|---|---|
| Estimated number in immigrant population (millions) | 6 | 9 | 11.970 | 0.810 | 4.800 | 2.520 | 20.100 | 11.970 | 4.800 | 2.520 | 19.290 |
| Total population (millions) | 234.307 | 234.307 | 255.407 | 255.407 | 255.407 | 255.407 | 255.407 | 255.407 | 255.407 | 255.407 | 255.407 |
| Percent of immigrant population in total population | 2.6 | 3.8 | 4.7 | 0.3 | 1.9 | 1.0 | 7.9 | 4.7 | 1.9 | 1.0 | 7.6 |
| **Estimated fiscal costs ($millions)** | | | | | | | | | | | |
| Law enforcement | 595 | 824 | - | 77 | 1,030 | - | 1,107 | na | na | na | na |
| Education | 1,573 | 2,360 | 12,050 | 1,370 | 5,320 | 1,130 | 19,870 | na | na | na | na |
| Health | 557 | 836 | 13,340 | 449 | 2,500 | 2,080 | 18,369 | na | na | na | na |
| Welfare | 1,778 | 2,668 | 2,590 | 901 | 820 | 700 | 5,011 | na | na | na | na |
| Other | - | - | 6,800 | 480 | 420 | 1,200 | 8,900 | na | na | na | na |
| Total | 4,503 | 6,688 | 34,780 | 3,277 | 10,090 | 5,110 | 53,257 | 34,780 | 10,090 | 5,110 | 49,980 |
| **Estimated Revenues ($millions)** | | | | | | | | | | | |
| Federal | na | na | 9,113 | 617 | 867 | 830 | 11,427 | 37,783 | 3,740 | 3,745 | 45,268 |
| State | na | na | 5,425 | 367 | 1,335 | 1,007 | 8,134 | 13,038 | 2,146 | 1,600 | 16,784 |
| County | na | na | 1,181 | 80 | 284 | 204 | 1,749 | 6,483 | 1,087 | 709 | 8,279 |
| Total | 5,970 | 8,955 | 15,719 | 1,064 | 2,486 | 2,041 | 21,310 | 57,304 | 6,973 | 6,054 | 70,331 |

**Table 5.3** (Continued)

| Author Year of estimates | INS 1983 | Huddle 1983a | Huddle 1992 | | | | | Passel 1992b | | | |
|---|---|---|---|---|---|---|---|---|---|---|---|
| Immigrant population Estimated number in immigrant population (millions) | Undoc. | Undoc. | Legal | New Legal | Undoc. | Amnest. | Total | Legal | Undoc. | Amnest. | Total |
| | 6 | 9 | 11.970 | 0.810 | 4.800 | 2.520 | 20.100 | 11.970 | 4.800 | 2.520 | 19.290 |
| Net revenues - Fiscal costs ($millions) | 1,467 | 2,267 | (19,061)" | (2,213)" | (7,604)" | (3,069)" | (31,947)" | 22,524 | (3,117)" | 944 | 20,351 |
| Estimated net per immigrant ($) | 245 | 252 | (1,592)" | (2,732)" | (1,584)" | (1,218)" | (1,589)" | 1,882 | (649)" | 375 | 1,055 |
| Estimated net per capita ($) | 6 | 10 | (75) | (9) | (30) | (12) | (125) | 88 | (12) | 4 | 80 |

a – Fiscal costs only (i.e., job displacement costs ignored). Most cost and revenue estimates were based on INS 1983 report, but Huddle assumed a larger undocumented immigrant population.

b – Fiscal costs only (i.e., job displacement costs ignored). Passel re-estimated revenues but used Huddle's estimates of costs and number in immigrant populations for comparative purposes only.

na = not ascertained, whereas a blank indicates value not estimated.

per immigrant. With respect to undocumented immigrants, Passel and Huddle appear to agree that revenues net of costs is negative, although Huddle's estimate is two-and-one-half times larger.

If there is a lesson to be learned from these studies, it is that estimates become rather elastic as the analysis relies upon extrapolation from and aggregation of local and state figures to produce national numbers. Furthermore, almost nothing can be said about the fiscal impact of Mexican immigrants in particular using national data. At present, the methodological problems appear too great to have much confidence in national-level estimates of the fiscal impact of immigration as presented in these studies or to make any specific claims about Mexican immigration.

## Cost-Benefit Studies at the State Level

Clark, Passel, Zimmermann, and Fix (1994) of the Urban Institute examined the fiscal impact of undocumented immigrants in seven states which contain an estimated 86 percent of the nation's undocumented population: Arizona, California, Florida, Illinois, New Jersey, New York, and Texas. The research was conducted at the request of the Office of Management and Budget in conjunction with the Department of Justice. The authors estimated the costs in three areas: incarceration, education for the children of undocumented parents, and emergency medical services. To determine benefits, revenues from state income and sales taxes and from state and local property taxes were estimated.

Using a combination of federal and state data sources, the authors calculated costs and benefits. INS estimates of undocumented immigrants were linked to state records on foreign-born prisoners. Using standard demographic techniques, the authors estimated the number of undocumented aliens enrolled in public schools and costs were generated per student from National Center for Education Statistics cost data. The authors assessed state Medicaid cost figures and used them as a benchmark for generating their own estimates. Indirect estimation techniques generated state income, sales, and property taxes paid from state-specific tax revenue reports.

Roughly 3.4 million undocumented aliens were estimated by the INS to be living in the United States, with 2.9 million residing in the seven states studied. Clark et al. found that the cost ($4 billion) to those seven states was over twice the tax revnues received ($1.9 billion). However, the authors clearly identified the limitations of their study, including its narrow focus on three cost categories and three tax-generated revenue categories.

The Government Accounting Office (GAO) (1994) conducted a comparative analysis of three estimates of the financial burdens of undocumented immigration

**Table 5.4**
**Fiscal Cost-Benefit Studies at the State Level**

| Author(s) | Clark, Passel, Zimmermann, and Fix Acc'ting | | | | | | | | U.S. Gov. and Office | Romero, Chang, Huddle Parker | | Policy | Illinois Immig. Project[a] |
|---|---|---|---|---|---|---|---|---|---|---|---|---|---|
| Year of estimates | 1993 | | | | | | | | 1994 | FY 1994-1995 | | 1994 | 1994 |
| State | Total | AZ | CA | TX | FL | IL | NJ | NY | CA | CA | CA | TX | IL |
| | Undocumented Immigrants Only | | | | | | | | Undoc. | Undoc. | Child. Citizen | Undoc. | Undoc. |
| Estimated number in immigrant population (millions) | 2.918 | 0.057 | 1.441 | 0.357 | 0.322 | 0.176 | 0.116 | 0.449 | 1.722 | 1.722 | 0.197 | 0.550 | 0.176 |
| Total population in area (millions) | 105.7 | 4.1 | 31.4 | 18.4 | 14.0 | 11.8 | 7.9 | 18.2 | 32.5 | 32.5 | 32.5 | 18.2 | 11.8 |
| Percent of immigrant population in total population | 2.8 | 1.4 | 4.6 | 1.9 | 2.3 | 1.5 | 1.5 | 2.5 | 5.3 | 5.3 | 0.6 | 3.0 | 1.5 |
| Estimated fiscal costs ($millions) | | | | | | | | | | | | | |
| Law enforcement | 471 | 11 | 368 | 23 | 12 | 6 | 7 | 45 | 360 | 474 | 10 | 39 | - |
| Education | 3,079 | 55 | 1,289 | 419 | 424 | 112 | 146 | 634 | 1,596 | 1,531 | 470 | 464 | 231 |
| Health | 211 | 8 | 113 | 9 | 22 | 7 | 1 | 51 | 395 | 395 | 50 | 84 | 8 |
| Welfare | - | - | - | - | - | - | - | - | - | 1,027 | 260 | - | - |
| Other | - | - | - | - | - | - | - | - | - | - | 107 | 107 | - |
| Total | 3,761 | 74 | 1,770 | 451 | 458 | 125 | 153 | 730 | 2,351 | 3,427 | 897 | 693 | 239 |

**Table 5.4** (Continued)

| Author(s) | Clark, Passel, Zimmermann, and Fix Acc'ting | | | | | | | | U.S. Gov. and Office | Romero, Chang, Huddle Parker | | Policy | Illinois Immig. Project[a] |
|---|---|---|---|---|---|---|---|---|---|---|---|---|---|
| Year of estimates | 1993 | | | | | | | | 1994 | FY 1994-1995 | | 1994 | 1994 |
| State | Total | AZ | CA | TX | FL | IL | NJ | NY | CA | CA | | TX | IL |
| | Undocumented Immigrants Only | | | | | | | | Undoc. | Undoc. | Child. Citizen | Undoc. | Undoc. |
| **Estimated revenues ($millions)** | | | | | | | | | | | | | |
| Federal | 1,886 | - | 732 | 202 | 277 | 94 | 130 | 422 | - | 1,309 | - | - | 397 |
| State | - | 29 | - | - | - | - | - | - | 1,100 | 739 | - | 150 | 145 |
| County | - | - | - | - | - | - | - | - | - | 139 | - | - | 61 |
| Total | 1,886 | 29 | 732 | 202 | 277 | 94 | 130 | 422 | 1,100 | 2,187 | - | 150 | 603 |
| Net revenues — fiscal costs ($mil) | (1,875) | (45) | (1,038) | (249) | (181) | (31) | (23) | (308) | (1,251) | (1,240) | (897) | (543) | (364) |
| Estimated net per immigrant ($) | (643) | (789) | (720) | (698) | (563) | (177) | (199) | (686) | (726) | (720) | (4,555) | (988) | (2,068) |
| Estimated net per capita ($) | (18) | (11) | (33) | (14) | (13) | (3) | (3) | (17) | (38) | (38) | (28) | (30) | (31) |

[a] Paral (1996) provided the cost estimates, Passell and Clark (1996) provided the revenues estimates for the Illinois Immigrant Policy Project.

on California, at the request of Senator Barbara Boxer. One of these estimates was derived from the Clark et al. (1994) study discussed above. The other two were developed by the Governor's Office of the State of California as part of their budget process, one in January 1994 and the second in September 1994. The authors considered the same public programs evaluated by Clark et al. (1994). The GAO authors evaluated the reasonableness of the assumptions and methodologies underlying the cost and revenue estimates in each study, extrapolated federal revenues based on previous state-level estimates, and convened a panel of experts to assess the merits of their own efforts.

The GAO report addressed only the costs and benefits of undocumented immigrants. Its overall cost estimate matched that of the September 1994 California report; however, the component costs differed, with public education being higher and incarceration costs lower. The GAO report concluded that it was very difficult to estimate tax revenues generated by undocumented immigrants. Still, the authors estimated that the total federal, state, and local tax contribution would roughly equal the costs undocumented immigrants impose on the government. But, while costs are immediately imposed upon state and local governments, a substantial part of the revenue generated flows to the federal government.

Romero, Chang, and Parker (1994), in collaboration with the California Department of Finance and the Office of Planning and Research, reported the costs associated with undocumented immigration and the taxes paid by undocumented immigrants in fiscal year 1994-95 for the state of California. Costs estimated were for education, criminal justice, health care, and other general services. Revenue estimates included those for federal and state income, payroll, gasoline, excise, and unemployment insurance taxes; state vehicle fees and lottery revenues; state and local sales taxes; and local property tax.

The researchers used state data as cost and revenue sources and the INS for estimates of the undocumented immigrant population. Tax contributions were extrapolated from several studies. Education costs were derived from "per pupil" costs multiplied by the undocumented school-age population. A similar method generated incarceration costs (undocumented inmates multiplied by "per inmate" costs). Health care costs were generated from regression models, and general state services from multiplying the costs of parks, roads, and police protection by the share of the state population estimated to be undocumented.

Total cost figures were $1 billion higher than the GAO estimates reported above, and revenue estimates were less than a third of GAO estimates. Thus, the study concluded that 1.7 million undocumented immigrants living in California in 1994 imposed a net cost of $2.7 billion on the California treasury.

The authors concluded that the costs to California

> arise exclusively because the federal government has failed to secure our na-
> tional border and enforce our existing immigration laws. They are exacer-
> bated because the Federal government has mandated that states provide costly
> services to undocumented immigrants and their citizen children.

Huddle (1994) examined the costs of immigration to Texas in 1992 based on immigration between 1970 and 1992. He estimated the costs of the 23 major federal, state, and local government assistance programs described in his earlier work. He also identified specifically those same costs and benefits not addressed in his previous work and included all levels of government within the state of Texas. Using a variety of data sources, administrative and academic, Huddle determined costs by multiplying "per-recipient" costs by estimates of the number of immigrant recipients. The author's basic conclusion was that the net cost of immigration to Texas in 1992 was $4.68 billion and would grow in the future.

Paral (1996) estimated the costs of providing welfare and education services to immigrants in Illinois, compared to providing them to U.S.-born persons. Major expenditures estimated were AFDC, SSI, Aid to the Aged, Blind and Disabled, Transitional Assistance, general education, school lunches, and K-12 bilingual education. The study focused on the entire immigrant population in the state of Illinois, although most of that population is concentrated in the Chicago metropolitan area. Data sources include population figures from Passel and Clark (1996) (see below), and fiscal data from the U.S. House of Representatives, the Illinois Department of Public Aid, the Illinois State Board of Education, and the U.S. Department of Agriculture.

The study estimates that 1.2 million immigrants were living in Illinois in 1994, and that total expenditures at all levels of government for that population were $854 million. Although they comprised 10.2 percent of the state's population, immigrants received only 6.3 percent of the federal and state spending on AFDC and 4.4 percent of state spending on transitional assistance. On the other hand, Illinois immigrants received approximately 14.8 percent of state spending on Aid to the Aged, Blind and Disabled and 14.8 percent of federal SSI expenditures. Education spending showed similar variation. Some 7.8 percent of immigrants were school-aged (5-19) versus 16.9 percent of the U.S.-born population, but immigrants comprised only five percent of K-12 enrollment figures. Approximately 5.5 percent of the combined federal, state, and local spending on education and 7.7 percent of federal and state school meals programs went to immigrants. However, over half of all federal, state, and local costs of bilingual education were spent on immigrants.

Passel and Clark (1996) estimated taxes paid by immigrants in Illinois to complement Paral (1996) for the Illinois Immigrant Policy Project. They estimated revenues from federal and state income taxes, FICA and Railroad Retirement, state and local sales tax, residential property tax, and unemployment insurance payments, using the Urban Institute's Transfer Income Model and data from the 1990 Census and the March 1994 Current Population Survey. The authors apportioned their estimates of taxes paid among all legal immigrants, refugees who entered the United States in 1980 and later, undocumented immigrants, and natives.

The authors concluded that immigrants in Illinois paid nearly $7.2 billion in taxes, an amount which represented approximately 10.6 percent of the total taxes paid by Illinois residents. Of those taxes, some $5 billion were paid to the federal government in the form of income tax and FICA. When combined with Paral (1996), the Illinois Immigrant Policy Project studies estimated that in 1994, immigrants in Illinois paid in over $7 billion in taxes while receiving less than $1 billion in services.

Espenshade and King (1994) examined the net fiscal impacts of all immigrants and U.S.-born households in New Jersey in 1979-80. They calculated state and local expenditures on direct state services, state aid, total public education and bilingual education, AFDC, Pharmaceutical Aid to the Aged, Medicaid, and general local services. They estimated state tax income revenue; sales tax; taxes from automobiles, fuel, alcohol, tobacco, inheritance, business property, and realty transfer; as well as local revenues from property and public utility taxes.

The authors used data from the Census Bureau's 1980 5 percent Public Use Micro Sample in conjunction with state data on the New Jersey population. They developed a fiscal impacts model to estimate household-level tax contributions and social services benefits received from state and local governments. They entered household records for the 127,516 households sampled, computed estimates, compared those estimates to public data, and made adjustments as necessary. Several comparisons were made. The authors not only compared all immigrants to U.S.-born households, but also households headed by a person 65 years of age and older to households headed by persons under 65, along with male-headed/female-headed household comparisons. They compared immigrant households by region of origin as well.

Espenshade and King found that, in 1980, all immigrants constituted a net fiscal burden to both the state and local governments of New Jersey. However, the authors pointed out the same was true for U.S.-born households, and that per-household net costs of immigrants were similar to those of natives. Differences occurred when comparing the immigrant groups by region of origin. For Latin-American immigrant-headed households, net cost per household was roughly 30 percent higher than for either U.S.-born households or for immigrant households as a whole.

Gumbleton, Appel, Bhargava, Morrow, and Wilhelm (1996) of the Tomas Rivera Center also studied the impacts of immigrants on California. They estimated costs of education and social welfare. To estimate benefits they calculated the lifetime contributions of state income and sales taxes, which amount to 80 percent of all taxes collected by the state. Additionally, the authors discussed, in broad terms, the costs of not providing general welfare services, such as immunization and education.

The authors relied primarily on California state government departmental sources, including the Department of Education, the California Post-Secondary Education Commission, the National Center for Education Statistics, and the state Department of Finance. They used a life-cycle approach, estimating median income over 40 years to compute tax contributions. They also calculated costs based on population estimates and the percentages of the state budget that go to education and welfare.

The authors concluded that, over the life cycle, immigrants more than repay the costs they incur in education and social welfare. They estimate that legal immigrants pay $1.43 in taxes for every $1.00 they receive in education, compared to $1.32 for U.S.-born Californians and $1.13 for undocumented immigrants. State education costs are $62,600 per person, while the lifetime tax contributions of legal immigrants are approximately $89,437. In terms of social welfare programs, 14.9 percent of immigrants use AFDC, 19.1 percent use SSI disability, 13.8 percent use food stamps, while 24.0 percent of the California population is non-citizen. In addition, though poverty rates among non-citizens in California are 20.2 percent, versus 11.2 percent for U.S.-born households, there is no statistically significant difference between participation rates by citizenship in means-tested social safety net programs. Immigrants do pay lower tax amounts than do citizens. Immigrants pay 74 cents in taxes for every dollar they receive in welfare benefits, versus 82 cents for the U.S.-born. The authors also note that immigrants add to the state's economic growth in terms of entrepreneurship, consumer goods, and housing market expansion.

Unfortunately the Paral (1996) methodology was not available, but it appears that this project was less comprehensive than other state-level studies in determining the basis for either expenditures or revenues. Although the target population of all foreign-born residents is similar to that used by Huddle, the scope of the two studies is quite different. It is impossible to determine whether the difference between the net fiscal cost of $4.68 billion estimated by Huddle for Texas and the net benefit of $6 billion for Illinois is due to methodological differences or differences in the national-origin composition of the state immigrant populations.

Only Huddle's Texas study and the California study from Gumbleton et al. focus on all immigrants, while the others examine undocumented immigration, making direct cross-study comparisons virtually impossible. If there is a common theme in the Southwestern studies, it is that fiscal impacts at the state and federal levels differ in ways that profoundly shape the political argument on immigration, with state and local burdens operating alongside federal net benefits. Without exception, estimates for undocumented workers point to a net cost in all of the states considered. To its credit, the Clark et al. study makes the most serious attempt in these state-level analyses to build in independent checks on the numbers being used and cautions readers against using the figures to assess net costs since the measures used are far from a complete set of those that might be included (e.g., only state revenue data is considered). The study does provide some basis for making comparisons between states. Arizona, California, and Texas, the three states in which the undocumented population would be expected to be primarily of Mexican origin, seem to be affected similarly on the same set of fiscal measures when considered in terms of net cost per immigrant (next to last row in Table 5.4) and more so than other states, although New York and Florida are not far behind.

## Cost-Benefit Studies at the County/Metropolitan Area Level

The Los Angeles County Internal Services Department (1992) undertook a study, mandated by the Board of Supervisors, attempting to estimate county costs attributable to immigration. The authors estimated the net county costs of public education and various county services, including health-care, criminal justice, and public social programs. The authors assessed revenues from federal and state income taxes, Social Security taxes, unemployment insurance, property taxes, vehicle license and registration fees, sales, gasoline and excise taxes, and state lottery revenues. The authors estimated immigrant population sizes as of the 1990 Census and projected forward to 1992 using several techniques, including those employed in the demography literature by Warren and Passel and by Woodrow.

The study examined all immigrant groups. The authors concluded that some 2.3 million immigrants cost Los Angeles County $947 million and generated $139 million in revenue, for a net burden of $808 million. However, the authors also found that the immigrant population generated $4.3 billion to all levels of government.

Parker and Rea (1993) conducted a study mandated by the California State Senate Special Committee on Border Issues. The study estimated net fiscal impact

## Table 5.5
## Fiscal Cost-Benefit Studies at the County Level

| | LA County Internal Services Department | | | | | Parker & Rea |
|---|---|---|---|---|---|---|
| Author(s) | | | | | | |
| Area | Los Angeles County | | | | | San Diego |
| Year of estimates | | | 1991-92FY | | | 1993 |
| Immigrant population | Total | Citizen children of undocumented | Legal | Amnestied | Undocumented | Undocumented |
| Estimated number in immigrant population (millions) | 2.301 | 0.252 | 0.632 | 0.718 | 0.699 | 0.222576 |
| Total population (millions) | 9.187 | 9.187 | 9.187 | 9.187 | 9.187 | 2.678 |
| Percent of Immigrant Population in total population | 25.0 | 2.7 | 6.9 | 7.8 | 7.6 | 8.3 |
| Estimated fiscal costs ($millions) | | | | | | |
| Law enforcement | 453.3 | 41.3 | 187.7 | 113.7 | 110.6 | 151.2 |
| Education | 1,484.8 | 662.3 | 331.1 | 123.5 | 367.9 | 60.0 |
| Health | 370.6 | 37.2 | 130.1 | 42.7 | 160.7 | 50.1 |
| Welfare | 1.7 | 0.5 | 0.9 | 0.2 | 0.2 | |
| Other | 121.1 | 12.6 | 33.5 | 37.9 | 36.9 | 31.1 |
| Total | 2,431.5 | 753.9 | 683.4 | 318.0 | 676.3 | 292.4 |
| Estimated revenues ($millions) | | | | | | |
| Federal | 2,599.6 | - | 1,212.6 | 909.7 | 477.3 | 162.6 |
| State | 1,236.9 | - | 486.4 | 451.0 | 299.5 | 59.7 |
| County | 134.3 | - | 54.1 | 45.2 | 35.0 | |
| City | 356.5 | - | 132.9 | 132.7 | 90.9 | |
| Total | 4,327.3 | - | 1,886.0 | 1,538.6 | 902.7 | 222.3 |

## Table 5.5 (Continued)

| Author(s) Area | LA County Internal Services Department Los Angeles County | | | | | Parker & Rea San Diego |
| --- | --- | --- | --- | --- | --- | --- |
| Year of estimates Immigrant population | Total | Citizen Children of Undocumented | 1991-92FY Legal | Amnestied | Undocumented | 1993 Undocumented |
| **CITY/COUNTY/STATE/FEDERAL** | | | | | | |
| Net revenues — fiscal costs ($millions) | 1,895.8 | (753.9) | 1,202.6 | 1,220.7 | 226.4 | (70.1) |
| Estimated net per immigrant ($) | 823.9 | (2,991.6)" | 1,902.9 | 1,700.1 | 323.9 | (314.8) |
| Estimated net per capita ($) | 206.4 | (82.1) | 130.9 | 132.9 | 24.6 | (26.2) |
| **CITY/COUNTY/STATE ONLY** | | | | | | |
| Net revenues — fiscal costs ($millions) | (703.8) | (753.9) | (10.0) | 311.0 | (250.9) | (232.7) |
| Estimated net per immigrant ($) | (305.9) | (2,991.6)" | (15.8) | 433.1 | (358.9) | (1,045.4)" |
| Estimated net per capita ($) | (76.6) | (82.1) | (1.1) | 33.8 | (27.3) | (86.9) |
| **CITY/COUNTY ONLY** | | | | | | |
| Net revenues — fiscal costs ($millions) | (1,940.7)" | (753.9) | (496.4) | (140.1) | (550.4) | (292.4) |
| Estimated net per immigrant ($) | (843.4) | (2,991.6)" | (785.4) | (195.1) | (787.4) | (1,313.6)"\ |
| Estimated net per capita ($) | (211.2) | (82.1) | (54.0) | (15.2) | (59.9) | (109.2) |

to the state and to local governments for providing public services to undocumented immigrants living in San Diego County. The authors focused on cost and revenue categories very similar to those of the Los Angeles County study listed above.

Parker and Rea used a variety of research methods. They interviewed self-identified undocumented immigrants; reviewed employer sanctions data from the INS; reviewed arrest records, court proceedings, and incarceration data; compared emergency room usage rates to non-emergency usage rates for undocumented immigrants; and interviewed education officials. They concluded that in fiscal year 1991-92 undocumented aliens paid $60 million in state and local taxes to offset $304 million in costs, for a net cost to San Diego County of $244 million. They further estimated that undocumented immigrants contributed $162 million in federal revenues while imposing $64 million in federal expenses, although they contended that unmeasured federal costs would serve to offset the net benefits at the federal level.

These studies may provide the closest approximation to the fiscal impact of Mexican immigration in particular that can be derived from the studies described in this chapter. Both studies used similar bases for estimating costs, but Parker and Rea were much more elaborate in estimating revenue flows; thus, the costs appear higher for the total immigrant population of Los Angeles than for the undocumented population of San Diego. Again, the research shows that costs borne on a local level are significant and immediate, while federal costs tend to be more remote (concentrated in old-age benefits), and are skewed toward legal rather than undocumented immigration.

## Other Types of Studies

Borjas and Hilton (1996) compared participation in welfare programs across nativity categories. The authors estimated immigrant and U.S.-born households on their usage rates for AFDC, SSI, general assistance, Medicaid, food stamps, Supplemental Food Programs for Women, Infants and Children (WIC), low-income energy assistance, housing assistance, and school meal programs. There was no effort to estimate revenues or assess net costs.

The level of analysis for this study is the household unit. The authors develop a regression model using data from the Survey of Income and Program Participation (SIPP) from 1984, 1985, 1990, and 1991. Analyses are restricted to those individual in the SIPP for the entire 32-month time frame. The number of persons in each household is multiplied times a per-recipient cost to determine the costs of each program attributable to immigrant and U.S.-born households. Immigrants are also disaggregated by refugee status.

Borjas and Hilton do not distinguish legal from undocumented immigrants, nor do they disaggregate national-origin groups. They conclude that the immigrant-native gap in cash benefits may be small, but the gap widens once other programs are included. Some 21 percent of immigrant households receive some type of assistance, compared to 14 percent of U.S.-born households. They also find a correlation suggesting that the types of benefits received by earlier immigrant cohorts affect the types received by newer immigrants, and conclude that ethnic networks may transmit information about the availability of particular benefits to newly arriving immigrants.

Van Hook, Glick, and Bean (1996) examine recipiency rates for three welfare programs: AFDC, SSI, and General Assistance, focusing on the household, family, and individual levels of analysis. The authors develop an algebraic formula to compare the relationships among household size, recipients per household, and household/family/individual-level welfare recipiency rates. Their data come from the 1980 and 1990 Public Use Micro Samples of the Census and the March 1994 and 1995 Current Population Surveys.

The authors focus on immigrants in general, without consideration of legal status. They conclude that research results are strongly affected by the level of analysis employed. Rates of public assistance receipt are higher among immigrant than U.S.-born households in 1979 and that difference grows over time. However, using the family as the unit of analysis shows a more modest difference, while individual analyses show negligible differences, with U.S.-born rates actually higher than immigrant rates in 1979 and 1989.

These studies do not treat the fiscal impact issue directly, nor do they deal with legal status issues or national-origin questions. However, both studies provide some insight as to how sensitive the whole modeling endeavor will be to specification decisions made by the research team. Those differences, in turn, can have very different policy implications regarding immigration restriction.

We find that, with notable exceptions, the fiscal impact literature concludes that the fiscal costs of immigration exceed the benefits derived. The disparity between the findings for most of the studies centered on the magnitude of the burden rather than the direction of the cost-benefit relationship.

Still, it is difficult to say with any certainty whether the studies outlined above can serve as useful guides to policymakers interested in the specific impact of Mexican migration to the United States. The most obvious constraints include the fact that none of the studies examine Mexican immigration specifically. Furthermore, the studies vary widely along the dimensions of (1) geographical scope, (2) types of costs and benefits included, (3) the specification of the immigrant target population, and (4) techniques for assigning dollar values to costs and benefits. With both the population estimates and the fiscal estimates varying so widely across studies, this entire literature begins to appear unstable. At the national level, the $70 billion difference between the Huddle and Passel estimates, for example, falls well beyond the boundaries of acceptable accounting error.

And the challenges do not stop there. Aside from the estimation problems inherent in any cost-benefit analyses, the "fiscal impacts" exercise offers additional challenges when Mexican immigrants are the target population. Taken together, the challenges that face researchers investigating Mexican immigration and its fiscal impacts on the United States are to increase the precision in the terms of the debate, and, in many cases, to shift the frame bounding the debate so that altogether new questions can be asked and answered.

## The Problem of Legal Status

Four of the studies listed in Table 5.1 deal only with the undocumented immigrant population. Each suggests a net cost of undocumented migration. Such findings are particularly relevant to those interested in Mexican migration, with its significant undocumented component.

The "legal status" issue within the Mexican immigrant population makes cost-benefit analyses more interesting and more difficult than they would be if the group were more homogenous. For instance, legal immigrants differ profoundly from their undocumented counterparts in their demographic profiles and eligibility profiles for public benefits. These differences bring differential burdens upon the public sector. While legal immigrants might be more inclined to use public assistance, for example, undocumented immigrants might be more likely to rely solely on emergency medical care. The question becomes, how would the composition of the burden change in the absence of an undocumented population? For that matter, how would one go about reducing that undocumented population? There are several ways to eradicate undocumented immigration, from "transformation" of undocumented stock to legal stock via amnesty and other new immigration benefits, to increased immigration law enforcement against undocumented entry and settlement. Each of these strategies has its own costs attached. The challenge is to specify the influence of legal status on the cost-benefit equation and to predict how various mechanisms for reducing undocumented immigration might be folded into that analysis. At present, the "fiscal impacts" exercises focusing on undocumented immigration do very little to simulate how the complex of costs and benefits might change under a variety of policy reform efforts, opting instead for the rather sanguine assumption that interdiction and deportation would reduce public assistance costs to zero and leave the rest of the system largely untouched.

## The Problem of Federalism

The fact that immigration costs and benefits are borne at different governmental levels is an inescapable part of this exercise. Put simply, both the "net cost" and the "net benefit" answers to the question of immigrant fiscal impact are true, depending on what level of government one is talking about. Enough information has accumulated demonstrating this fact that it may now be time to ask a new question. If, indeed, much of the concern over immigration's fiscal impacts comes from the fact that federal immigration policy sets the parameters for what then become state and local funding problems, more attention should be paid to the "what if" question. What if fiscal impacts were restructured along the lines that state and local policymakers in high-settlement sites have been calling for? How would the fiscal equation—and the politics—around Mexican immigration change under a different financing system? Continued attempts to quantify the cost-benefit ratio may be a necessary part of the policy space in which Mexican immigration is situated, but those attempts may not be sufficient to ease intergovernmental conflicts and solve policy problems. Such calming of the discourse will be promoted only when scholars can also contribute suggestions for models that might optimize the distribution of costs and benefits of immigration across levels of government.

## Taking Household and Family Structure into Account

Some of the research outlined above took household and family structure into account when modeling public assistance recipiency (Borjas and Hilton 1996; Van Hook, Glick, and Bean 1996). Most of the research did not. Those studies relying on the household as the unit of analysis demonstrated large immigrant/native differences in income assistance recipiency. The differences shrank when the unit of analysis dropped to the individual level. Clearly, the ways in which poor immigrants and poor natives form households may explain much about the difference in their public assistance dependence. If immigrants are broken into more households with members receiving assistance than is true for U.S.-born households, they will show higher recipiency rates even if the same proportion of individual recipients exists in both populations.

This observation becomes important for understanding Mexican immigrant fiscal impacts for several reasons. As the migration stream from Mexico has matured beyond the phase at which most entrants are young male target-earners, both intergenerational household formation and an increasing presence of women can be expected. Public assistance systems geared toward income maintenance for the elderly and for female household heads will be very sensitive to changes in the household and family composition of the Mexican immigrant population along these dimensions. The potential for divergent results stemming from unit-of-analysis choices may well increase as the Mexican immigrant population becomes more diverse. The challenge for scholars will be to model public assistance recipiency rates at all meaningful units of aggregation and treat all of those results with comparable weight in the policy dialogue.

## Taking the Life Course into Account

The studies reviewed in this chapter share a basic methodological feature—they are all snapshots in time. Several of the studies modeled cost-benefit ratios or public assistance recipiency rates with multiple cross-sectional panels of data, but none of these studies are truly longitudinal over a significant period of time.

The policy implications of this reliance on cross-sectional data are considerable. Public assistance burdens are imposed at distinct points in the life course. Young and old people are at greatest risk for economic dislocation, and the U.S. welfare system is biased toward them accordingly. Criminal justice costs are often concentrated on those in young adulthood and among males. Likewise, contributions to the public revenue base take place at distinct points in the life course, and there is no accounting for intergenerational effects in a static model. In short, a dynamic process is being modeled within static research frameworks in most of the extant literature.

The challenge posed by including the "life course" perspective in discussions of Mexican immigration to the United States is a substantial one. To track a representative sample of Mexican immigrants through time, with detailed attention to their transitions into and out of public assistance recipiency, would be an ambitious and time-consuming enterprise. It would require both extensive data collection and a reframing of the fiscal impact model from a static accounting perspective to a more dynamic model that captures equilibrium and disequilibrium in the face of changing conditions.

It is with the "life course" perspective, also, that the insights of qualitative and case studies can add important texture to the cross-sectional data readily available. Until now, most of the attempts to model fiscal impacts have gone "broad" rather than "deep." The result has been a series of estimations that are somewhat removed from the direct information provided by actual immigrants and U.S. natives. Along with more direct attempts to track immigrant and U.S.-born samples over time, researchers can benefit from drawing upon ethnographic methods to become more familiar with the ways in which public assistance receipt and revenue-generation unfold during the settlement process.

## Comparisons to Whom and When to Compare?

Whether particular nationality groups are overconsumers of public services is part of the political problematic, and is of some consequence theoretically. We think the question is more complex than it may seem. To provide a useful response to the problem requires that at least three methodological issues be resolved: (1) costs and benefits must be disaggregated by national origin; (2) apparent costs and benefits at any given point in time must be reconciled with accumulated costs and benefits over the life course; and (3) comparisons must be made with an appropriate reference group. The reflexive response of many a researcher is to assume that the white, U.S.-born, U.S.-parentage, English-speaking population is the appropriate reference group. But, different national origin populations not only reflect different cultural situations, but are differentially located in U.S. social structure. Their "fiscal" profiles are likely to differ, particularly over the life course, and different age cohorts in the same national origin group may have fiscal profiles that vary substantially in ways that we do not know enough about.

Although the problem is complex, much of the relevant data are available in time series, and the problem may not be difficult to model. An idealized version of a fiscal cost-benefit profile for a particular age cohort would be like a sine wave with a peak in the middle during the cohort's working life and two troughs, one during childhood and another during old age, when the cohort would consume more than it contributed to the public treasury. The burden in the early trough would fall on state and local government (e.g., for education, law enforcement, and some social welfare programs), whereas the burden in the later period would be on the federal government (e.g., for Medicare, Medicaid, and Social Security). The main expenditures during the middle period would primarily be for health, unemployment benefits, and some social welfare programs, and be offset somewhat, if not completely, by taxes on earnings, sales, and the like.

Apparent overconsumption of public resources when an immigrant population is compared to the U.S.-born may say more about the structure of U.S. society than about the immigrant group. Thus, comparing the same age cohort of undocumented Mexican immigrants with their legal counterparts may be a more relevant contrast for both policy and analytic purposes. If deficit reduction is the policy focus, and if Mexican immigrants are poorer, they raise costs. If they are less likely to be legal, they are more likely to lower costs given less access to available services. A comparison of either group with non-Hispanic, U.S.-born populations would obscure that analysis. Since so little is known about variations in the fiscal profile of different national origin populations over the life course, we are not convinced that static analyses really tell us much. None of the studies we reviewed tackled this problem in a serious way.

## Knowledge for What and for Whom?

As several of the studies demonstrated, immigrant/native comparisons on public assistance variables are highly sensitive to the estimation procedure. The most benign outcomes suggest that individual immigrants are about as likely as individual U.S.-born persons of comparable characteristics to receive public assistance (Van Hook, Glick and Bean 1996). The most extreme outcomes reported suggest a monumental burden is being placed on the public sector by today's immigrants (Huddle 1993). A few of the studies suggest that immigrants are a net fiscal benefit (Paral 1996; Passel 1994; Gumbleton et al. 1996).

It becomes quite difficult to know what to do with the information on fiscal impacts when so much of it is contradictory. However, even if the research and policy communities take the conflicting reports at face value, there is some benefit to be gained from going through the exercise of considering what policy implications flow from the results.

If immigrants really are a fiscal benefit to the public coffers, as some of the authors suggested, then the policy job is simply deciding how to preserve that positive balance sheet. This is more difficult than it might appear, however, requiring the research community to unpack the balance sheet and identify the sources of the net benefit. At that point, the debate expands from the economic to the political; for, if the net benefits derive from qualified immigrants failing to access assistance to which they are entitled by law, then the black ink is purchased at a social cost. If instead, the benefits are derived from the fact that immigrants are indeed contributing more to the public sector than they need from or demand of it, those aspects of immigration and labor policy that afford immigrants the opportunity to make those contributions should be protected.

But what if immigrants are, at best, equivalent to U.S.-born persons in their use of public services, and, at worst, a heavy drain on the public coffers? Accepting that immigrants are equally likely as other poor people to use public services, the fact remains that immigrants are, as a whole, and Mexican immigrants in particular, more likely to be poor than are non-Hispanic white U.S.-born persons. This fact makes Mexican immigrants a volatile part of the political debate around public assistance. The volatility increases to the extent that immigrants are perceived as much more likely than U.S.-born natives to seek public assistance.

What bears remembering is that more than one policy flows from the fact situation just presented. One solution is an immigration policy approach—one that limits the ability of poor, at-risk immigrants to enter the United States at all. A second solution is an "immigrant" policy approach—one that might hold immigrants to a higher eligibility standard than natives for public assistance. That is, the basic principles governing entry to the United States might remain the same, but the conditions under which those immigrants settle will change. A third solution is a more general domestic policy approach—one that restructures policies that help all working people with modest resources to avoid poverty and public assistance in the first place. Such policies include tax and wage policies that make low-skill work more rewarding than use of public assistance, child and family policy that makes work feasible for single parents, and education and training policies that allow workers to meet employer demands. To the extent that such investments in workers, U.S. and foreign-born, improve their employ-ability and productivity, the costs of public assistance over the life course may be dwarfed by the benefits generated.

An irony emerges in these competing visions of solutions to the "net cost" problem of U.S. immigration. The first two options reinforce the boundaries be-tween immigrants and the U.S.-born. The third option dissolves those bound-aries and adopts a more broad-based class approach to poverty prevention and economic independence. At present, it seems unlikely that policymakers will bring immigrants inside the domestic policy fold in such a way. From the right and the left, immigrants are being pitted against the U.S.-born regarding labor market dynamics and fiscal impacts. The wide disparity across assessments of fiscal impact outlined here, and the political uses to which that information has been put, makes it likely that those battle lines will only become more marked in the next round of policymaking.

In sum, considerable challenges face those attempting to model the fiscal impact of immigration generally and Mexican immigration in particular. Some of those challenges might be readily surmounted with new data collection techniques and new models. Other challenges are inherent in the nature of the exercise—most notable among those, the fact that costs and burdens are borne at different government levels. In the absence of substantive reform in the financing of immigration-related mandates, those aspects of the debate are unlikely to subside.

## Notes

1. Prostitutes and criminals in 1875, the mentally ill ("lunatics, idiots, and persons unable to take care of themselves without becoming a public charge") in 1882, the physically ill (persons suffering from "loathsome or dangerous contagious disease") and

vagrants in 1891, physically and mentally handicapped persons (epileptics and people with a prior history of insanity) in 1903, imbeciles, feeble-minded persons, and anyone with a physical or mental handicap that might affect their ability to make a living in 1907, and children unaccompanied by their parents in 1907 (Harper and Chase 1975: 5).

2. Additional reviews of different aspects of this literature may be found in Rothman and Espenshade (1992), Edmonston and Lee (1995), and Vernez and McCarthy (1995).

3. Changes and corrections to the table cited by Huddle are in italics in Table 5.2, the most significant of which are the net figures when job displacement costs are discounted (bottom row).

4. See Bean, Vernez, and Keely (1989), Bean, Edmonston, and Passel (1990), Heer (1990), and Espenshade (1995) for commentaries on the problems in estimating undocumented immigration to the United States.

# References

Bean, Frank D., Barry Edmonston, and Jeffrey S. Passel (Editors). 1990. *Undocumented Migration to the United States: IRCA and the Experience of the 1980s*. Washington, D.C.: Urban Institute Press.

Bean, Frank D., Georges Vernez, and Charles B. Keely. 1989. *Opening and Closing the Doors: Evaluating Immigration Reform and Control*. Washington, D.C.: Urban Institute Press.

Borjas, George J., and Lynette Hilton. 1996. Immigration and the Welfare State: Immigrant Participation in Means-Tested Entitlement Programs. *Quarterly Journal of Economics* 11 1(2):575-604.

Bustamante, Jorge. 1978. Commodity Migrants: Structural Analysis of Mexican Immigration to the United States. In Stanley Ross (Editor), *Views Across the Border: The United States and Mexico*. Albuquerque: University of New Mexico Press, pp. 183-203

Calavita, Kitty. 1994. U.S. Immigration and Policy Responses: The Limits of Legislation. In Wayne A. Cornelius, Phillip L. Martin, and James F. Hollifield (Editors), *Controlling Immigration: A Global Perspective*, Stanford, CA: Stanford University Press, pp. 55-82.

Clark, Rebecca L., Jeffrey S. Passel, Wendy N. Zimmermann, and Michael E. Fix. 1994. Fiscal Impacts of Undocumented Aliens: Selected Estimates for Seven States. Washington, D.C.: The Urban Institute.

Edmonston, Barry, and Ronald Lee, eds. 1995. Local Fiscal Impacts of Illegal Immigration: A Workshop Report. Unpublished Draft.

Espenshade, Thomas J. 1995. Unauthorized Immigration to the United States. *Annual Review of Sociology* 21: 195-216.

Espenshade, Thomas J., and Vanessa E. King. 1994. State and Local Fiscal Impacts of U.S. Immigrants: Evidence from New Jersey. *Population Research and Policy Review* 13:225-256.

Fix, Michael, Jeffrey S. Passel, with Marfa E. Enchautequi and Wendy Zimmermann. 1994. *Immigration and Immigrants: Setting the Record Straight*. Washington, D.C.: The Urban Institute Press.

Gumbleton, Kathleen, Morgan Appel, Anoop Bhargava, Laura Morrow, and Tony Wilhelm. 1996. Why They Count: Immigrant Contributions to the Golden State. Claremont, CA: Tomas Rivera Center.

Harper, Elizabeth, and Roland F. Chase. 1975. *Immigration Laws of the United States*, 3rd edition. Indianapolis, IN: Bobbs-Merrill.

Heer, David M. 1990. *Undocumented Mexicans in the United States*. Cambridge: Cambridge University Press.

Huddle, Donald. 1994. The Net Costs of Immigration to Texas. Washington, D.C.: Carrying Capacity Network.

———. 1985. Illegal Immigration: Job Displacement and Social Costs. Alexandria, VA: American Immigration Control Foundation.

———. 1993. The Costs of Immigration. Washington, D.C.: Carrying Capacity Network.

Jenks, Jeremiah W., W. Jett Lauk, and Rufus D. Smith. 1922. *The Immigration Problem: A Study of American Immigration Conditions and Needs*. New York: Funk & Wagnals.

Latino Institute. 1996. Illinois Immigrants Pay 10 Percent of Major Taxes, Use Only 7 Percent of Major Social Programs. Chicago: Latino Institute (May 16 news release).

Los Angeles County Internal Services Department. 1992. Impact of Undocumented Persons and Other Immigrants on Costs. Revenues. and Services in Los Angeles County. Los Angeles: Los Angeles County Internal Services Department.

Paral, Rob. 1996. Estimated Costs of Providing Welfare and Education Services to the Native Born and to Immigrants in Illinois. Chicago: A Latino Institute Technical Paper produced for the Illinois Immigrant Policy Project.

Parker, Richard A., and Louis M. Rea. 1993. Illegal Immigration in San Diego County: An Analysis of Costs and Revenues. Report to the California State Senate Special Committee on Border Issues. San Diego.

Passel, Jeffrey S. 1994. Immigrants and Taxes: A Reappraisal of Huddle's "The Cost of Immigrants." Washington, D.C.: The Urban Institute.

Passel, Jeffrey S., and Rebecca L. Clark. 1996. Taxes Paid by Immigrants in Illinois. Washington, D.C.: Urban Institute Technical Paper Produced for the Illinois Immigrant Policy Project.

Romero, Philip, Andrew Chang, and Theresa Parker. 1994. Shifting the Costs of a Failed Federal Policy: The Net Fiscal Impact of illegal Immigrants in California. Sacramento, CA: Governor's Office of Planning and Research.

Rothman, Eric S., and Thomas J. Espenshade. 1992. Fiscal Impacts of Immigration to the United States. *Population Index* 58(3):381-415.

Simon, Julian L. 1996. Public Expenditures on Immigrants to the United States, Past and Present. *Population and Development Review* 22(1):99-109.

U.S. General Accounting Office. 1995. Illegal Aliens: National Net Cost Estimates Vary Widely. Washington, D.C.: GAO/HEHS-95-133.

———. 1995. Welfare Reform: Implications of Proposals on Legal Immigrants' Benefits. Washington, D.C.: GAO/HEHS-95-58.

———. 1994. Illegal Aliens: Assessing Estimates of Financial Burden on California. Washington, D.C.: GAO/HEHS-95-22.

———. 1993. Illegal Aliens: Despite Data Limitations, Current Methods Provide Better Population Estimates. Washington, D.C.: GAO/PEMD-93-25.

Van Hook, Jennifer V. W., Jennifer E. Glick, Frank D. Bean. 1996. Nativity Difference in Public Assistance Receipt: What Difference Does the Unit of Analysis Make? Austin, TX: Population Research Center Paper #95-96-08, University of Texas.

Warren, Robert, and Jeffrey S. Passel. 1987. A Count of the Uncountable: Estimates of Undocumented Aliens Counted in the 1980 United States Census. *Demography* 24(3): 373-393.

Woodrow, Karen A. 1991. A Consideration of the Effect of Immigration Reform on the Number of Undocumented Residents in the United States. Washington DC: Population Division, Bureau of the Census, December 1972.

Vernez, Georges, and Kevin McCarthy. 1995. The Fiscal Costs of Immigration: Analytical and Policy Issues. DRU-958-1-IF, February. Santa Monica, CA: RAND Corporation.

# 6.
# Labor Market Implications of Mexican Migration:
## Economies of Scale, Innovation, and Entrepreneurship

*Michael J. Rosenfeld and Marta Tienda*

T his chapter addresses what is known about the impacts of immigrants on the U.S. economy, with special focus on Mexican immigrants. To stimulate critical thinking about whether Mexican migration warrants special policy consideration, it is necessary to first identify what is unique or distinctive about U.S.-bound Mexican migration. This a fair question because historically, U.S. immigration policy has considered national origins in setting admission guidelines. Sometimes administrative policies for immigrants from different countries have been used to reinforce controversial international policies, as in the case of immigrants and asylum seekers from Central America during the 1980s, when refugees from El Salvador and Guatemala were systematically turned away, while refugees from Nicaragua were welcomed (see Teitelbaum and Weiner, 1995). The different treatment of unauthorized migrants from Haiti and Cuba during the 1990s offers another stark example of the intersection of foreign policy and immigration policy.

Our discussion of U.S. immigration begins by recognizing that migrant characteristics differ according to source regions and countries, and that these characteristics directly influence migrants' integration prospects and labor market impacts in the host society. Most studies about migration make the simplifying assumption that the U.S. is a single, or perhaps divided (high-wage and low-wage), labor market. Frequently ignored are the reception factors, especially community-level circumstances, that facilitate the integration of new arrivals and organize links between immigrant enterprises and the mainstream economy. Most Mexican immigrants come not to an alien Anglo environment, but rather to Mexican-American communities within the United States where Spanish is spoken and where the customs and consumer tastes of the neighbors are well understood. This is relevant for understanding the labor market impacts of Mexicans along with several additional factors that distinguish Mexican migrants from those who come to the U.S. from other source countries.

## Mexican Migrants

### Size of the Flow

Among the 18 million foreign-born people living in the U.S. in 1990, more than 4 million, or 24 percent, came from Mexico (see Table 6.1). Mexico contributes a larger share to the foreign-born population of the U.S. than any other country, and roughly as much as the entire continents of Asia and Europe.

### Duration of the Flow

In the decade 1911-1920, 219,000 Mexicans legally immigrated to the U.S. (Bean and Tienda, 1987). In the 1920s, this flow more than doubled. The 1930s and 1940s were slow times for all kinds of international migration except for war refugees. Migration from Mexico picked up again in the 1950s (299,000), and the flow has steadily increased to more than a million legal Mexican immigrants in the 1980s. The share of legal migration of Mexican origin is lower than the Mexican proportion of foreign-born in the U.S. because the foreign-born population also includes undocumented (i.e., illegal) immigrants.

### Residential Concentration and "Sister" Communities

For historical reasons, the Mexican-origin population is residentially concentrated in the five Southwestern states and Illinois. Within these locations, Mexican immigrants tend to reside in the largest metropolitan areas. Moreover, there are sizeable established Mexican-American communities in cities such as Los Angeles, Chicago, San Antonio and Houston. In 1990 there were just under 9 million U.S. natives of Mexican descent (see Table 6.1).

## Motives for Migration

The Mexican immigrant flow includes negligible numbers of refugees or political asylum seekers. Virtually all Mexican immigrants seek better economic opportunities in the United States. However, social and familial ties to established Mexican-American communities in the U.S. also draw immigrants across the U.S.-Mexico border.

## Undocumented Immigration

Mexicans represent the bulk of undocumented migrant flows. Data on undocumented migrants is necessarily sketchy. However, studies of legalization authorized by the Immigration Reform and Control Act (IRCA) of 1986 indicate that 70 percent of those who were legalized under the amnesty program were of Mexican origin (see Tienda et al., 1991; Singer, 1994).

## Educational Attainment

The Mexican immigrant population comes to the U.S. with low levels of formal education. Male Mexican immigrants average nine years of education (see Table 6.2), which is substantially less than most other native and immigrant groups, who average a high school education. Because Mexico has been the single largest source of migrants to the U.S. for 30 years, and because migrants from Mexico have low levels of formal education, there has been much concern in recent years about declining skills of recent immigrants, and Mexican streams in particular.

## Low Wage Workers

As a corollary to the low educational attainment of Mexican immigrants, Table 6.2 shows that male Mexican immigrant workers (excluding farm workers) averaged an hourly wage rate of only $8 in 1993, which is considerably lower than most other native and immigrant groups. The annual average wage and salary income of male Mexican immigrant workers hovered around $15,000 in 1993, almost 50 percent below that earned by non-Hispanic white immigrants and 24 percent below that earned by U.S.-born Mexicans.

Table 6.1
The Distribution of Foreign- and Native-Born Persons, by Ethnicity from the 1990 Census

A) U.S.-Born Population

| | California | Florida | Illinois | New York | Texas | Other S.W. AZ+CO+NM | Other US | US Total |
|---|---|---|---|---|---|---|---|---|
| Mexican | 3,474,080 | 97,400 | 280,540 | 35,540 | 3,103,620 | 1,001,400 | 986,400 | 8,978,980 |
| Puerto Rican | 124,580 | 230,520 | 113,120 | 837,940 | 42,620 | 16,240 | 897,280 | 2,262,300 |
| Cuban | 25,700 | 147,920 | 5,900 | 23,100 | 7,480 | 3,080 | 63,720 | 276,900 |
| Other Hispanic | 491,620 | 136,060 | 38,980 | 256,000 | 195,080 | 439,900 | 572,080 | 2,129,720 |
| Non-Hispanic Whites | 15,728,680 | 9,401,480 | 9,019,020 | 12,845,480 | 10,932,720 | 5,982,780 | 124,548,880 | 188,459,040 |
| Non-Hispanic Blacks | 1,754,560 | 1,488,600 | 1,246,180 | 1,501,800 | 1,825,560 | 211,180 | 16,696,940 | 24,724,820 |
| Non-Hispanic Asian | 871,940 | 39,120 | 73,580 | 138,380 | 72,740 | 45,280 | 1,071,460 | 2,312,500 |
| Non-Hispanic Other | 329,080 | 50,660 | 27,740 | 68,660 | 81,840 | 389,920 | 1,520,180 | 2,468,080 |
| *Total Persons* | 22,800,240 | 11,591,760 | 10,805,060 | 15,706,900 | 16,261,660 | 8,089,780 | 146,356,940 | 231,612,340 |

B) Foreign-Born Population

| | California | Florida | Illinois | New York | Texas | Other S.W. AZ+CO+NM | Other US | US Total |
|---|---|---|---|---|---|---|---|---|
| Mexican | 2,535,300 | 61,120 | 234,980 | 42,140 | 924,480 | 234,760 | 310,640 | 4,343,420 |
| Puerto Rican | 3,480 | 3,260 | 1,200 | 10,780 | 820 | 340 | 6,960 | 26,840 |
| Cuban | 47,460 | 490,820 | 9,660 | 40,020 | 9,920 | 1,980 | 103,860 | 703,720 |
| Other Hispanic | 718,440 | 311,040 | 45,580 | 508,120 | 116,620 | 24,100 | 571,840 | 2,295,740 |
| Non-Hispanic Whites | 1,143,320 | 443,060 | 337,700 | 974,100 | 178,240 | 147,160 | 2,645,700 | 5,869,280 |
| Non-Hispanic Blacks | 59,740 | 176,660 | 15,580 | 356,620 | 28,140 | 5,220 | 288,040 | 930,000 |
| Non-Hispanic Asian | 1,772,800 | 100,120 | 166,880 | 453,440 | 202,560 | 65,140 | 1,381,160 | 4,142,100 |
| Non-Hispanic Other | 39,440 | 3,660 | 1,760 | 13,380 | 5,260 | 2,640 | 49,280 | 115,420 |
| *Total Persons* | 6,319,980 | 1,589,740 | 813,340 | 2,398,600 | 1,466,040 | 481,340 | 5,357,480 | 18,426,52 |

Source: 1990 U.S. Census Public Use Micro Samples.
Tabulations performed by Emilio Parrado.

## Labor Force Participation

Adult male immigrants from Mexico participate in the labor force at a rate of about 80 percent (see Table 6.2), which is higher than the average rate of both native and immigrant men of comparable ages. One reason for Mexican immigrants' higher labor force participation than other immigrants is age structure. Mexican immigrants are relatively young: only 1.4 percent of all Mexican immigrant male adults are retired, as compared with 7.8 percent for all immigrant male adults, and 12.9 percent for all native-born adult males. Mexican immigrants may also work more in their older years or perhaps may not live long enough to enjoy a lengthy retirement (or may retire back to Mexico); the sample size of the Current Population Survey (on which Table 6.2 is based) is not large enough to allow for deeper study of this question.

All of these features of U.S.-bound Mexican migration—its volume, history, and socioeconomic and demographic composition—would appear both to justify and warrant bilateral policy considerations. This is all the more so because the 2,000-mile shared border facilitates unregulated entry and poses special challenges for both the Mexican and U.S. governments. Because Mexican immigration does not include many refugees (whose entry into the United States satisfies humanitarian or global political criteria), it is reasonable, as a first step, to address the policy issues of Mexican immigration as a simple cost and benefit problem for the U.S. economy: if Mexican migrants are beneficial for the U.S. economy, then less restrictive immigration policies would be appropriate. If Mexican immigration is harmful to the U.S. economy, then restrictive policies are justified.

Before turning to a discussion of the different ways that international migration, and Mexican immigration in particular, may affect the U.S. economy, we offer two comments. Our reading of the recent literature about the economic impacts of immigration, and our own research (including a survey of households and businesses in the mostly Mexican Chicago neighborhood called Little Village), leads us to believe that immigrants in general, and Mexican immigrants in particular, are probably beneficial to the U.S. economy. We will endeavor to justify this assertion in the remainder of this paper.

The second comment relates to the efficacy of restrictive policies toward Mexican immigration. Rather than discuss specific policies in this chapter, we simply note that the duration of U.S.-bound Mexican migration and the resultant size and vibrancy of the established Mexican-American communities in the United States makes control very difficult because migrants can tap into social and familial contacts in the established Mexican-American communities (which lowers the cost of migration). Massey, Donato and Liang (1990) have expressed

### Table 6.2
### Wages and Work Force Participation for Males

#### A) U.S.-Born Male Workers

| | LFPR | Number of workers in (000) | Workers' mean years education | Mean 1993 wages | Mean number of weeks worked 1993 | Hours worked per week | Mean constructed hourly wage |
|---|---|---|---|---|---|---|---|
| *Ethnic group* | | | | | | | |
| Mexican | 73.51% | 1,195 | 12.10 | $19,429 | 44.40 | 38.90 | $10.51 |
| Other Hispanic | 67.93% | 775 | 12.50 | $20,497 | 46.00 | 40.10 | $10.59 |
| Non-Hispanic Black | 63.54% | 4,176 | 12.50 | $19,976 | 44.20 | 38.50 | $10.83 |
| Non-Hispanic White | 76.92% | 48,445 | 13.50 | $27,287 | 46.00 | 41.60 | $14.68 |
| Non-Hispanic Other | 73.83% | 1,178 | 13.00 | $17,668 | 37.50 | 38.70 | $15.71 |
| TOTAL | 75.65% | 55,769 | 13.37 | $26,274 | 45.65 | 41.23 | $14.27 |

#### B) Foreign-Born Male Workers

| | LFPR | Number of workers in (000) | Workers' mean years education | Mean 1993 wages | Mean number of weeks worked 1993 | Hours worked per week | Mean constructed hourly wage |
|---|---|---|---|---|---|---|---|
| *Ethnic group* | | | | | | | |
| Mexican | 79.87% | 1,427 | 9.40 | $14,855 | 46.00 | 38.90 | $8.10 |
| Other Hispanic | 74.51% | 870 | 12.10 | $20,045 | 44.70 | 40.80 | $10.73 |
| Non-Hispanic Black | 67.24% | 315 | 14.00 | $19,664 | 44.10 | 41.90 | $10.29 |
| Non-Hispanic White | 71.72% | 1,825 | 14.00 | $28,823 | 44.70 | 40.60 | $15.51 |
| Non-Hispanic Other | 80.79% | 1,582 | 14.70 | $27,847 | 46.50 | 39.70 | $15.94 |
| TOTAL | 76.20% | 6,019 | 12.82 | $23,507 | 45.45 | 40.06 | $12.90 |

Source: March, 1994 Current Population Survey. Labor Force Participation Rates include all adult males. All other columns apply only to non agricultural adult male workers.

informed skepticism about the deterrent effects of IRCA. Massey's work on immigration has emphasized the strength of social and familial ties as factors that draw Mexican immigrants to the United States, and the impotence of governmental policies that attempt to restrict immigration after sister communities are established in the United States. Zolberg (1995) has called attention to the perverse effects and unintended consequences of U.S. immigration policies. We raise this point simply as a cautionary note for policy discussions; the complexity of the real world is humbling for those of us who work on policy issues, particularly when framed in narrow economic terms.

## The Economic Impacts of Immigration

Academic studies about the economic impacts of immigration are concerned with various different types of impacts. Accordingly, we adopt Greenwood's (1994) language in which he refers to separate and distinct channels of influence through which immigration affects the economy of the host society. In this chapter we discuss a few these channels of influence, paying special attention to labor market impacts. We will treat only briefly the most commonly studied channel of influence, that is, the direct effect of immigrants on the wages of natives. One common view of immigration sometimes found in the mass media is that immigrants take jobs away from native workers, or exert a downward force on wages by accepting lower wages than comparably skilled native workers. Immigrants, however, also create jobs by their own demand for goods and services, and immigrant workers can be complements as well as substitutes for native workers. The net effects of immigrants on the wages of natives is therefore difficult to measure, although many have tried.

The second most frequently studied channel of influence focuses on the direct fiscal impact of immigrants, and we will again be brief with this topic. Fiscal impacts concern the current account balance between what immigrants pay in taxes and fees and what they consume in tax-supported amenities and services. Mexican immigrants earn low wages, and therefore pay lower than average income tax. Mexicans also have larger than average families, so they may consume more in public education services than they pay in local taxes. The issue is complicated, as we note below, by the fact that Mexican (and other) immigrants pay their share of Social Security taxes, a regressive tax, and many immigrants are ineligible for Social Security benefits. We will take up the issue of fiscal channel of influence with a brief literature review below.

Instead of focusing on the labor market channel of influence or the fiscal channel of influence, both of which have been extensively analyzed, albeit inconclusively, we focus instead on the channels of influence that derive from economies of scale, and the special contributions that immigrants may make through their inventiveness, motivation, and self-selection for willingness to work hard in order to improve their lot in life. The former consideration is important for Mexican immigration because of the sheer volume of the flow, while the latter is relevant because the low educational attainment of Mexicans relative to other immigrants and U.S. natives leads to the partly inaccurate inference that Mexican immigrants are unlikely to be entrepreneurial. To make our case on these two points, we draw on a recent survey of entrepreneurship in the Mexican neighborhood of Little Village, Chicago.

## The Labor Market "Channel of Influence": A Brief Comment

Borjas and Tienda (1987) summarize many of the empirical studies of wage and labor market impacts of immigration, with the general finding that immigrants' impact on the wages of natives are barely significant, while impacts on the wages of earlier cohorts of immigrants are discernible, albeit small. Greenwood and McDowell (1993) also provide an extensive survey of this literature, therefore we provide only a few comments. The first point is that, as Borjas (1994) notes, there are some methodological and empirical shortcomings of this line of work. Most of the labor market studies use the number of immigrants in a city as a measure of the immigrants' influence in a particular labor market. One problem is that natives may migrate internally in response to immigration (for instance, to avoid immigrants) so that the correlation of immigrant presence with low native wages may simply represent the effect of selective internal migration by natives.

A second problem has been highlighted by Card's (1990) empirical study of the massive and sudden wave of Cuban migration to Miami in 1980, known as the Mariel boat lift. Card has shown that this sudden wave of mostly low-skilled migrants, which in the course of six months increased Miami's work force by 7 percent (60,000 people), had no perceptible impact on Miami's labor market for either natives or for previous Cuban migrants. This surprising result implies that the economic impacts of migrants are not so easily isolated to their city of entry or residence, as has been previously assumed. Considering that the Mariel boat lift corresponded to a wave of migration that was a full order of magnitude larger (relative to the work force of Miami) than most of the empirical studies are able to contemplate, and that no impacts were found, Card's study raises fundamental questions about the efficacy of the econometric literature on labor market impacts of migration.

## The Fiscal Channel of Influence

Empirical studies about fiscal channels of influence have been weighted down by studies that examine only part of the fiscal picture (i.e., welfare) and studies that examine only local impacts. Simon (1984, 1989, and 1996) has presented a series of analyses based on the most comprehensive data source available—the 1976 Study of Income and Expenditures. He showed that immigrants are net fiscal contributors to the U.S. economy mainly because they contribute to, but do not receive benefits from, the Social Security program. This is because immigrants have a high worker-to-dependent ratio, and because immigrants of retirement age are generally not eligible for benefits. Social Security is a federal program, and Simon points out, as do Greenwood and McDowell (1993), that much of the fiscal burden of immigration is felt by states and localities.

The peculiarities of the distribution of the fiscal effects of immigration implies that local and state governments probably *are* burdened by immigration, but that this burden is more than balanced by immigrants' support of Social Security. The fiscal burden felt by states and localities in regard to immigration is, therefore, not a real "cost" of immigration, but rather a problem in the fiscal balance between the federal government and the states, and more specifically between the states with few immigrants (whose retirees are partly subsidized by immigrants) and the immigrant-receiving states. Precisely because they ignore federal programs like Social Security, studies that focus on local fiscal impacts, such as Mines and Martin (1986), Muller and Espenshade (1985) and McCarthy and Valdez (1986), have left the possibly mistaken impression that immigrants are a fiscal drain on the U.S. economy. Rothman and Espenshade (1992) were rather critical of Simon's analysis for two reasons. One reason is that Simon aggregated immigrants of all national origins, and the second is that he applied national average figures for taxation and per pupil school expenditure to populations that are not evenly distributed across the country. Neither criticism invalidates Simon's inference that Social Security payments by immigrants make them net fiscal assets to the U.S. economy (although the lack of national disaggregation does pose some problems for applying Simon's findings to the case of Mexican immigrants only).

In the particular case of Mexican immigrants, the issue of fiscal impacts is complicated by the fact that there are legal and illegal immigrants, who use services and transfers at very different rates and whose contributions to Social Security and to federal taxes differ depending on whether they are formally or informally employed, and depending on their legal status in the United States.

Heer (1990) and Weintraub and Cardenas (1984) claimed that undocumented Mexicans use fewer services or transfers (because they are either not eligible for them or are wary of any contact with officials). This implies that undocumented workers are essentially a fiscal windfall for employers and also for state and national coffers (because they do pay taxes). Weintraub and Cardenas (1984) estimated that the state of Texas received a fiscal benefit of at least $120 million per year from undocumented aliens (mostly Mexicans), although Rothman and Espenshade (1992) point out that Weintraub and Cardenas' data is based on a non-random interview sample. Undocumented workers occupy a peculiar space in the rhetoric about immigration. Undocumented workers, or illegal immigrants, are the object of much political backlash against migration, yet (if Heer and Weintraub and Cardenas are correct) they may be the most fiscally beneficial of migrants.

## Economies of Scale and Innovation

The first modern essay on population growth and the economy is credited to Malthus, who assumed that natural resources were fixed and that therefore a larger population would necessarily mean a lower standard of living for everyone. Simon (1993) notes that Malthus wrote five different editions of his famous essay, and each subsequent edition was less alarmist about the consequences of larger populations. Adam Smith and the other early innovators of modern economic theory took a different view. For Smith, a greater population meant a greater division of labor, which implied greater efficiency and product per person, and therefore positive returns to scale. One of Smith's famous examples is the pin factory, where the manufacture of pins is divided into eighteen different tasks, each performed by one person.

Simon (1993) cites a number of nineteenth-century economists who directly confronted Malthus' initial supposition that natural resources are fixed; he quotes Henry George, who wrote "Both the jayhawk and the man eat chickens, but the more jayhawks the fewer chickens, while the more men the more chickens." This same anti-Malthusian view is developed at some length in Simon (1989). The basic premise is the classical economic notion that the price mechanism ensures that as demand for a given natural resource rises while supply falls, technology and innovation will be applied to find more or to create substitutes for the important resource. Simply put, the greater the human demand for chickens, the more farmers will devote themselves to new and more efficient ways to produce chickens. Technology, in other words, overcomes some of, if not all, the apparent limits of natural resources. Not all resources are as easy to replenish as chickens, of course, and Simon takes his argument considerably further. He argues that, despite the claims of the environmentalists, natural resources from fresh water to forests to oil reserves have never been more plentiful (at least in terms of the resources that are directly accessible by society).

The past two centuries of history in the developed world have proven that Malthus' alarmist view of population growth is insufficient. Therefore, Preston (1989), Simon (1989) and others have reemphasized the positive economic potential of population growth. Some public goods, such as national defense, do not depend directly on the size of the population. An increase in population ought not to increase the need for national defense, but would increase the number of people paying for defense, thus lowering the cost per capita and lessening the burden on the native residents. This would be experienced as a direct positive return to scale. Most services are not like national defense, however, so that population growth would require an increase in services provided. Education, police protection, health care, electricity and sewer service are noteable examples. In the case of these basic services, the question is whether the additional services are provided at increasing or decreasing marginal cost. If the marginal cost of providing a service decreases as the population grows (holding the quality of the service constant, which is easier to do in theory than in practice), then population growth will lower the per capita cost of that service, and everyone will benefit from returns to scale.

In theory (and usually in practice), an increasing population leads to higher population density, and higher density areas receive most services at a lower cost per person. For example, rural electrification costs much more per person served than urban electrification. Some rural schools may be less costly per pupil than urban schools, but unlike the provision of electricity, the quality of education services is not easily comparable. Preston (1989) points out that in the United States, which has a relatively low average population density, the majority of the population is crowded around large metropolitan areas, leaving many rural counties almost vacant. Population concentration, therefore, is a precondition for positive returns to scale. Both Preston and Simon cite the powerful Japanese economy, with high population density and few natural resources, as an example of the importance of returns to scale. The Japanese enjoy minimal transportation and communication costs because their population density is so high.

On the question of returns to scale and economic history, the central figure is Simon Kuznets. Kuznets (1960, [1967] 1973, [1972] 1973) argued that not only are there positive returns to scale in industry because of greater specialization and because of technological innovation, but that technological innovation itself is subject to a scale economy. The reasoning is as follows: there are a fixed proportion of innovators and geniuses in any population. Because different branches of knowledge are interrelated, and because engineering and technical innovations rest on an established base of knowledge (the cumulative effects of earlier innovations), it stands to reason that larger societies will have a greater number of innovators and geniuses (because of sheer numbers). Furthermore, this larger number of innovators and geniuses will feed off each other's work to create an economy of scale for innovation, which will in turn make the entire society more efficient. As Kuznets writes (1960: 328), "The greatest factor in growth of output per capita is, of course, the increasing stock of tested, useful knowledge."

If there are in fact positive returns to scale as Kuznets and Simon and the classical economists claimed, the implication for immigration is fairly clear: more people make the whole society more efficient, and immigration, on balance, should be beneficial to the host society. The issue is, of course, more complex because there can also be diseconomies of scale, and because the extent of positive or negative returns to scale is the subject of substantial disagreement in the empirical literature. The question of returns to scale is central, however. The pro-immigration studies generally assume, as Simon (1989) does, a positive return to scale for population growth. And most anti-immigrant work emphasizes over crowding, overuse of limited resources, and other implicit negative returns to scale for population growth.

The economic literature that employs explicit models for the impacts of immigration, such as Borjas (1995), almost invariably assumes zero returns to scale in the production functions. Despite the fact that the measurement of real returns to scale presents many empirical problems, and therefore the assumption of zero returns to scale is a defensible assumption, we believe that this common assumption builds an inherent bias against possible economic benefits of immigration. Kuznets' economic history of the United States makes a strong case for the importance of returns to scale over time, and Simon has pointed out that there is little reason to believe these historical arguments are any less relevant today.

The returns to scale issue is further complicated for the case of Mexican immigrants because Mexicans are, on average, the immigrant group with the fewest years of formal education (see Table 6.2 and also Chiswick, 1986; Borjas, 1992; Borjas and Freeman, 1992). This means that arguments about the innovative capacity of Mexican migrants may be a bit harder to make. On the other hand, the size and duration of the flow of migrants from Mexico (and the resultant size, development, and division of labor within the established Mexican-American communities) provides many possibilities for scale economies internal to the Mexican-American neighborhoods themselves.

As we will see in the vignettes from our Little Village (Chicago) survey, this immigrant Chicago neighborhood has enough Mexicans to support a fully differentiated economy of goods and services. Because the Little Village community is growing, and because the consumer tastes and language of the Little Village residents is best understood by other co-ethnic residents, there are ample opportunities for business, entrepreneurship, and economic innovation in Little Village and in other Mexican-American communities. Little Village, in other words, is conducive to myriad formal and informal economic activities which are largely invisible to formal accounting systems and surveys. Moreover, there is more economic innovation in these communities than the low level of formal education of the Mexican migrants might lead one to believe.

Arguments about national-level diseconomies of scale generally rest on the inefficiency of large enterprises due to inertia and the inability to change and adapt. Robinson (1960) presents multinational data on the cost of national administration (health, education, services and defense), and argues that the large countries (which in most of his samples, means the United States) are not necessarily more efficient in providing services than the smaller countries (Great Britain, France, Italy, Jamaica). Robinson's data shows that United States spends less per capita on national administration except for defense, where the United States spends far more. The problem with this kind of data is that there is no way to account for differences in the quality of the services provided, so one does not know whether India is either a tremendously efficient provider of national services, or a provider of very sparse administrative services (the latter is probably closer to the truth). Robinson (1960: xvii) makes the rather bold claim that "it seemed to be our general impression that most of the major industrial economies of scale could be achieved by a relatively high-income nation of 50 million," which would imply, of course, that the U.S. is far too big to enjoy any further advantages from scale economies. The problem, however, is that the 50-million-person limit is arbitrary, and no empirical data or sound reasoning is cited to support it.

Jewkes (1960) makes an argument about the diseconomies of scale that seems to contradict Kuznets directly on the issue of economies of scale for innovation. Jewkes argues that although there are some examples of large corporate research and development making technological breakthroughs that would have been impossible for individual inventors to make (he cites the DuPont corporation's invention of Nylon), most inventions are made by individuals working alone. Jewkes points out that the aircraft jet engine was invented simultaneously by a British air force cadet and a German undergraduate, working by themselves. In terms of Kuznets' theory, what is relevant for our argument is that the inventors of the jet engine lived in the well-populated developed countries, and were therefore able to take advantage of a stock of knowledge, and had access to other innovators and ideas that would not have been available to an equally talented inventor living in Costa Rica or Belize. The invention of the jet engine by two separate individuals does not, therefore, undermine the idea of scale economies in knowledge.

When Kuznets refers to innovation and technology as the engines for economic growth (see Kuznets [1972] 1973), he mainly refers to technologies like the steam engine, the light bulb, the telephone, the internal combustion gasoline engine, or the more recent advent of atomic energy. These technological advances have had profound and lasting effects on the economy, without doubt (although the legacy of atomic energy may not be as clear as Kuznets imagined). But Kuznets' emphasis on the highest levels of technological input leave open the question of whether working-class immigrants can be considered as advantages in a scale economy of knowledge, which according to Kuznets' examples, would seem to favor mainly the immigration of physicists, engineers, doctors and other highly trained people.

Simon (1989: 175) offers one answer to this question. In his words:

> It cannot be emphasized too strongly that "technological advance" does not mean only "science" and scientific geniuses are just one part of the knowledge process. Many technological advances come from people who are neither well educated nor well paid: the dispatcher who develops a slightly better way of deploying the taxis in his ten-taxi fleet; the shipper who discovers that garbage cans make excellent cheap containers; the supermarket manager who finds a way to display more merchandise in a given space; the supermarket clerk who finds a quicker way to stamp prices on cans; the market researcher in the supermarket chain who experiments and finds more efficient and cheaper means of advertising the store's prices and sale items and so on.

Simon appropriately acknowledges that it is not only the Enrico Fermis and Albert Einsteins who contribute to knowledge and hence economic efficiency, but also motivated, entrepreneurial and innovative immigrants who, despite a lack of formal education, may contribute to a society's economic well-being. It is well to remember that much of the economic literature assumes that years of schooling is a direct measurement of skill and hence of worker productivity. Simon (1989) argues that immigrants bring with them knowledge based on the experience of how things are done in other places, and may therefore be highly productive in their host society despite a limited formal education. The burgeoning literature on ethnic enterprise in America would appear to support this view.

Supplementary to Simon's argument about working-class innovation and entrepreneurship are studies that consider how immigrants may be self-selected for entrepreneurial spirit and work ethic. Chiswick (1978: 901) argues that the good performance (in excess of what their moderate schooling levels would lead one to expect) of immigrants in the U.S. economy is evidence that the immigration process self selects migrants for "motivation" and "innate ability." Chiswick's empirical findings have been repeatedly questioned by Borjas (1992, 1994) who argues that Chiswick confused an assimilation effect with a cohort effect; Borjas' point is that there has been a decline in immigrant skills rather than an assimilation of immigrants over time.

Borjas (1992) refers to the declining skills of recent immigrant cohorts, but his own tables show that overall immigrant educational attainment has risen steadily over time (from 9.5 years in 1940 to 12 years in 1980). U.S. native educational attainment has simply risen faster. Hence it is not immigrant skills that are declining, but rather U.S. native skills (measured by years of education) that are outpacing the skills of the immigrants, and precisely at a time when returns to skills have been rising markedly. The educational attainment of Mexican male immigrants to the United States has crept up from about 7 years in the 1950s to a bit less than 9 years today (in Table 6.2, their educational attainment is reported as 9.4 years, but this is for only non-agricultural workers; the full sample of Mexican male immigrants averaged 8.7 years of education). As such, the "skills" of Mexican immigrants (as measured by education) have not declined over time. The education gap between Mexican immigrants and natives may have increased over time, but Chiswick's analysis still rests on immigrants' advantages stemming from self-selection on determination and creativity, if not formal schooling. Since both Chiswick and Borjas rely mainly on cross-sectional data from the decennial census, it is not entirely possible to adjudicate between their competing conclusions or interpretations because neither can adequately model period effects which have greatly altered opportunities for earning a living.

Kao and Tienda (1995) have recently demonstrated a result which bolsters Chiswick's idea that immigrants are self selected for innate skill and motivation. Using the National Education Longitudinal Survey (NELS:88), they showed that the children of first-generation immigrants have higher scholastic aspirations and test scores than their native-born counterparts of similar socioeconomic standing. Although the effect that Kao and Tienda measure is strongest for the children of Asian immigrants, the children of Hispanic immigrants also seemed to benefit from this optimism and strong immigrant work ethic.

If Mexican immigrants are self selected for innate skill and motivation, it is partly due to the fact that Mexican immigrants come to the United States for economic opportunity rather than fleeing Mexico for political reasons. Political refugees, as Chiswick (1978) notes, migrate for noneconomic reasons, and therefore would not necessarily represent the most fit, able, or motivated citizens. Economic migrants (like the Mexican migrants), who assume the costs and risks of migration, would naturally be most likely to migrate if they considered their own abilities and determination would produce higher returns in the destination country. This, at any rate, is the rationale for believing that economic immigrants might be self selected for innate ability. There is, of course, no direct way to measure innate skills. What we offer, instead, is a glimpse into the Little Village neighborhood of Chicago, which shows substantial levels of economic activity and entrepreneurship.

## Mexican Immigrants' Entrepreneurship and Innovation

The Little Village Household Survey, hereafter LVHS, consists of in-depth interviews from 330 households in Chicago's mostly Mexican Little Village community (see Tienda and Raijman, 1996, for a more detailed description). The survey uncovered considerably higher rates of self-employment and informal employment for Mexicans (especially Mexican immigrants) than had been previously found. According to 1980 U.S. Census figures (Fratoe, 1986), 4.9 percent of all Americans were self-employed. Some ethnic groups, such as Russians and Lebanese, were self-employed at rates approaching 10 percent, while for Mexicans the self-employment rate hovered around 2 percent. According to the LVHS, self-employment rates for Mexicans in Little Village were about 10 percent. While the higher rate of self-employment may be partly due to the urban setting of the Little Village community (which excludes the farm worker population, almost none of whom would be self-employed), the LVHS in-depth interviews also uncovered that much self-employment occurs in the informal economy, which is a kind of economic activity that standard surveys seldom detect.

Following Portes and Sassen-Koob (1987), we note that the level of self-employment, and especially self-employment via informal activities, can be viewed as a source of economic innovation at the margins of a developed economy (there is considerable debate about the value of the informal sector in both developing and developed countries; see Portes and Schauffler, 1993, for a review). In fact, according to preliminary analysis of the LVHS, many Mexican migrants have charted a labor market history that starts with low-wage employment, proceeds to a mixture of low-wage jobs with informal self-employment to smooth income levels, and sometimes proceeds to full-time informal self-employment. A sizeable proportion of the formally self-employed Mexican immigrants in Little Village started those businesses in the informal sector, so that the informal economy can also be seen as a pipeline into the formal economy. By definition, informal businesses do not pay taxes and license fees, which is seldom examined by analyses that estimate the fiscal balance between immigrants and natives. Before going further into the possible benefits and drawbacks that immigrant entrepreneurship entails for the wider economy, we turn to the LVHS interviews themselves for examples. Consider the case of Yolanda (now age forty), who immigrated from the Mexican state of Jalisco to Chicago in 1975. She has a second-grade education, and is married with eight children. The following is a verbatim excerpt from her interview.

> She came to the U.S. with economic necessity and she had always liked the fruit business. She went to Maxwell Street [a flea market in Chicago] where there was a man who sold fruit. She started selling fruit (tomatoes) for the man without him telling her to do so. He liked the way she sold fruit and within three weeks, he looked for her to ask her to help him sell in the flea market. He paid her $25 per day. One day, he made her cry in front of everyone.

He accused her of stealing $25. She held in her anger and stayed there, but she started thinking that maybe she, too, could sell fruit and that way nobody would humiliate her. She told the man she was going to steal whatever she could. Within three weeks she stole $100. She returned the money to him to show him that she was no thief. But because he had humiliated her, he gave her the money. Then she began to study the way he sold, where he got his merchandise, how much he sold it for, etc. Then she asked him to pay her with vegetables instead of with money so that she could sell them. She got a grocery cart (she said she found it in the street— she stressed that she didn't steal the cart). She sold the merchandise that he gave her and made almost twice the amount she earned by working with the man. She saved a little and bought whatever she could from the man so that she could sell it. With $250 she set up a stand at Maxwell Street. In three years she saved $1000, plus $10,000 for a down payment on a house. When she found out that Maxwell Street would be closing, she decided to open up a store. With $1000 she started the store two years ago and until now, she has invested $30,000 in it. She has no debts; she didn't ask for loans because she doesn't like debt. She started the business on her own and she continues to develop it on her own.

The first point to be made about Yolanda's story is that, as Simon (1989) has pointed out, economic innovation can originate among persons of all social classes. Yolanda's second-grade education and modest income did not keep her from finding a better way to sell tomatoes. The second point concerns how much immigrants "take" from the host society in their endeavors to find a better life for themselves. For this question, we take Yolanda's shopping cart as a metaphor. If, as Yolanda claims, her shopping cart (with which she started her fruit-selling business) was indeed simply "found in the street," we see immigrants taking resources that are essentially wasted and returning them into the economy by dint of their own hard work and innovative use.

If, for a moment, we imagine that Yolanda (perhaps a different Yolanda) had stolen the cart, we get the other side of the economic argument. If the cart had been stolen, then Yolanda was not contributing to efficiency but simply cutting in on an already existing market for retail fruit, and perhaps undercutting the sales of a legitimate retail fruit store by selling fruit from a stolen cart without paying any sales tax to the state.

The question of fiscal contributions is a bit more complex, but it seems that Yolanda eventually is also contributing through this economic channel of influence. At first, Yolanda works for the other fruit merchant, and we can assume that no income taxes are being paid from Yolanda's $25 a day salary, and no sales taxes are paid from sales in the Maxwell Street flea market. In the second stage, Yolanda is selling fruit from her own cart, and again we can assume that no sales taxes are being paid. In the third and final stage, Yolanda is reinvesting her money in a house and her own fruit store, which denotes a shift from the informal to the formal economy. In the final stage, Yolanda is presumably paying taxes on a business and a property that were capitalized out of her own effort and creativity. Sassen-Koob (1989) describes the tension between immigrant informal economies that innovate, create and incubate entrepreneurial ideas (and are presumably an asset to the overall economy) versus informal sectors that simply represent tax and regulation avoidance by subcontractors tied to larger, formal firms (this kind of informal business is presumably a drain on the overall economy). Both kinds of informal businesses exist in Little Village.

As Yolanda's story is a bit unusual, we offer a few other representative stories taken from the Little Village survey. Hugo, age 48, was born in Mexico and has a U.S.-born wife, two children, and a Mexican high school education. His father worked on the railroads in Mexico. Hugo started his own business because he did not want to work for others.

> I started this business in 1985 after working for the Lawndale Bank as a vice president. There I discovered that many people wanted to send documents and letters to Mexico and since no one offered this kind of service I decided to establish this business. It took me a year to acquire sufficient understanding of this area. I decided to start this business because of the demand by the people for the service; in this area there are many people that come to make deposits and I think that if they had more education it would work better but none the less we are growing.

Jesus was born in Mexico, immigrated to Chicago in 1965, and now lives with his wife, one child, and his mother-in-law. Jesus had a third-grade education in Mexico. He had been part-owner of a restaurant in Nuevo Laredo, Mexico, and sold it to come to the United States; he says he thinks about business all the time.

> In 1968, there was no latinos here, I was one of the first. The neighborhood was Polish. I rented a garage in which I sold tortas and food. I began to let them taste my food—tacos and everything—and I began to do better and better. It was a small place—a garage. I formed it into a restaurant. I paid rent to a Polish man, when he saw me working hard, he promised to sell it to me. In 1972, the owner of the building financed and sold it to me. It's been 25 years.

José and Efigenia are from Tamaulipas, Mexico, and are both over 50 years old. José reports zero formal education. He says he went into business to be independent.

I came illegally to the U.S. from Mexico, where I was a barber. I started working as a barber in my house, and when I had sufficient clientele I rented a
small place which was completely equipped, and that's how I got to the first
level. After a long time, I got my savings together and started my own business with my own equipment, although I still rent the space.

The modest stories of Hugo, Jesus, José and Efigenia illustrate a few important
points about Mexican migration to the United States. Despite a lack of formal
education, both Jesus and José exhibit the traits of entrepreneurship. Both
abandoned businesses in Mexico in order to come to the United States, where,
presumably, they expected to receive better returns for their skills. Admittedly,
this is circumstantial evidence for the theoretical proposition that immigrants
from Mexico, and other non-refugee countries are self selected for innate skill,
or entrepreneurial spirit. But absent direct empirical evidence, many have
concluded that low education levels are inconsistent with innovation and
entrepreneurial activity.

A second point relates to the size of Chicago's Mexican-American community,
and the differentiated economy that is implied by residential concentration within
the city limits. Because Little Village was (or became) populous and diversified,
there were ample opportunities for new and innovative kinds of businesses, like
Hugo's document and currency transmission service. The information that Hugo
needed in order to start his business was an experiential knowledge based on
having lived in Mexico and the United States, and having contact with the consumer
needs of households in Little Village, rather than formal education.

## Conclusion

The literature on the effects of population growth on economic development
is justifiably modest in its claims and predictions. Kuznets himself ([1967] 1973)
readily admitted that increased population could have different impacts on an
economy, depending on many factors, and that therefore there is no single "population effect." Mexican migrants to the United States are almost always viewed
in the recent literature as low-wage labor market drones—people who are willing
to work picking lettuce or sewing pants in a factory for just a few dollars a day.
The bulk of the literature then turns on whether this low-wage labor is more
beneficial to the United States, or detrimental because the migrants exert a downward pressure on wages and also use state services. Our point in this paper is that
Mexican migrants, despite their low average formal education, may contribute
significantly to the U.S. economy through economic and cultural innovations,
and returns to scale for a larger population.

Direct national returns to scale may be due to a greater national division of labor, or to a larger number of persons to share fixed costs such as defense, or to a decreasing marginal cost for transportation, communication and other basic services. These scale economies would be created regardless of the origin or profile of the immigrants. The country as a whole may also benefit from a larger population due to an increased number of technical and practical innovations. This is Kuznets' theory, and Simon has reminded us that beneficial innovations can come from people of any class or educational background. While the flow of immigrants from Mexico may provide a somewhat lower yield of scientific innovations (because of the low proportion of Mexican immigrants who have postgraduate education), many Mexican migrants are able to take advantage of a different, local kind of scale economy. Because of the size and duration of the flow of migration from Mexico, Mexican migrants are integrated into the U.S. economy through Mexican-American communities that are themselves large enough and diverse enough (especially the urban neighborhoods like Little Village in Chicago) to support innovative new businesses.

Mexican immigrants are workers; their labor force participation is high because they come to the United States in their prime working years. Because the flow of Mexican migrants is so heavily weighted toward young workers and contains so few retirees, Mexican immigrants make an especially positive fiscal contribution to the national Social Security program. Mexican migrants may also be self selected for talent, motivation and innate skill, as Chiswick would argue, which would imply that the low educational attainment of Mexican immigrants underestimates their real skill and productivity. We cannot deny, however, that the low educational attainment of Mexican migrants also correlates with low annual and hourly wages, so that the economic returns to this (supposed) high level of innate skill and motivation is not easily detected in the Current Population Survey. Chiswick would argue that the respondents in the CPS (especially the Mexican immigrants) are weighted to the most recent immigrants (because the flow of immigration from Mexico has been increasing over time—see Table 6.3), and that it takes time for the innate skills of immigrants to lift their earnings to the level of native workers. Chiswick (1986) reports that the earnings of Mexican immigrants exceeds the earnings of native workers when the Mexican immigrants have been in the U.S. labor market for 15 years.

We have not considered migrants' possible effect on the U.S. economy through their consumer purchases. Migrants not only increase the size of the U.S. consumer market but they also have particular tastes and needs that may affect the tastes of natives. Immigrants, as Simon (1989) points out, have throughout history been viewed as the bearers of new ideas, new ideas that have been tested in other societies and contexts. Despite the fact that the effect of population growth

## Table 6.3
## Historical Trends in Legal Mexican Migration to the U.S.

| Period | Number of legal Mexican immigrants | Total (all countries) legal immigrants | Mexican immigration as % of total |
|---|---|---|---|
| 1901-1910 | 49,642 | 8,273,667 | 0.60% |
| 1911-1920 | 219,004 | 5,763,263 | 3.80% |
| 1921-1930 | 459,287 | 4,100,777 | 11.20% |
| 1931-1940 | 22,319 | 531,405 | 4.20% |
| 1941-1950 | 60,589 | 1,044,638 | 5.80% |
| 1951-1960 | 299,811 | 2,519,420 | 11.90% |
| 1961-1970 | 453,934 | 3,313,387 | 13.70% |
| 1971-1980 | 640,294 | 4,509,113 | 14.20% |
| 1981-1989 | 974,200 | 5,801,600 | 16.79% |

Sources: Bean and Tienda (1987), Statistical Abstract of the United States, and Statistical Yearbook of the U.S. Immigration and Naturalization Service

on economic growth is quite resistant to formal quantification because of the myriad ways that population increase can trigger economic effects, we urge that questions about economies of scale be considered more systematically. There is no sound reason to think that the United States has passed some magic population density that makes it immune to any further benefits from economies of scale. The implications of positive returns to scale are simply that, other things being equal, a larger population will tend to increase the economic efficiency of the entire society.

## Note

This research has been supported by the U.S.-Mexico Binational Commission on Immigration. The Little Village Household Survey on which we draw is part of a project, "Entrepreneurship in Chicago's Ethnic Neighborhoods," (Marta Tienda, Richard Taub and Robert Townsend, Principal Investigators) supported by a grant to the Center for the Study of Urban Inequality from the Rockefeller, the Ford and the Macarthur Foundations. We acknowledge institutional support from the Ogburn-Stouffer Center of NORC and the University of Chicago, and the technical assistance of Fay Booker. The usual disclaimers apply.

# References

Bean, Frank D., and Marta Tienda. 1987. *The Hispanic Population of the United States.* New York: Russell Sage Foundation.

Borjas, George. 1995. "The Economic Benefits from Immigration." *Journal of Economic Perspectives* 9: 3-22

————. 1994. "The Economics of Immigration." *Journal of Economic Literature* 32: 1667-1717.

————. 1992. "National Origin and the Skills of Immigrants in the Postwar Period." Chapter 1 in *Immigration and the Work Force,* edited by George Borjas and Richard Freeman. Chicago: University of Chicago Press and NBER.

Borjas, George, and Richard Freeman. 1992. "Introduction and Summary." *Immigration and the Work Force,* edited by George Borjas and Richard Freeman. Chicago: University of Chicago Press and NBER.

Borjas, George, and Marta Tienda. 1987. "The Economic Consequences of Immigration." *Science* 235: 645-651

Card, David. 1990. "The Impact of the Mariel Boat Lift on the Miami Labor Market." *Industrial Labor Relations Review* 43: 245-57

Chiswick, Barry. 1978. "The Effects of Americanization on the Earnings of Foreign-Born Men." *Journal of Political Economy* 86: 897-921

————. 1986. "Is the New Immigration Less Skilled than the Old?" *Journal of Labor Economics* 4: 168-192

Fratoe, Frank. 1986. "A Sociological Analysis of Minority Business." *Review of Black Political Economy* 15: 5- 29

Greenwood, Michael J. 1994. "Potential Channels of Immigrant Influence on the Economy of the Receiving Country." *Papers in Regional Science* 73: 211-240.

Greenwood, Michael J., and John McDowell. 1993. "The Labor Market Consequences of U.S. Immigration." Submitted to U.S. Department of Labor.

Heer, David. 1990. *Undocumented Mexicans in the United States.* Cambridge: Cambridge University Press.

Jewkes, J. 1960. "Are Economies of Scale Unlimited?" Chapter 6 in *Economic Consequences of the Size of Nations.* edited by E.A.G. Robinson. London: Macmillan.

Kao, Grace, and Marta Tienda. 1995. "Optimism and Achievement: The Educational Performance of Immigrant Youth." *Social Science Quarterly* 76: 1-19

Kelley, Allen. 1972. "Demographic Changes and American Economic Development: Past, Present and Future." In *U.S. Commission on Population Growth and the American Future,* edited by Elliot Morss and Ritchie H. Reed. Washington, D.C.: U.S.

Government Printing Office.

Kuznets, Simon. [1972] 1973. "Innovations and Adjustments in Economic Growth." In *Population, Capital and Growth.* New York: Norton

———. [1967] 1973. "Population and Economic Growth." *Proceedings of the American Philosophical Society* III: 170-93. Reprinted in *Population, Capital and Growth.* New York: Norton.

———. 1960. "Population Change and Aggregate Output." In *Demographic and Economic Change in Developed Countries,* 324-340. Princeton, NJ: Princeton University Press for NBER.

Massey, Douglas, Katherine Donato, and Zai Liang. 1990. "Effects of the Immigration Reform and Control Act of 1986: Preliminary Data from Mexico." Chapter 6 in *Undocumented Migration to the United States: IRCA and the Experience of the 1980's,* edited by Frank Bean, Barry Edmondston and Jeffrey S. Passel. Washington D.C.: Urban Institute Press.

McCarthy, Kevin F., and R. Briciaga Valdez. 1986. *Mexican Immigration in California: Dispelling the Myths about Migrants.* Santa Monica. Rand Corporation.

Mines, Richard, and Philip L. Martin. 1986. "A Profile of California Farmworkers." In *Giannini Information Series* 86-2, University of California.

Muller, Thomas, and Thomas J. Espenshade. 1985. *The Fourth Wave: California's Newest Immigrants.* Washington, DC: Urban Institute Press.

North, David S., and Marion F. Houstoun. 1976. *The Characteristics and Role of Illegal Aliens in the U.S. Labor Market: An Exploratory Study.* Washington, DC: U.S Dept. of Labor.

Portes, Alejandro, and Saskia Sassen-Koob. 1987. Making It Underground: Comparative Material on the Informal Sector in Western Market Economies. *American Journal of Sociology* 93: 30-61.

Portes, Alejandro, and Richard Schauffler. 1993. Competing Perspectives on the Latin American Informal Sector. *Population and Development Review* 19: 33-60

Preston, Samuel H. 1989. "The Social Sciences and the Population Problem." In *Demography as an Interdiscipline,* edited by J. Mayone Stycos. New Brunswick, NJ: Transaction Publishers.

Robinson, E.A.G. 1960. *Economic Consequences of the Size of Nations.* London: Macmillan.

Rothman, Eric S., and Thomas J. Espenshade. 1992. "Fiscal Impacts of Immigration to the United States." *Population Index* 58: 381-415

Sassen-Koob, Saskia. 1989. New York City's Informal Economy. Chapter 3 in *The Informal Economy: Studies in Advanced and Less Developed Countries,* edited by Alejandro Portes, Manual Castells, and Lauren A. Benton. Baltimore, MD: Johns Hopkins University Press.

Simon, Julian. 1996. "Public Expenditures on Immigrants in the United States, Past and Present." *Population Development Review (in press).*

———. 1993. "Economic Thought about Population Consequences: Some Reflections." *Population Economics* 6: 137-152.

———. 1989. *The Economic Consequences of Immigration.* Cambridge, MA: Basil

———. 1984. "Immigrants, Taxes, and Welfare in the United States." *Population and Development Review* 10: 55-69.

Singer, Audrey. 1994. "Changes in the Employment and Earnings of the Legalized Population." Report to the U.S. Department of Labor.

Teitelbaum, Michael S., and Myron Weiner. 1995. "Introduction" to Weiner and Teitelbaum, eds., *Threatened Peoples, Threatened Borders: World Migration and U.S. Policy.* New York: Norton.

Tienda, Marta, and Rebeca Raijman. 1996. "Forging Mobility: Immigrants' Socioeconomic Progress in a Low-Wage Environment." Paper presented at SSRC conference on International Migration to the United States

Zolberg, Aristide. 1995. "From Invitation to Interdiction: U.S. Foreign Policy and Immigration since 1945." Chapter 3 in Weiner and Teitelbaum, eds., *Threatened Peoples, Threatened Borders: World Migration and U.S. Policy.* New York: Norton.

# 7.
# Policy, Politics and Emigration:
## Reexamining the Mexican Experience

*Rodolfo O. de la Garza and Gabriel Szekely*

E migration and immigration are issues on which state policy matters. States can impede or facilitate emigration, just as they can welcome or reject immigrants. Disputes arise when sending and receiving states act in contradictory ways, e.g., when one promotes emigration and the other restricts immigration.

U.S. responses to Mexican emigration are a major source of tension in the U.S.-Mexico relationship. Indeed, no issue has more frequently caused problems for the relationship, and none has proven more intractable. To date, however, while numerous studies have examined the origin and impact of U.S. immigration policies, few have examined how Mexican politics and the policies of the Mexican state affect emigration. The objective of this chapter is to begin to fill this void.

The chapter is divided into four sections. The first examines why the literature on emigration has been so inattentive to the effects of Mexican policy and politics. Part two offers a framework illustrating the relationship between domestic politics, state policy and emigration from 1910 through today. The third section uses that framework to describe variations in Mexican emigration in three periods, 1910-1930, 1930-1970, and 1970-1995 (and beyond). The chapter concludes by suggesting the kinds of political and policy reforms that the Mexican state should enact and the Mexican people should demand that would contribute to managing the emigration/immigration issue.

## Why Mexican Emigration Policy Has Been Unanalyzed

From 1910 forward, that is, since the beginning of the first major wave of Mexican emigration, Mexican and American governmental preferences have been aligned for more years than they have been in opposition. Throughout this period, official American policies toward both legal and undocumented immigration have remained consistent. Regarding legal immigration, U.S. policies have always been even more generous vis-à-vis Mexico than they have been toward other countries. Mexico, for example, has been exempted from the restrictions that applied to non-European countries between 1921 and 1965 (Cafferty et al. 1983, 54-55; Bean and Freeman 1966). Official policy regarding illegal immigration has also been consistent since 1917, when Mexican immigration began to be regulated: any Mexican who did not meet the requirements of the immigration laws was an illegal immigrant.

The policy toward illegal immigration has never been consistently enforced, however. It was first implemented against Mexico when the Border Patrol, which was created by National Origins Act of 1924, was empowered to arrest any alien attempting to enter the country illegally (Cafferty et al. 1983, 54). Since then, it has often been ignored or selectively enforced in ways that benefit employers and disadvantage the immigrants (Calavita 1992); on a few occasions it has been vigorously and uniformly enforced within specific geographic locations (McKay 1984). Never, however, has Congress or the public been willing to fund federal agencies so that they could either prevent the great majority of illegal entries or identify and remove all undocumented immigrants already in the country.

The Mexican position, however, has been much more consistent. Although it has had no official policy regarding emigration, the Mexican government has officially (1942-1964) and unofficially (1965-1996) continuously supported high and continuous outflows of legal emigrants, and, except for a brief period prior to and during the early years of the Bracero program, it has also supported undocumented emigration, knowing that many who left would become permanent U.S. residents. Additionally, it has with intermittent vigor defended the right of Mexicans, regardless of their immigrant status, to seek work in the United States and to be treated respectfully while they are in this country.

Thus, since 1924, when U.S. and Mexican policy preferences have coincided, it has been because U.S. officials have not enforced the nation's immigration laws. When the United States and Mexico conflict, as in the 1930s, the 1950s and today, it is because the United States government has changed its attitude toward enforcement and attempted to control illegal immigration. Again, as will be described below, the only exception to this pattern occurred during the early years of the Bracero program when Mexico unsuccessfully called for more vigorous enforcement of U.S. immigration laws so as to discourage illegal emigration. This exception aside, these patterns suggest why efforts to understand how emigration/immigration becomes an issue in U.S.-Mexico relations and how it is addressed have focused primarily on explaining changes in U.S. enforcement practices (Lowell et. al 1986; Calavito 1993; Masey and Espinosa 1995; Bean et al. 1990).

This concern with changes in U.S. policy has diverted attention from understanding how domestic politics affect Mexican emigration policy. Indeed, with important exceptions (Craig 1971; Cross and Sandos 1981), analysts have ignored or dismissed the role politics and policy have played in shaping emigration policy. Leading demographers, for example, seem to have concluded that the Mexican state has had no role in Mexican emigration, and that emigration has not been or is not now a significant issue in Mexico's domestic politics (Massey and Espinosa 1995). Political analysts share this view. Two recent texts make no mention of emigration as a political issue or policy outcome (Levy and Székely 1987; Cornelius 1996), while a third raises it only briefly (Camp 1993, 48-49).

We reject this perspective and argue instead that, as is true in other states (Wiener 1995) Mexican state policy and domestic politics have significantly affected emigration. Furthermore, we argue that this impact is not constant but instead varies as a function of these two factors. Thus, different eras of Mexican political history have produced different types of emigration—emigration in 1910-1930, the violent years of the Revolution, differs in significant ways from emigration during the Mexican Miracle (1940-1982), just as emigration since 1970 is significantly different from prior emigration. In other words, while there has been a continuous flow of emigrants that has varied in size since 1910, there have been significant variations in the types of emigrants who have left Mexico in these different periods.

## Three Types of Emigrants

Central to our argument is the recognition that there are three major types of emigrants, refugees, economic migrants and political migrants; and each is defined by its relationship to state policy and domestic politics. Refugees are individuals who flee their homeland out of fear for their lives (Zolberg et al. 1989, 269), e.g., Jews who left Germany and its allies during the reign of the Third Reich and Mayans who left Guatemala from the late 1970s through the 1980s. Nineteenth-century Italian and Irish immigrants to the United States are examples of economic migrants, i.e., individuals who voluntary migrate to improve their economic situation (Portes and Bach 1985, 73). The distinction between refugees and economic migrants is not always clear, however. Portes and Bach, for example, argue that "it would be hard to prove that the movement out of Cuba was significantly less 'economic' than that out of Mexico or that the latter was much less 'political'" (Portes and Bach 1985, 85). It is also important to note that all of these examples identify emigrants in terms of the conditions in the country of origin rather than on how the receiving country officially classifies them.

The third category, political emigrants, is one that has been ignored in the literature on international migration (Zolberg et al. 1989; Portes and Rumbaut 1990) but which is of particular relevance to recent Mexican emigration. Political emigration is defined as migration that is the result of the failure of the political system to incorporate and respond to publicly articulated demands for participation and policy in ways that reflect governmental accountability and responsiveness. When such demands exist and are articulated, incorporating them requires the government to formulate policies to implement them, to draw on them to modify existing policies, or to explain why they are rejected. In policies that incorporate public demands the great majority of citizens will have some of their demands satisfied some of the time, but few are likely to have all of their demands met. This combination of incorporating demands and partially satisfying them produces efficacy among citizens and legitimizes the state. Citizens whose preferences are either never heard or heard but continuously rejected will feel neither efficacious nor supportive of the state and could, depending on their resources, become alienated and permanently non-participatory, mobilize and threaten the state via urban protests or guerrilla movements, or emigrate (Hirschman 1970).

Political emigrants, thus, are distinct from refugees and economic migrants. Refugees either flee widespread but untargeted violence such as occurs during any revolution, or they emigrate to escape persecution (Zolberg et al. 1989). Refugees migrate because political processes have broken down and been replaced by widespread or targeted violence. Economic migrants leave to improve their economic conditions and are unconcerned about political processes. Thus, as is illustrated by most nineteenth-century Italian and Irish immigrants to the United States, economic migrants are "subjects" rather than "participants" in their home country's politics (Almond and Verba 1963). That is, they are esentially unconcerned about political processes but are instead focused exclusively on governmental outcomes. Their departure may reflect the failure of a government's economic development program or be integral to its implementation and is therefore politically relevant to the state, but such emigration is not in and of itself political from the perspective of the individual (Portes and Bach 1985, 74-75). Political emigration, by contrast, may be linked to economic concerns but it is rooted in dissatisfaction with both governmental policies and the political processes by which government is held accountable. Thus, it may be best understood as the most extreme but non-violent form of political protest available to citizens (Hirschman 1970).

Political emigration is an historical and contemporary phenomenon. Its most significant historical example is evidenced in the seventeenth-century European migration to America (Hartz 1955). Today, Hong Kong and South Africa are major sources of political emigrants. In these cases, emigrants are leaving not because they are poor or because they are being persecuted; they are leaving because they are dissatisfied with extant or potential state policies and have virtually no chance of changing them. The most effective way for them to express their views and defend their economic and social interests is to emigrate.

The United States "owes its very existence and growth to millions" who chose exit over voice (Hirschman 1970, 106), i.e., to political emigrants. Once the nation was established, furthermore, citizens continued to exercise this option by moving west. "Even after the closing of the frontier, the very vastness of the country combined with easy transportation make far more possible for Americans than for most other people to think about solving their problems through 'physical flight' than either through resignation or through ameliorating and fighting in situ the particular conditions into which one has been 'thrown'" (Hirschman 1970, 107).

Clearly, U.S. immigration patterns combine a rich mixture of refugees, economic migrants and, in particular, political emigrants. Given that history and the dramatic changes that Mexico has experienced since 1910, it is puzzling that almost all studies of Mexican migration, especially those by Americans, have ignored the political roots of Mexican emigration and assumed instead that all Mexicans are economic migrants. It is equally noteworthy that the literature on Mexican politics pays considerable attention to the role of the state in Mexico's economic development and to various aspects of political participation including voting, social movements, urban protests and guerilla movements. There are, however, few studies explicitly linking state policy to emigration and none focusing on political emigration. In our judgment these oversights have produced an incomplete and incorrect understanding of Mexican politics and of the interrelationship among domestic politics, state policy and emigration. In the remainder of this chapter, therefore, we will attempt to illustrate the historical relationship among politics, policy and emigration. We will also pay particular attention to how political emigration has developed and begun affecting Mexican domestic politics, official emigration policies and U.S.-Mexico relations.

## Domestic Politics and Emigration

### Refugees, 1910-1930

Large-scale emigration begins following the eruption of the Mexican Revolution of 1910. At that time Mexico's labor force was "primarily agricultural, secondarily artisan, and only thirdly industrial" (Knight 1986, 79). By 1910, the great majority of the agricultural labor force was "not simply landless, but were also subject to the political and social control of the estate. . . . " (Knight 1986, 96). In other words, those Mexicans who would have been the most likely to emigrate were prevented from doing so by the nation's political structures. The Revolution had two powerful consequences: 1) it essentially destroyed the rural economy and the demand for all but the poorest quality jobs, an, 2) it almost immediately broke the chains that tied workers to the hacienda and ended the ability of *hacendados* to control the fate of their workers. Prior to the Revolution, then, agricultural workers (i.e., the majority of Mexicans) lived in poverty but could do little about it. With the Revolution, the economic situation worsened for many, but now they could act in their own self-interest. Political change, in sum, made it possible for Mexico's peasants to consider a variety of alternatives for improving their lives.

The Revolution brought widespread violence to Mexico. "Moderate estimates" indicate that between 1.5 and 2 million people died between 1910-1920. (Meyer and Sherman 1983, 552). Generalized violence diminished for several years and then exploded again in the Cristero Rebellion of 1926-1929 and was concentrated in north and west-central Mexico, and especially in the states of Michoacán, Jalisco, Guanajuato and San Luis Potosi, where approximately 100,000 more died (Cross and Sandos 1981, 9).

One of the ways Mexicans responded to these violent episodes was to move. Many migrated within the nation. However, it was at this time that emigration to the United States began to become institutionalized. Official records indicate that between 1910-1930 almost 700,000 Mexicans entered the United States (Bean and Freeman 1996). This, however, is a conservative estimate since records were so poorly kept at this time and entering the United States was so simple (Balderama 1982, 5).

Political upheavals from 1910-1930, thus, explain the origins of Mexican emigration. Because most of those who left between 1910 and 1920 were fleeing widespread violence, and many (most?) of those who fled in the late 1920s were escaping violence and anti-Catholic persecution before and through the Cristero Rebellion, it is fair to conclude that this first wave of emigrants consisted primarily of refugees (Zolberg et al. 1989, 33). Given that Mexico was in the throes of a civil war, however, politics rather than governmental policy was the factor behind emigration. That is, during these years there was no effective government in Mexico, and therefore the state per se was not involved in promoting this emigration.

## Economic Migrants, 1930-1970

By the 1930s, the modern Mexican state was being consolidated, and with that, governmental policy began shaping emigration patterns. From an economic perspective, the goals of the "Revolutionary Family" quickly focused on the long-term industrial development and urbanization of the nation at the expense of the countryside (Brandenburg 1965). Ironically, this was effected through policies that initially emphasized the break-up of the haciendas and an agrarian reform that favored the peasants. By the 1960s, however, Mexico's peasants would become the least influential sector within Mexico's ruling party. By 1994, despite an extensive land reform program or, what is more likely, perhaps because of how it was implemented, the economic viability of the peasantry was not much greater than it was before 1930 (Cornelius 1996, 79 ).

Politically, the nation's political leaders needed an acquiescent if not actively supportive peasantry. This was guaranteed via the agrarian reform that was most energetically enforced under President Lazaro Cardenas (1934-40) and continued into the Salinas regime, which officially terminated the government's commitment to the *ejido* in 1992. During that half-century the government maintained its commitment to these policies with a combination of practices that initially combined substance with symbol, and that by the 1990s, as the Zapatista protests clearly illustrate, consisted almost entirely of symbolic manipulations and virtually no substance (Oppenheimer 1996, 48-60).

There can be no doubt that these policies stimulated migration and emigration by undercutting *ejidos* while promoting and subsidizing private agriculture. The *ejidos* were often too small to be efficient; by the mid 1960s those that had access to irrigation and thus might be productive averaged 4.54 hectares and thus were too small to be productive. Meanwhile, private land holdings easily found ways to exceed the legal maximum of 100 hectares. For example, in the 1970s the average private farm size in Sonora's Yaqui River valley was estimated at 500 hectares. Private lands, thus, became the focus of the state's agricultural development program. More significantly for the purposes of this chapter, from 1941-1970, almost half of all public funds for irrigation went to Baja California, Sonora, Sinaloa and Tamaulipas, where almost one million hectares of new irrigated land were created. Yet in 1960, these states were home to only 9.3 percent of the nation (Cross and Sandos 1981, 16-26). Mexico's development policy, in sum, made it impossible for the great masses of the rural population to maintain themselves as farmers or agricultural workers, even as it was incapable of providing them employment in the cities. Millions therefore pursued the only jobs that were available, and many of these were beyond the Rio Bravo.

In addition to providing the state with a means for realizing its developmental objectives, these policies also were implemented so as to weaken if not eliminate the Revolution's major opposition. In its first phases, international migration came primarily from the states of Michoacán, Guanajuato, Jalisco, and Zacatecas, "curiously the same region in which were generated, simultaneously, two social movements that had transcendental significance for the future of Mexican reality in the twentieth century, the agrarian movement and the Cristero movement. The study of peasant migration in this region can not be separated from these types of historical determinants" (Rionda Ramirez 1992, 23).

Movement out of this region began in the 1910-1930 period when approximately one-fifth of the population moved to other parts of Mexico and to the United States. This accelerated after 1940 as a result of how the government implemented its agrarian policy and the Bracero program. For example, while the number of *ejidos* in Guanajuato, Jalisco and Michoacán grew by 217 percent from 1930 to 1940, between 1941 and 1970 this region received only 15 percent of the nation's investment in irrigation even though it had 25 percent of the nation's population (Cross and Sandos 1981, 11-22). More significantly, the Catholic conservatism that gave rise to the Cristeros reappeared as the Sinarquista political party in 1937 and became a major threat to the state. The government responded carefully but effectively, and by 1944 the party was outlawed and went underground. Its future was destroyed in large part because of how the state implemented the *Bracero* program (1942-1964). Two-thirds of all *Bracero* contracts were allocated to peasants from the Sinarquista region (Cross and Sandos 1981, 42). The central government was responsible for allocating these contracts, and thus it appears that the state used the *Bracero* program to further both its economic and political objectives. Removing so many potential and real opponents from this area effectively killed Sinarquismo in Mexico and brought peace to the region once more.

Nonetheless, emigration policy, particularly as it became formalized in the *Bracero* program, did not go uncontested in Mexico. Indeed, the nation's three major economic sectors opposed the program. Industrialists protested against exporting workers on the grounds that it deprived them of needed labors. Unions were opposed because it depleted their potential ranks and made no provision to have Braceros unionize once they were in the United States. Agricultural entre-preneurs complained that they were losing workers and that Mexican workers were helping American cotton growers produce a surplus that would undermine the Mexican cotton industry (Craig 1971, 20-21). Additionally, the *Bracero* pro-gram was attacked on nationalistic grounds. Critics were embarrassed at the need to send workers to the United States, Mexico's bitterest historical enemy. Also, there were fears about the social and political values that those *Braceros* who returned might bring back with them (Craig 1971, 22). These protests had no discernible effect, however.

It must also be emphasized that the Mexican government actively participated in the design, implementation and evaluation of the program. Indeed, for political, nationalistic and humanitarian concerns Mexican officials tried to use the *Bracero* program to regulate emigration and protect emigrants so as to avoid a repeat of the repatriations of the 1930s and their great human and financial costs (Scruggs 1961). This is why, given Texas' widespread discriminatory practices, Mexico initially prohibited *Braceros* from going there. Government officials also tried albeit unsuccessfully to guarantee the highest possible wages for *Braceros* (Galarza 1964, 49-50). Central to this effort were several attempts to prevent undocumented emigration because those workers were the most likely to be exploited. In 1944, Mexican officials considered establishing federal policy forbidding non-contract laborers (i.e., undocumented workers) from leaving Mexico (Scruggs 1961, 154-155). While no such policy was enacted, they tried in a variety of ways, including using federal forces, to prevent non-contract laborers from crossing the border (Galarza 1964, 65-68). These efforts proved futile in the face of persistent recruitment efforts by American growers and were quickly terminated.

Mexico's efforts to protect workers were undermined by the great increase in undocumented emigration that the *Bracero* program itself spurred. Moreover, the influx of migrants to the border also was causing problems in border cities from Juarez to Tijuana. In response to protests that U.S. recruiters were the source of these problems, the American ambassador blamed Mexico for not controlling emigration and warned that unless Mexico was more successful in reducing the flow of illegal emigrants, the guest worker program would be terminated. Mexico responded by arguing that the only way to control the situation was for the U.S. government to establish a policy of employer sanctions: "Without presuming to suggest action to the Government of the United States, if the problem were attacked at its economic source, imposing sanctions on American employers who employ illegal entrants would generate the result that Mexican workers would not in the future embark upon a venture made both difficult and unprofitable." (Scruggs 1961, 157). The dispute subsided and the program continued without employer sanctions.

Mexico's advocacy of workers' rights was not always consistent, however. For example, little effort was made to work with American unions who were challenging the agricultural industry. To the contrary, Mexican officials voiced no protest against decisions by U.S. agencies that invalidated strikes by American labor unions to protect wages and working conditions affecting U.S. and Mexican workers (Craig 1981).

Perhaps what most clearly illustrates the extent to which the state was utilizing temporary and permanent emigration as a domestic policy tool is the government's response to the ending of the *Bracero* program. As it became likely in 1963 that the program would be terminated, Mexican officials, in keeping with nationalistic posturing, initially acknowledged that termination would cause problems but that Mexico could manage them. Subsequently, Antonio Carillo Flores, Mexico's ambassador to the United States, officially expressed the government's opposition to ending the program. Among his reasons were that:

1. Terminating the program would not end emigration; it would merely convert it from legal to undocumented emigration.

2. Terminating the program would likely result in an increased number of permanent emigrants, and this would deplete Mexico's rural labor market.

3. Terminating the program would create an unemployment crisis in Mexico (Craig 1971, 186-87).

Despite these arguments, Congress voted to end the *Bracero* program effective December 31, 1963.

Ambassador Carillo Flores' worst fears were not realized, i.e., Mexico did not experience an unemployment crisis. This may be because his first two predictions proved more accurate than he expected, that is, undocumented emigration increased, as did the number of emigrants who settled in the United States.

The Mexican state's economic policy, nonetheless, remained constant. That is, the development policy that was underway by 1940 continued through the end of the Lopez Portillo sexenio in 1982, when the bank nationalization signaled the end of the "Mexican Miracle" (Levy and Szekély 1987, 151-162). Similarly, from 1940 until 1982, Mexican policy regarding emigration also remained functionally consistent despite formal changes. Prior to 1964 the *Bracero* program allowed Mexican policy to promote legal emigration even though it also generated high levels of illegal emigration. Because of the end of the *Bracero* program, after 1964 the government would, in effect, promote undocumented emigration by defending under the mantle of human rights the right of Mexican workers to seek jobs in the United States and by interpreting the Mexican Constitution as prohibiting the government from preventing Mexican citizens from leaving the country at will. In view of how development policies continued to displace rural workers and how deeply institutionalized emigration patterns were by 1964, there was nothing else state policy needed to do to promote continued emigration.

It is, furthermore, reasonable to question state's explanation of its current posture. The sincerity of the claims regarding labor and human rights is challenged by the abuse and violence that the state inflicts on its own citizens. Also, some analysts have argued that Mexico could respect its constitutional requirement regarding the right of Mexicans to immigrate at will while regulating emigration by requiring Mexicans to exit through officials ports of entry/exit as it tried to do in the 1940s. The political consequences of such a policy would, however, probably be disastrous.

Nonetheless, to a level equal to or greater than existed during the *Bracero* program, Mexican consuls continued to defend the human and civil rights of Mexican workers in the United States, whatever their immigration status. There is no doubt that they had the right and obligation to defend their countrymen from American racism, and that there was ample need for them to do so. Nonetheless, in view of the extent to which the state has violated the civil and human rights of Central American immigrants in Mexico as well as those of its own citizens, official protests against similar and, in recent years, far less systematic violations sometimes ring hollow (Wambaugh 1966). A victim of governmental repression in Morelos has made this clear: "If the Government is going to demand justice for Mexicans in another country, it has to begin by protecting the rights of its own people at home." President Zedillo, it should be noted, recognizes the legitimacy of such criticisms (DePalma 1996, 5).

From 1930 to 1982, then, state policy played a major role in shaping emigration (Portes and Bach 1985, 85-86). Nonetheless, the majority of emigrants during this period were economic migrants. They left in pursuit of economic advancement and not because they were politically mobilized against the state. These emigrants, thus, became a "safety valve" for the regime, i.e., their departure prevented the generation of economic demands to which the state could not have responded. If these emigrants had remained in Mexico, their eventual politicization could have produced widespread political discontent.

The *Bracero* program and undocumented emigration played a major role in preventing this from developing.

## Political Emigrants, Economic Migrants and Refugees, 1970-1995 (and Beyond)

Because the factors explaining Mexican emigration today are more varied than they have been historically, the composition of today's emigrants is also more heterogenous. From 1910-1930, they were primarily refugees. From 1930-1982, they were primarily economic migrants. Beginning in the 1970s and greatly increasing since 1982, the mix includes refugees, economic migrants and political emigrants. Given the difficulty of determining the total number of Mexican immigrants currently in the United States, it is simply impossible at the present time to know the proportion of all immigrants that each category represents. Nonetheless, there is little doubt that economic migrants, including peasants and a greatly increased number of better educated and more highly skilled urban workers (Roberts and Escobar 1966), still constitute the majority. Political migrants are, in our judgment, the second largest group, and refugees are the smallest.

Although there is no way to generate a reliable estimate of the number of political emigrants, how they evolved is quite clear. They are the product of the development policies that began in 1930 and produced the "Mexican Miracle" that by the mid-1970s had created an expanding and thriving urban middle class (Roberts and Escobar 1996). Ironically but predictably, the economic downturns that began with the Echeverria regime (1970-1976), continued through the Lopez Portillo sexenio (1976-1982) and culminated in the financial disaster of 1994 that was the legacy of the Salinas administration most immediately affected the groups that had most benefitted from the Mexican Miracle—the new middle class, including professionals, entrepreneurs, intelligentsia, and new economic elites. These recurring economic crises recruited these new groups into the ranks of potential and real emigrants along with peasants who throughout these years continued to emigrate. With that, emigration once more became a salient issue for the nation and began to play an important role within domestic politics, and the state's role in emigration and particularly with respect to emigrant communities gained importance as a domestic political issue (Gonzalez Gutierrez 1995).

The middle- and upper-class potential and actual emigrants differed from most of their peasant counterparts in a fundamentally significant way, however. They were "political participants," i.e., real or incipient members of Mexico's political class. Unlike the majority of peasants, in other words, they were attentive to political and governmental processes as well as to policy outcomes. Thus, their anger at the state's failed economic policies was exacerbated by their inability to hold public officials accountable and to influence the state's future policies. In the mid 1980s, for example, most Mexicans expressed low efficacy and only a minority believed their votes mattered or that government officials sought to serve the public (Camp 1993, 59-60). Such feelings of political impotence were not new (Almond and Verba 1963); what was new was that many Mexicans were increasingly insisting on exercising democratic rights and on controlling if not ending governmental corruption and unrestrained Presidential power. Perhaps the first and most dramatic example of this new attitude may be found in the public response to President Echeverria's attacks on the private sector (Arriola 1981; Pozas 1993). Other examples include the protests against electoral fraud that began in the 1970s with municipal elections in the north (Aziz 1994) and that inexorably grew into a national movement following the debacle of the 1988 presidential elections, and the increasingly loud and widespread criticisms of governmental influence over and censorship of the media (Skidmore 1993).

It must be emphasized that what was at issue in these and related protests was not new. To the contrary, it consisted of well-established state practices. What was new is that large numbers of citizens began publicly protesting these practices. For the purposes of this chapter, this illustrates how from 1970 forward, failing state policies combined with a newly developed middle class and an expanding participant political culture to stimulate "political emigration."

Nonetheless, even though political emigration becomes an important category in the 1970s and its members continue to increase, it is unlikely that it will ever become the majority category. Political emigrants emerge from the ranks of political dissenters. Since 1970, or perhaps since the student protests of 1968, as political dissenters have increased in number, their protests have become sufficiently salient to stimulate the state to enact reforms that have mollified some of the dissenters (Loeza 1994) and reduced the likelihood that they would emigrate. Because the state's capacity to enact such reforms is greater than its capacity to solve the nation's economic problems (Urquidi 1994), economic problems produce a continuous migration flow while political emigration is probably intermittent. Additionally, many Mexicans who are likely candidates for becoming political emigrants do not do so because they have the ability to do business, and regularly escape to the United States and thus have no need to emigrate (Castaneda 1996). This type of interaction has increased and been strengthened as a result of NAFTA, which went into effect in January, 1994. NAFTA does not address the massive migration of workers, yet a political agreement was reached and guidelines established to facilitate the free flow of businessmen and professionals across the borders of the three countries. These individuals receive a set number of visas every year that allows them to perform their tasks wherever needed. Those who benefit from this situation include a small but significant number doctors, businessmen and journalists.

The significance of political emigrants is less a function of their numbers than of who they are, what they represent and the potential they have as political actors even if they are in the United States. They are important in part because they represent the contemporary failures of the Mexican state. Political emigrants come primarily from the new middle class, from the new generation of university-trained intelligentsia, from economic elites, from the new citizens that fledgling and hard-won political reforms have produced—in sum, political emigrants are the very Mexicans in which the nation has invested for its future. This is the group that should be most loyal to the nation. Their leaving focuses attention on the failures of the polity and generates demands for further reforms.

Additionally, political emigrants are in a position to mobilize previously unpoliticized economic emigrants against the Mexican state and to protest Mexican political practices in ways that could affect U.S. public opinion and public policy toward Mexico (de la Garza and DeSipio 1996; Dresser, 1993). The opportunities to engage in such activities will be greatly enhanced by two recent developments. The first is the electoral reform agreed to in August 1996 between the Mexican government and all major opposition parties, particularly the provision that will allow all Mexican citizens residing abroad to vote in the presidential election in the year 2000. In 1988 and 1994, thousands of emigrants were mobilized around the candidacy of Cuauhtemo Cardenas, the PRD's nominee, and by the PRI. The objectives of these efforts included raising funds for the campaigns in Mexico. When emigrants receive the right to vote, the parties will surely be even more energetic in their outreach. The second development is the proposed constitutional reform that will grant Mexicans the right to maintain their nationality even if they become citizens of another country. The reason for this change, according to Mexican official and non-official governmental sources, is to provide emigrants with a tool for protecting their rights in the United States, especially in the current anti-immigrant environment.

What is noteworthy from the perspective of this chapter is that both of these developments will greatly increase the clout of political emigrants. Both initiatives extend Mexico's politics into the United States (Dresser 1993). Political emigrants, therefore, will be excellently situated to disrupt PRI rallies and generate increased attention from the U.S. press to governmental and electoral irregularities. They could also mobilize fellow emigrants to vote against the PRI and this could lead to its defeat. To a greater extent than they have previously (de la Garza and Vargas 1991), they could persuade Latino organizations to join their protests, or, if they become American citizens, they could attempt to go directly to U.S. elected officials to influence the nation's policies toward Mexico. The impact of such efforts will be determined in large part by how many political emigrants participate in them and how intense they are in their sentiments.

As we have indicated, however, there is no way at this time to determine how much political emigration Mexico has experienced. The Secretaría de Gobernación, the Secretaria de Relaciones Exteriores (SRE), El Colegio de la Frontera Norte (COLEF), and the political parties confirm that they have conducted no studies that ask the emigrants about their attitudes toward the Mexican political system and politics in their local communities. Nor is there evidence regarding the weight that frustration with government corruption or the bad treatment they received from the authorities has had in decisions to emigrate, just as there are no data on whether emigrants are interested in the right to vote, what their partisan preferences are and other issues of a political nature. SRE sources, however, indicate that consular officials in the United States report that in their daily contact with emigrants they have detected on many occasions a very negative attitude toward the Mexican government, especially with regard to police officers and customs agents who attempt to blackmail them when they go back to Mexico. Such criticisms do not necessarily indicate that those who voice them are political emigrants, however.

It is, nonetheless, possible to suggest the parameters of the size of the group based on immigrant demographics and what we know about Mexican political participants. As of 1990, 61 percent of adult Mexican immigrants had less than eight years of school, 25 percent completed nine or more years of school in Mexico, and only 4 percent had thirteen or more years of school (de la Garza et al. 1992, 29; 150). Given that education and being a "political participant" are highly correlated (Almond and Verba 1963), it is reasonable to expect that most political participants have at least nine years of school. Furthermore, political emigrants are most likely to emerge from the ranks of political participants. Therefore, if only those with more than nine years of school are likely to be political emigrants, then at a maximum only 29 percent of emigrants fall into this category. Clearly, however, some of these individuals are not political emigrants.

Many individuals who are usually thought of as economic migrants may also have emigrated for political reasons, however. The reaction of Primitivo Rodriguez, an advisor on emigration issues to the Mexican Congress, to the possiblity of absentee voting suggests he agrees this is likely: "Mexicans will no longer vote with their feet, but with their hearts and minds." Comments from emigrants themselves lend further credence to this view: "I know firsthand the pain and suffering that we as immigrants must endure, being away from our families and seeing in disgust what those politicians are doing to our country. We may finally have a say in the kind of country we want to build and return to someday"

(Corchado and Iliff 1996, 1). The point, then, is that the total number of political emigrants is not trivial and in our assessment probably includes from 10 to 33 percent of all Mexican immigrants.

Another group about which we have very limited information and which may include many political emigrants is made up of Mexican professionals who have found job opportunities in the United States. This would include many who make up what has come to be known as the "brain drain." Unappreciated in their own land, partly because of the meager salaries they are offered but mainly because of their rebellious attitude toward a hierarchical and partisan system, many professionals have left Mexico. Perhaps a symbol of this phenomenon that has increased in recent decades is Mario Molina, a researcher at the Massachusetts Institute of Technology who became a U.S. citizen and was awarded the Nobel Prize for Chemistry in 1995. Additionally, it is very likely that many political emigrants would be found among the large number of Mexican professionals, such as teachers and doctors, who have emigrated since the 1994 crisis. This includes teachers who prefer earning $200 weekly as fruit pickers to $140 monthly as teachers in Mexico. It also includes many college graduates who remain unemployed or have limited professional success. According to a dentist who graduated in 1986, 25 percent of his classmates have emigrated and most are not working as dentists (*Migration News* 1966).

Many such professionals who left following the devaluation in 1982 returned to Mexico during the early 1990s, attracted by a promising economic outlook and a special program devised for the "repatriation of brains" sponsored by the National Council for Science and Technology (CONACYT). This effort included financial assistance from CONACYT to many research institutions and universities, which in turn have recruited one thousand researchers. It is unclear whether, given the current crisis, they will want or be able to remain.

Whatever their total numbers, moreover, political emigrants are also economically significant because they constitute a substantial loss of human resources and, in noteworthy cases, significant capital flight. The most salient examples of the latter occurred between 1976 and 1982, when political disorder (kidnapping, expropriations, anti-business governmental rhetoric) and successive devaluations prompted several thousand of Mexico's economic elite to express their dissatisfaction with their government by crossing the border. Some of the favorite destinations for these Mexicans have been La Jolla, California, especially among those who lived in Mexico City and Guadalajara; and Padre Island and other destinations in Texas, among those who lived in Monterrey. In the early 1990s, many of them returned, in part because they considered that NAFTA and other parts of the Salinas reforms justified such a move; because they were uneasy about their children attending high school in the United States, where the drug problem is very severe; or because they were worried that their children might lose their family values.

This exodus could not be repeated in the 1994-95 economic crisis because the types of individuals who left in the 1970s found themselves without any liquid resources after the December 1994 economic crisis. They were, in sum, victimized by their belief in the government's economic plan. Thus, they were completely unprepared for the devaluation, and the nature of the crisis made it virtually impossible for them to convert their resources to pesos in order to exchange them for dollars and exit as they did previously.

Political refugees are the smallest group among current immigrants and, like political emigrants, little is known about them. As Table 7.1 illustrates, the number of asylum applicants increased greatly in recent years. It is noteworthy that this extraordinary growth preceded the outbreak of violence in Chiapas in 1994, and then expanded by an additional 50 percent following those events. This upturn must, therefore, include an increase in the number of claims by Partido de Acción Nacional (PAN) and Partido Revolucionario Democrático (PRD) militants and members of social organizations who were the subject of abuse in their home states by diverse authorities. Additionally, it surely includes large numbers of desperate economic migrants and political emigrants attempting to capitalize on such events to obtain legal residency.

What must be emphasized, however, is that there is probably a great discrep-

### Table 7.1
### Asylum Applications Filed by Mexican Nations, FY 1991-1996*

|  | 1991 | 1992 | 1993 | 1994 | 1995** | 1996** |
|---|---|---|---|---|---|---|
| Applications filed | 185 | 614 | 6397 | 9323 | 9304 | 3825 |
| Cases completed | 60 | 177 | 1,245 | 8,043 | 11,188 | 3,995 |
| Approvals | 0 | 0 | 0 | 5 | 54 | 17 |
| Denials | 5 | 10 | 501 | 4,470 | 1,016 | 18 |
| In process | NA | NA |  |  | 55,323 | 2,969 |
| Administratively closed | 55 | 107 | 744 | 3,568 | 4,795 | 991 |

*Applications may be filed in one year but not adjudicated until subsequent years.
** FY1995 data are preliminary; FY 1996 data cover October 1995-March 1996.
Source: Office of International Affairs, U.S. Immigration and Naturalization Service

ancy between the number of asylum applications approved and the number of legitimate asylum requests. INS officials emphasize that asylum claims are considered on their own merit and that there is no directive instructing them to deny asylum to Mexicans. In the past, however, the criteria for validating such claims have been affected by State Department priorities and other political factors that are independent of an individual's personal circumstances, as is illustrated by the ease with which Cubans and Nicaraguans received asylum compared to the extreme difficulty encountered by Guatemalans and Salvadorans (Zolberg et al. 1989, 210-220). The extent to which that continues to be true is unclear, however. Senior INS officials indicate that such factors have become essentially irrelevant under the new refugee policies that went into effect in January 1995. Yet, one INS official anonymously notes that "there is no question that there is a sensitivity (among Mexican officials) to seeing asylum (to Mexicans) granted, and there is a sensitivity (among U.S. officials) to not seeing our friends upset." Foreign policy, however, is only one such consideration. Increased undocumented immigration is another: "If Mexicans claimants start succeeding in any number, this could spark a much greater influx." Whether these comments reflect how asylum decisions were made prior to 1995, as a senior INS official insists, or whether they continue to be relevant today, is uncertain. What seem indisuptable is that, while there is no doubt that refugees make up only a small proportion of all immigrants, the group is growing and the number of those who are eligible for asylum probably exceeds the number of those who receive it.

Finally, there is the mass of economic migrants. The conventional perspective is that all emigrants fall in this category. As we have argued, however, this assessment must be revised to account for political emigrants and refugees. There are hundreds of studies financed by U.S., European, and Asian foundations, as well as numerous international organizations that focus on how many emigrants there are, what kind of ill-treatment they have to withstand to cross the border and find work, where they come from, what is their gender and social class, in what economic sector do they work, what is their occupation now, how much money do they send back to Mexico, how much taxes do they pay in the United States, what public services do they utilize, among other things. Unless similar energies are committed to exploring the political asepects of emigration, such studies will be of diminishing significance because they ignore the most significant new developments affecting the emigrant communities.

For example, existing research offers no insights into how emigrants will respond to Mexican governmental efforts to promote absentee voting or dual citizenship. Will emigrants take advantage of this opportunity? For which party will they vote? What will be the consequences for U.S.-Mexico relations of Mexican campaigns conducted within the United States (Ayon 1966)?

Similarly, they cannot inform us about how emigrants will respond to the growing interaction between state officials, including several governors, and their compatriots residing in the United States. Ernesto Ruffo, Baja California's first PAN governor, made extensive inroads into California's immigrant community, something that can also be said about other PAN governors. At the present time, the most ambitious program to establish these kinds of contacts is that of Vicente Fox, the PAN governor of Guanajuato. With the advice of the SRE, he has opened eleven offices across the United States and distributed thousands of flyers regarding sources of support in Guanajuato among Guanajuatense emigrant communities.

The state/PRI has been even more energetic in its dealings with emigrants. The Salinas administration institutionalized the Program for Mexican Communities Living Abroad, a major initiative that provides a wide range of services to emigrants in the United States (de la Garza 1996). That program in combination with Salinas's "Solidarity" programs successfully worked with emigrants in the United States to develop and invest in community development projects in their communities of origin (Smith 1995). Such collaborations create an additional incentive for emigrants, regardless of their legal status, to stay in the United States—as long as they remain, they earn much more than they could at home and this benefits not only their families but their communities as well.

Many emigrants believe that such outreach and support constitutes better treatment than what they received in their communities of origin. Will such efforts strengthen the political ties between emigrants and the governments that initiate or carry them out? Would this positive impact outweigh the anti-state/PRI sentiments that motivated, in whole or in part, the departure of such political emigrants? The answer to these questions could become very important when absentee voting goes into effect.

Will communities convert these programs into mechanisms for increasing their political clout, that is, could emigration increase because communities and individuals conclude that they have more access to government officials when they are in the United States than when they are in Mexico? Will such programs stimulate further emigration by reducing the costs of leaving and returning to Mexico? The answer to these inquiries will help explain future emigration patterns.

## Conclusion

The message is clear. Mexican political practices and state policies have significantly influenced the size and composition of the emigrant flow and continue to affect individual decisions about returning or staying in the United States. Sometimes, as during the Revolution, politics rather than state policy stimulated emigration. On other occasions, state policies have explicitly promoted emigration or attempted to shape it, as was evident during the Bracero period. More often, however, the state has directly stimulated emigration even if its policies were not explicitly designed to do so. This is obvious in the consequences of national economic program from the 1940s through NAFTA as well as in current efforts to recover from the 1994 economic crisis. Since 1968, this has also been the effect of how the state has managed the nation's political life.

Given this historical and continuing influence over emigration, what, if anything, should the Mexican state do to affect future emigration? What can it do? Few Mexican or American officials and analysts have been willing to seriously consider these questions. Instead, Mexican officials and most Mexican and American academics respond by saying 1) the Mexican Constitution guarantees all Mexicans the right to leave their nation at will and therefore it would be illegal and wrong for the state to prevent emigration, 2) the Mexican government could not prevent undocumented emigration even if it tried, 3) Mexicans emigrate in response to U.S. demands for labor over which the Mexican government has no control, and 4) there is no reason for Mexico to try to control emigration because the U.S. government and the nation's key political actors support undocumented immigration because it is beneficial to the U.S. economy. Many opponents of undocumented immigration respond by calling for unilateral efforts to stop illegal immigration, including militarizing the border, intensified employer sanctions, expanded efforts to identify and deport undocumented immigrants, and denying undocumented immigrants access to all except emergency social services.

All of these answers and proposals are irrelevant or misguided because they begin from the premise that the Mexican state is powerless regarding emigration. We reject that premise for two reasons. First, given the rising anti-immigrant sentiment in the United States, Mexican officials cannot afford the luxury of feigning impotence as they have in the past. All indications are that U.S. efforts to reduce undocumented immigration will continue and intensify for the foreseeable future. If Mexican officials refuse to engage the issue in concrete ways, U.S. officials are even more likely to act unilaterally in ways that will inevitably damage U.S.-Mexico relations and expose Mexico's emigrants to the mercy (of which there appears to be little) of the American public. Second, we believe the Mexican state could develop, initiate and implement a variety of policies that could increase the willingness of U.S. officials to work with Mexico to manage this issue as well as affect the composition and number of emigrants.

Its unclear whether Mexican officials recognize the need to change their approach to the issue. At an operational level, e.g., to prevent the abuse of emigrants on the Mexican side of the border and to repatriate undocumented immigrants to the interior of Mexico, Mexican officials have been extremely cooperative. At a more fundamental level, it is unclear whether senior officials are willing to abandon their traditional posture. For example, President Zedillo appears to justify maintaining Mexico's traditional posture by relying on studies from the Colegio de la Frontera Norte (COLEF) that assert emigration is decreasing. COLEF's reports, however, contradict the findings of the Mexico-U.S. Binational Migration Study Commission on Immigration, which includes the leading experts from Mexico and the United States.

The first step Mexico must take is to recognize the new realities, and this requires policies based on the best information available. Unless officials use such research to inform their policies, it is unlikely that U.S. officials will respond positively to efforts to develop collaborative responses to the immigration issue.

Second, the state must restructure the political system in ways that guarantee governmental accountability and insure that public policies are informed by public preferences. The consequences of such reforms will, of course, affect not only the interests of refugees and political emigrants but of the entire nation. Restructuring must go beyond institutionalizing honest elections to include meaningful campaign finance reform and disclosure, and meaningful media access for all political parties. It must also attack and greatly reduce governmental corruption. If implemented, the recent political reforms that the major political parties have agreed upon would constitute a major step in this direction.

Third, the state must redesign its economic program. The Zedillo administration's inflexible adherence to the policies of his predecessor have accelerated the impoverishment of Mexico. Even advocates of liberalization and privatization such as Governor Fox of Guanajuato, a likely PAN presidential nominee in 2000, has called for a halt to privatization and for increased expenditures to provide at least temporary relief from the economic crisis by creating short- and medium-term job opportunities. Such efforts could be a first step in developing an economic strategy that would address the needs of the entire nation and thus reduce the incentives to emigrate, rather than continue with programs that exacerbate unemployment, increase economic inequalities and spur migration. During the Salinas regime, for example, the number of Mexican billionaires increased to thirteen; only the United States, Germany and Japan had more (Oppenheimer 1996, 8). On the other hand, a 1992 study by agencies of the United Nations found 43.8 percent of the nation's total population "living at or below the official poverty line (Cornelius 1996. 106). Additionally, a 1996 study by the Centro de Estudios Económicos del Sector Privado estimates that between 1988 and 1993 the number of new workers exceeded the number of new jobs by 4,481,000. "Whatever statistical base is used, it is clear that the new, market-oriented development model thus far has exacerbated—not alleviated—Mexico's poverty and inequality problems, even when the model was apparently working well in macroeconomic terms (that is, from 1989 through 1992) (Cornelius 1996, 106). Furthermore, the Ministry of Agriculture estimates that NAFTA and PROCAMPO, the government's program to support rural development, will contribute to reducing the rural population from 26 million in 1993 to 10-15 million in 2005. This means that during the coming decade 10 million Mexicans will have to find new jobs in an economy that cannot meet current demands. Those programs, which are part of the state's ongoing economic project, will greatly increase migration to urban areas and, inevitably, to the border and beyond. Of course, whether or not the state modifies these policies and develops new ones will depend on the extent to which genuine political reforms are instituted.

Finally, it must be emphasized that for the Mexican state to develop the kinds of policies we propose will require U.S. support and pressure. U.S. policy makers are already deeply implicated in Mexico's decision making process; indeed, if they are not the architects of the State's current policies, they have played a major role in their design and implementation. For Mexico to reorient its economic policies, therefore, it is necessary for U.S. officials to also alter their demands. Given how deeply involved U.S. officials already are with Mexican policymaking, this is not advocating a new or increased form of intervention. It is, instead, a call for changing the objectives of U.S. involvement.

In the past, the United States has been complicit in the maintenance of what is now a clearly discredited political regime. This is as evident in the endorsement of state claims that Carlos Salinas won the 1988 elections, as in the $50-billion bailout of the Zedillo administration in 1995. As a former U.S. deputy assistant secretary of state states, "No U.S. administration wants to hear the bad things about Mexico. It would be put in a domestic political position to have to do something about them" (Oppenheimer 1996, 308-309). Now the United States must help those forces in Mexico, including perhaps President Zedillo, that are trying to change the political system. American officials must also be prepared for the consequences that such reforms might produce. A government that is genuinely reflective of Mexican interests and accountable to the Mexican people is much more likely to have an economic program that will target poverty and unemployment and thus reduce emigration. As suggested by Governor Fox's proposals, such a program would also surely include initiatives that will trouble key American political actors.

In our judgment, such initiatives would incorporate the long-term objectives of the current economic plan, i.e., increasing high-paying jobs in the manufacturing sector and promoting exports. But it would also include policies that would deal with the short-and medium-term dislocations that have resulted from NAFTA and Mexico's participation in GATT. Without such interventions,

Mexico's impoverishment will continue, and that will maintain or increase today's high emigration. Together, these developments will fuel discontent on both sides of the border and undermine the support that is essential if Mexico's economy is to expand and provide good jobs for Mexicans in Mexico as NAFTA initially promised.

In the long run, the governments of the United States and Mexico must work together to find ways to manage emigration/immigration. Mexico's ability to engage in the negotiations that this will require will depend on the extent to which its government represents and is accountable to its people. We only hope that, as that becomes a reality, the U.S. government will have the maturity to deal with Mexico with the respect that a democratic Mexico would deserve.

# References

Almond, Gabriel A., and Sidney Verba.1963. *The Civic Culture*. Princeton, N. J.: Princeton University Press.

Arriola, Carlos. 1981. *Las organizaciones empresariales y el Estado*. Mexico City: Fonda de Cultura Económica.

Ayon, David. 1996. Democratization Imperils U.S. Latino Empowerment. *Los Angeles Times*, May 26.

Aziz, Alberto. 1994. *Chihuaha: historia de una alternativa*. Mexico City: La Jornada, Serie Disidencias.

Balderama, Francisco E. 1982. *In Defense of La Raza: The Los Angeles Mexican Consulate and the Mexican Community, 1929-1936*. Tucson: University of Arizona Press.

Bean, Frank D., Barry Edmonston and Jeffrey S. Passel, eds. 1990. *Undocumented Migration to the United States: IRCA and the Experience of the 1980s*. Washington, D.C.: Urban Institute Press.

Bean, Frank D., and Gary Freeman. 1996. Mexico and U.S. Worldwide Immigration Policy. Paper presented at the conference on Mexican Migration and U.S. Policy. Washington, D. C.

Brandenburg, Frank. 1964. *The Making of Modern Mexico*. Englewood Cliffs, N. J.: Prentice Hall.

Cafferty, Pastora San Juan, Barry R. Chiswick, Andrew M. Greeley and Teresa A. Sullivan. 1983. *The Dilemma of American Immigration: Beyond the Golden Door*. New Brunswick: Transaction Books.

Calavita, Kitty. 1992. *Inside the State: the Bracero Program, Immigration and the I.N.S.* New York: Routledge.

Camp, Roderic A. 19943. *Politics in Mexico*. New York: Oxford University Press.

Castaneda, Jorge G. Mexico's Circle of Misery. *Foreign Affairs* 75 (July/August), 92-105.

Cook, Maria Lorena, Kevin J. Middlebrook and Juan Molinar Horcasitas, eds. *The Politics of Economic Restructuring*. San Diego: Center for U.S. Mexico Studies, University of California at San Diego.

Corchado, Alfredo, and Laurence Iliff. 1966. Mexicans living abroad may be allowed to vote. *The Dallas Morning News*, June 6, p. 1.

Cornelius,Wayne. 1996. *Mexican Politics in Transition: The Breakdown of a One-Party Dominant Regime.* San Diego: Center for U.S.-Mexico Studies, University of California, San Diego.

Craig, Richard B. 1971. *The Bracero Program.* Austin: University of Texas Press.

Cross, Harry E., and James A. Sandos. 1981. *Across the Border: Rural Development in Mexico and Recent Migration to the United States.* Berkeley: Institute of Governmental Studies, University of Californa, Berkeely.

de la Garza, Rodolfo. 1966. Foreign Policy Comes Home: The Program for Mexican Communities Abroad. Paper presented at the Conference on Mexico's New Foreign Policy, Centro de Investigaciones y Docencia Económica, January 15. Mexico City.

de la Garza, Rodolfo, and Louis DeSipio. N.D. Interests not Passions: Mexican American Attitudes Toward Mexico and Issues Shaping U.S.-Mexico Relations. In Michael Clough, ed. *Ethnics and the New Foreign Policy.* New York: Council on Foreign Relations.

de la Garza, Rodolfo, Louis DeSipio, F. Chris Garcia, John Garcia and Angelo Falcon. 1992. *Latino Voices: Mexican, Puerto Rican and Cuban Perspectives on American Politics.* Boulder: Westview Press.

de la Garza, Rodolfo, and Claudio A. Vargas. 1991. Paisanos, pochos o aliados políticos? *Revista Mexicana de Sociología* 2 (Abril-Junio de 1991), 185-206.

DePalma, Anthony. 1996. Policy Brutality in Mexico, Echoing California, Puts Zedillo on the Spot. *New York Times.* April 13, p. 5.

Dresser, Denise. 1993. Exporting Conflict: Transboundary Consequences of Mexican Politics. In Abraham F. Lowenthal and Katrina Burgess, eds. *The California-Mexico Connection.* Stanford: Stanford University Press.

Galarza, Ernesto. 1964. *Merchants of Labor: The Mexican Bracero Story.* Santa Barbara: McNally & Loftin, West.

Gonzalez Gutierrez, Carlos. 1993. The Mexican Diaspora in California: Limits and Possibilities for the Mexican Government. In Abraham F. Lowenthal and Katrina Burgess, eds. *The California-Mexico Connection.* Stanford: Stanford University Press

Hartz, Louis. 1955. *The Liberal Tradition in America: An Interpretation of American Political Thought Since the Revolution.* New York: Harcourt, Brace.

Hirschman, Albert O. *Exit, Voice and Loyalty: Responses to Decline in Firms, Organizations and States.* Cambridge: Harvard University Press.

Knight, Alan. *The Mexican Revolution: Volume 1: Porfirians, Liberals and Peasants.* Cambridge: Cambridge University Press.

Levy, Daniel, and Gabriel Székely. 1987. *Mexico: Paradoxes of Stability and Change.* Boulder: Westview Press.

Loeza, Soledad. 1994. Political Liberalization and Uncertainty in Mexico. In Maria Lorena Cook, Kevin J. Middlebrook and Juan Molinar Horcasitas, eds. *The Politics of Economic Restructuring.* San Diego: Center for U.S. Mexico Studies, University of

California at San Diego.

Lowell, B. Lindsay, Frank D. Bean and Rodolfo O. de la Garza. 1986. Undocumented Immigration: Analysis of the 1984 Simpson-Mazzoli Vote. *Social Science Quarterly* 64 (March):118-127.

Massey, Douglas S., and Kristin E. Espinosa. 1995. What's Driving Mexico-U.S. Migration? A Theoretical, Empirical and Policy Analysis. Paper presented at Social Science Research Council Conference on Becoming American/America Becoming, January 18-21, 1996.

McKay, R. Reynolds. 1984. The Impact of the Great Depression on Immigrant Labor: Repatriation of the Bridgeport, Texas, Coalminers. *Social Science Quarterly* 65, no. 2: 354-364.

Meyer, Michael C., and William L. Sherman. 1983. *The Course of Mexican History*. New York: Oxford University Press.

*Migration News*. 1966. University of California at Davis. Vol. 3 (4) April.

Openheimer, Andres. 1996. *Bordering on Chaos: Guerrillas, Stockbrokers, Politicians, and Mexico's Road to Prosperity*. Boston: Little, Brown and Company.

Portes, Alejandro, and Robert L. Bach. 1985. *Latin Journey: Cuban and Mexican Immigrants in the United States*. Berkeley: University of California Press.

Portes, Alejandro, and Ruben G. Rumbaut. 1990. *Immigrant America: A Portrait*. Berkeley: University of California Press.

Pozas, Mary. 1993. Industrial Restructuring in Mexico: Competitive Adaptation, Technological Innovation, and Changing Patterns of Industrial Relations in Monterrey. La Jolla, Calif.: Center for U.S.-Mexico Studies.

Rionda Ramirez, Leon Miguel. 1992. *Y jalaron pa'l norte*. Mexico City: Instituto Nacional de Anthropología e Historia, El Colegio de Michoacán.

Roberts, Bryan R., and Agustin Escobar Latapi. 1996. Mexican Social and Economic Policy and Emigration. Paper presented at the conference on Mexican Migration and U.S. Policy. Washington, D. C.

Scruggs, Otey M. The United States, Mexico and the Wetbacks, 1942-1947. *Pacific Historical Review* 30 (May): 149-164.

Skidmore, Thomas. 1993. Television Politics and the Transition to Democracy in Latin America. Washington, D. C.: Woodrow Wilson Center for International Scholars.

Smith, Robert Courtney. 1995. Los Ausentes Siempre Presentes: The Imagining, Making and Politics of a Transnational Migrant Community Between Ticuani, Puebla, Mexico and New York City. Ph.D. dissertation, Columbia University.

Urquidi, Victor L. 1994. The Outlook for Mexican Economic Development in the 1990s. In Maria Lorena Cook, Kevin J. Middlebrook and Juan Molinar Horcasitas, eds. The Politics of Economic Restructuring. San Diego: Center for U.S.-Mexico Studies, University of California at San Diego.

Weiner, Myron. 1995. *The Global Migration Crisis: Challenges to States and to Human Rights*. New York: HarperCollins College Publishers.

Zolberg, Aristide R., Astri Suhrke and Sergio Aguayo. 1989. *Escape from Violence: Conflict and the Refugee Crisis in the Developing World*. New York: Oxford University Press.

# 8.
# U.S. Public Perceptions and Reactions to Mexican Migration

*Thomas J. Espenshade and Maryann Belanger*

Americans have seldom displayed an overwhelming enthusiasm for immigrants, especially new immigrants. The syndicated columnist Ben Wattenberg once quipped, "I'm convinced that when the second boatload of pilgrims landed in Massachusetts, those on the *Mayflower* said, 'There goes the neighborhood.'" Ever since the founding of the new colonies there have been persistent efforts by former immigrants to keep out newcomers and to preserve this country for those who were already here (Simon, 1985). New England Puritans disliked the Quakers, Episcopalians and Catholics. The English were troubled by German and Irish immigrants who in turn wanted to pull up the drawbridge before too many more Italians, Jews and Russians arrived.

Recent poll data suggest that sentiment against a continuation of current levels of immigration has returned to historic highs. Two-thirds of those interviewed in separate public opinion surveys conducted by the Gallup Organization in the summer of 1995 said that immigration to the United States should be reduced, and just 7 or 8 percent preferred an increase. Similar disapproval levels were registered in 1980-81 when the U.S. unemployment rate reached close to 10 percent

(Espenshade and Hempstead, 1996). These episodes are merely symptomatic, however, of a return to a more generalized set of restrictionist attitudes toward immigration that began to crystallize soon after 1965, when the Immigration and Nationality Act was amended in ways that permitted more Asian and Latin American immigrants to enter the United States at the expense of migrants from Europe. These attitudes have intensified with a persistent weakness in the earning power of many Americans (Espenshade, 1996).[1]

Respondents to public opinion polls are increasingly being asked, and do in fact appear able, to make a conceptual distinction between immigrants who are in the United States legally and those who are here illegally. Nearly half of all participants in a June 1986 CBS News/*New York Times* poll believed that most recent U.S. immigrants were in the country illegally, versus one-third who thought the majority of recent immigrants were legal. By June 1993 the proportion responding that most were illegal had risen to two-thirds, whereas less than 20 percent of the sample believed most recent immigrants were legal. Several facets of these results are interesting. First, very few people had no opinion about whether recent migrants were legal or illegal. That proportion was already low in the 1986 survey (13 percent), and it fell to below 10 percent by 1993. Second, the public mind vastly exaggerates the importance of illegal immigration in annual U.S. immigration flows. By the best estimates, net illegal or undocumented migration accounts for roughly 30 percent of total net U.S. immigration (Fix and Passel, 1994).[2] Third, Mexico and illegal immigration are highly intertwined in public attitudes. In a March 1995 survey, for example, 32 percent of those interviewed said that illegal immigration into the United States was their "greatest worry about the future of Mexico." The next greatest concern was the U.S. economy (28 percent), while issues associated with civil war or having a government unfriendly to the United States captured many fewer responses.[3]

The distinction between legal and illegal migrants carries over to people's attitudes. Americans are significantly more likely to view undocumented migration as a serious problem than they are legal immigration. In a September 1993 national survey conducted by Yankelovich Partners, 15 percent of respondents said the presence of legal aliens in the United States concerned them "a great deal," but 48 percent gave this response when the same question was asked about illegal aliens.[4] A *Los Angeles Times* survey taken during the same month asked how "big a problem" legal and illegal immigration were. Legal immigration was considered a major problem by 30 percent of those sampled, whereas 62 percent considered illegal immigration a major problem. Finally, two-thirds of respondents in a July 1993 poll believed that the United States has a more serious problem with legal immigration than it did in the past. When asked the same question about illegal immigration, 85 percent gave an affirmative response.[5]

The purpose of this chapter is to explore what is known about attitudes and reactions toward Mexican migration to the United States. Although much of this migration is unauthorized, much is also legal. Mexico is now the most important source country for U.S. immigration. According to data from the 1990 census, 21.7 percent (or 4.3 million) of the total U.S. foreign-born population of 19.8 million persons were born in Mexico (U.S. Bureau of the Census, 1993). By March of 1995 this proportion had increased to 29.3 percent, and the estimated size of the foreign-born population originating in Mexico had grown to 6.7 million (Hansen, 1996). The Philippines was in distant second place with 1.2 million migrants. Mexico sends more legal migrants to the United States than any other country. The U.S. Immigration and Naturalization Service (INS) granted 804,000 permanent resident visas (or "green" cards) during fiscal year 1994, of which persons born in Mexico received 111,000 or nearly 14 percent. The total European share in 1994 barely exceeded 160,000 (U.S. Immigration and Naturalization Service, 1996). The Mexican numbers were largely unaffected by the legalization program surrounding the 1986 Immigration Reform and Control Act (IRCA). Only 6,000 of the 804,000 visas were IRCA related.

As is well known, Mexico has typically sent more undocumented migrants to the United States than any other country. Of the estimated 2.06 million undocumented aliens enumerated in the 1980 census, 1.13 million (or 55 percent of the total) were born in Mexico (Warren and Passel, 1987). Many of these illegal immigrants took advantage of an amnesty program that was a condition of IRCA's passage. In a study of a sample of nearly 6,200 newly legalized aliens who had lived in the United States continuously since January 1, 1982, the INS found that the great majority (70 percent) came from Mexico (U.S. Immigration and Naturalization Service, 1992). Despite the fact that close to 3 million formerly illegal migrants eventually received temporary legal resident status under IRCA, there were still an estimated 3.4 million undocumented migrants resident in the United States in the fall of 1992, 1.3 million (or 39 percent) of whom were born in Mexico. El Salvador ranked second on the list with just 327,000 undocumented migrants (Warren, 1995).

Given the prominence of Mexican migration, it is surprising that so little direct information exists on how the American public feels about it. The opinion results presented in this chapter are based on data from the Public Opinion Location Library (POLL) database, a comprehensive on-line retrieval system for polling data provided by Dialog Information Services, Inc., and compiled from survey data collected by the Roper Center for Public Opinion Research at the University of Connecticut. POLL currently contains the full-text and complete responses to more than 230,000 survey questions.[6] Specifying keywords relating to Mexico or Mexican and to immigration, migration, or migrant identified just 14 questions that had appeared on national public opinion polls between 1979 and 1995. Many of these related to how respondents thought the North American Free Trade Agreement (NAFTA) was likely to affect Mexican migration to the United States. This information proved inadequate to support a complete analysis, so we broadened the search to include other identifiers, including Hispanic, Latin American, Latino, and illegal, and we eliminated any time constraints on survey dates.

In the end, our search netted close to 300 questions having something to do with immigration to the United States. From this group, we discarded questions that pertained to attitudes toward or the perceived consequences of immigration in general. To be candidates for analysis, questions minimally had to make reference to particular kinds of immigrants (for example, legal versus illegal, Latin American versus Asian). Our main results are included in a set of appendix tables. They are based on national surveys conducted by nine different polling organizations during a 30-year period between 1965 and 1995. The findings are grouped into two broad categories: (1) those questions assessing respondents' attitudes toward particular kinds of migrants and (2) items that ask how people feel about various measures to control illegal immigration. Ten different issues are explored in the appendix tables, encompassing 28 separate survey questions. In many cases, the same (or nearly the same) question was asked several times during the 30-year period under study, making it possible to gauge trends in the responses.

We will argue that the results support two broad conclusions. First, when given a choice, the American public prefers European immigrants to those from Asia or Latin America. When the choice is restricted to the latter two groups, Asian migrants are generally considered superior along several dimensions. Second, whereas the American public is concerned about illegal U.S. immigration, they are generally willing to support only the mildest measures to try to control it. Measures that might have a greater chance of being efficacious are generally deemed too unattractive to the majority of American adults.

In the next section we examine how Americans feel about immigrants from particular parts of the world, concentrating on migrants from Mexico and Latin America and contrasting attitudes with those toward migrants from other major sending regions. We also examine whether the public thinks levels of immigration from different regions should be increased or decreased. The following section focuses on attitudes toward a variety of measures for controlling illegal immigration. Some of these, such as enhanced border security and the use of something akin to a national identification card, are presently being discussed as part of proposed reforms of national immigration policy. The final section summarizes our findings.

## Attitudes toward Different Immigrant Groups

Our analysis of how the American public feels toward immigrants from different parts of the world is based on answers to survey questions 1-15 in the appendix tables. A general assessment of the public's knowledge of where immigrants come from and their likes and dislikes of immigrants of particular kinds are shown in questions 1-3. Most respondents—approximately two-thirds of the total—identified either Latin America or Asia as the source of most of today's recent immigrants. Immigrants from Latin America were mentioned somewhat more often than those from Asia. A comparison of these perceptions with census data shows that these beliefs are essentially correct at the aggregate level. The March 1995 Current Population Survey (CPS) identified 23 million foreign-born individuals resident in the United States. Nearly one-quarter (5.4 million) of these came to this country in 1990 or later. Nearly half of these "recent" immigrants (47.8 percent) came from Mexico, Central or South America, and another quarter (24.8 percent) originated from Asia. Just 15 percent came from a European country (Hansen, 1996).

Respondents' reactions to particular immigrant groups are identified in question 2. The great majority of persons interviewed in 1965 felt most favorably toward European immigrants, and only 11 percent of the sample mentioned Mexico, Latin America or Asia. By 1993 (third column) the proportion feeling most favorably toward Latin American or Asian migrants surpassed the percentage citing Europe (36 versus 20). In the last column of question 2, more than 50 percent of the sample who named a specific country toward whose migrants they felt most favorable cited Mexico or Asia. In general, there appears to have been a strong preference for European immigrants in 1965. But the strength of this inclination waned, and the acceptability of Latin American and/or Asian migrants intensified by 1993. Of course, the ethnic and racial mix of the U.S. population was changing during this time, too, which may have influenced trends in preferences.

In question 3 respondents are asked to identify the immigrants they like the least. Migrants from Mexico and the Caribbean receive a disproportionate share of negative votes. In 1965 the number of respondents who mentioned Europe as the homeland of their least favorite immigrants was less than half the number who mentioned it as their favorite source for migrants. On the other hand, the proportions that gave Mexico, Latin America or Asia as their least favorite place were three times as large as those who preferred immigrants from these regions (35 versus 11 percent). In 1993 Asian migrants were clearly preferred to those from Mexico. A comparison of the last columns for questions 2 and 3 shows that the proportion of respondents citing a specific Asian country as their favorite source of immigrants was twice the proportion who gave Mexico as a response (35 versus 18 percent). The overall ratios go the other way when people are asked about their least favorite countries for migrants. Twice as many cite Mexico as cite a specific Asian country. In short, when Mexican immigrants are compared with immigrants from Asia, those from Asia have the upper hand in the public mind.

Questions 4-6 ask respondents to indicate whether they think the presence of various immigrant groups has generally benefitted the United States or more often created problems. The results, reported separately for Latin American/Caribbean, Asian and European migrants, support the following conclusions. First, the proportion of people who had formed a definite impression increased between 1985 and 1993 because the fraction responding "don't know" declined. This suggests that immigration has become a more salient issue. Second, immigration took on a somewhat less favorable reputation during this period, because the proportion of survey participants thinking immigration benefitted the country declined while the proportion believing that immigrants usually create problems rose. The Haitians provide a striking example of these trends. Third, the increase in unfavorable ratings appears greater than the decline in favorable ones, suggesting that persons who responded "don't know" in 1985 would have been more likely to express an unfavorable opinion by 1993. Fourth, European immigrants are viewed most positively in 1993. Next come migrants from Asia, and last are Latin American and Caribbean immigrants. For example, 75 percent of respondents in 1993 believed that Irish immigrants generally made a positive contribution to the United States, versus 59 percent for the Chinese, and just 29 percent for Mexican migrants. One exception to this pattern is that Japanese were viewed more positively than Russians in 1985. Finally, among Latin American/Caribbean migrants, Mexicans "did better" than Cubans or Haitians in 1993. Some of the negative attitudes toward Cubans and Haitians may be related to the extensive media coverage that was given to the Cuban and Haitian boatlifts and to fears over AIDS among these migrant groups.

Concerns that immigrants lower the earnings and labor market opportunities of native workers are often among the surest predictors of negative attitudes toward immigrants (Espenshade and Hempstead, 1996). Question 7 asks whether respondents believe that illegal immigrants compete for jobs with U.S. workers. Survey results for both 1980 and 1981 suggest that roughly half of all Americans believe that illegal migrants take jobs away from natives. The results for 1986 in the third column pertain specifically to undocumented Mexican migrants and reinforce our central conclusion. It is difficult to know what to make of the responses in the final column, however, because the survey item poses a double-barreled question. It is not clear what part of the question is being answered—the kinds of jobs Mexican illegals hold or the degree of job competition. The kind of job may be more influential in determining responses.

The next set of questions (8-13) asks about immigrants' perceived characteristics, including welfare use, criminal involvement, work ethic, degree of competitiveness, school performance, and family values. Each question contains a comparison between Latin American and Asian immigrants. A majority of respondents think that "ending up on welfare" is an accurate characterization of recent immigrants (question 8). Immigrants were perceived as somewhat less of a welfare burden in 1993 than in 1985. This result is interesting, especially in light of current immigration reform proposals to restrict the eligibility of legal immigrants' access to public benefits. Latin American migrants are clearly believed to be significantly more likely than Asian immigrants to use welfare. A somewhat larger majority of respondents associates immigrants with a crime problem in question 9 (60 versus 54 percent). Asians are again viewed more favorably than Latinos. The number of respondents who think that immigrants add to the crime problem rises by 50 percent when the question is posed about Hispanics instead of Asians (62 versus 43 percent).

Recent immigrants are generally seen as hard working (question 10), which partially contradicts the stereotype that immigrants end up on welfare. However, by a margin of three-quarters to two-thirds, Asians are more likely to be viewed as hardworking than Latino immigrants. Question 11 asks whether recent U.S. immigrants are too competitive. A majority of respondents in 1993 disagreed with this depiction, both for Latin American and Asian immigrants. But Asians were roughly 50 percent more likely than Latinos to be seen in this light.

Some of the attributes we have mentioned are negative stereotypes (end up on welfare, add to crime, too competitive). Questions 12 and 13 inquire about more positive traits—doing well in school and having strong family values. School performance is an area where Asian competitiveness is perceived to pay dividends. Asian immigrants are viewed as much more likely to do very well in school than Latinos. Moreover, recent immigrants are believed to possess strong family values. Three-quarters of respondents in 1993 felt this way. Along this dimension there is no apparent difference between the two immigrant groups.

One way perhaps of summarizing people's overall attitudes toward Latin American and Asian immigrants is to ask whether the United States is admitting too many, too few, or about the right number from these regions. Responses from six surveys, taken between 1984 and 1995, are tabulated under questions 14 and 15. At least one-half of all survey participants feel we are letting in too many immigrants from both Latin America and Asia. The sentiment against immigrants builds to a peak in 1992-93 and then tapers off. This pattern is similar to the behavior of U.S. employment rates and suggests that concerns about the presence of immigrants may grow in response to a perception of diminished labor market opportunities among native workers (Espenshade and Hempstead, 1996). The proportion of respondents who think that we are letting in too few immigrants is relatively stable at around 4-7 percent over the 11-year period. This means that the increase in the percent saying "too many" comes at the expense of people saying "don't know" and, to a lesser extent, those responding "about right." In any given survey, nearly identical proportions of participants say the number of immigrants from Latin America and from Asia is either too many or about right. However, within this group, there is a greater likelihood of responding "too many" when Latin America immigrants are mentioned, suggesting in another way that immigrants from Latin America are seen as less desirable in some sense than Asian immigrants.

## Attitudes toward Ways to Control Illegal Immigration

Additional perspective on the American public's reactions to Mexican migration is gained by examining their attitudes toward measures for controlling illegal immigration because, as we have already noted, Mexico is the major source country for undocumented migrants in the United States. Americans generally feel that the United States has a problem with border security. In a 1990 Roper survey, three out of five respondents agreed that we have a serious problem with illegal aliens crossing our country's border; only 30 percent considered our border security to be "pretty good." Eighty percent of respondents in the same survey believed that the United States was doing either a fair or poor job controlling illegal immigration, and just one percent rated the federal government's job performance as "excellent."

There is additional evidence suggesting that the American public feels the federal government should and can do more to cope with the problem. Three-quarters of respondents in a 1993 Yankelovich poll felt the government was not doing enough to keep illegal immigrants out of the country, and roughly 70 percent of participants in a 1993 Gallup survey were of the opinion that the government could be doing significantly more to reduce illegal immigration. The American public clearly favors doing more as well. Whereas 60 percent of respondents in a 1993 survey indicated they would favor changes in federal laws to reduce the number of immigrants who enter the country legally, 85 percent supported changes to cut down on the number who enter illegally.

The remainder of this section deals with the public's attitudes toward a variety of measures to reduce the flow of undocumented migrants into the country. Some of these measures are features of IRCA and most have been recommended in one form or another by the U.S. Commission on Immigration Reform (1994). As we shall see, whereas many Americans support the general principle of controlling illegal immigration, this support sometimes wavers when respondents are confronted with specific tactics.

In question 16 people are asked whether they think "patrolling U.S. borders and coastlines more strictly" is a good or bad idea as a way of dealing with illegal aliens. Phrased in this very general way, the option commands broad support. Roughly 90 percent of respondents in 1985 and 1993 thought it was a good idea. Support was somewhat less uniform (down to 80 percent) when in 1986 one group (illegal Mexican migrants) was singled out for attention. More importantly, when people were reminded in 1993 that greater border security was likely to be reflected in higher taxes, support was dramatically reduced. When the answers to question 16 are compared with those to items 17-20, the conclusion that emerges is that people are much more likely to agree to something in the abstract (for example, the need to have greater border security) than they are when they hear about the actual implementation.

Question 17 asks whether increasing enforcement manpower along the border would be a good way of tightening border security. People generally favor adding more Border Patrol agents; 4 out of 5 respondents supported this option in 1992. Support drops when the military is substituted for the Border Patrol, but the idea still garners a two-thirds approval rating. Not surprisingly, there is stronger support for both the Border Patrol (94 percent) and the military personnel (80 percent) option among those who think illegal immigration is a serious problem.

Just two-thirds of respondents favor the idea of erecting fences in high-traffic areas to discourage illegal immigrants who cross the border on foot (question 18). This is less than the 81 percent who supported using more Border Patrol agents. A proposal to build a fence along the entire U.S.-Mexico border was opposed by two-thirds of those interviewed in 1993. The suggestion of digging ditches in high-entry areas to discourage illegal vehicle traffic receives about the same level of approval as fences in high-entry areas (question 19). Nearly two-thirds of respondents favor the proposal. Support in 1992 for ditches is somewhat weaker than a selective fence option, but it still has a clear majority of the American public behind it.

People are asked in question 20 how they feel about building a wall along the border with Mexico. A majority opposes a wall. Roughly two-thirds of respondents are against the idea in 1993 and 1995. Approximately the same response pattern was elicited when the idea was proposed of building a fence along the entire border with Mexico. The wall option commands the least support of all the measures we have discussed. A wall, in contrast to a fence, may be seen as too impenetrable. If this is correct, what the responses to the various options suggest is that people are willing to support token or symbolic measures to control illegal immigration, but enthusiasm declines for measures seen as too extreme (even if they might work).[7] It is interesting that there is less opposition to a wall in 1995 than in 1993. Perhaps the seriousness with which illegal immigration is perceived rose thereby permitting people to tolerate stronger measures.

In question 21 respondents are asked how they feel about charging a small toll of $2.00 to cross U.S. borders if the money is used to enhance border security. A user fee could have a deterrent effect on undocumented migration. A $2.00 toll might discourage some daily commuters, and the accumulated funds could support more Border Patrol agents and equipment. Three-quarters of respondents favor the idea, nearly as high as the four-fifths approval rating for more Border Patrol agents in the same poll. There is slightly less support for a user fee when the measure is made more specific (i.e., to land borders in the 1993 survey).

IRCA made it illegal for the first time for employers knowingly to hire unauthorized alien workers.[8] In addition, IRCA established penalties including fines and potential jail time for a "pattern and practice" of violations. Questions 22 and 23 ask respondents how they feel about employer sanctions. There is not much of a trend in the 15-year pattern of responses to question 22. Indeed, there is remarkable consistency both before and after IRCA. Roughly three-quarters of the respondents think hiring an illegal alien should be against the law. When respondents are presented with penalizing employers as a specific means of enforcing the law, support is reduced in comparison with the degree of interest shown for the abstract principle in item 22. A majority of Americans still supports penalties for employers of illegal aliens, but the extent of agreement drops closer to 65 percent than the three-quarters endorsement registered for question 22.

Amnesty for approximately 3 million former undocumented migrants is the feature of IRCA that seems to have had the most lasting impact. Numerous times prior to IRCA's enactment in November 1986 polling questions were asked about people's attitudes toward amnesty. The pattern of responses shown with question 24 indicates that, with the exception of 1985-86, a slim majority of Americans consistently opposed amnesty for illegals. Support for amnesty increased just prior to IRCA. The change in response patterns is not due to changes in question wording. It may be that respondents were reacting to congressional debates and saw amnesty as a price they were willing to pay for expanded measures to control illegal immigration. A more likely possibility is that the concept became less foreign (and therefore perhaps more agreeable) to many adults as talk of amnesty accelerated prior to IRCA's final debate and passage. Many of the questions about amnesty specify different residency requirements (0, 2 or 7 years). These details appear to have had little impact on respondents. People seem to have reacted instead to the general concept of forgiveness.

The INS now has in operation several pilot projects designed to allow employers to use computerized data systems to verify the legal status of noncitizen job applicants (Schmitt, 1996). Proponents of these programs say they are needed to weed out from U.S. labor markets illegal immigrants using counterfeit identification papers. Critics complain that using national data bases, including possibly those of the Social Security Administration, could eventually lead to a national identification card that would threaten individual freedoms. How the American public views these matters is indicated by responses to questions 25-27.

Question 25 asks whether individuals think it is a good idea to issue national identification (ID) cards to every U.S. citizen at birth or when they become naturalized as a way of detecting who is in this country legally.[9] The 1977 and 1984 Roper poll percentages are virtually identical, even though seven years separate the surveys. When the same question is posed, one-half of respondents favor national ID cards, one-third are opposed, and the remainder either have mixed feelings or are not sure. Both Yankelovich surveys in 1985 and 1993 also asked the same question. During this 8-year period, support for a national ID card increased so that one-half of all respondents favored the proposal by 1993. Paradoxically, there is considerably less support for a national ID card in the May 1985 Yankelovich survey than in the August 1984 Roper poll. However, the former survey carries stronger language (i.e., "require" and "carry"). The Gallup polls of 1993 and 1995 asked similar questions, too. Roughly three-fifths of respondents supported ID cards. Here the verb "carry" has been softened to "have," which may help to account for somewhat higher levels of support in the Gallup surveys. Overall, however, support for the general national ID card is very mixed.

Restricting the use of a national ID card to employment purposes does not appear to enhance its popularity (question 26). The 1990 and 1994 Harris polls phrased the question in the same way, and over these four years support for an ID card increased—rising from a small majority opposed in 1990 to a slim majority in favor by 1994. This result parallels those during the 1990s in question 25. Finally, a forge-proof social security card is favored by stronger margins—roughly two-thirds of American adults—possibly because of the greater familiarity of the social security card and the fact that U.S. residents use social security numbers so frequently for identification purposes (question 27).

In November 1994 voters in California approved Proposition 187 by a 3-2 margin. The initiative denies public education (including K-12, community colleges, and higher education), health care (except emergency medical services), and social services to undocumented immigrants. In November 1995 a federal judge ruled large sections of Proposition 187 unconstitutional, citing individual rights and the fact that "the state is powerless to enact its own scheme to regulate immigration" (Ayres, 1995a: A10). Nevertheless, it is interesting to observe how U.S. residents in general feel about these issues, especially because interest in Proposition 187 has spilled over into other states.[10]

Question 28 asks how people feel about proposals to deny social services (in particular, American schools and hospitals) to illegal immigrants as a way of controlling undocumented migration. Support rose between the 1993 and July 1995 Gallup surveys. By 1995, one-half of American adults favored these measures, although the publicity surrounding Proposition 187 may have helped to increase support. On average, it appears that somewhat more than half of all respondents favor measures denying education and health benefits to illegal immigrants.[11] Enthusiasm for these proposals seems to be greater at mid-decade than earlier in the 1990s. This result parallels those surrounding many other measures to control illegal immigration. It is possible that many people are viewing undocumented U.S. migration as an increasingly serious problem.

## Conclusion

Two broad conclusions emerge from our analysis of attitudes toward Mexican migration. One is that Latin American/Caribbean migrants in general, and Mexican migrants in particular, rank somewhere near the bottom in terms of how Americans view immigrants from different parts of the world. European immigrants are most favored and Asians fall in the middle. In comparison with Latin American migrants, Asian immigrants are perceived to be less likely to use welfare, less likely to commit crimes, more likely to work hard, and more likely to do well in school. Only in terms of being overly competitive (assuming a pejorative connotation for this phrase) are Asians viewed less favorably than Latino migrants. Although the American public feels that the United States is admitting too many migrants from both Latin American and Asian countries, they are more likely to feel this way about Hispanic migrants.[12]

Second, individuals are significantly more concerned about problems surrounding illegal migration than they are about legal immigration. They feel that the federal government can and should be doing more to control the flow of undocumented migrants into the country. By margins of roughly 9 to 1, Americans believe that stricter control of our borders and coastlines is a good idea. But support begins to waver once specific measures are introduced. Overall, there seems to be a tradeoff between policy measures that are effective and those that will receive broad approval. Many measures that might be expected to cut rather deeply into illegal immigration are seen by the American public as too harsh and are not supported.

# Appendix

CBS/NYT: Columbia Broadcasting System/*New York Times*
GALLUP: Gallup Organization
HARRIS: Louis Harris and Associates
LAT: *Los Angeles Times*
PSRNEW: Princeton Survey Research Associates
ROPER: Roper Organization
YANK: Yankelovich, Skelly and White
YANKCS: Yankelovich Clancy Shulman
YANKP: Yankelovich Partners, Inc.

## Survey Results:
## Attitudes toward Immigrants by Countries and Regions of Origin

### Likes and Dislikes

1. *CBS/NYT, GALLUP, YANKP*: These days, where do most new immigrants
   to the United States come from—Latin America, Asia or somewhere else?

| | CBS/*NYT* 6/86 (%) | GALLUP 5/88[a] (%) | CBS/*NYT* 6/93 (%) | YANKP 9/93[b] (%)[c] |
|---|---|---|---|---|
| Latin America | 46 | 49 | 35 | 42 |
| Asia | 17 | 27 | 30 | 30 |
| Other | 4 | 7 | 10 | 12 |
| All over | 8 | – | 12 | – |
| Europe | 2 | 5 | – | 4 |
| Caribbean | 1 | 11 | – | 12 |
| Don't know | 22 | – | 13 | 11 |
| N | 1,618 | 1,611 | 1,363 | 1,108 |

[a]"Where would you say most immigrants to the U.S. come from today?" Latin America = Mexico/Central America; Other = South America; Caribbean = Cuba.
[b]"Where would you say the majority of [recent immigrants who have come to this country, legally or illegally, in the past ten to fifteen years] came from—Latin America, Asia, Africa, India, Arab countries in the Middle East, Eastern Europe, or the Caribbean?" Asia = Asia, India; Other = Africa, Arab/Middle East; Europe = Eastern Europe.
[c]Adds to more than 100% due to multiple responses.

2. *HARRIS, ROPER, YANKP:* Think about the group of recent immigrants you feel most favorable toward. Where would you say the majority of those recent immigrants came from—Latin America, Asia, Africa, India, Arab countries in the Middle East, Eastern Europe, or the Caribbean?

| | HARRIS 5/65[a] (%)[b] | ROPER 6/86[c] (%) | YANKP 9/93[d] (%) | YANKP 9/93[e] (%) |
|---|---|---|---|---|
| Mexico | 5 | – | – | 18 |
| Latin America | 4 | 12 | 15 | – |
| Asia | 2 | 6 | 21 | 35 |
| Other | 3 | 7 | 11 | 23 |
| All over | 34 | – | – | – |
| Europe | 136 | 44 | 20 | 8 |
| Caribbean | – | – | 7 | 12 |
| Don't know | 13 | 31 | 26 | 7 |
| N | 1,250 | 1,003 | 1,108 | 1,108 |

[a]"Here is a list of countries and parts of the world. If we are going to allow more people into this country as immigrants, which places on this list would you most prefer they come from . . .?" Other = Middle East; Europe = Canada, England or Scotland, Scandinavia, Germany, Ireland, France, Italy, Poland, Eastern Europe, Russia.

[b]Adds to more than 100% due to multiple responses.

[c]"Which of these four areas of the world would you like to see the greatest part of our future immigration come from—Africa, Asia, Europe, or Latin America?" Other = Africa.

[d]Asia = Asia, India; Other = Africa, Arab/Middle East; Europe = Eastern Europe; Don't know = None (17), Not sure (9).

[e]"Which country is that which stands out in your mind as the country the group of recent immigrants you feel most favorable toward came from?" Asked of those who named where the group of recent immigrants they feel most favorable toward came from and said it was one particular country (17% of those who named where group was from, 13% of sample, roughly 140 respondents).

3. *HARRIS, YANKP:* Think about the group of recent immigrants you feel least favorable toward. Where would you say the majority of those recent immigrants came from—Latin America, Asia, Africa, India, Arab countries in the Middle East, Eastern Europe, or the Caribbean?

| | HARRIS 5/65[a] (%)[b] | YANKP 9/93[c] (%) | YANKP 9/93[d] (%)[e] |
|---|---|---|---|
| Mexico | 11 | – | 28 |
| Latin America | 9 | 19 | – |
| Asia | 15 | 13 | 14 |
| Other | 14 | 29 | 23 |
| All over | 30 | – | – |
| Europe | 62 | 2 | 2 |
| Caribbean | – | 11 | 29 |
| Don't know | 15 | 27 | 6 |
| N | 1,250 | 1,108 | 1,108 |

[a]"Which countries or places would you least like to see immigrants into the United States come from . . .?" Other = Middle East; Europe = Canada, England or Scotland, Scandinavia, Germany, Ireland, France, Italy, Poland, Eastern Europe, Russia (26).

[b]Adds to more than 100% due to multiple responses.

[c]Asia = Asia, India; Other = Africa, Arab/Middle East (26); Europe = Eastern Europe; Don't know = None (17), Not sure (10).

[d]"Which country is that which stands out in your mind as the country the group of recent immigrants you feel least favorable toward came from?" Asked of those who named where the group of immigrants they feel least favorable toward came from, and said it was one particular country (27% of those who named where group was from, 20% of sample, roughly 218 respondents).

[e]Caribbean includes Haiti (18); Other includes Iraq (12).

## Benefit-Cost Comparisons

*YANK, GALLUP:* I'm going to read you a list of people of various nationalities, races and religions who have immigrated to the United States. As I read each one, please tell me whether you believe their presence has generally benefitted the country or generally created problems for the country.

### 4. Latin America/Caribbean

|  | More benefits/ Benefitted (%) | More problems/ Created problems (%) | Both (volunteered) (%) | Don't know/No opinion (%) | N (%) |
|---|---|---|---|---|---|
| **Mexicans** |  |  |  |  |  |
| YANK 5/85 | 44 | 37 | – | 20 | 1,014 |
| GALLUP 7/93 | 29 | 59 | 5 | 7 | 1,002 |
| **Cubans** |  |  |  |  |  |
| YANK 5/85 | 29 | 55 | – | 17 | 1,014 |
| GALLUP 7/93 | 24 | 64 | 3 | 9 | 1,002 |
| **Haitians** |  |  |  |  |  |
| YANK 5/85 | 31 | 35 | – | 34 | 1,014 |
| GALLUP 7/93 | 19 | 65 | 2 | 14 | 1,002 |
| **Colombians** |  |  |  |  |  |
| YANK 5/85 | 32 | 31 | – | 37 | 1,014 |
| **Salvadorans** |  |  |  |  |  |
| YANK 5/85 | 30 | 33 | – | 38 | 1,014 |

## 5. Asia

| | More benefits/ Benefitted (%) | More problems/ Created problems (%) | Both (volunteered) (%) | Don't know/No opinion (%) | N (%) |
|---|---|---|---|---|---|
| Chinese | | | | | |
|   YANK 5/85 | 69 | 13 | – | 18 | 1,014 |
|   GALLUP 7/93 | 58 | 31 | 2 | 7 | 1,002 |
| Koreans | | | | | |
|   YANK 5/85 | 52 | 23 | – | 25 | 1,014 |
|   GALLUP 7/93 | 53 | 33 | 3 | 11 | 1,002 |
| Vietnamese | | | | | |
|   YANK 5/85 | 47 | 30 | – | 23 | 1,014 |
|   GALLUP 7/93 | 41 | 46 | 3 | 10 | 1,002 |
| Japanese | | | | | |
|   YANK 5/85 | 70 | 14 | – | 16 | 1,014 |
| Pakistanis | | | | | |
|   YANK 5/85 | 37 | 25 | – | 38 | 1,014 |

## 6. Europe

| | More benefits/ Benefitted (%) | More problems/ Created problems (%) | Both (volunteered) (%) | Don't know/No opinion (%) | N (%) |
|---|---|---|---|---|---|
| Irish | | | | | |
|   YANK 5/85 | 78 | 5 | – | 17 | 1,014 |
|   GALLUP 7/93 | 75 | 11 | 3 | 11 | 1,002 |
| Poles | | | | | |
|   YANK 5/5 | 72 | 7 | – | 21 | 1,014 |
|   GALLUP 7/93 | 65 | 15 | 2 | 18 | 1,002 |
| Italians | | | | | |
|   YANK 5/85 | 74 | 10 | – | 16 | 1,014 |
| Russians | | | | | |
|   YANK 5/85 | 51 | 26 | – | 22 | 1,014 |
| Greeks | | | | | |
|   YANK 5/85 | 72 | 7 | – | 22 | 1,014 |

## Job Competition

7. *LAT, YANKCS*: Do you think illegal aliens take jobs that nobody wants, or do you think they take jobs away from Americans who need them?

| | LAT 10/80 (%) | LAT 3/81 (%) | YANKCS 7/86[b] (%)[c] | YANKCS 7/86[d] (%) |
|---|---|---|---|---|
| Take jobs nobody wants | 39 | 40 | 26 | 70 |
| Compete with Americans | 52 | 48 | 71 | 16 |
| Some of both (vol.) | – | – | – | 10 |
| Not sure | 9[a] | 12 | 3 | 3 |
| N | 2,853 | 1,681 | 1,017 | 1,017 |

[a]Includes 1% who refused to answer.

[b]"Illegal aliens often come to this country to find jobs. To what extent do you feel illegal aliens from Mexico take jobs away from American workers—a lot, sometimes, only a little, or not at all?"

[c]Take jobs nobody wants = only a little (21) and not at all (5). Compete with Americans = a lot (38) and sometimes (33).

[d]"Do you think that illegal aliens from Mexico mostly take menial jobs that American workers don't want, or do they mostly compete with American workers for good jobs?"

**Perceived Characteristics**

8. *YANK, GALLUP, YANKP:* I am going to read you some statements that are sometimes made about people who have immigrated from other countries in the last ten years. Tell me, in general, whether you think that statement applies to immigrants moving here in the past ten years or does not apply. . . . End up on welfare.

|  | (Latin America) | | (Asia) | |
|  | YANK 4/85 (%) | GALLUP 7/93[a] (%) | GALLUP 7/93[b] (%) | YANKP 9/93 (%) |
| --- | --- | --- | --- | --- |
| Applies | 59 | 60 | 38 | 54 |
| Does not apply | 21 | 27 | 53 | 30 |
| Applies to some/not others | 15 | – | – | 10 |
| Not sure | 5 | 13 | 9 | 5 |
| N | 1,014 | 1,002 | 1,002 | 1,108 |

[a]Please tell me whether each of the following characteristics does or does not apply to immigrants from Latin American countries. . . . Often end up on welfare.

[b]Please tell me whether each of the following characteristics does or does not apply to immigrants from Asian countries. . . . Often end up on welfare.

9. *GALLUP, YANKP:* Tell me in general whether you think the statement applies to immigrants moving here in the last ten to fifteen years. . . . Add to the crime problem.

| | (Latin America) GALLUP 7/93[a] (%) | (Asia) GALLUP 7/93[b] (%) | YANKP 9/93 (%) |
|---|---|---|---|
| Applies | 62 | 43 | 60 |
| Does not apply | 28 | 48 | 29 |
| Applies to some | – | – | 8 |
| No opinion | 10 | 9 | 4 |
| N | 1,002 | 1,002 | 1,108 |

[a]"Whether the following characteristics do or do not apply to immigrants from Latin America. . . . Significantly increase crime."
[b]"Whether the following characteristics do or do not apply to immigrants from Asian countries. . . . Significantly increase crime."

10. *GALLUP, YANKP:* Tell me in general whether you think that statement applies to immigrants moving here in the past ten to fifteen years or does not apply. . . . Are hard-working.

| | (Latin America) GALLUP 7/93[a] (%) | (Asia) GALLUP 7/93[b] (%) | YANKP 9/93 (%) |
|---|---|---|---|
| Applies | 65 | 74 | 79[c] |
| Does not apply | 27 | 20 | 12 |
| No opinion | 8 | 6 | 4 |
| N | 1,002 | 1,002 | 1,108 |

[a]Whether each of the following characteristics does or does not apply to immigrants from Latin America. . . . Work very hard.
[b]Whether each of the following characteristics does or does not apply to immigrants from Asian countries. . . . Work very hard.
[c]79% (67% = applies, 12% = applies to some).

11. *GALLUP:* Whether. . . the following characteristic does or does not apply to immigrants moving here in the past ten to fifteen years. . . . Are too competitive.

|  | (Latin America) GALLUP 7/93[a] (%) | (Asia) GALLUP 7/93[b] (%) |
|---|---|---|
| Applies | 26 | 40 |
| Does not apply | 64 | 52 |
| No opinion | 10 | 8 |
| N | 1,002 | 1,002 |

[a]Latin American countries.
[b]Asian countries.

12. *GALLUP:* Whether . . . the following characteristic does or does not apply to immigrants moving here in the past ten to fifteen years. . . . Do very well in school.

|  | (Latin America) GALLUP 7/93[a] (%) | (Asia) GALLUP 7/93[b] (%) |
|---|---|---|
| Applies | 42 | 74 |
| Does not apply | 42 | 17 |
| No opinion | 16 | 9 |
| N | 1,002 | 1,002 |

[a]Latin American countries.
[b]Asian countries.

13. *GALLUP:* Whether. . . the following characteristic does or does not apply to immigrants moving here in the last ten to fifteen years. . . . Have strong family values.

|  | (Latin America) GALLUP 7/93[a] (%) | (Asia) GALLUP 7/93[b] (%) |
|---|---|---|
| Applies | 72 | 77 |
| Does not apply | 19 | 16 |
| No opinion | 9 | 7 |
| N | 1,002 | 1,002 |

[a]Latin American countries.
[b]Asian countries.

## Preferred Levels of Immigration

*GALLUP, PSRNEW:* Thinking about immigration into this country from various parts of the world, do you think the number of immigrants now entering the U.S. from each of the following areas is too many, too few, or about the right amount?

14. Latin American countries

|  | Too many (%) | Too few (%) | About right (%) | Don't know (%) | N (%) |
|---|---|---|---|---|---|
| GALLUP 5/84 | 53 | 5 | 30 | 12 | 751 |
| GALLUP 6/84 | 54 | 5 | 30 | 12 | 751 |
| GALLUP 8/90 | 54 | 7 | 28 | 11 | 767 |
| GALLUP 2/92 | 69 | 5 | 22 | 4 | 1,002 |
| GALLUP 7/93 | 62 | 5 | 29 | 4 | 1,002 |
| PSRNEW 2/95 | 56 | 3 | 27 | 14 | 758 |

15. Asian countries

|  | Too many (%) | Too few (%) | About right (%) | Don't know (%) | N (%) |
|---|---|---|---|---|---|
| GALLUP 5/84 | 49 | 6 | 33 | 12 | 751 |
| GALLUP 6/84 | 48 | 6 | 33 | 12 | 751 |
| GALLUP 8/90 | 49 | 7 | 31 | 13 | 767 |
| GALLUP 2/92 | 58 | 4 | 32 | 6 | 1,002 |
| GALLUP 7/93 | 62 | 4 | 29 | 5 | 1,002 |
| PSRNEW 2/95 | 44 | 3 | 38 | 15 | 758 |

**Attitudes toward Measures for Controlling Illegal Immigration**

**Border Security**

16. *YANK, YANKCS, ROPER, GALLUP, YANKP:* There have been various proposals offered for dealing with illegal aliens. I'm going to read you a list of these. Please tell me whether you think it is a good idea or a bad idea. . . . Patrol U.S. borders and coastlines more strictly.

|  | YANK<br>4/85<br>(%) | YANKCS<br>7/86[a]<br>(%) | ROPER<br>4/90[b]<br>(%) | GALLUP<br>7/93<br>(%) | YANKP<br>9/93[d]<br>(%) |
|---|---|---|---|---|---|
| Good idea | 87 | 80 | 94[c] | 90 | 65 |
| Bad idea | 9 | 15 | 4 | 9 | 32 |
| Don't know | 4 | 6 | 3 | 1 | 3 |
| N | 1,014 | 1,017 | 1,144 | 1,002 | 1,108 |

[a]"Do you think the U.S. should increase its efforts to patrol the Mexican border to keep out illegal immigrants from Mexico?"

[b]"To improve the situation (of illegal aliens crossing our country's borders), do you think border security needs to be increased a great deal, a fair amount, or only a little?" Asked of those who think this situation is a serious problem (62%).

[c]94% (60% = a great deal, 34% = a fair amount).

[d]"Spend more federal tax money to tighten security at the border between the U.S. and Mexico."

17. *ROPER:* I'm going to read you a few ways that have been suggested to increase our border security. For each one I'd like you to tell me if you would or would not be in favor of it. . . . Increase the Border Patrol manpower.

| | ROPER 4/90[a] (%) | ROPER 4/90[a,b] (%) | ROPER 4/92 (%) | ROPER 4/92[b] (%) |
|---|---|---|---|---|
| Favor | 94 | 80 | 81 | 65 |
| Oppose | 4 | 17 | 14 | 32 |
| Don't know | 2 | 3 | 5 | 3 |
| N | 1,144 | 1,144 | 1,100 | 1,100 |

[a]Asked of those who think the situation of illegal aliens crossing our country's borders is a serious problem (62%).
[b]"Use military personnel to patrol the border."

18. *ROPER, YANKP:* I'm going to read you a few ways that have been suggested to increase our border security. For each one I'd like you to tell me if you would or would not be in favor of it. . . . Construct fences in high entry areas to discourage crossing the border on foot.

| | ROPER 4/90 (%) | ROPER 4/92 (%) | YANKP 9/93[a] (%) |
|---|---|---|---|
| Favor | 64 | 62 | 29 |
| Oppose | 33 | 34 | 68 |
| Don't know | 3 | 4 | 4 |
| N | 1,144 | 1,100 | 1,108 |

[a]Build a fence along the entire border between the U.S. and Mexico.

19. *ROPER:* I'm going to read you a few ways that have been suggested to increase our border security. For each one I'd like you to tell me if you would or would not be in favor of it. . . . Dig ditches in high entry areas to discourage crossing the border in a vehicle.

|  | ROPER 4/90 (%) | ROPER 4/92 (%) |
|---|---|---|
| Favor | 63 | 58 |
| Oppose | 33 | 38 |
| Don't know | 3 | 4 |
| N | 1,144 | 1,100 |

20. *GALLUP:* Please tell me whether you would generally favor or oppose each of the following steps which have been proposed as a way of reducing illegal immigration into the U.S. . . . Erecting a wall along the border with Mexico.

|  | GALLUP 7/93 (%) | GALLUP 7/95 (%) |
|---|---|---|
| Favor | 27 | 35 |
| Oppose | 71 | 62 |
| Don't know | 2 | 3 |
| N | 1,002 | 801 |

21. *ROPER, YANKP:* Would you favor or oppose charging everybody who crosses a U.S. border a small user toll of $2.00 if the money were used for improving border security?

|  | ROPER 4/92 (%) | YANKP 9/93[a] (%) |
|---|---|---|
| Favor | 76 | 70 |
| Oppose | 20 | 27 |
| Don't know | 4 | 4 |
| N | 1,100 | 1,108 |

[a]"Charge a small fee to each person who crosses the border between the U.S. and Mexico or Canada in order to pay for tighter security at those borders."

**Employer Sanctions**

22. *GALLUP, ROPER:* Do you think it should or should not be against the law to employ a person who has come into the U.S. without proper papers?

|  | Should be against the law/Favor (%) | Should not be/ Oppose (%) | Don't Know (%) | N (%) |
|---|---|---|---|---|
| GALLUP 3/77 | 82 | 14 | 5 | 1,550 |
| GALLUP 10/77 | 72 | 23 | 5 | 1,509 |
| GALLUP 11/80 | 76 | 18 | 6 | 1,556 |
| GALLUP 9/82[A] | 65 | 35 | – | 1,486 |
| GALLUP 10/83 | 79 | 18 | 3 | 1,549 |
| GALLUP 6/84 | 75 | 20 | 5 | 1,522 |
| ROPER 4/90BV | 71 | 23 | 6 | 1,144 |
| ROPER 4/92[c] | 69 | 26 | 5 | 1,100 |

[a]"Do you favor or oppose a law making it illegal to hire an immigrant who has come to the U.S. without proper papers?"

[b]"Do you favor or oppose a law that forbids the hiring of illegal aliens?"

[c]See (b) for question wording. Sample includes 1,000 nationwide plus an additional oversample of 100 interviews in California.

23. *LAT, GALLUP, YANK, CBS/NYT:* Do you think the government should penalize employers who hire people who are here illegally?

| | LAT 3/81 (%) | GALLUP 5/84 (%) | GALLUP 6/84 (%) | YANK 5/85[b] (%) | CBS/NYT 6/86 (%) |
|---|---|---|---|---|---|
| Yes/Good idea | 62 | 61 | 61 | 76 | 69 |
| No/Bad idea | 28 | 28 | 28 | 17 | 20 |
| Don't know | 10[a] | 11 | 11 | 6 | 11[c] |
| N | 1,681 | 751 | 751 | 1,014 | 1,618 |

[a]Includes 1% who refused to answer.

[b]"There have been various proposals offered for dealing with illegal aliens. I'm going to read you a list of these and for each one, please tell me whether you think it is a good idea or a bad idea. . . . Impose strict penalties on employers who hire illegal aliens."

[c]Includes 5% who volunteered "Depends."

## Amnesty for Illegal Aliens

24. *ROPER, GALLUP, LAT, YANK, CBS*/NYT: The law requires that illegal aliens be deported. Do you think an exception should be made for those who have lived here for several years without breaking any laws?

| | Favor/Amnesty for those here (%) | Oppose/Arrest and deport (%) | Don't know (%) | N (%) |
|---|---|---|---|---|
| ROPER 9/77 | 41[a] | 51 | 8 | 2,004 |
| GALLUP 10/77[b] | 39 | 52 | 9 | 1,509 |
| GALLUP 11/80[b] | 37 | 52 | 11 | 1,556 |
| LAT 3/81[c] | 39 | 50 | 11[d] | 1,681 |
| GALLUP 10/83[b] | 41 | 52 | 7 | 1,549 |
| GALLUP 10/83[e] | 41 | 52 | 7 | 1,549 |
| GALLUP 5/84[f] | 34 | 55 | 11 | 751 |
| GALLUP 6/84[f] | 34 | 55 | 10 | 751 |
| GALLUP 6/84[g] | 42 | 49 | 10 | 1,522 |
| GALLUP 6/84[h] | 35 | 55 | 10 | 1,522 |
| GALLUP 7/84[h] | 35 | 55 | 10 | 1,532 |
| YANK 5/85[e] | 59 | 34 | 7 | 1,014 |
| CBS/NYT 6/86 | 58 | 32 | 10[i] | 1,618 |

[a]Amnesty after two years of residence (31%); amnesty for all illegals (10%).
[b]Seven years.
[c]Amnesty for all "illegal aliens who are presently in the U.S."
[d]Includes 1% who refused to anwer.
[e]Six or more years.
[f]"Some people say that there are too many illegal immigrants living in this country for the authorities to arrest and deport them. They feel we should have an amnesty to let most of them live here legally. Others say that the government should do everything it can to arrest and deport those living in this country illegally. Which view comes closer to your own?"
[g]Since 1980.
[h]Since 1982.
[i]Includes 6% who volunteered "Depends."

## National Identification Card

25. *ROPER, HARRIS, GALLUP, YANK, YANKP:* At the present time there is no foolproof way of determining if a person is legally or illegally in this country. Illegal aliens can get forged driver's licenses, Social Security cards, etc. It has been proposed that a national identity card be issued to every U.S. citizen at birth or on naturalization, as they do in Europe. You would have to show this card to an employer to get a job, or to a policeman on request, etc. Some people are in favor of a national identity card as a means of cutting down on illegal immigration. Others are opposed to it as being a violation of people's privacy and civil rights. How do you feel—would you like to see national identity cards issued to all citizens or not?

| | Yes/Issue ID card (%) | No/Oppose ID card (%) | Mixed feelings (vol.) (%) | Don't know (%) | N |
|---|---|---|---|---|---|
| ROPER 9/77 | 51 | 33 | 12 | 5 | 2,004 |
| HARRIS 12/78[a] | 37 | 57 | – | 5 | 1,513 |
| GALLUP 5/84[c] | 42 | 52 | – | 6 | 751 |
| GALLUP 6/84[c] | 42 | 52 | – | 7 | 751 |
| ROPER 8/84 | 49 | 35 | 13 | 3 | 2,000 |
| YANK 5/85[d] | 39 | 57 | – | 4 | 1,014 |
| GALLUP 7/93[c] | 57 | 41 | – | 2 | 1,002 |
| YANKP 9/93[d] | 50 | 48 | – | 2 | 1,108 |
| GALLUP 7/95[e] | 62 | 37 | – | 1 | 801 |

[a]"Identity cards should be issued by the government to all Americans so that it would be easier to find suspected criminals and illegal aliens."

[b]Yes includes favor strongly (23%) and favor somewhat (14%). No includes oppose somewhat (15%) and oppose strongly (42%).

[c]"Some people propose that the federal government issue identity cards to all citizens and legal immigrants to distinguish them from those who are in the country illegally. Others oppose this plan on the grounds that it would give the federal government too much knowledge and control over all Americans. Which view comes closest to your own?"

[d]"In order to control the flow of illegal aliens into the U.S., require all U.S. citizens to carry a national identification card."

[e]"As a way of reducing illegal immigration into the U.S., require all U.S. citizens and legal residents to have a national I.D. card to distinguish them from illegal immigrants."

26. *LAT, CBS/NYT, HARRIS, ROPER:* Do you think that every worker should be required to have some kind of national identification before he or she can get a job, or not?

| | LAT 3/81 (%) | CBS/NYT 6/86[a] (%) | HARRIS 1/90[b] (%) | ROPER 4/90[c] (%) | HARRIS 8/94[b] (%) |
|---|---|---|---|---|---|
| Favor ID card | 54 | 46 | 43 | 62 | 53 |
| Oppose ID card | 41 | 44 | 56 | 32 | 46 |
| Don't know | 5 | 10 | 2 | 6 | 2 |
| N | 1,681 | 1,618 | 2,254 | 1,144 | 1,005 |

[a]"So that illegal aliens could not get jobs here, would you be willing to carry a new government issued identity card that would have to be shown to employers, or would this be a violation of your freedoms?"
[b]"Would you favor the government requiring a national work identification card for all working Americans, both citizens and non-citizens? Supporters believe this would help to identify illegal aliens. Opponents see this as a dangerous threat to privacy. Would you favor or oppose such a requirement?"
[c]"Do you favor or oppose the federal government issuing a forge-proof, easily verifiable identification document to all U.S. citizens and legal aliens that would have to be shown only when applying for a job?"

27. *ROPER, GALLUP:* Another proposal (besides one that a national identity card be issued to every U.S. citizen at birth or on naturalization) is that all citizens be issued a forge-proof Social Security card which you would only have to show a prospective employer at the time you were being hired, but wouldn't have to carry with you at all times, and wouldn't have to show to police or anyone else on demand. Would you like to see forge-proof Social Security cards issued to all people who work or are looking for jobs, or would you be against this?

| | ROPER 9/77 (%) | GALLUP 10/77[b] (%) | GALLUP 10/83[b] (%) | GALLUP 6/84[b] (%) | ROPER 8/84 (%) |
|---|---|---|---|---|---|
| For | 29 | 65 | 66 | 63 | 31 |
| Against | 9 | 30 | 31 | 34 | 10 |
| Have mixed feelings (vol.) | 8 | – | – | – | 8 |
| Don't know | 4 | 5 | 3 | 3 | 3 |
| Not asked[a] | 51 | – | – | – | 49 |
| N | 2,004 | 1,509 | 1,549 | 1,522 | 2,000 |

[a]Respondents favored national identity card.
[b]"Do you believe everyone in the United States should be required to carry an identification card such as a Social Security card, or not?"

## Denying Social Services

28. *GALLUP, YANKP:* Please tell me whether you would generally favor or oppose each of the following steps which have been proposed as a way of reducing illegal immigration into the U.S. . . . Not allowing illegal immigrants to use American schools and hospitals.

| | GALLUP 7/93 (%) | YANKP 9/93[a] (%) | GALLUP 12/94[b] (%) | GALLUP 12/94[c] (%) | GALLUP 6/95[d] (%) | GALLUP 7/95 (%) |
|---|---|---|---|---|---|---|
| Favor | 40 | 47 | 57 | 63 | 28 | 50 |
| Oppose | 57 | 48 | 39 | 34 | 67 | 45 |
| No opinion | 3 | 6 | 4 | 4 | 5 | 4 |
| N | 1,002 | 1,108 | 1,016 | 1,016 | 1,311 | 801 |

[a]"Stop providing government health benefits and public education to immigrants and their children."

[b]"Would you favor or oppose a proposal to eliminate all forms of public assistance, including education and health benefits, to all illegal immigrants and their children?"

[c]"Voters in California recently approved a proposal to eliminate those benefits (public assistance including education and health benefits) for illegal immigrants. Would you favor or oppose a similar proposal in your state?"

[d]"Are you in favor of or opposed to providing free public education, school lunches, and other benefits to children of immigrants who are in the U.S. illegally?"

# Notes

Partial support for this research was provided by grants from the Andrew W. Mellon Foundation and the National Institute of Child Health and Human Development. The authors gratefully acknowledge useful comments from Stanley Presser and the capable technical assistance of Melanie Adams and Emily Niebo.

1. A brief history of American attitudes toward U.S. immigration from the late nineteenth century to the present may be found in Cornelius (1983), Espenshade and Calhoun (1993), Espenshade and Hempstead (1996), and Simon and Alexander (1993).

2. This incongruence between beliefs and reality is possibly related to other misperceptions. For example, Gallup Poll items show that the public greatly overestimates the size of U.S. minority populations, including blacks and Hispanics (Nadeau, Niemi, and Levine, 1993).

3. This may be partly a function of how the question was asked. If the survey item had not mentioned Mexico but instead asked what or who worries you when it comes to immigrants, many fewer respondents might mention Mexico.

4. Unless otherwise noted, all survey data reported in this chapter come from nationally representative samples of adults.

5. To some extent, responses may be patterned by cues attached to the adjectives "legal" and "illegal" that have nothing to do with immigration. In other words, knowing nothing about an issue, respondents may be more likely to express concern over its "illegal" aspects than its "legal" ones.

6. Some of these pertain to immigration, but POLL covers the full spectrum of public interest (for example, politics, government, public institutions, international affairs, business, social issues and attitudes, and consumer issues and preferences).

7. IRCA had as its prime objective reducing illegal immigration from Mexico by, among other things, increasing the number of Border Patrol agents and expanding the physical resources used in the apprehension process (including high-technology equipment, vehicles, and fences). Evaluations of the effectiveness of IRCA suggest it had a short-term impact in 1986-88, but that within two or three years the undocumented flow had returned to near-normal levels (Espenshade, 1990). Some authors are skeptical that effective control of undocumented migration from Mexico is a realistic possibility (Cornelius, 1996).

8. Prior to IRCA it was unlawful for undocumented migrants to hold a job in the United States, but not illegal for a U.S. employer to hire them.

9. As a technical matter, item 25 overlooks the status of legal aliens. Would they also receive an ID card that testifies to their legal (albeit alien) status?

10. Groups in Arizona, Florida, New York and Texas have expressed an interest in similar ballot initiatives in the 1996 elections.

11. The June 1995 Gallup results are consistent with all the rest. But one needs to check the question wording carefully.

12. Parallel results from the General Social Survey show that whites express greater social distance from and more negative stereotypes about Hispanics than Asians over a broad range of issues (Wilson, 1996).

# References

Ayres, Jr., B. Drummond. 1995. California Immigration Law is Ruled to be Partly Illegal, *The New York Times*, November 21, p. A10.

Cornelius, Wayne A. 1996. Appearance and Realities: Controlling Illegal Immigration in the United States, International Migration Working Paper Series, Center for International Studies, Massachusetts Institute of Technology. Cambridge, MA.

————. 1983. America in the Era of Limits: Migrants, Nativists, and the Future of U.S.-Mexican Relations, in Carlos Vasquez and Manuel Garcia y Griego, eds., *Mexican and U.S. Relations: Conflict and Convergence*. UCLA Chicano Studies Research Center and UCLA Latin American Center Publications. Los Angeles, CA: University of California, pp. 371-396.

Espenshade, Thomas J. 1996. Fiscal Impacts of Immigrants and the Shrinking Welfare State, in Josh DeWind and Charles Hirschman, eds., *America Becoming/Becoming American: International Migration to the United States*, Social Science Research Council, forthcoming.

————. 1990. Undocumented Migration to the United States: Evidence from a Repeated Trials Model. Pp. 159-181 in Frank D. Bean, Barry Edmonston, and Jeffrey S. Passel, eds., *Undocumented Migration to the United States: IRCA and the Experience of the 1980s*. Washington, D.C.: The Urban Institute Press.

Espenshade, Thomas J., and Charles A. Calhoun. 1993. An Analysis of Public Opinion Toward Undocumented Immigration, *Population Research and Policy Review*, vol. 12, no. 3 (1993): 189-224.

Espenshade, Thomas J., and Katherine Hempstead. 1996. Contemporary American Attitudes Toward U.S. Immigration, *International Migration Review*, Summer, 30(2): 1-36, forthcoming.

Fix, Michael, and Jeffrey S. Passel. 1994. *Immigration and Immigrants: Setting the Record Straight*. Washington, D.C.: The Urban Institute.

Hansen, Kristin A. 1996. Profile of the Foreign-Born Population in 1995: What the CPS Nativity Data Tell Us, paper presented at the Annual Meetings of the Population Association of America, New Orleans, Louisiana, May 9-11, 1996.

Nadeau, Richard, Richard G. Niemi, and Jeffrey Levine. 1993. Innumeracy About Minority Populations, *Public Opinion Quarterly*, Fall, 57(3): 332-347.

Schmitt, Eric. 1996. U.S. Expands Status Checks on Job Seekers, *The New York Times*, May 24, p. A1.

Simon, Rita J. 1985. *Public Opinion and the Immigrant: Print Media Coverage, 1880-1980*. Lexington, MA: Lexington Books, D.C. Heath and Company.

Simon, Rita J., and Susan H. Alexander. 1993. *The Ambivalent Welcome: Print Media, Public Opinion and Immigration*. Westport, CT: Praeger.

U.S. Bureau of the Census. 1993. *The Foreign-Born Population in the United States: 1990*. Subject Report CP-3-1, July. Washington, D.C.: U.S. Government Printing Office.

U.S. Commission on Immigration Reform. 1994. *U.S. Immigration Policy: Restoring Credibility. A Report to Congress*. 1994 Executive Summary, September. Washington, D.C.: U.S. Commission on Immigration Reform.

U.S. Immigration and Naturalization Service. 1996. *1994 Statistical Yearbook of the Immigration and Naturalization Service*, February, M-367. Washington, D.C.: U.S. Government Printing Office.

———. 1992. *Immigration Reform and Control Act: Report on the Legalized Alien Population*, March, M-375. Washington, D.C.: U.S. Government Printing Office.

Warren, Robert. 1995. Estimates of the Undocumented Immigrant Population Residing in the United States, by Country of Origin and State of Residence: October 1992, paper presented at the Annual Meeting of the Population Association of America, San Francisco, California, April 1995.

Warren, Robert, and Jeffrey S. Passel. 1987. A Count of the Uncountable: Estimates of Undocumented Aliens Counted in the 1980 United States Census, *Demography*, August, 24(3): 375-393.

Wilson, Thomas C. 1996. Cohort and Prejudice: Whites' Attitudes Toward Blacks, Hispanics, Jews, and Asians, *Public Opinion Quarterly*, Summer, 60(2): 253-274.

# 9.
# NAFTA and Mexican Migration

*Peter H. Smith*

Negotiation of the North American Free Trade Agreement (NAFTA) aroused soaring expectations in both Mexico and the United States. It was predicted that formation of a free trade zone among Mexico, the United States, and Canada would accelerate and perpetuate rates of economic growth in all three member countries. The integration of technology, capital, and natural and human resources would enhance the competitiveness of the entire region, and especially of the United States, vis-à-vis competitors in Europe and around the Pacific Rim. For Mexico, NAFTA would attract direct investment from all parts of the world, stimulate development, and assure social peace; it would extend the process of economic liberalization, strengthen the cause of political reform, and draw the country into the much-cherished ranks of the "first world." As officials and pundits repeatedly proclaimed, NAFTA would create a "win-win-win" situation. Such exaggeration was part and parcel of political reality: In order to be sold at all, NAFTA would have to be monumentally oversold.[1]

Amid all this hyperbole, one of the most persistent claims was that implementation of NAFTA would lead to an immediate and continuous reduction in the flow of illegal immigrants from Mexico to the United States.[2] Free trade would foster economic growth, according to this argument, economic growth would expand employment, and increasing job opportunities in Mexico would reduce incentives for emigration to the United States. (A distorted version of this idea was propounded by Texas billionaire Ross Perot, who mournfully predicted that a massive relocation of U.S. investments south of the border would emit a giant "sucking sound" and transfer millions of U.S. jobs to Mexico.) By creating jobs in Mexico, NAFTA would have two beneficial effects: it would retain some of the most energetic and entrepreneurial elements of the Mexican labor force within Mexico, and it would reduce unemployment and job competition within the United States. Both countries stood to gain as a result.

In contrast, skeptics asserted that NAFTA would lead to an increase in Mexican migration to the United States. According to this view, free trade would bring about the devastation of Mexican small- and medium-sized business, which tends to use more labor-intensive production techniques than does big business—and which would be unable to compete with U.S. corporations. This process would intensify concentration in Mexico's already oligopolistic business sector and simultaneously displace employees who, in the absence of alternatives, would head for the United States. These dynamics would be especially apparent in the countryside, where traditional producers of grain (especially corn and wheat) would find it impossible to compete with U.S. agribusiness. Dislocated from the land, *campesinos* would set out in search of work, and thousands would trek north toward the United States.

Intermediate positions emerged in this debate. One held that NAFTA would have no visible effect on net emigration from Mexico. Free trade would lead to the displacement of some workers in Mexico and to the employment of others; NAFTA would encourage some to migrate and others to stay at home. Theoretically, at least, these effects could cancel each other out, and the net result would be a continuation of recent and historic trends. (There was uncertainty about the long-term direction of such trends, however, so agreement about a null "NAFTA effect" did not necessarily lead to agreement about the likely path of migration.)

Another intermediate position held that NAFTA would exert differential impacts over time. In the short to medium term, NAFTA would lead to an increase in illegal migration from Mexico—either (a) because it would lead to displacement of workers and *campesinos* who would seek employment in the United States, or (b) paradoxically, because it would generate economic development that would enable Mexican workers to accumulate the resources needed for the northward trip.[3] As long as the wage differential between the two countries remained very high, according to this interpretation, either or both of these processes would stimulate emigration. If and as the wage differential were to decline, however, emigration would eventually diminish as well. A key question, of course, was whether and how long it might take to begin closing the gap in wages.[4]

In summary, debates and expectations have yielded four major hypotheses about the impact of NAFTA on emigration from Mexico:

$H_1$:   Implementation of NAFTA would lead to a steady reduction in the flow of undocumented workers from Mexico to the United States.

$H_2$:   Implementation of NAFTA would lead to an acceleration in the flow of undocumented workers (and peasants) from Mexico to the United States.

$H_3$:   Implementation of NAFTA would have no observable effect on the flow of undocumented workers from Mexico to the United States, which would either (a) continue at current levels, or (b) increase at a gradual rate.

$H_4$:   Implementation of NAFTA would have a curvilinear effect on the flow of undocumented workers from Mexico to the United States—increasing the flow in the short- to medium-term, thereafter reducing the flow.

Conspicuously, and revealingly, this entire debate relies upon conjecture. NAFTA itself says nothing about the question of labor migration. The treaty called for a free flow of goods between member countries by eliminating duties, tariffs, and trade barriers over a period of 15 years. It addressed the question of investments, permitting U.S. banks and securities firms to establish branch offices in Mexico and allowing U.S. citizens to invest in Mexico's banking and insurance industries. It established rigorous "rules of origin" in order to provide preferences for signatory countries (to the dismay of Japan and other Asian nations). One item, however, was most conspicuous by its absence: beyond a narrowly written provision for movement of corporate executives and selected professionals, the treaty made no reference at all to labor migration. Apparently sensing that there was no ground for reasonable compromise, NAFTA negotiators decided to avoid the question altogether.

## Background: Trends and Policies Prior to NAFTA

The United States has prospered as a nation on the basis of migration. From the 1950s through the 1980s, as Washington attempted to set strict limits on migratory flows, patterns of legal immigration underwent substantial change. There was a steady increase in the volume of legal migration, from 2.5 million in the 1950s to 6.0 million in the 1980s—the highest figure in the world, it might be said, but well below the proportional levels of the early 1900s. There also occurred a precipitous decline in the share of immigrants from Europe and Canada (mostly Europe), from 66 percent in the 1950s to 14 percent in the 1980s, and a concomitant rise in Asian immigration from 6 percent to 44 percent. Legal immigration from Mexico held steady, around 12-14 percent of the total, while flows from elsewhere in Latin America increased sharply during the 1960s and subsequently hovered around 26-27 percent of the total.

These trends underline important points. First, there was—and continues to be—a significant volume of legal migration from Mexico and Latin America to the United States. Indeed, the inflow of Mexicans in the 1920s was just about as large as during the 1960s, and legal admissions increased markedly in the 1970s and 1980s. Even in the absence of illegal immigration, these flows would have a considerable impact on American society.

Second, alterations in the composition of the immigrant stream—especially the relative decline of the component from Europe—prompted xenophobic, nativistic reactions among the U.S. public. Often this response took overtly racist form. As conservative presidential candidate Patrick J. Buchanan opined in 1992, "I think God made all people good, but if we had to take a million immigrants in, say Zulus, next year, or Englishmen, and put them in Virginia, what group would be easier to assimilate and would cause less problems for the people of Virginia?" In some parts of the country, particularly California, racist feelings erupted in widespread denunciation of Mexicans, virulently condemned as "illegal aliens" in a land that once was theirs.

Third, the establishment of numerical quotas proved to be an illusory exercise. Even the increase in legal entries—which nearly doubled between the 1960s and the 1980s—could not accommodate growing pressures for migration to the United States. As a result many people chose to enter the United States without official authorization, in violation of U.S. law. It is by definition impossible to gauge the magnitude of this population with much precision, but responsible demographers have settled on a rough estimate of a stock of 2.5 to 4.0 million "illegal aliens" from all parts of the world as of early 1992. (This was lower than the estimated range of 3.0-5.0 million for 1986, but higher than the figure of 1.8-3.0 million for 1989.) Particularly conspicuous was illegal migration from Mexico, estimated to account for 55-60 percent of unauthorized residents in the United States by the early 1990s. Others came from all points of the globe, from Haiti to Ireland to China, frequently entering the country legally and then overstaying their visas.

## Patterns in U.S. Policy

Within the Americas, U.S. policy on migration devoted special attention to Mexico. From the turn of the century until the 1930s, an informal "open border" policy toward Mexico provided U.S. employers with an immense pool of unskilled workers to accommodate seasonal and cyclical variations in labor demand, primarily in agriculture, mining, and construction. Mexican workers met special needs for temporary labor during World War I and, more generally, played a valuable role in the development of the American Southwest. Restrictions during the 1930s came as a direct consequence of the Great Depression. Not only did Mexican migration come to a screeching halt; amidst anti-Mexican sentiment, the forcible deportation of a half-million Mexicans led to a reversal of the flow. Despite its unseemly conclusion, this first migration cycle convinced U.S. employers of the economic advantages that derived from access to an unregulated, flexible, and inexpensive supply of labor.

World War II initiated a second cycle of Mexican immigration. In response to labor shortages in agriculture, the U.S. government in 1942 proposed a formal agreement to utilize Mexican workers. Formally legislated as U.S. Public Law 45, but more popularly known as the *Bracero* program, this temporary-worker agreement between Mexico and the United States began as an emergency measure to replenish labor lost to military service. Despite minor modifications, the accord continued without significant interruption until 1964, when Washington allowed the agreement to lapse.

The Walter-McCarran Immigration Act of 1952 continued and tightened the quota system first established in the 1920s. By establishing a preference system which gave priority to prospective immigrants with special skills in short supply in the United States, Walter-McCarran explicitly acknowledged the principle that immigration should be coordinated with labor demand in the United States. But the statute also revealed internal contradictions. Most glaring was the so-called "Texas Proviso" of 1952, which enabled growers in that state (and elsewhere) to hire undocumented field hands from Mexico; Walter-McCarran thus made it illegal to *be* an undocumented alien but not to *hire* one. As a result, the enforcement against illegal entry by Mexican agricultural workers was frequently lax.

Next came the immigration reforms of 1965. Passed in the midst of the Civil Rights movement, this legislation set the stage for dramatic changes in the size and composition of migrant streams. To abolish the discriminatory quota system, the 1965 amendments nearly doubled the worldwide number of annual U.S. visas, from 158,000 to 290,000; established a more equitable distribution of visas by region, allotting 170,000 to the Eastern Hemisphere and 120,000 to the Western Hemisphere; and reordered priorities for visa preference categories, giving relatively greater emphasis to family reunification over labor market considerations. The original legislation set a maximum of 20,000 visas per nation from the Eastern Hemisphere but placed no ceiling on individual countries in the Western Hemisphere, a provision which allowed Mexico to acquire a disproportionate share. In 1976, however, supplementary legislation applied the 20,000 limit to nations of the Western Hemisphere—to the direct detriment of Mexico.

## Impacts of IRCA

Against this backdrop, the Immigration Reform and Control Act (IRCA) of 1986 culminated a succession of attempts to curtail undocumented immigration. Passage came amidst a national clamor to "take control of our borders," in President Reagan's telling phrase, and as persistent unemployment fueled public resentment against workers from Mexico and other countries. Attorney General Edwin Meese III also proclaimed, in the face of both logic and fact, that restrictions on illegal immigration would reduce the flow of illicit drugs to the United States. Sponsored by Alan Simpson (R-Wyoming) and Peter Rodino (D-New Jersey), the bill contained three principal provisions:

- economic sanctions against U.S. employers who "knowingly employ, recruit, or refer for a fee" undocumented workers,

- permanent amnesty for undocumented workers who could prove continuous residence in the United States since any time prior to January 1, 1982, and

- partial amnesty for undocumented workers in the agricultural sector who had worked for at least 90 consecutive days in the three consecutive years prior to May 1986 (SAW I) or during the year between May 1985 and May 1986 (SAW II); and a provision for the readmission of "replenishment agricultural workers" (RAWs) in 1990-92.

Ultimately, IRCA represented a compromise between those political forces opposing unauthorized migration (from organized labor to racist reactionaries), those who benefited from its existence (mostly employers), and Hispanic leaders expressing concern about the potential aggravation of ethnic prejudice.

IRCA achieved mixed results. The employer-sanctions portion of the law proved to be toothless. It remained possible for employers to comply with the law—and still hire undocumented workers. For instance, Simpson-Rodino obliged employers to request official papers from job applicants, but did not require them to verify the authenticity of the documents: merely by inspecting any one of twenty-plus possible documents, widely available in counterfeit form, employers could technically satisfy their legal requirements. As a result, employer sanctions had only marginal impact on illegal migration.

In contrast, the amnesty portion of IRCA turned out to be highly effective. Partly seeking to improve its public image, INS gave high priority to the program, opening 109 new offices in order to handle an eventual volume of 3.9 million inquiries. Approximately 1.7 million applications were submitted under the "pre-1982" program and 1.3 million under the SAW program. More than 90 percent of the pre-1982 applicants had their status adjusted from temporary to permanent resident. All SAWs approved for temporary residence automatically received permanent resident status. In other words, nearly 3 million people acquired legal status in the United States as a result of Simpson-Rodino.

In the meantime there continued a historic shift in the nature and composition of *indocumentados* from Mexico, away from the temporary or seasonal migration of single working-age males toward the longer-term settlement of families, women, and children. But as Wayne A. Cornelius has concluded, "There is no evidence that IRCA has reduced the total pool of Mexican migrants employed or seeking work in U.S. labor markets."[5] While sharpening the distinction between migrant workers with and without legal status, in fact, IRCA might even have served to increase the size of the overall pool and, in so doing, it may have exacerbated social and political tensions within American society over unauthorized immigration.

## Changing the Context: The NAFTA Era

Negotiation and implementation of NAFTA in the early 1990s led to major alterations in the tone and conduct of the U.S.-Mexican relationship. In economic terms, NAFTA was expected to increase trade between the two countries and to stimulate foreign direct investment (FDI) in Mexico from the United States and from other industrial nations. According to U.S. data, in fact, two-way trade jumped from $81 billion in 1993 to $100 billion in 1994, the first year of NAFTA, an increase of 23 percent. Even in 1995, with Mexico mired in recession, two-way trade continued to expand since the increase in Mexican exports to the United States was greater than the decline of U.S. exports to Mexico. Two-way trade for 1995 amounted to $108 billion.

Similarly, FDI in Mexico grew from $4.4 billion in 1992 to $4.9 billion in 1993 and $8.0 billion in 1994.[6] And in 1995, with Mexico's GDP falling by almost 7 percent, FDI came to more than $5 billion, still much higher than levels obtained prior to the NAFTA negotiations. While the free trade accord accomplished its short-term objectives, the long-term goal of sustained economic growth would prove more elusive.

Throughout 1994 and 1995 Mexico suffered from a distressing combination of trends and events. The downward spiral included a regional uprising in the poverty-stricken state of Chiapas in January 1994, partly in protest against NAFTA itself; a series of high-level political assassinations, including the murder of the official-party presidential candidate, Luis Donaldo Colosio; the appearance a yawning deficit in the current account of the balance of payments (amounting to 8 percent of GDP in 1994), which made Mexico vulnerable to the shocks of that year; and a large short-term debt indexed to the dollar, through government-issued *tesobonos,* which investors used as a hedge against devaluation. Throughout 1994 the Salinas administration made strenuous efforts to sustain the value of the peso, so that foreign-exchange reserves by December 1994 were considerably less than the value of *tesobonos* outstanding. This created doubt that the Mexican government (under newly inaugurated President Ernesto Zedillo) would be able to meet its obligations, and financiers responded by moving portfolio investments out of the country. Instead of stabilizing the market, the Zedillo administration only exacerbated the situation through its ill-timed and poorly managed peso devaluation on December 20, precipitating an exodus of panic proportions.[7]

Clearly, the existence of NAFTA did not prevent Mexico from plunging into year-long economic crisis. (Indirectly, in fact, the treaty might even have contributed to Mexico's difficulties by stimulating large amounts of portfolio investment—"hot money," in contrast to FDI—that abandoned the country at its moment of trial.) Just as clearly, however, NAFTA helped shape official responses to Mexico's collapse. In contrast to its previous encounters with balance-of-payment crises, the Mexican government did not increase restrictions on imports in its 1995 stabilization program; instead it relied on orthodox macroeconomic measures of fiscal and monetary austerity, alongside the peso devaluation. Although the ensuing hardships were substantial and widespread, signs of recovery began to appear in early 1996.

For its part, the United States provided $20 billion in credit and pressured the International Monetary Fund to provide an additional $18 billion. The scale of this assistance was without precedent: there had been U.S. financial-support packages after previous Mexican crises, as in 1982, but none as massive as this. NAFTA surely encouraged this largess.

In sum, NAFTA succeeded in stimulating two-way trade and direct investment in Mexico, but it could not prevent the peso crisis of late 1994. This experience has led some experts and analysts to raise the question of whether NAFTA needs to be strengthened through close and regular trilateral consultation on macroeconomic issues, particularly on fiscal and monetary policy and on exchange-rate matters. These are sensitive and complex matters, of course, but by mid-1996 it seemed entirely possible that NAFTA would lead to increasingly institutionalized and "deeper" forms of economic integration between Mexico and the United States.

## Immigration Policy in the NAFTA Era

Not so with regard to labor migration. At virtually every level, the U.S. government has been attempting to curtail Mexican immigration throughout the 1990s. A tough stand against undocumented migration has in fact become a hallmark of the Clinton administration, which took office in the midst of a crisis over an influx of rafters from Haiti.[8] Encouraged by hard-line reports from the U.S. Commission on Immigration Reform (established by the Immigration Act of 1990, and chaired by the late former Congresswoman Barbara Jordan), the Clinton administration has given high priority to immigration control—increasing the INS budget from $1.4 billion in FY 1992 to $1.85 billion in FY 95 and proposing a 24 percent increase to $2.6 billion for FY 1996. As Attorney General Janet Reno declared in a September 1994 speech: "We *are* securing our nation's borders, we are aggressively enforcing our nation's borders, and we are doing it *now.* We will not rest until the flow of illegal immigrants across our nation's border has abated."

### Strengthening the Border Patrol

Apparently seeking a high-profile strategy, the Clinton administration has taken deliberate steps to bolster interdiction along the U.S.-Mexican border. The government increased the overall size of size of the Border Patrol by 51 percent from 1993 to 1995, bringing the number of agents to more than 4,500 and establishing a target of 7,000 by 1998. In mid-1995 Congress also approved a special $328 million enhancement for concentrated border enforcement operations.

It was not just a matter of adding more agents. In September 1993 the administration proclaimed Operation Hold-the-Line in El Paso, Texas (formerly known as Operation Blockade), an effort to curtail illegal entrants by deploying Border Patrol agents at close intervals along the border itself, and in September 1994 Attorney General Reno proclaimed the initiation of Operation Gatekeeper in San Diego. Due to topography and settlement patterns in the local area, Gatekeeper would employ a wide variety of measures: floodlighting, fingerprinting, extension of a wall, increased prosecution of smugglers (*coyotes*), and, of course, deployment of more agents. Despite budgetary uncertainty, the INS strategic plan called for a long-term, phased effort to extend concentrated enforcement operations to encompass the entire southwestern border. Even so, it remained unclear whether such an effort could ever be effective—or whether it would simply encourage would-be entrants to seek new modes of access.[9]

## Reducing Incentives for Migration

A second strategy adopted in the 1990s has been to reduce or eliminate reasons for migration. The most conspicuous example has been the malodorous Proposition 187, a measure presuming to reduce the flow of illegal migrants into the state of California by depriving them (and their children) of social services—such as non-emergency health care and public education. Advocates of Proposition 187 even predicted that effective implementation would induce voluntary self-deportation by illegals already resident within the state. Ardently supported by Governor Pete Wilson, soon to announce his short-lived candidacy for the presidency, Proposition 187 garnered support from 59 percent of the California electorate in November 1994.

Movements in favor of similar measures soon appeared in other southwestern states. And while the California measure quickly became entangled in complex litigation, it was doubtful that its application could have a significant deterrent effect. Its premise held that migrants came from Mexico in order to take advantage of social services and public education in the United States; to the contrary, however, virtually every piece of respectable research on the subject has shown that that migrants come in search of jobs. Despite this limitation, however, Proposition 187 and look-alikes elsewhere performed an important if unsavory political function: providing bigots and racists with a socially acceptable means of expressing anti-Mexican feeling. Largely for this reason, the movement continued to spread throughout the mid-1990s.[10]

An alternative kind of deterrent could come from strict application of employer sanctions. As envisioned in the 1986 IRCA legislation, this provision would increase the risk to employers (who would face the possibility of fines and/or arrest), impose additional burdens on migrants (who would have to obtain fraudulent papers), and, as a result, reduce the number of jobs available to undocumented migrants. Though fraught with potential weaknesses and loopholes, this approach had the distinct advantage of directly addressing fundamental reasons for migration. Cross-national research has shown that employer sanctions, though rarely applied with rigor anywhere around the world, can in principle have a significant impact on illegal immigration.[11]

Curiously enough, however, the Clinton administration has been reluctant to pursue this strategy. The number of INS agents charged with inspecting the more than 7 million employers throughout the country actually dropped from 448 in 1989 to 245 in 1994, while the corresponding amount of fines declined from

$18.5 million in 1990 to $10.9 million in 1994. In southern California, only 30-35 INS inspectors by the mid-1990s were supposed to monitor nearly 500,000 employers.[12] In his 1996 state-of-the-union address President Clinton grandly announced that the government would undertake to prosecute employers of illegal aliens, as though this were a novel step, while neglecting to observe that the IRCA statutes had been in place for nearly ten years. Clearly, application of employer sanctions would be a herculean task; just as clearly, the U.S. government was doing little about it.

## Reducing Legal Immigration

A third general strategy to emerge during the 1990s was an effort to reduce the volume of *legal* migration to the United States, and to redefine the criteria for eligibility. Revealingly, the Jordan Commission recommended in mid-1995 a reduction in the core level of legal admissions from approximately 725,000 per year to 550,000 per year. Entries would be allocated by category: 400,000 for nuclear family reunification; 100,000 for skill-based immigration; and 50,000 for refugee resettlement. Conspicuous among these recommendations was a proposal to recast the criteria for family reunification, eliminating siblings and adult children from eligibility, a measure that would have a disproportionate impact on Mexican-born citizens and legal residents in the United States.[13]

## Congressional Action

Apparently responding to the sentiments of their constituencies, both houses of the U.S. Congress showed strong support for efforts to curtail unwanted migration. In 1994 the House of Representatives approved, by a 417-12 vote, an amendment to a crime bill authorizing the addition of 6,000 agents to the Border Patrol, bringing the total up to 10,000. And in March 1996, by a vote of 333-87, the Republican-led House approved a sweeping immigration bill that would add 5,000 new agents to the Border Patrol; increase penalties for smugglers and document counterfeiters; authorize the construction of 14 miles of triple fencing in the San Diego area; restrict public benefits for illegal immigrants; permanently ban individuals who enter the country illegally; and, in the spirit of Proposition 187, permit states to deny public education to illegal-immigrant children.

Surprisingly, however, the House voted against a provision that would have cut legal immigration by 30 percent, as proposed by the Jordan Commission, and that would have disallowed adult children and siblings of U.S. citizens from receiving family visas. The tally on this measure was 238-183 and cut sharply across party lines. "Americans got the whole loaf on illegal-immigration reform and half the loaf on legal-immigration reform," said Representative Lamar Smith (R-Texas). "Three-fourths of a loaf tastes pretty good."[14]

For its part, the Senate approved (by 97-3) a similarly large-scale bill that would double the size of the Border Patrol, authorize the triple fence along the California border, develop a pilot project for employers to check with a federal agency to determine employment eligibility; set federal standards for driver's licenses, identification cards, and birth certificates (to make them less susceptible to misuse); and deny federal aid in health care, education, and other needs-based programs to legal immigrants if sponsors are able to pay. "This is a big piece of lumber here," said a proud Alan R. Simpson (R-Wyoming), the legislator who had cosponsored IRCA a decade before.

As the two bills headed for reconciliation in mid-1996, the principal difference concerned authorization for states to deny public education to illegal-immigrant children. The Clinton White House dismissed the idea as "nutty," and Attorney General Reno and Education Secretary Richard W. Riley declared their intention to recommend a presidential veto. "We're trying to keep it out of the final bill, and I will do everything I can to keep it out," Clinton himself was quoted as saying.[15] Attentive observers noted that this statement stopped short of proclaiming a definite veto.

Amid this political jockeying, scant attention focused on one fundamental fact: the underlying contradiction between NAFTA and the anti-immigration movement. On the one hand, the Clinton administration (and the U.S. government in general) was reaching out to Mexico with an expansionist, inclusive economic policy; on the other hand, it was containing Mexico with a restrictive, exclusive social policy. The United States has been embracing and rejecting Mexico at one and the same time.

This contradiction emerged on three levels. One was symbolic (and hence political): the construction of a wall along the U.S.-Mexican border seemed utterly inconsistent with the spirit of a newfound economic partnership. A second was procedural and institutional: although NAFTA made no provision for labor migration, the U.S. emphasis on unilateral assertion appeared to undermine the principles of cooperation and consultation established by the free trade agreement. The third plane was substantive: experience around the world has shown that economic integration tends to foster social integration. Freer trade encourages investment which generally stimulates cultural interaction and, ultimately, labor migration. By endorsing anti-immigration measures, the Clinton administration was tacitly attempting to restrict and curtail the social consequences of the economic policy that it so strongly endorsed. Eventually, if not immediately, this inconsistency was bound to become self-evident: You cannot have it both ways.

## Realities of Immigration under NAFTA

What has happened so far? Has NAFTA exerted any discernible impact on migration from Mexico?

There are at least three major impediments to comprehensive analysis of causal relationships between free trade and rates of migration. The first stems from the fact NAFTA went into effect in January 1994; little time has passed since then, which means that there exist very few data points. This is especially important because most hypotheses on the subject envision long-term or lagged effects, which would be impossible to capture over such a short span of time. A second obstacle relates to quality of the data. There are no direct measurements of levels or rates of illegal migration (which would be the dependent variable); the closest approximation comes from numbers of apprehensions, which can be a highly misleading proxy. The third impediment derives from the simultaneous presence of multiple potential causes (or independent variables), which are extremely difficult to disentangle. As a result, it is impossible to perform the kind of time-series analysis that would meet prevailing standards in the social sciences.

With all these caveats in place, Figure 9.1 presents month-by-month data on INS apprehensions of illegal aliens along the U.S.-Mexican border from January 1990 through August 1995.[16] It must be said, once again, that the number of arrests provides a less-than-perfect guide to the number of illegal entries. Apprehension statistics refer to *events*—that is, to the number of arrests—rather than to *people*. They make no allowance for multiple arrests (anecdotal evidence indicates that individuals can be arrested more than once in the same day).[17] They make no adjustment for voluntary returns to Mexico or other homelands (while survey data indicate that the majority of migrants come only for temporary periods). And they are bound to respond to the varying intensity and magnitude of enforcement efforts by the U.S. Border Patrol.

Despite these imperfections, the data offer some suggestive hints. First, Figure 9.1 provides no evidence that NAFTA had much immediate impact on rates of migration. Monthly statistics throughout 1994 are close to pre-NAFTA levels, though a little bit lower, and they reveal the same seasonal cycle evident in prior years. (This furnishes preliminary support for Hypothesis 3, that NAFTA would have little impact on migration.) Second, the data show a marked increase by around 30 percent throughout the first half of 1995, apparently in response to the peso crisis of December 1994 and the ensuing depression in Mexico. (Popular opinion in Mexico increasingly holds NAFTA to blame for the crisis, which would indicate an indirect causal relationship between free trade and emigration, thus giving implicit credence to Hypothesis 2; in view of the complex origins of the peso crisis, however, I tend to discount this argument.[18])

An alternative explanation for variations in apprehensions might focus on deployment of the Border Patrol, which has nearly doubled the number of agents under the Clinton administration. INS data provide partial substantiation for this interpretation: the monthly average for agent hours deployed along the entire border was 404,666 in 1993, when apprehensions were at a periodic high; 359,593 in 1994, after NAFTA went into effect; and 428,411 during the first eight months of 1995, after Operation Gatekeeper and other measures had taken hold. In somewhat more rigorous terms, the correlation between agent-hours and apprehensions over the 68-month span from January 1990 to August 1995 comes out to +.299 (a positive association, but not overwhelmingly strong). Not surprisingly, intensity of enforcement appears to be related to the number of arrests.

Even so, the substantive meaning of these figures remains far from clear. Prior to the Clinton administration, INS officials routinely held that there were two or three undetected entries for each actual arrest; multiplied by one of these ratios, data on apprehensions thus yielded semi-official estimates of unauthorized flows. According to this logic, low apprehension rates offered a measure of success. Under Clinton, however, INS officials have begun to claim that apprehension figures demonstrate the U.S. capacity for interdiction and deterrence. As a result high numbers, not low ones, indicate a measure of success. As Border Patrol agent Steve McDonald claimed in Tucson: "We hold people in custody for less than an hour, so you are seeing us arrest the same people four or five times per day. When you catch

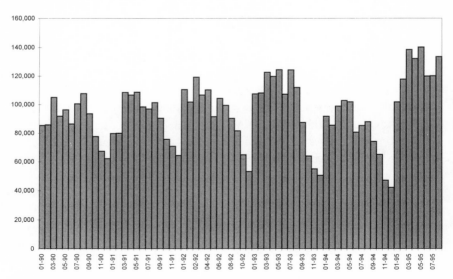

**Figure 9.1. Apprehensions along the U.S.-Mexican Border,
1990-1995 *(by month)***

the same guy five times a day they are not getting through . . . . We are catching a greater percentage of people than we have in the past."[19] With all due respect, this sounds more like an article of faith than a scientific deduction.[20]

There was, however, one clear-cut effect of such stepped-up operations as Gatekeeper and Hold-the-Line: relocation of routes of access into the United States. In the San Diego area, for instance, Gatekeeper slowed transit through long-standing avenues and pushed migration eastward.[21] Within a year or so, apprehensions along the coastal area of Imperial Beach dropped by nearly 20 percent, apparently reflecting a decline in numbers of attempted crossings.[22] Apprehensions meantime shifted to the east: In 1994 Border Patrol agents made only 20,000 arrests along the 20-mile stretch of inland border between Otay Mesa and Tecate; in 1995, as Gatekeeper blocked traditional routes, agents in this area made 51,000 arrests. As INS officials have explained, this was precisely the point: "Operation Gatekeeper has made it more difficult than before for aliens to get across the San Diego section of the Southwest Border illegally. Forced out of Imperial Beach, potential illegal crossers encounter considerable personal adjustments as they move eastward toward Tecate or Mexicali."[23] The presumption is that the added hardship (and potential expense) of traversing unfamiliar and dangerous terrain would provide an effective deterrent against illegal crossing.

One unintended consequence of Gatekeeper was to endanger an area slated for preservation as part of the San Diego National Wildlife Refuge, as streams of would-be migrants struggled to make their way through the wilderness: "What is the point of protecting it?," asked one frustrated naturalist. "Because of Operation Gatekeeper, we have more people out there than ever before. There are thousands of people coming through."[24] While it is not apparent that the Clinton border operations have reduced overall levels or rates of illegal immigration, in other words, there is little doubt that they have altered routes for immigration.

A final effect of strengthened border enforcement, and of the contradiction between free-trade policies and immigration control, has been heightened political tension. This is especially evident along the border with California, the cradle of Proposition 187 and like-minded movements throughout the American Southwest. In March and April 1996, a vicious beating of undocumented migrants by local police in Riverside was followed by the high-speed crash of a renegade truck that was attempting to evade the Border Patrol, an accident leading to the loss of eight Mexican lives. As Sidney Weintraub has noted, this made immigration into a human rights cause for the Mexican government, even prompting the mild-mannered President Ernesto Zedillo to denounce the Riverside beatings as "absolutely reprehensible."[25]

But it was at the societal level, rather than in official circles, where tensions and resentments became most palpable. On the U.S. side of the border, especially in California, anti-Mexican sentiment was rapidly growing; and on the Mexican side, throughout the country, disillusionment with NAFTA and with Mexico's new "partnership" with the United States was also on the rise. Almost certainly, NAFTA was not the cause of all these problems; just as certainly, it was not the panacea that many had predicted with such confidence in the early 1990s.

## Conclusion

What are the policy implications of this analysis? Any effort to design public policy measures in this area must first assume postures of abject humility. All kinds of evidence, anecdotal and systematic, historical and cross-national, suggest that governmental action is notoriously ineffective in deterrence of migration flows. If people want to go somewhere, they will usually find a way to get there. So long as unemployment and underemployment persist in Mexico—and, more to the point, so long as wage differentials approach ratios of 10:1—citizens of that country will seek employment in the United States. And so long as U.S. employers want to take advantage (in many senses) of this labor pool, there will be jobs available. There are limits to what governments and policies can do.

That said, this brief sketch of Mexican migration under NAFTA leads to several policy recommendations for the U.S. government:

### Stick with NAFTA

Over the long term, only economic growth in Mexico will lead to reduction in rates of emigration; and for the foreseeable future, NAFTA offers the best available hope for sustained development in Mexico. To be sure, numerous un-certainties remain. As Wayne Cornelius and Philip Martin pointed out some time ago: "How much and how fast NAFTA retards migration depends on how the jobs created in Mexico by free trade will be distributed among communities, regions and sectors of the economy."[26] NAFTA is not a perfect instrument and it can use refinement. But NAFTA is here to stay, and we must make the best of it.

### Give Special Attention to Mexico

It seems neither appropriate nor necessary to treat Mexico the same as Co-lombia, Honduras, India, Nigeria, or Bangladesh with regard to migration. Mexico is a neighboring country with deep historic ties to the United States and, even more to the point, a member of NAFTA. These facts provide ample justification for uniquely tailored policies.

## Engage in Bilateral Consultations with Mexico

The United States has long asserted its sovereign right to make and enforce its own laws. That is not in dispute. The question is how best to manage (or control) migration from Mexico to the United States. Evidence and a priori logic suggest that this requires bilateral cooperation and consultation at the highest levels of government. As a beginning, two subjects could provide bases for negotiation: (a) creation of a guest-worker program for Mexican nationals in the United States, and (b) apprehension and repatriation of smugglers, or *coyotes*. There is nothing to be gained from pressuring the Mexican government to prevent its citizens from leaving the country, as many U.S. citizens demand, since that would constitute flagrant infringement of a fundamental human right.

## Adopt a Multi-Faceted Deterrent Strategy

Perhaps in search of political gain, the Clinton administration has stressed interdiction and apprehension of would-be migrants at the border. By itself, this strategy is doomed to failure. At least two other approaches are needed: (a) rigorous application of employer sanctions in the United States, and (b) promotion of economic development in traditional sending areas in Mexico, including the stimulation of nonagricultural jobs (perhaps through tax incentives for investments or other opportunities that might be made available through NAFTA). This latter point could also be a subject for bilateral negotiation.

## Lower the Political Heat

There is an understandable (if unpraiseworthy) temptation for U.S. politicians to seek advantage by blaming Mexican immigrants for joblessness, crime, drugs, rising costs of social services, and other social ills. This should be stopped. Otherwise resentments are liable to grow and bilateral cooperation will become all the more difficult. Political leadership, from the highest office in the land, would have the most effect in this regard. In the vast majority, U.S. citizens are fully capable of responding constructively to public information and to education on key issues. Mexico should be seen as a partner, not as an enemy.

## Reconcile Immigration Policy with Trade Policy

In these and other ways, the United States should undertake to make its immigration policy compatible with the spirit as well as the letter of NAFTA. Operations Hold-the-Line and Gatekeeper do not meet this test. This does not mean that it is illegitimate or inappropriate for the United States to enforce its own laws; it means that immigration and trade policy are currently at cross-purposes. Washington should make serious efforts to resolve this inconsistency at distinct levels—political, institutional, and substantive. Otherwise there remains the danger that anti-immigrant sentiment and policy in the United States will undermine the promise and purpose of NAFTA.

## Notes

I want to thank Sidney Weintraub for careful and constructive comments on an early draft of this paper.

1. See M. Delal Baer and Sidney Weintraub (eds.), *The NAFTA Debate: Grappling with Unconventional Trade Issues* (Boulder: Lynne Reinner, 1994).

2. For background, see Wayne A. Cornelius and Philip L. Martin, "The Uncertain Connection: Free Trade and Rural Migration to the United States," *International Migration Review* 27, no. 3 (Fall 1993): 484-512; and Dolores Acevedo and Thomas J. Espenshade, "Implications of a North American Free Trade Agreement for Mexican Migration into the United States," *Population and Development Review* 18, 4 (December 1992): 729-744.

3. Researchers at El Colegio de la Frontera Norte indicate that would-be migrants from central Mexico must now be prepared to spend $1,000 before landing a job in Southern California, and that *coyotes* are more than ever in demand.

4. One blue-ribbon commission has predicted that "development, if sustained, can eventually reduce emigration pressures, but it may take several generations for this process to run its course. In the interim, it can be expected to exacerbate emigration pressures." Commission for the Study of International Migration and Cooperative Economic Development, *Unauthorized Migration: An Economic Development Response* (Washington DC: July 1990), p. 35.

5. Wayne A. Cornelius, "From Sojourners to Settlers: The Changing Profile of Mexican Immigration to the United States," in Jorge A. Bustamante, Clark W. Reynolds, and Raúl A. Hinojosa Ojeda (eds.), *U.S.-Mexico Relations: Labor Market Interdependence* (Stanford: Stanford University Press, 1992), p. 184.

6. Council on Foreign Relations, *Lessons of the Mexican Crisis: Report of an Independent Task Force* (New York: Council on Foreign Relations, 1996), p. 9.

7. See Peter H. Smith, "Politics, Pesos, and the Mexican Crisis," paper prepared for the World Bank (Washington DC, 1996).

8. On this episode, see Peter H. Smith, *Talons of the Eagle: Dynamics of U.S.-Latin American Relations* (New York: Oxford University Press, 1996), pp. 284-290.

9. For an excellent discussion of these initiatives, see Wayne A. Cornelius, "Appearances and Realities: Controlling Illegal Immigration in the United States," forthcoming in Myron Weiner and Tadashi Hanami (eds.), *Immigration, Refugees, and Citizenship: Japanese and U.S. Perspectives* (New York: New York University Press, 1997).

10. Yet another purpose behind Proposition 187 was to oblige the U.S. federal

government to help states and local governments cover costs of immigrant-related social services, but this was a separate question.

11. Wayne A. Cornelius, Philip L. Martin, and James F. Hollifield (eds.), *Controlling Immigration: A Global Perspective* (Stanford, CA: Stanford University Press, 1994).

12. Cornelius, "Appearances and Realities," p. 21 and Figure 4.

13. U.S. Commission on Immigration Reform, *Legal Immigration: Setting Priorities* (Washington, DC: U.S. Government Printing Office, June 1995).

14. *Los Angeles Times,* March 22, 1996.

15. *Los Angeles Times,* May 26, 1996.

16. INS data supplied by Charles W. Haynes and Gordon Hanson, both of the University of Texas at Austin.

17. In recognition of this fact, the INS has begun using fingerprint technology to estimate numbers of individuals apprehended from the frequency of apprehensions. However, this does not address the longstanding question about the relationship between apprehensions (or number of people apprehended) and the number of unimpeded crossings (or successful crossers) into the United States.

18. Except insofar as NAFTA encouraged large sums of portfolio investment, which may have created a false sense of confidence within Mexican policy making circles—and which abruptly fled the country in November-December 1994.

19. North County *Times Advocate,* March 25, 1995.

20. For a contrasting opinion, see Cornelius, "Appearances and Realities," p. 7.

21. See San Diego Dialogue, "Enforcement and Facilitation: An Analysis of the San Ysidro Port of Entry and the Implementation of Gatekeeper Phase II" (La Jolla: San Diego Dialogue, University of California, San Diego, 1996).

22. It has been charged, however, that Border Patrol agents have been encouraged to undercount arrests around Imperial Beach in order to exaggerate the success of Operation Gatekeeper. *Los Angeles Times*, July 6 and 9, 1996.

23. U.S. Immigration and Naturalization Service, *Operation Gatekeeper: Landmark Progress at the Border* (Washington DC: Immigration and Naturalization Service, October 1995).

24. *San Diego Union-Tribune,* May 26, 1996.

25. *Los Angeles Times,* April 14 and 17, 1996.

26. Cornelius and Martin, "Uncertain Connection," p. 487.

# 10.
# U.S. Foreign Policy and Mexican Immigration

## Sidney Weintraub

*"Mexican migrants make a very important contribution to the economy of the United States and the great majority do not compete with the local work force, but rather fill a critical gap in the U.S. economy that cannot otherwise be met in a satisfactory way. . . ."*

President Ernesto Zedillo, Tijuana, April 26, 1996.[1]

*"The credibility of immigration policy can be measured by a simple yardstick: people who should get in, do get in; people who should not get in are kept out; and people who are judged deportable are required to leave."*

U.S. Commission on Immigration Reform,
"U.S. Immigration Policy: Restoring Credibility," September 1994.

The problems that require the immediate attention of policy makers in the United States and Mexico are often quite trivial. The United States has a bilateral trade surplus in some years, Mexico in others, and the issue, while it generates much heat, is of little lasting consequence in the overall relationship. The chemistry between presidents is good in some periods (such as between Presidents George Bush and Carlos Salinas), and horrible in others (such as between Presidents Jimmy Carter and José López Portillo), but this is the stuff of ephemeral gossip and not lasting importance.

Other changes are significant because they shape the workings of the two economies. What was once unthinkable, the negotiation of the North American Free Trade Agreement, represented a Mexican shift from maintaining a distant relationship with the United States to an effort to exploit proximity, and a U.S. decision to give Mexico a higher profile in U.S. foreign policy priorities. U.S. direct investment, once shunned by Mexico or, at best, tolerated, is now avidly sought.

Many problems are not amenable to complete correction. Mexico, because of the long border with the United States, is a logical route for narcotics traffic. Because the U.S. Southwest and the Mexican Northwest are arid regions, techniques to share water and maintain its quality are essential for mutual well-being. Environmental pollution along the border can be minimized only by separate and joint efforts. The growth of industry in northern Mexico, and the population this attracts, inevitably has repercussions in the U.S. Southwest. These perennial problems are not solved; at best, they can be managed to minimize damage.

The tension created by migration from Mexico to the United States is perhaps the most intractable theme in the relationship between the two neighbors, one highly developed, the other less developed. At times, the friction between the two countries over this issue is modest and, at others, incandescent, but it is never absent. Right now—in the mid-1990s—differences between the two countries on migration matters play a prominent role in the relationship.

In some regions of the two countries, this migration actually dominates all other foreign policy issues. Proposition 187 in California demonstrated this. So does the erection of fences at critical points where Mexican migrants seek to enter the United States clandestinely. The combination of NAFTA and fences creates an immense contradiction of simultaneous opening for trade in goods and services and flows of investment, and closing with respect to movement of people. There is no simple solution to this contradiction, certainly not as long as the pull of economic benefit makes emigration from Mexico to the United States a rational act for an enterprising individual.

The discussion that follows tries to place the migration issue into its proper foreign/domestic policy context. It is an issue over which both countries have been ambivalent, at times encouraging migration and at others seeking to curtail it. There are competing national, regional, and sectoral interests in each nation. Many alliances for policy choices cross national lines, such as between fruit and vegetable growers in California and the Pacific Northwest and idle workers in Mexican rural areas. At times, the issue erupts into harsh antagonisms, and at others the migration proceeds with hardly any official notice. The aggravation of problems is cyclical in that attention to migration rises as economic conditions in either of the countries deteriorates.

Efforts to control the level of clandestine migration invariably have failed. Different palliatives have been tested at various times, such as fences and penalties against employers who knowingly hire illegal aliens, and these have worked imperfectly or not at all. Each has unintended consequences. It is hard to know whether an active policy in this field is better than no policy, but efforts at management are inevitable. Some conclusions from this experience will be provided.

## Key Repetitive Themes in U.S. Policy

Three patterns recur in U.S. immigration policy, and each of these affects migration from Mexico with particular force. They are:

1. A conscious decision not to completely close access to the United States by unauthorized immigrants.

2. A tendency to base entry eligibility on specific domestic regional or sectoral interests, those that can exert concerted political pressure.

3. Repeated policy turnarounds, from welcome to rejection, when the U.S. economy falters.

To turn first to the third theme, there is a long history of inviting foreign workers to the United States to meet the labor needs of employers, only to reject them at times of economic downturns.[2] This is an oft-repeated story.[3] Although the practice of seeking foreign workers goes back much further in time, a good place to start in modern U.S.-Mexican migration relations is the *Bracero* program that was instituted in 1942 and lasted in various iterations until 1964. Much has been written about this experience, some of it favorable (for example, that it legalized temporary foreign workers who were coming in any event), but mostly highly critical (for example, that the program served to teach *Braceros* enough so that the temporary expedient was transformed into a permanent stream).[4] This legal recruitment of temporary foreign workers was justified originally on the proposition that U.S. agriculture needed foreigners to compensate for the labor shortages during World War II, but *Bracero* recruitment continued for almost 20 years after the war was over in order to recruit Mexican workers at peak U.S. harvest seasons.

Another regular pattern is that when unemployment rises in the United States, immigrants invited earlier—either explicitly or with a wink and a nod—are disinvited, even forcibly ejected. This happened during the Great Depression.

It happened again in 1954—even as *Bracero* programs were being renewed— in what was callously called "Operation Wetback," instituted when U.S. unemployment rose to 5.5 percent.[5] A wetback was a Mexican who swam or waded across the Rio Grande without explicit invitation, whereas a *Bracero* was deliberately recruited.[6]

When the Immigration Reform and Control Act (IRCA) was passed in 1986, two of the recurring themes (catering to specific interests and not fully closing the door to unauthorized entry) were incorporated. IRCA made provision for Special Agricultural Workers (SAWs) not available for other sectors, and also instituted a deliberately nonworkable program of penalties for employers who knowingly hired illegal aliens. In the period since, through U.S. fiscal year 1994, more than one million persons were granted legal residence status under the SAWs provision.[7] The employer-penalty program was vitiated from the outset by the inability to reach agreement on a secure means for determining whether an employer knowingly hired an illegal alien. In addition, enforcement of the employer-penalty program by the Immigration and Naturalization Service (INS) was lax. No thorough effort was made to really close off access to illegal entrants to the United States.

Then in 1994, the third theme that has typified U.S. immigration practice (rejection, when economic conditions worsen, of persons previously welcomed) was repeated when California voters approved Proposition 187 to deny illegal aliens access to health, education, and other benefits. Governor Pete Wilson, who advocated support for Proposition 187 in his campaign for reelection as governor, had earlier supported the SAWs program when he was in the U.S. Senate.

These past patterns may not repeat themselves indefinitely into the future because domestic circumstances in the United States are changing. The INS is building up its prevention and detection assets at the Mexican border, making clandestine access more difficult. An experimental program will be instituted to permit verification of the legal status of job seekers and perhaps giving some teeth to the employer-penalty program. There is considerable concern in many states and localities about the costs of providing public services to immigrants, especially those here illegally, and this may deter some clandestine entries.[8]

However, it probably is still a good bet that the past will be a reliable guide to the future, that concern over immigration will diminish as the economy prospers and that specific national groups who favor particular kinds of immigrants will get their way—will be able to recruit low-wage foreign labor for agriculture, have a larger labor pool for many industrial producers and service providers, and admit many skilled foreign practitioners for U.S. knowledge and high-level service activities.

# Recurring Pattern of Mexican Responses

Three themes recur in the official articulations of the Mexican position on undocumented migration to the United States:

1. The migration meets a legitimate need in the United States and does so without significant damage to American workers. The headnote quoting President Ernesto Zedillo captures this sentiment.

2. Rather than be seen as an illegal act, which is the U.S. position, the migration obeys fundamental market forces of supply and demand.[9]

3. The Mexican government's highest obligation is to protect the "physical integrity and dignity of its nationals who emigrate abroad, regardless of their migration situation in the country where they are."[10]

During the past several years, however, there has been an important addition to the Mexican posture, namely, the willingness to examine jointly the issue of undocumented migration with U.S. authorities. Earlier, it was nearly impossible to engage the Mexican authorities in such discussions. The Mexican government remained silent for all practical purposes when IRCA was under examination in the U.S. Congress. The Mexican rationale was that immigration was a domestic issue for the United States, as it was for Mexico, and Mexico did not interfere in the internal affairs of other countries. President Carlos Salinas had suggested that immigration be put on the table during the negotiation of NAFTA, but he never made clear what he had in mind substantively.[11]

There is now a binational U.S.-Mexico study in progress to review most facets of the migration issue—numbers, causes, labor-market effects, social and human rights matters, results of past efforts to deal with the issue—with the objective of reaching some joint conclusions, perhaps by the end of 1996 or early 1997. Mexican authorities now talk openly of their country's shortcomings in meeting the job and economic opportunity needs of their co-nationals.

However, while there is now much discussion, there is no comprehensive Mexican position on how to deal with the U.S. concerns. The U.S. position is that persons who cross clandestinely into the United States or overstay nonimmigrant visas are illegally in the country; and, consequently, the heart of the problem is the excess supply. The Mexicans, in contrast, emphasize the U.S. demand for these workers, which implicitly assumes that the migration is the market solution rather than the problem. Each side knows intellectually that supply and demand are not completely separable in practice, but there is no easy way to bring the two starting conceptual positions together.

The Mexicans, for the most part, react to developments in the United States rather than take positions on their own. When the U.S. temperature on this issue rises to fever levels, the Mexicans demonstrate their willingness to talk about the issue, but without presenting meaningful new suggestions.[12] The Mexican authorities reacted strongly and resentfully to the approval of Proposition 187, and they did so again in April 1996 after the events in Riverside County in California (see below). The main element of these responses has been the need to respect the rights and dignity of Mexicans in the United States.

In truth, it is hard to know how the Mexicans could do more. If the problem is lack of opportunity at home for venturesome persons, which Mexico admits, the long-term solution is economic growth. It is asking too much of the Mexican authorities to insist that they forcibly prevent their own nationals from leaving, a practice the United States has condemned in other parts of the world. The United States can put up fences on its side of the border, but this is not a feasible solution on the Mexican side. The United States can deploy more border patrol agents with more sophisticated equipment, but it goes too far to expect Mexico to do the same on its side of the border.[13] Mexico can cooperate in the capture of *coyotes* who help Mexicans enter clandestinely into the United States, but it is mainly U.S. law that is being flouted.

Discussion, yes. Better understanding, yes. Cooperation in the detection of persons who violate the laws of both countries, yes. But a direct attack in Mexico on the supply side of the problem, no, not in the short term. This then leaves most action on the U.S. side, either by seeking to seal the border or reducing demand by an employer-penalty program with teeth. There are, in fact, limits on effective joint actions if the objective is to slow the unauthorized entry of Mexicans into the United States.

## Complicating the Relationship

U.S. Mexican relations have a troubled history going well beyond the migration problem. The facts are well known to even casual students of the relationship. They date particularly from the seizure of half of Mexican territory, as embodied in the Treaty of Guadalupe-Hidalgo of 1848 ending the war with Mexico; invasions of Mexico in this century; and pressure on Mexico in favor of U.S. oil companies, which contributed to the popularity of the nationalization of oil company assets in 1938. One consequence of this history was deep-seated mistrust of the United States, particularly among intellectuals and reflected in the media. For many years, the Secretariat of Foreign Relations (SRE from its initials in Spanish) was considered the center of anti-Americanism in the Mexican government.

A conscious effort was made during the De la Madrid and Salinas administrations to change the bilateral atmosphere. Entering into NAFTA represented an effort to forge cooperative interaction with the United States, to alter what Alan

Riding in his 1985 book referred to as a "distant" relationship into a closer one. On its part, the United States welcomed the Mexican free-trade initiative as much for its favorable political consequences as for its potential economic benefits. The pervasive low-key anti-American rhetoric diminished markedly. Politicians from the governing party, the Partido Revolucionario Institucional, stopped using anti-American rhetoric in their speeches and the press gave much less prominence to news stories that put the United States in a bad light.

The official effort to maintain good relations continues, as is evident from statements by President Zedillo and even from SRE, but it is badly frayed by now. One reason is that the economic collapse of 1995 dimmed the luster of NAFTA—which epitomizes the new, more cooperative relationship—and made Mexicans skeptical of the tangible benefit from the new relationship with the United States. A more solid reason, however, has been the anti-Mexican rhetoric of U.S. politicians during the 1996 presidential campaign, preceded by some nasty anti-Mexican measures of the past several years.[14] One of these was the highly public debate reflecting official U.S. agonizing as to whether Mexico should be decertified for lack of cooperation in curbing narcotics trade.[15] The certification process is seen as a form of scapegoating by an egotistical United States.

However, the actions that most enraged Mexicans—public officials, intellectuals, the media—dealt with migration. Mexicans see great inconsistency in the building of fences along the border while simultaneously freeing trade and investment, but official statements on this contradiction are rare and usually subdued in light of Mexico's long tradition of not interfering in the internal affairs of other countries.

Proposition 187, which would deny most public services to illegal immigrants, particularly education and non-emergency health care, was a different matter. Here, non-interference had its limits. The core of the official statement from Los Pinos, the presidential residence, was that "Mexico will continue to respect its traditional principle of non-interference in the internal affairs" of the United States, but then emphasized the international requirement to respect the fundamental rights of migrants.

Senior Mexican officials went on to emphasize the fact that the harshness of Proposition 187 was a California initiative and not a federal U.S. policy and made clear that Mexico did not want to see this California project become a national problem. In an interview with the editors and staff of the *Washington Post*, then President-elect Zedillo stated explicitly: "We are rather offended by Proposition 187."[16] Andrés Rozental, the subsecretary of SRE, made much of two points, the hypocrisy of persons who sought the services of illegal Mexican workers and later supported Proposition 187, and the cruelty of wanting to deny education to children.[17]

Mexican rage simmered when Proposition 187 was approved, but it boiled over following the two incidents in Riverside County in early April 1996. In the first of these, on April 1, 1996, following a high-speed, 80-mile chase of a pickup truck with 19 illegal Mexican aliens, two sheriff's deputies were photographed from a helicopter for a Los Angeles television station beating two of the Mexicans apprehended, one of them a woman. In the second incident, on April 6, seven Mexicans out of 25 on board were killed when the speeding truck on which they were riding crashed and turned over trying to get away from the U.S. Border Patrol.

The first of these incidents, the beating with clubs, was widely interpreted in Mexico as evidence of underlying U.S. anti-Mexican racism which had become acceptable as a result of the passage of Proposition 187 and the anti-Mexican rhetoric of many U.S. politicians. Official Mexican statements were harsh, but they maintained the traditional emphasis on the need to do more to protect the rights and dignity of Mexican nationals. Indeed, the Mexican press and public felt that the reaction of the Foreign Secretary, José Angel Gurria, had been too mild.[18] Gurria felt obliged to issue further and stronger statements. He gave an interview to the newspaper *Reforma* in which he blamed the anti-immigrant sentiment on actions by Governor Pete Wilson, Proposition 187, the effort to replicate its provisions in other states, and electoral pressures in the United States.[19] In early May, when the cabinet-level U.S.-Mexico Binational Commission held its annual meeting in Mexico City, the migration issue took pride of place, particularly the matter of protecting the rights of Mexicans in the United States.

President Zedillo put a different twist on the adequacy of the Mexican response to the incidents when he said that "We cannot confuse diplomacy with machismo."[20] However, President Zedillo's effort to keep the incidents in perspective did not impede the rash of anti-Americanism that apparently had only gone into the closet for a number of years. It is impossible to cite here all the news stories and op-ed articles that attacked the United States because they dominated the media for days, even weeks. The flavor of the coverage was that "racial discrimination and xenophobia are increasing in that country" (the United States)[21]; that Mexican hesitancy in defending the human rights of its nationals in the United States is based on the desire not to "contaminate" issues of higher priority for the Zedillo government, namely foreign credits[22]; and that Mexico must strengthen its programs to protect the rights of its emigrants.

The incidents in Riverside County, coming on top of Proposition 187 and the anti-Mexican content of much U.S. political debate, undoubtedly have cooled the warmth that was developing in U.S.-Mexican relations in the aftermath of NAFTA, at least for now. Nevertheless, some mitigating elements do exist. The first is that both President Zedillo and Secretary Gurria are trying to combine their annoyance over behavior in the United States with respect to Mexican migrants with the maintenance of good relations generally. Thus, a key Mexican reaction to Proposition 187 was to suggest the bilateral study of the migration issue that is now taking place. The official emphasis after the Riverside County events was to focus on the central theme—how to protect the rights of Mexicans in the United States—and not make broadside attacks on the U.S. character. These attacks are coming from commentators and some politicians, but not from the Mexican government.

A second reaction of a number of commentators is that Mexican treatment of illegal aliens from Guatemala can also be quite harsh. This may not excuse the U.S. actions, but it at least raises the issue of whether Mexico enters into this matter with entirely clean hands. Finally, the *Reforma/El Norte* survey referred to in note 18 makes clear that the overwhelming majority of Mexicans place the reason for undocumented migration on Mexican economic conditions and are not overwhelmed by the anti-U.S. rhetoric.

## Intractability of the Issue

It is self-evident that immigration laws are based on national considerations but, because they deal with the entry of non-nationals, have foreign repercussions. Temporary workers are sought outside the country not out of concern for the workers or foreign relations, but because of demands by nationals with political influence. Foreigners are rejected in times of economic downturns without giving much heed to the welfare of the countries to which they are returned, as U.S. expulsions of Mexicans during the Great Depression amply illustrated.

Yet, it is illuminating to examine the domestic agendas that give shape to immigration laws and the immigration consequences of laws and actions on seemingly unrelated themes.[23] Students of immigration have long since discovered that prior colonial relationships affect immigration (they explain why North Africans migrate mainly to France, South Asians earlier to Great Britain, and Filipinos to the United States). Mexicans were chosen as the cheap labor for the *Bracero* program because of geographic convenience, and this then stimulated a long-term Mexican presence in the United States, as did German postwar recruitment of Turkish guest workers. U.S. intervention in Viet Nam and later in Central American civil wars led in due course to immigration into the United States from those countries.

Mexico, however, is a special case for the United States because of the combination of a shared border and great economic differences. Temporary worker programs undoubtedly gave impetus to the flow of Mexicans, but these probably would have taken place in any event. Economic downturns in Mexico lead to migration to the United States whereas such hardships in other regions do not affect the United States to the same extent. The kinship relationships between Mexicans in Mexico and the United States are by now more extensive than with other ethnic groups seeking to migrate to the United States. When anti-immigrant fervor rises in the United States, the main target country is normally Mexico.

The U.S. domestic agenda driving immigration issues, consequently, normally affects Mexico more than any other country. Mexican instability or economic insecurity affects the United States more than any other foreign country. This connection was given explicit form in IRCA, which directed the establishment of a bipartisan commission to explore "mutually beneficial, reciprocal trade and investment programs to alleviate such conditions [of underdevelopment which contribute to unauthorized migration to the United States]." The main recommendation of the commission was to bring Mexico into a North American free-trade area.[24] NAFTA was subsequently created and the desire to dampen immigration flows from Mexico was one of the motivations, even if not the main one.

It was recognized in the report of the bipartisan commission, as well as in other analyses of the consequences of NAFTA, that dampening the migration flow was, at best, a long-term proposition. The per capita incomes differences were too great to overcome rapidly. Philip Martin, based on his own analysis and the empirical work of others, concluded that there would be what he called a hump in immigration from Mexico due primarily to changes in Mexico's agricultural scene, some of which were the consequence of NAFTA.[25] This type of analysis led to opposition to NAFTA by many in California, including the state's two federal senators, on the grounds that it would lead to greater immigration into the state, at least in the short to medium term.

For all these reasons—the domestic U.S. forces driving immigration legislation, the migration consequences of other domestic developments, and the anxieties caused when the U.S. economy, or the economy of a state as important as California, declines—it is impossible to "solve" immigration problems. Management of the issue also is complicated by the opportunism that the issue generates. There is the drive by specific groups who wish the inflow of migrants for their particular reasons, and of others who wish to curtail the inflow for fear that it is harming them. Politicians take positions that clearly are opportunistic, seeking cheap labor when this suits their agenda and then railing against illegality when their priorities change.

As these contests are played out on the domestic U.S. scene, Mexico has its own internal conflicts. Economic policy in Mexico probably has greater force on the flow of migrants than does U.S. policy. It is hard to contain the push forces at any time, given the economic disparities between the two countries, but the pressure to emigrate takes on greater gravity when the Mexican economy suffers a free fall, as it did in 1995. The networks between individuals, families, and villages in Mexico and compatriots and families in the United States are now firmly established. It is particularly hard to stifle the initiative of an enterprising, rational young person who is determined to emigrate and obtain higher income.

These clashes of interests and motives within and between the two countries lead regularly to unfortunate incidents, like those in Riverside County, which aggravate the difficulties. Relations between the two countries thereby become hostage to inevitable but unpredictable incidents. Hate groups on both sides of the border, those with a visceral dislike of those in the other country, are then quick to pounce on each incident to further their agenda of animosity. Governments are often forced to react to these stimuli, as the Mexican SRE was to complaints that it did not protest strongly enough over the Riverside County incidents, or the United States to assertions during the presidential primaries and before that not enough was being done to seal the border.

This chapter was written at a moment of high tension between the two countries on the immigration issue. The best hope is that this moment will pass as Mexican economic performance improves and the U.S. economy sustains healthy growth.

## Conclusion

The following ten conclusions, which are a mixture of observations and recommendations, are predicated on the belief that the migration problems between Mexico and the United States will persist well into the future—that they cannot be disposed of the way a specific trade or investment dispute can—but that the tensions can be reduced and the deleterious fallout in bilateral relations minimized.

1. In the normal course of events, the tensions will vary with the times and circumstances. The main conditioning features are the state of the U.S. economy, or that of particular states and regions and the state of the Mexican economy and job and wage opportunities at home. Thus, the heightened emotions that affected California and led to the approval of Proposition 187 in 1994 were caused by a temporarily declining economy. Texas, another neighbor of Mexico and an important recipient of unauthorized immigration, did not at that time take anti-immigrant or anti-Mexican actions; and it is not mere coincidence that the Texas economy was then prospering.

2. The foregoing observation leads to the conclusion that every effort should be made not to over-react, to scapegoat immigrants for economic

woes in the United States or particular states. Economic conditions will change. It became impossible not to over-react in California once the immigrant bugbear was made one of the main issues, perhaps the main issue, in the gubernatorial election. Over-reaction was institutionalized and remains to some extent even as the California economy has rebounded. The trashing of Mexico in 1995 and 1996 by U.S. politicians who dislike NAFTA came at the worst time in Mexico's modern economic history and served no real purpose other than to embitter relations.

3. The evidence is quite strong that the anti-Mexican atmosphere created by Proposition 187 and the harsh anti-Mexico statements by U.S. politicians contributed to the tense atmosphere that exploded when officers from the Riverside Country sheriff's office unnecessarily beat two undocumented immigrants they had captured. There is a lesson here both for U.S. and Mexican political figures and elites: their own nationals will also reap the whirlwind when they agitate xenophobia.

4. The two governments, those of Mexico and the United States, have for the most part kept their balance during the past several years at particularly tense moments concerning immigration. When Proposition 187 was approved, Mexico's main reaction was to call for a binational study and focus its grievance on the obligation to protect the human rights of Mexican nationals. The U.S. government did not make a major issue of the harsh media commentary in Mexico depicting the United States as inherently racist following the Riverside County incidents, but instead emphasized that the bilateral relationship remained fundamentally sound. One payoff of this U.S. restraint was the internal commentary in Mexico that its record of treatment of Guatemalans illegally in Mexico no more made it a racist country than did a particular incident by a local sherrif's office in California make all Americans racist.

5. Emotional words are best avoided. Those Mexican commentators who used the word "racist" to condemn the United States as a whole for the treatment of the Mexican undocumented immigrants in Riverside County did inflame some domestic passions, but they contributed nothing to improving the bilateral relationship. The word "illegal," when stressed by those who condemn the undocumented migrants, is troublesome to Mexicans. The migrants are illegal in that they are violating U.S. law, but they are not seen in Mexico as criminals.

6. The importance of overall friendly and cooperative relations between Mexico and the United States does much to temper the adverse reaction of particular incidents. Those who would turn back the clock to the pre-1980 mutual suspicions could do much harm. The fallout from migration problems would be far greater if the bilateral relationship as a whole were a deeply troubled one, as it was for many years.

7. Whatever NAFTA's faults and accomplishments in the economic sphere, the agreement has spawned a series of cooperative binational institutions (trinational in some cases, to include Canada) that have profoundly changed the way Mexico and the United States now carry out their business with each other. There is an ease of communication that did not exist earlier. This makes possible frank interchange on migration issues, among others, of a type that did not take place earlier. More meetings and discussions do not necessarily lead to the resolution of problems, but the lack of discussion forecloses any resolution.

8. The changes taking place in Mexican agriculture are speeding the exodus from rural areas. Viewed more deeply, however, this exodus is inexorable in that upwards of 25 percent of Mexico's population is still rural and agriculture contributes less than 10 percent of the nation's GDP. NAFTA may or may not hasten this departure to urban areas and across the border, but the rural to urban migration has been and will be a fact of life for years to come.

9. When considering immigration laws and policy, one certainty is that there will be unintended consequences. The *Bracero* program stimulated later undocumented immigration. IRCA legalizations are leading to family reunions and further immigration. Who knows what fences will bring. Most probably, those Mexicans who make it across the border successfully are more likely to stay put in the United States rather than make repeated journeys back and forth, which was the normal practice earlier.

10. Finally, there is a need for each side to understand the pressures that exist on the other. Mexican policy makers can do little to prevent enterprising Mexicans from crossing over to the United States to seek greater opportunities. U.S. policy makers cannot ignore wholesale violation of the country's border. There are political limits that must be taken into consideration when either side makes demands on the other.

Immigration is one facet of U.S.-Mexican policy. The reality is that problems will flare up from time to time and complicate the entire relationship. These problems are durable, although not necessarily eternal. They need not, however, eclipse all other issues in the relationship, as they did during the consideration of Proposition 187 in California.

## Notes

1. President Zedillo's remarks were taped, and my translation, while loose, captures the meaning of what he said.

2. The title of an essay by Aristide R. Zolberg captures this practice. See "From Invitation to Inderdiction: U.S. Foreign Policy and Immigration since 1945," in Michael S. Teitelbaum and Myron Weiner, eds., *Threatened Peoples, Threatened Borders: World Migration and U.S. Policy* (New York: Norton for the American Assembly, 1995), pp. 117-159.

3. A Mexican version of this history from 1966 to 1986 can be found in Carlos Rico, "Migration in U.S.-Mexican Relations, 1966-1986," in Christopher Mitchell, ed., *Western Hemisphere Immigration and U.S. Foreign Policy* (University Park, PA: Pennsylvania State University Press, 1992), pp. 221-283. Rico brings out that U.S. management of immigration from Mexico has ranged from open, even encouraging, periods to harsh restrictionism.

4. Michael J. Piore, *Birds of Passage: Migrant Labor and Industrial Societies* (New York: Cambridge University Press, 1979) makes the point that most streams of clandestine migration from less- to more-developed countries got started at the invitation of employers in the importing country. This was certainly true of the *Bracero* program.

5. This level of unemployment, 5.5 percent, is now considered by many to be the "natural" rate in that as the percentage gets much lower, inflation will follow.

6. The distinction was blurred during the *Bracero* program because even though it was illegal for a foreigner to be in the United States without papers, under the Texas Proviso in the then U.S. legislation, it was perfectly legal for an employer to hire an illegal immigrant. The United States invited *Braceros*, but the official policy was to make sure that the door remained largely open to Mexican and other foreign non-*Braceros* who were willing to work.

7. U.S. Immigration and Naturalization Service, *Statistical Yearbook of the Immigration and Naturalization Service, 1994* (Washington, D.C.: U.S. Government Printing Office, 1995), p. 32.

8. George Vernez and Kevin F. McCarthy, *The Costs of Immigration to Taxpayers: Analytical and Policy Issues* (Santa Monica, CA: RAND, 1996).

9. Manuel Rodriguez Arriaga, Subsecretary for Population and Migratory Services, said the following to the Grand Commission of the Mexican Senate on March 28, 1996 (author's translation): "For the [U.S.] government, the undocumented [migrants] are a problem of legality, of violation of migration norms, which in principle should be curbed. For Mexico, it [the migration] deals with a phenomenon that in its fundamentals obeys the forces of supply and demand of a binational labor market that, whether it is recognized or not, exists."

10. Statement of the Mexican Secretariat of Foreign Relations, April 9, 1996, following the two incidents affecting Mexican nationals in Riverside County, California, on April 1 and 6, 1996.

11. The U.S. suspicion was that Mexico was making a conceptual and not a practical argument, that if there was to be free movement of capital, why not have similar treatment for labor, another factor of production? Many anti-NAFTA Mexican intellectuals made this argument. When the United States refused to include the migration issue in the NAFTA discussions, except for temporary entry of businessmen and technicians, the issue was dropped.

12. When President Zedillo visited the White House on October 10, 1995, his remarks included the following paragraph (official Mexican translation): "Mexico is also fully determined to intensify the cooperation efforts to tackle the problems of illegal migration and trafficking of individuals. In no way do we pretend to limit law enforcement in other countries, nor would we advocate illegality. But we will always defend respect for basic human rights and individual dignity."

13. Recent measures to strengthen U.S. detection and apprehensions at or near the border are discussed in U.S. General Accounting Office (GAO), *Border Patrol: Staffing and Enforcing Activities* (Washington, D.C.: GAO, March 1996).

14. This includes the anti-Mexican rhetoric of Patrick Buchanan during the Republican Party presidential primaries, the constant sniping against Mexico by Senators Jesse Helms and Alphonse D'Amato, and the effort by Senator Diane Feinstein to remove drug-cooperation certification from Mexico.

15. Decertification would have disqualified Mexico for U.S. financial assistance, such as from the Export-Import Bank of the United States, and would have triggered negative U.S. votes on credits to Mexico in the international financial institutions, unless President Clinton provided a national security waiver for Mexico.

16. *Washington Post*, November 23, 1994.

17. *La Jornada*, October 30, 1994. Governor Pete Wilson of California fit this description.

18. A survey by and published in the sister newspapers *Reforma* of Mexico City and *El Norte* of Monterrey on April 10, 1996, indicated that two-thirds of those polled felt that the Mexican government response was unsatisfactorily weak.

19. *Reforma*, April 12, 1996.

20. From taped remarks at a private meeting on migration issues at the Colegio de la Frontera Norte, Tijuana, April 26, 1996.

21. Raymundo Riva Palacio, *Reforma*, April 8, 1996.

22. Adolfo Aguilar Zinser, *Reforma*, April 12, 1996.

23. *La Jornada*, April 8, 1996, p. 4. The first eight pages of this issue of the newspaper were almost completely taken up with the migration problem, with an emphasis on U.S. racist attitudes against Mexicans.

24. Sergio Díaz-Briquets does this in "Relationships between U.S. Foreign Policies and U.S. Immigration Policies," in Teitelbaum and Weiner, eds., *Threatened Peoples, Threatened Borders*, pp. 160-189.

25. Report of the Commission for the Study of International Migration and Cooperative Economic Development, *Unauthorized Migration: An Economic Development Response* (Washington, D.C.: U.S. Government Printing Office, 1990).

26. Philip L. Martin, *Trade and Migration: NAFTA and Agriculture* (Washington, D.C.: Institute for International Economics, 1993).

# Conclusion

*Frank D. Bean, Rodolfo O. de la Garza,
Bryan R. Roberts, and Sidney Weintraub*

M exican migration into the United States, especially undocumented migration, has become a topic of increasing regional and national concern. Traditionally, the United States has taken an attitude of benign tolerance toward undocumented migration and thus managed to serve the competing interests of various groups. But in the last ten years, a climate of insecurity, heightened by economic globalization and downsizing, together with the perception that migrants take jobs from U.S. citizens and take advantage of social services, has created in the public mind and among many politicians a need to more tightly control the entry of and benefits available to undocumented migrants. In response, the U.S. Congress has moved toward clarifying and enforcing immigration policy. The federal government passed two significant pieces of legislation, IRCA in 1986 and the Immigration and Naturalization Act (INA) of 1990. State governments have reacted as well. In 1994, California citizens passed Proposition 187, which has attempted to restrict severely services to migrants.

Any success in regulating migration the United States may strive for cannot be achieved solely on U.S. terms. Mexico must be consulted and its involvement enlisted. Reversing a trend of at least 150 years, the North American Free Trade

Agreement (NAFTA) represents a new willingness for Mexico and the United States to work toward mutually beneficial ends. Solid economic growth and a more equitable distribution of income within Mexico, outcomes that NAFTA may encourage, offer the prospect of reduced migration. The instability within the Mexican economy, however, provides a recent illustration of how past Mexican economic progress has often been rendered ineffective, with the result that migrants continue to stream across the border. To move too drastically against migrants now could disrupt the nascent trust between the two nations that made NAFTA possible and its success plausible. To move too slowly could undermine any U.S. public support for continuing to build a beneficial relationship with Mexico. In either case, migration issues remain unresolved.

Other factors, however, may ease migration pressures within Mexico within ten years or so. Mexican birth rates are rapidly diminishing and rural-to-urban migration is likely to have soon run its course. These more optimistic conditions need to be kept in mind when policy options are weighed. Serious consideration of the pros and cons both of policies emphasizing the restriction of Mexican migration and the limitation of further economic integration between the two countries and of policies emphasizing the regulation (or perhaps even the slight expansion of) migration flows and the development of greater economic integration must also consider a number of other issues. As the foregoing chapters make clear, these include the implications for immigration policy of (a) labor market structures and processes, (b) immigrant integration and use of social services, (c) trade and economic development, (d) foreign policy, and (e) immigration trends and border management.

## Labor Markets

Most Mexicans migrate to the United States for economic reasons, whether "pulled" by U.S. labor demand or "pushed" by lack of opportunities in Mexico. These migrants, in turn, stimulate supplementary migration by their families and from their "home" regions. Increasingly, however, "push" seems to be a more important element in spurring migration. Income inequality has deepened. Today many Mexican workers (an estimated nine million) earn $300 or less each month. In 1995, inflation rose to 50 percent, although it has now dropped to no more than half that. While wage differentials may not be driving immigrants to the United States as strongly as in the past, the inability of Mexican urban labor markets to absorb migrants apparently is. And for the first time in memory, economic contraction in 1995 led to large-scale lay-offs.

Patterns of migration have also become more complex and widespread. The level of migrant education and work experience is increasing. Mexicans with service or manufacturing experience are now taking even agricultural jobs in the United States, which are better-paying than their alternatives in Mexico. Migrants no longer come from only certain states, but increasingly from all over Mexico.

U.S. policy has not effectively addressed these changes in migration patterns or numbers. Some provisions of IRCA have actually encouraged immigration. Nor have U.S. employer sanctions and other labor controls dampened migration rates. In 1995, the INS removed only 50,000 illegal workers (Graham, 1996). Sanctions affect only those who knowingly hire illegal laborers, a situation aggravated by the constant availability of counterfeit documents.

The regulation of the immigrant marketplace may be getting worse, although the INS is now beginning to test seriously employer sanctions in industries that hire large numbers of undocumented migrants. Moreover, both employers and employees have found economic benefits in noncompliance, especially in the informal sector which may be absorbing increasing numbers of illegal immigrants and is the most difficult to regulate. The availability of labor, promoted by a broad migrant job network, enables employers to hire at lower wages and under worse labor conditions. The Department of Labor oversees undocumented labor as a part of its mandate to review workplace conditions, but migrant workers do not report poor conditions.

Sanctions do not require 100 percent compliance to work, but they do need to be tried under more favorable conditions. More resources (the INS budget has been increased to $2.6 billion) and a better understanding of differences in formal labor markets and industries would allow for more consistent and effective enforcement. Still, employer sanctions probably offer the best method for discouraging illegal migrants because it is precisely the search for employment that attracts them to this country.

Implementing a guest worker program might be another effective strategy. Opponents point out a number of flaws: Such plans only serve as a safety valve on Mexico's unemployment problems. They are supported by U.S. employers who cite labor shortages as a justification but use such workers to suppress wages. There are no ways to guarantee the "guests" would ever leave. (As many as half of the illegal residents in the United States enter on legal visas through interior ports of entry and simply fail to leave [Graham, 1996].) An identification program, insurance for immigrants, and the expenses of enforcement all would contribute to the high cost of administering a program. Those in favor of guest worker plans simply argue that they are the only feasible way to regulate undocumented workers and to meet the demand for low-skilled labor not met by U.S. natives.

# Immigrant Integration and
# Social Service Usage

Studies suggest that the availability of social services does not draw migrants to the United States. Yet, restriction of services is one of the major ways in which the United States has attempted to discourage immigration. Economic conditions, fear of crime, a failure to consider that, even with cutbacks and restrictions, life in the United States may still be better for immigrants than it was in Mexico, and perhaps racism, have all helped create in the public's mind an equation between uncontrolled migration and costly social services. Exacerbating the situation is the fact that a highly disproportionate share of the costs of immigrant services are borne at the state and local governmental levels, whereas a disproportionate share of the taxes they pay goes to the federal level.

The federal government has done little to remedy these problems. Besides legislation greatly restricting the ability of illegal immigrants to become legal, legislation to prevent migrants from participating in job training and from receiving health care or food stamps has been passed, and legislation to restrict other social services is currently pending. A trend toward transferring fiscal responsibility, but not federal funds, to individual states both reflects and contributes to the deterioration of public sentiment. An Urban Institute study found that the seven states with the largest concentration of immigrants spend $2 billion/year on emergency health care, Medicaid, and education for illegal immigrants. Regional conditions complicate the picture. For instance, the anti-immigrant fervor in California, exemplified in Proposition 187, is largely absent in Texas, where there have been fewer political gains to be won from such a stance, where less money has gone to services for immigrants, and where the economy has improved coincident with a rise in immigration.

As a consequence of governmental policies and public mood, the debate over providing social services to immigrants has conflated a complex set of issues into a single matter of immediate financial cost. This may prove short-sighted and harmful to U.S. interests. It excludes recognition of social or economic contributions the Mexico-educated worker may make to the community. Some advantages are immediate. For example, Mexican labor keeps agricultural prices to the consumer low. Others may accrue over time, as second and third generations of Mexicans living in the United States become able to contribute to the economic and social welfare of local communities. Additional benefits may be just over the border, where, for instance, less-expensive Mexican-trained dentists, doctors, and pharmacists provide less expensive services for U.S. citizens.

New, more-sophisticated cost-benefit analyses that examine the intergenerational and life-course impacts of immigrants on the economy and on different governmental levels, not merely short-term budgetary impacts, might help rationalize discussions. But analysts disagree about the value of updating current studies, which are frequently poorly conceived and executed. Many argue that the public has already made up its mind.

Nonetheless, a far-sighted assessment of immigrants' role in the United States must be more vigorously pursued. A simple example illustrates the point. Congress's intent in proposing cuts to social services has been to save money. Yet, even before being passed into law, the action has helped to stimulate an unforeseen and unprecedented boom in naturalization. Proposition 187 seems to have had a similar effect. Statistically, Mexican immigrants have had one of the lowest rates of naturalization. Many have intended to return at some point to Mexico. Once naturalized, they must give up their Mexican citizenship (Mexico has only quietly and unenthusiastically considered changing its Constitution to allow dual citizenship) and may then claim full social and economic benefits of U.S. citizenship for themselves and their families. These new citizens become part of the aging U.S. population and work force, adding to already substantial social service, health, and elder-care costs.

As with other migration issues, the problem of providing social benefits to immigrants needs to be solved in order to prepare a climate more receptive to finding viable, long-term answers to questions posed by Mexican migration in general. This requires constructing a more balanced understanding of the contributions made and received by both the Mexican and U.S. economies. NAFTA has fostered greater cooperation between local, state, and national governments from both countries. It might provide a model for negotiating a "grand bargain" in social service contributions, an important but controversial idea about which both nations have become increasingly divided. But even if this could be done, it would take more than a generation to achieve.

## Trade and Economic Development

Increased trade and further economic development may eventually decrease Mexican migration, but not soon. Pressures may get worse as Mexico continues to struggle through a difficult economic transition. The new government has had little success in reversing the massive restructuring of its rural areas that accelerated in the 1980s. Indeed, Mexico will have to surmount serious political and economic problems before it can stop providing the "push" toward U.S. labor markets. Economic disparity, dislocation, and development, especially in rural Mexico, persist and continue to drive its residents to migrate. To survive, Mexico must develop and implement a comprehensive plan to solve its systemic economic problems, looking beyond trade and NAFTA to encompass all sectors of its economy. At the least, economy. At the least, Mexico's economy must grow consistently at a rate of 5-6 percent per year in order to absorb the growth of its labor force, and grow more than that to absorb underemployment and accumulated unemployment.

The economic cooperation represented in NAFTA accelerates the operation of forces that complicate the relationship between the Mexican economy and migration. NAFTA allows free entry of goods and services, but it was not intended to encompass the free movement of labor. Scholars never expected NAFTA to slow migration in the short run by improving the Mexican economy. In fact, the agreement hastens the exodus of migrants from rural areas because of the relative noncompetitiveness of Mexican agriculture. Migration may slow down in the medium-term if Mexican growth rates can be sustained at relatively high levels.

The conflict of regional versus national interests also complicates the scenario. Migration is often a local phenomenon and may bear little or no connection to NAFTA's bi-national economy. Yet U.S. public impression joins border issues with NAFTA trade, and demands that for NAFTA to succeed, action must be taken to secure the border. Perhaps the only solution to this problem in which the success of either migration controls or NAFTA relies on the prior success of the other is to tackle the challenges of economic integration and migration regulation at the border through incremental rather than radical migration policy changes. These may be the only responses that will not upset a fairly delicate balance of interests.

## Foreign Policy

The health of the Mexican economy, nationalism, and the effect of the economies of both countries on migration influences the ways in which the United States and Mexico will deal with immigration. Mexico has survived a series of recent economic crises (1976, 1982, 1987-88), but the current one is by far the worst (Casteñeda, 1996). This has led some to doubt the wisdom of the United States pursuing broader economic integration. Some observers have abandoned the European Economic Union (EU) as a reasonable comparison, finding the relationship between Europe and Turkey to be more appropriate. However, the consensus seems to be that more effort should be invested in developing a productive Mexico-U.S. relationship. Mexico, after all, is not going to disappear from the southwestern border of the United States. The two countries have yet to expore fully the ways in which they can work together to the benefit of each.

The interrelationship of the Mexican and U.S. economies also modifies the way in which migration is viewed, but there is no clear understanding about how economic conditions affect movement. While it is generally agreed that migration increases when the Mexican economy falters, there are also indications that some kinds of movement across the border increase as the economy improves. Other surveys discern no difference in migration patterns when periods of vastly different levels of economic output are compared. NAFTA has created another tier to the Mexican economy and trade has increased significantly. Nationalism and a history of distrust also direct the way in which the two nations view migration and interact. Perceived racism against Mexican immigrants, recent California legislation, and anti-Mexican remarks about the 1995 loan guarantee have all affected Mexico's willingness, especially among its elite, to cooperate on migration issues. Mexicans, some fear, may use these perceptions as a justification for balking at full participation in migration talks.

The U.S. mood of anti-immigration also affects the potential for success. This sentiment has been magnified in the political arena as politicians play on the confluence between changing migration patterns and the general perception that social inequality is worsening even as economic opportunities seem to be contracting. Neither the current administration nor its critics has proved able to guide public debate or opinion on the issue. Despite these obstacles, talks between Mexico and the United States have not broken down. Both countries are tentatively setting aside mistrust and suspicion and recently have begun to undertake serious discussions on migration and many other issues. These are modest beginnings, but important in that they are largely without precedent.

The ability of both nations to work together to manage immigration issues will be enhanced as the public accountability of the Mexican state continues to increase. The American public may be less willing to support arrangements that facilitate Mexican emigration (thus reducing Mexico's internal economic and political pressures) if such efforts are seen as perpetuating Mexico's current political system. And to the extent that the Mexican government functions in ways that undermine its legitimacy, it will reduce its political capacity to enter into new agreements with the United States that the Mexican public sees as involving compromises in national sovereignty. In practice, the Mexican public and many Mexican officials are increasingly advocating and implementing governmental and political reforms. This provides an opportunity for the United States to support these officials and to suggest further reforms. In the long run, Mexico and the United States will both be better served by a more democratic Mexico. And a more democratic Mexico is more likely to develop economic and social policies that will reduce emigration.

## Immigration Trends and Border Management

Creating a Mexico-specific plan for immigration and border management would enable the United States to address better its unique and evolving relationship with Mexico. NAFTA stimulates economic integration and a more penetrable border in the interests of trade. The use of inexpensive Mexican labor in U.S. agriculture and other industries encourages a Mexican presence in the United States. At the same time, public hostility to "illegals" spills over to Mexicans in general, pressuring the government to take action. This climate of ambiguity gives rise to inconsistent immigration enforcement and inflated rhetoric.

A Mexico-specific policy directed to settling these difficulties could facilitate the new binational relationship. But its precedent must be examined. Such a policy would run counter to the official immigration philosophy of universalism, which the United States has asserted since the late 1970s. It might be viewed as a "slide backward" toward older policies that relied on racial and ethnic distinctions and that encouraged other groups and nations to demand their own special arrangements. In practice, however, the United States has often engaged in specific de facto policies toward Mexican immigration. Enough flexibility may already inhere within existing policy frameworks to deal effectively with the special circumstances of Mexico.

Any policy changes, whether under cover of new acts or old practices, must address the public perception that the solution to migration troubles lies at the border. More than half a million migrants will be apprehended along this 2,000-mile boundary this year (Graham, 1996). The United States has tried a number of strategies to slow or stop illegal entries. It has raised walls, hired bigger patrols, and expanded administration. While some of these tactics have worked in isolated venues, they have not altered the larger picture, at least up to now. Mexicans continue to cross illegally, and once in the United States, stay longer.

Changes in current policy might help exert more control at the border. For example, streamlining port-of-entry procedures would encourage legal entry. (Customs and the DEA, who insist on thorough inspections, would have to be placated for this to work.) The U.S. public may hope that the border can be controlled and may measure government success in regulating all immigration against that standard; but ultimately, it may prove impossible that the border can be so tightly managed that illegal immigration would end. It may simply seek other avenues of entry than crossing the land border.

A more comprehensive immigration policy must be sought that reflects specific goals and a broad-gauge strategy through which to realize them. The first step would be to clarify what the United States hopes to achieve through migration control. For example, border management may be seen as a way to enforce legal wages, a way to exclude Mexicans, a way to stop crime, or in any number of different lights. Broadening the definition of "legal" or establishing "tolerable levels" of undocumented migration might make expectations of border control more realistic, and perhaps lead to calmer discussions over the practicality of simply opening the border. Once goals have been articulated, solutions about dealing with the border will become much more evident. As it is, the "line" that constitutes the U.S.-Mexico border is simply not substantial enough either as an idea or a geographical barrier to stop immigrants from entering the United States illegally.

Better regulation of migrant job markets opens additional possibilities for regulation. Stronger enforcement of employer sanctions against those who knowingly hire undocumented workers might help slow illegal migration by depressing the job market. This would depend on the creation of a simple, portable, easily identifiable worker identification or a national ID system—one that respected individual rights—in order to distinguish more easily between authorized and unauthorized workers. Given the expense and current levels of technology, however, such programs would be hard to monitor, especially outside the agricultural sector. Stricter documentation requirements tend to push the undocumented worker farther underground. The most significant opposition to implementing an identification system, though, rises from the public, which fears that this sort of monitoring could potentially violate its own civil rights.

Whatever strategies the United States considers cannot be undertaken without bilateral approaches to seeking solutions. Traditionally, Mexico has either regarded immigration as a U.S. domestic problem or has contended that it refuses to compromise the rights and freedoms of its citizens by discouraging their free movement. As distrust of the United States has gradually dissipated, Mexico and the United States have begun to work together, if only indirectly so Mexico may avoid outcry from its people to control emigration. For instance, Mexico now broadcasts an INS infomercial that warns about the dangers of crossing the border illegally. It has also created an elite police, "Grupo Beta," to help control crime among (and against) migrants waiting to cross into the United States. Cooperative efforts have enabled both countries to address sensitive migration issues, including fundamental disputes over immigration statistics, in newly opened talks between various governmental representatives and agencies.

In order to achieve an overarching and viable migration policy, the United States and Mexico will each have to make concessions that will be politically and socially acceptable to both sides. Some argue that both effective border control and new immigration programs must be discussed simultaneously. Others believe the political climate in the United States requires that border management has to be effective before it is politically feasible to discuss new immigration policies. Indeed, public perception is key to making any policy change, since neither political support nor specific policymaking is possible without the sense that, given the will and the right approach, the border can be controlled. At the same time, it is clear that no full control will ever be established even with bilateral cooperation.

The cooperative optimism symbolized in NAFTA indicates the dramatic change in U.S.-Mexican relations. Yet the existing de facto U.S. immigration policy, full of contradictions, has not changed to accommodate new, more demanding social, political, and economic conditions that the bi-national relationship entails. Mexican and U.S. interests, as perceived by the public, understood by regional and national policymakers, and insisted upon by economic players must be acknowledged fully in order to find acceptable solutions.

The most promising policy options are those of engagement that more directly foster authorized migration and employment rather than policies that confirm strategies of restriction and containment. Such plans would recognize the role of the labor market in drawing Mexicans to the United States and seek to legitimate it so as to regulate it. This might entail better use of employer sanctions, worker identification plans, somewhat increased legal Mexican immigration, and creation of guest worker programs. Plans that made more useful distinctions between legal and illegal migrants and possibly broadened the definition of "legal" could not only assist interior enforcement, but also take pressure off current efforts which seek to address the issue by regulating illegal border crossing.

Two important considerations temper any efforts to modify existing policy. Favorable public opinion on both sides of the border and the bilateral involvement of both countries are essential to the success of any migration policy. Indeed, the precarious state of the Mexican economy makes bilateral efforts all the more important. If the United States hopes to be able to gain control over the magnitude and kind of migration coming to the country, Mexico must become economically capable of reversing, or at least modifying, migration trends whose origins stem from conditions within Mexico but whose direction is guided by U.S.-Mexico social and economic relations. Only bilateral approaches offer the prospect of success.

## References

Casteñeda, Jorge G. 1996. Mexico's Circle of Misery. *Foreign Affairs* July/August, pp. 92-105.
Graham, Wade. 1996. Masters of the Game. *Harpers* June, pp. 38, 49.

# Index

# W

# About the Contributors

**Susan Gonzalez Baker** received her Ph.D. from the University of Texas at Austin in 1989, where she has been employed as an assistant professor in the Department of Sociology since 1995. Before that she was at the Urban Institute in Washington, D.C., and at the School of Public Administration and Policy at the Mexican American Studies and Research Center at the University of Arizona in Tucson.

**Frank D. Bean** is Ashbel Smith Professor of Sociology and Public Affairs and director of the Population Research Center at the University of Texas at Austin. Formerly at the Urban Institute in Washington, D.C., where he served as Director of the Program for Research on Immigration Policy, he works on U.S./Mexico relations, Mexican migration to the United States, international migration, the demography of racial and ethnic groups, and population policy. His recent books include *Undocumented Migration to the United States: IRCA and the Experience of the 1980s* (edited with B. Edmonston and J. Passel), and *Illegal Mexican Migration to the United States and the U.S./Mexico Border* (with several University of Texas colleagues).

**Maryann Belanger** is director of the Population Research Library at the Office of Population Research, Princeton University, where she has served as information specialist for six years. She received a BA in social studies from Notre Dame of Ohio and a master's degree in library science from

Rutgers University, and is a former president of the Association of Population/
Family Planning Libraries and Information Centers International.

**Marion Carter** received her Bachelor of Arts with a degree in international studies
at the University of North Carolina at Chapel Hill in 1995. She is currently
serving as an intern at the Population Council, South and Southeast Asia
Regional Office, in New Delhi, India, assisting in the development of a regional program on youth issues and in organizing regional and national con-
ferences on reproductive health issues.

**Robert G. Cushing** received his Ph.D. in sociology from Indiana University in
1967. He is a professor in sociology at the University of Texas at Austin and
director of data services at the Population Research Center. His academic
interests include crime, deviance, social control, and legal systems; economic
development and social change; ethnic stratification; labor flows and international migration; and quantitative analysis and computer processing techniques.

**Rodolfo O. de la Garza** is Mike Hogg Professor of Community Affairs in the
Department of Government at the University of Texas at Austin and vice-
president of the Tomás Rivera Policy Institute. Professor de la Garza combines interests in American and comparative politics, specializing in political behavior (especially the study of Latino populations) and Mexico. The
editor, co-editor, or co-author of five books, he is currently directing studies
on Latino-African American relations, immigrant incorporation, and Latinos
and U.S. hemispheric integration.

**Thomas J. Espenshade** is professor of sociology and a faculty associate of the
Office of Population Research at Princeton University. He was formerly
senior research associate and director of the Program in Demographic Studies at the Urban Institute. He is author of *Investing in Children: New Estimates of Parental Expenditures* (1984) and co-author of *The Fourth Wave:
California's Newest Immigrants* (1985). His research interests include patterns of undocumented migration to the United States, the fiscal impacts of
new immigrants, and attitudes toward U.S. immigration.

**Gary P. Freeman** received his education at Emory University and the University
of Wisconsin, Madison, where he earned the doctorate in political science.
He has been in the Government Department of the University of Texas for
twenty years and has also taught at the University of Pennsylvania. His published work ranges over comparative politics in Europe and the other Western democracies and covers not only immigration policy, but also the development of the welfare state. He is the author of *Immigrant Labor and Racial*

*Conflict in Industrial Societies* and the co-editor of *Nations of Immigrants: Australia, the United States, and International Migration.*

**Alene H. Gelbard**, Ph.D., director of international programs for the Population Reference Bureau, holds a doctorate in population dynamics from Johns Hopkins University. She has worked on population and health issues world-wide for more than 25 years—including residencies in the Philippines, Brazil, France, and Bolivia. Dr. Gelbard, who specializes in population policy, has worked in both the public and private sectors as well as for international organizations.

**Charles W. Haynes** is a graduate student, researcher, and teaching assistant in the Department of Sociology at the University of Texas at Austin. A retired Air Force major who holds master's degrees in public affairs form the Lyndon Baines Johnson School of Public Affairs at the University of Texas at Austin and in business administration from Southwest Texas State University, his primary interests are migration and development.

**Agustín Escobar Latapí** received his Ph.D. in Sociology from the University of Manchester in 1984. He is currently employed as a profesor-investigador titular at Centro de Investigaciones y Estudios Superiores en Anthropología Social de Occidente in Guadalajara, Jalisco, and as a postdoctoral visiting research fellow in anthropological demography at the Population Research Center, University of Texas at Austin. His main topics of research are labor markets, informality, international migration, and social mobility.

**Philip L. Martin** is professor of agricultural economics at the University of California, Davis. He was a staff associate at the Brookings Institute 1978, and an economist for the Selection Commission on Immigration and Refugee Policy in 1979. He has conducted research on immigration and labor market issues in the U.S. and in Germany, Turkey, Egypt and Mexico. He is a member of the Commission on Agricultural Workers established by the Immigration Reform and Control Act of 1986.

**Bryan Roberts** holds the C. Smith Sr. Centennial Chair in U.S.-Mexico Relations and is professor of sociology at the University of Texas at Austin. After completing his doctorate at the University of Chicago in 1964, he returned to the United Kingdom and taught at the University of Manchester for 22 years until 1986. His research concentrates on social and economic development, primarily in Latin America, but also including Europe and the border region of the United States.

**Michael J. Rosenfeld** is a doctoral student in sociology at the University of Chicago.

**Peter H. Smith** is professor of political science, Simon Bolivar Professor of Latin American Studies, and director of Latin American studies at the University of California in San Diego. His interests focus on comparative methodologies, Latin American politics, and U.S.-Latin American relations. He is editor of *The Challenge of Integration: Europe and the Americas* and *Latin America in Comparative Perspective: New Approaches to Methods and Analysis*, co-editor of *Cooperation or Rivalry? Regional Integration in the Americas and the Pacific Rim* and author of *Talons of the Eagle: Dynamics of U.S.-Latin American Relations*.

**Gabriel Székely** received his Ph.D. in political science from George Washington University. Székely, a specialist in the global telecommunications industry, served as associate director of the Center for U.S.-Mexican Studies at the University of California, San Diego (1986-91), and currently teaches at El Colegio de México. He is also a guest conductor in the prime-time news analysis program at CN140 in Mexico City, and has a weekly column in the City's largest circulation daily, *El Universal*. He is the author and editor of a large number of books and articles, including *Teléfonos de México: Una empresa privada* and *Japan, the United States and Latin America: A New Trilateralism in the Western Hemisphere?*

**Marta Tienda** is Ralph Lewis Professor of Sociology and research associate of the Population Research Center of NORC and the University of Chicago. She is co-author of *The Hispanic Population of the United States* (Russell Sage, 1987), and co-editor of *Divided Opportunities: Poverty, Minorities and Social Policy* (Plenum, 1988) and *Hispanics in the U.S. Economy* (Academic, 1985). Her research interests and writings focus on race and gender inequality and various aspects of the sociology of economic life, and include demographic and social change in developing countries, persistent poverty and welfare participation, labor market processes, and the economic and social consequences of immigration.

**Sidney Weintraub** holds the William E. Simon Chair in Political Economy at the Center for Strategic and International Studies. Before joining CSIS, he was Dean Rusk Professor of International Affairs at the Lyndon B. Johnson School of Public Affairs, the University of Texas at Austin. Professor Weintraub was a career diplomat for many years before joining the faculty of the LBJ School, serving in a number of foreign posts, including Mexico City. He has written extensively on international trade, finance, and Mexico.